PRINCIPLES OF INTERNATIONAL LAW

by HANS KELSEN
PROFESSOR OF POLITICAL SCIENCE
UNIVERSITY OF CALIFORNIA

THE LAWBOOK EXCHANGE, LTD.
Clark, New Jersey

ISBN 9781584773252 (hardcover)
ISBN 9781616193058 (paperback)

Lawbook Exchange edition 2003, 2012

The quality of this reprint is equivalent to the quality of the original work.

THE LAWBOOK EXCHANGE, LTD.
33 Terminal Avenue
Clark, New Jersey 07066-1321

Please see our website for a selection of our other publications and fine facsimile reprints of classic works of legal history:

www.lawbookexchange.com

Library of Congress Cataloging-in-Publication Data

Kelsen, Hans, 1881-1973.
   Principles of international law / by Hans Kelsen.
      p. cm.
   Originally published: New York: Rinehart & Co., Inc., c1952.
   ISBN 1-58477-325-1 (cloth: alk. paper)
    1. International law. I. Title.

KZ3375.K45A37 2003
341—dc21   2003047462

Printed in the United States of America on acid-free paper

PRINCIPLES OF INTERNATIONAL LAW

by HANS KELSEN
PROFESSOR OF POLITICAL SCIENCE
UNIVERSITY OF CALIFORNIA

RINEHART & COMPANY · INC.
NEW YORK

Third Printing, March, 1959
Copyright, 1952, Hans Kelsen
Printed in the United States of America
Designed by Stefan Salter
All Rights Reserved
Library of Congress Catalog Card Number: 52–5587

To *Josef L. Kunz*

PREFACE

This book is designed as an introduction to the study of international law. As it shall serve not only law students, but all those who are interested in social and especially in political science, the first part deals with certain legal concepts, the knowledge of which is indispensable for an understanding of the problems of international law.

I have chosen the title *Principles of International Law* because I thought it necessary to present, in addition to the most important norms which form this branch of the law, a theory of international law, that is to say, an examination of its nature and fundamental concepts, an analysis of its structure, and the determination of its position in the world of law.

It is usual to divide international law into two main parts, the law of peace and the law of war. I have abandoned this systematization. For it was justified, if at all, only as long as it was possible to conceive of the state of war as existing on the same legal level as the state of peace. However, in view of the Kellogg-Briand Pact and the Charter of the United Nations, war can be considered legal only if it is a reaction against a violation of international law. Hence the law of war is dealt with in this treatise in connection with the problem of the sanctions provided for in international law.

It is in the first place general international law to which the *"Principles"* refer. Particular international law created by treaties is discussed merely in order to show the possibilities of developing international law in a technically progressive way.

Among the treaties recently concluded, the Charter of the United Nations is of decisive importance. Since it claims to be valid not only for states that are members of the Organization but also for nonmember states, it may be—or is about to be—recognized as general international law. This explains the careful consideration given to the law of the United Nations in this treatise.

It seems to be an empty pleonasm to assert that a treatise on international law deals with the problems concerned only from a juristic, and that means from a legal point of view. If international law is law in the true sense of the term—and this is assumed in this book—which other method, but a juristic one, could be applied in the description and explanation of this object? If, nevertheless, I think it necessary to emphasize the purely juristic character of this book, I do so in opposition to a tendency widespread among writers on international law, who—although they do not dare to deny the legal character and hence the binding force of this social order—advocate another than a legal, namely a political approach as adequate. This view is in my opinion nothing but an attempt to justify the nonapplication of the existing law in case its application is in conflict with some interest, or rather, with what the respective writer considers to be the interest of his state. If he thinks that it is his duty to suggest to his government a power policy, that is to say a policy determined only by the real or assumed interest of his state and restricted only by its actual power, he may do so under his own responsibility. But if he tries to make his readers believe that this policy is in conformity with international law interpreted "politically" he does not present a scientific theory of international law but a political ideology.

As to the formulation of the norms of positive international law and their traditional interpretation I have used the works referred to on page xvii, especially the English standard work by L. Oppenheim and H. Lauterpacht.

I wish to express my sincere gratitude to Professor Erwin N. Griswold, Dean of Harvard Law School, for the permission to use certain parts of my *General Theory of Law and State*, Harvard University Press, 1945, and to Professor H. Lauterpacht for the permission to cite a number of cases presented in the *Annual Digest of Public International Law*. I wish also to thank Professor Leo Gross, Professor Josef L. Kunz, and Professor Robert W. Tucker for their valuable suggestions.

H. K.

Berkeley, California
March, 1952

TABLE OF CONTENTS

Preface	vii
Table of Cases	xiii
List of Comprehensive Works on International Law	xvii

I. The Nature of International Law: International Delicts and International Sanctions

  A. The Concept of Law 3
    1. The Two Kinds of Social Order 3
    2. Sanctions: Criminal and Civil 5
    3. Legal Norm and Rule of Law: The "Ought" 6
    4. The Delict 7
    5. Obligation (Duty) and Right 7
    6. Responsibility: Individual and Collective 9
    7. Culpability and Absolute Responsibility 11
    8. The Force Monopoly of the Community 13
    9. Self-help and Collective Security 15
    10. Retribution and Prevention 17
    11. Law and Peace 17
  B. Is International Law "Law" in the True Sense of the Term? 18
    1. Meaning of the Question 18
    2. International Delicts 19
    3. International Sanctions 20
    4. Reprisals 23
    5. War: Its Concept 25
    6. War: Its Legal Interpretation 33

7. War (Use of Force) under the Charter of the United Nations 44
8. War: Regulation of Its Conduct 64

II. The Spheres of Validity of International Law

A. The Spheres of Validity of a Legal Order 93
B. The Territorial and Temporal Spheres of Validity of International Law 94
C. The Personal Sphere of Validity of International Law: The Subjects of International Law 96
　1. Juristic Persons as Subjects of Law 96
　2. The State as Subject of International Law 100
　3. The Subjects of Obligation and Responsibility in International Law 114
　4. The Subjects of Rights in International Law 139
　5. The So-Called Fundamental Rights of the State 148
　6. Communities Not Having the Character of States as Subjects of International Law 158
　7. General and Particular International Law 188
D. The Material Sphere of Validity of International Law 190
　1. International and National (Domestic) Jurisdiction 191
　2. Implementation of International Law by National Law 192
　3. Transformation of International Law into National Law 194
　4. Article 2, Paragraph 7, of the Charter of the United Nations 196
　5. Definition of International Law 201
　6. Exclusive International Jurisdiction 202

III. The Essential Function of International Law: The Determination of the Spheres of Validity of the National Legal Orders (Legal Existence of the State) by the International Legal Order

A. Determination of the Territorial Sphere of Validity of the National Legal Order (Territory of the State) by International Law 207

Table of Contents xi

    1. The Territory of the State as the Territorial Sphere of Validity of the National Legal Order   207
    2. The Restriction of the Territorial Sphere of Validity of the National Legal Order   209
    3. The Territory of the State in a Narrower and in a Wider Sense   212
  B. Determination of the Personal Sphere of Validity of the National Legal Order (the People of the State) by International Law   227
    1. The People of the State as the Personal Sphere of Validity of the National Legal Order   227
    2. Exterritoriality   228
    3. No State Has Jurisdiction over Another State   235
  C. Determination of the Material Sphere of Validity of the National Legal Order (Competence of the State) by International Law   240
    1. No Natural Limits to the Competence of the State   240
    2. Protection of Organs and Citizens of Foreign States   242
    3. Citizenship (Nationality)   248
    4. Conflict of Laws (Private International Law)   254
  D. Determination of the Temporal Sphere of Validity of the National Legal Order (Existence of the State in Time) by International Law   257
    1. Time as Element of the State   257
    2. Birth and Death of the State   258
    3. The Identity of the State   259
    4. Recognition of a Community as a State   264
    5. Recognition of a Government   279
    6. So-Called Governments in Exile   288
    7. Recognition of Insurgents as a Belligerent Power   291
    8. Recognition and Nonrecognition of Illegally Established Situations (Stimson Doctrine)   293
    9. Succession of States   295

IV. Creation and Application of International Law

  A. The Creation (Sources) of International Law   303
    1. The Concept of "Source" of Law   303

2. The So-Called "Gaps" in the Law	304
3. Custom	307
4. Treaties	317
5. Decisions of International Agencies	365
B. The Application of International Law	367
1. Settlement of International Disputes by Agreement	367
2. Settlement of International Disputes by Organs of the League of Nations and of the United Nations	368
3. Settlement of International Disputes by International Tribunals	377

V. International and National Law

A. The Differences between International and National Law	401
B. The Relationship between International and National Law (Monism and Pluralism)	403
1. The Monistic and the Pluralistic Theory	403
2. The Subject Matter of National and of International Law	404
3. The "Source" of National and of International Law	406
4. The Reason of Validity of National and of International Law	408
5. Conflicts between National and International Law	419
6. The Unity of National and International Law as a Postulate of Legal Theory	424
7. Primacy of National Law or Primacy of International Law	428
8. Sovereignty	438
9. The Philosophical and Juristic Significance of the Two Monistic Interpretations	444
Index	451

TABLE OF CASES

Admission to the United Nations	177	Buron v. Denman	118
Adriaenssens v. Ministère Public	74	Canevaro	252
		Carinthia	74
Alabama Claims	82	Caroline, The	59, 236
Altman & Co. v. United States	318	Cherokee Tobacco	421
Anna, The	220	Chung Chi Cheung v. The King	233 f., 421, 433
Antelope, The	310, 425		
Appam, The	83	Civilian War Claimants Association Ltd. v. The King	142
Attorney-General for Canada v. Attorney-General for Ontario	354	Clipperton Island Arbitration	215, 225
Austrian Empire (Succession)	299	Colombian-Peruvian Asylum	266
Austrian Pension	261	Competence of the General Assembly regarding Admission to the United Nations	177
Baja California, The	234	Corfu Channel	219 f., 222
Bayot, *In re*	211	Cristina, The	228
Beamten Abkommen	143	Cutting	211
Bermuda, The	82	Czechoslovak Agrarian Reform (Swiss Subject)	351
Bernstein v. Van Heyghen Frères S.A.	239 f., 257		
Bigelow v. Zizianoff	237	De Brabant and Gosselin v. T. and A. Florent	73
Blonde, The	148 f.		
Blumhardt v. Mexico	247	Dickinson v. Del Solar	229 f.
Bochart v. Committee of Supplies of Corneux	73	Dickson Car Wheel Co. v. Mexico	247 f
Born, Baron F. de, v. Yugoslavia	252	Dougherty v. Equitable Life Assurance Society	240, 280 f.
Brown, Robert E., Claims	298	Drummond Wren, *In re*	144

Table of Cases

Duff Development Co. v. Government of Kelantan 112

Eastern Carelia 380
Eastern Extension Telegraph Co. Claim 306
Eastern Greenland 325 f.
Eheleute K. v. Deutsche Reichsbahngesellschaft 351, 353
Elida, The 220 f.
Eliza Ann, The 28, 331 f.
État Russe v. Cie Ropit 240
Exchange, The, v. McFaddon 232 f.

Factory of Chorzow 20
Foster v. Neilson 353 f.
Four Packages of Cut Diamonds v. United States 318
Free Zones of Upper Savoy and District of Gex 325
French National Railway Company v. Chavannes 421

Gagara, The 272
Geipel v. Smith 81
Gelbtrunk Claim 121
German Interests in Polish Upper Silesia 329, 348
German Major War Criminals (Nuremberg Trial) 138, 239
German Settlers in Poland 298
Government of Spain v. The Chancery Lane Safe Deposit Ltd. 281
Governor Collot 236
Greco-Bulgarian "Communities" 421
Gschwind v. Swiss Confederation 246

Hawaiian Claims 298
Helena, The 124 f.
High Command Trial 137

Hoogstraten v. Low Lum Seng 162
Interpretation of Peace Treaties 200
Invincible, The 236 f.
Island of Palmas 96, 215

Janes, Laura M. B. 121
Jessie, The 123
John, The 68
Jones v. Garcia del Rio 281
Jurisdiction of the Courts of Danzig 195

Kalisyndikat Gesellschaft, Deutsche 237 f.
Kandiliotes v. The Commonwealth 245
Katz and Klump v. Yugoslavia 261
Kennett v. Chambers 271
Kontinental-Gasgesellschaft, Deutsche 267
Kotzias v. Tyser 68

La Jeune Eugénie 310
Lazard Bros. v. Midland Bank Ltd. 256
Lehigh Valley Railroad Co. v. State of Russia 280
Llandovery Castle, The 135
Lotos, The 211
Lusitania, The 80
Luther v. Sagor & Co. 239, 257, 287

Macintosh v. United States 44
Mathot v. Longué 74
Mavrommatis Palestine Concessions 243
Megalidis v. Turkey 329
Menge v. Polish Railway Administration 143

Table of Cases

Mexican Union Railway	244	Reparation for Injuries suffered in the Service of the United Nations	184
Military Decoration Pension	261 f.		
Mortensen v. Peters	420		
		Republic of Panama (Compania de Navigacion Nacional) v. United States of America	221
Naulilaa, The	24		
Nayade, The	28		
Nishimura Ekiu	242		
North American Dredging Co.	244 f.	Reservations to the Convention on Genocide	334
North Atlantic Coast Fisheries Arbitration	345 f.	Rhineland Ordinances	351
		Riera et al., *In re*	421
		Roberts, H., v. Mexico	243
Oder Commission	332	Romano v. Comma	250
Ottoman Debt Arbitration	261	Rothschild & Sons v. Egyptian Government	360
Over the Top, The	421, 433		
		Roy, R.T., The	247
Pablo Najera	339	Russian Socialist Federated Soviet Republic v. Cibrario	280, 286
Papadopoulos v. Koninglijke Nederlandsche Stoomboot Maatschappij	353		
Paquete Habana, The	435		
Parlement Belge, The	222, 234	Salem	252 f.
Pearson v. Allis Chalmers Co.	82	Salimoff & Co. v. Standard Oil Co.	287
Pearson v. Parson	82		
Pesaro, The	234	Santissima Trinidad, The	82
Petrogradsky M.K. Bank v. National City Bank	287	Sei Fujii v. State of California	144
Philippine Sugar Estates Development Co. v. United States	297	Serbian Loans	318
		Sigwald, Charles, v. Germany	141 f.
Pinson, Georges	420	Sokoloff v. National City Bank	280, 283, 287
Piracy *jure gentium*	125		
Polites v. The Commonwealth	245	South-West Africa, International Status	164
Prometheus, The	23	Soviet Government v. Ericsson	286 f.
Queen v. Keyn	23	State of Spain v. The Chancery Lane Safe Deposit Ltd.	281
Quirin et al., *Ex parte*	129 f.		
R. v. Bottril, *ex parte* Kuechenmeister	76	Steiner and Gross v. Polish State	142 f.
R. v. Gordon-Finlayson	223	Stoeck v. Public Trustee	250
Railway Traffic between Lithuania and Poland	342 f.	Switzerland–France Arbitration	325

Tellech v. Austria and Hungary	251	United States–Norway Arbitration	305 f.
Thomas v. Gay	421		
Three Friends, The	292 f.		
Tinoco Arbitration	282	West Rand Central Gold Mining Co. Ltd. v. The King	315 f., 435
Totus et al. v. United States et al.	421	Wimbledon, The	346
Treatment of Polish Nationals in the Danzig Territory	195, 423	Wulfsohn v. Russian Socialist Federated Soviet Republic	280, 286
Tunis–Morocco Nationality Decrees	197		
Underhill v. Hernandez	236	Youmans Claim	120
United States v. Bank of New York & Trust Co.	256		
United States v. Germany (Nationality of Claims)	246	Zamora, The	237, 420
		Zoppot Street-Crossing	350

LIST OF COMPREHENSIVE WORKS ON INTERNATIONAL LAW

Oppenheim, L. *International Law.* 6th ed., edited by H. Lauterpacht, Vol. I (1947), Vol. II (1944).
Hyde, Charles Cheney. *International Law, chiefly as interpreted and applied by the United States.* 3 vols., 2d ed. (1945).
Fauchille, Paul. *Traité de droit international public.* 2 vols., 8th ed. (1921–1926).
Scelle, George. *Précis de droit des gens* (1932–1934).
Verdross, Alfred von. *Völkerrecht* (1937).
Guggenheim, Paul. *Lehrbuch des Völkerrechts.* Vol. I (1947), Vol. II (1951).
Anzilotti, Dionisio. *Corso di diritto internazionale.* 3d ed. (1923).
Pallieri, Balladore. *Diritto internazionale publico* (1937).
Sanchez de Bustamante y Sirven, Antonio. *Derecho internacional publico.* 5 vols. (1933–1938).

I.

THE NATURE OF INTERNATIONAL LAW: INTERNATIONAL DELICTS AND INTERNATIONAL SANCTIONS

INTERNATIONAL Law or the Law of Nations is the name of a body of rules which—according to the usual definition—regulate the conduct of the states in their intercourse with one another. These rules are designated as law. If we speak of law in daily life, we think of national or municipal law, the law which prevails within the state. But is so-called international law, the rules prevailing in the relations among the states, law in the same sense as national or municipal law? The answer to this question depends on the definition of the concept of law.

Any attempt to define a concept must proceed from a certain usage of language, from the usual meaning of the word by which we intend to designate the concept. One must see whether the social phenomena called "law" present a characteristic in common, distinguishing them from other social phenomena of a similar kind —a characteristic which is sufficiently significant to constitute a general concept for the rational understanding of social life. Such a characteristic can be found.

It is an element, the only one, by which we are able to differentiate definitely and successfully between a legal and a moral or a religious order. It is this element which constitutes a fact of fundamental importance in the mutual relations of men; it is this element which is suited in all regards to form the decisive criterion for an investigation into the nature of law. What is this criterion?

A. THE CONCEPT OF LAW

1. *The Two Kinds of Social Order*

It is the function of every social order—and law is a social order—to bring about certain reciprocal behavior of men, that is to induce men to refrain from certain acts which for one reason or another are deemed detrimental to society, and to perform others which for one reason or another are regarded as useful to society. One can seek to attain this goal in two fundamentally different ways: without or with the threat and use of force.

He who wants to induce another to adopt a certain conduct may do so by requesting the other, in the hope that the latter, from respect for or love of the one making the request, will fulfill his wish. He may enlighten another as to the appropriateness of the conduct demanded, in the expectation that the understanding thus acquired will supply the motive for corresponding action or abstention from action. He may set an example by his own behavior; or promise reward in case of obedience. In all these cases, obedience to the social order is voluntary.

There is, however, an entirely different method of bringing about a desired human behavior. In order to induce individuals to a certain conduct, an authority may threaten them with an evil to be forcibly inflicted upon them in case they act contrarily. The threatened evil consists of depriving men of certain possessions, such as life, freedom, property, or other values. In so doing the social authority assumes that the individuals whose conduct is to be regulated will, in order to avoid the threatened evil, refrain from the undesired actions, and will perform the desired ones.

The threatened evil we call a sanction. If, in the belief of men, the sanction emanates from a superhuman authority, if it has a transcendental character, the order providing for such sanctions is a religious order. The social orders which prevailed in early times in primitive societies were of this type. Men behaved in conformity with the order because they believed that superhuman powers would punish violations of it with misfortune of every kind, such as bad harvest, sickness, and death. Transcendental sanctions are to be distinguished from socially organized sanctions, i.e., sanctions to be executed by men according to a social order established by men. Such sanctions have the character of acts of coercion; for they are to be carried out against the will of those subject to the order, by the employment of physical force, if necessary. The use of physical force ensues if the application of the sanction meets with resistance, which is only exceptionally the case where the authority applying the sanction has sufficient power. But the admissibility of employing physical force, in case the individual offers resistance against the measure by which he is to be deprived of certain values, is essential. Only if the employment of physical force

The Nature of International Law

is admissible we speak of a sanction as of a coercive act or enforcement action. A social order that attempts to bring about the desired conduct of individuals by sanctions we call a coercive order, in the sense that it provides for coercive acts as sanctions. It stands in the sharpest contrast to all the other social orders, which rest on voluntary obedience. The various systems of morals insofar as they do not provide for transcendental or socially organized sanctions are such noncoercive orders. Thus the antagonism of freedom and coercion—fundamental to social life—supplies the decisive criterion.

It is the criterion of law; for law is a coercive order. It provides for socially organized sanctions and thus can be clearly distinguished from a religious order on the one hand, and a merely moral order on the other hand. As a coercive order the law is that specific social technique which consists in the attempt to bring about the desired social conduct of men through the threat of a measure of coercion which is to be taken in case of contrary, i.e., legally wrong, conduct. This conduct, which is the specific condition of the sanction, is called "illegal act," "crime," "tort," "delict." The last-mentioned term covers all possible kinds of legally wrong conduct. The individual who commits a delict is called the delinquent.

2. Sanctions: Criminal and Civil

In modern national law two different kinds of sanction exist: punishment and civil execution. Punishment is forcible deprivation of life—capital punishment; or forcible deprivation of freedom—imprisonment; or forcible deprivation of property—fine. These are the sanctions of criminal law. Civil execution, the sanction of civil law, also consists in forcible deprivation of property. If a man does not pay his debt or does not repair the damage which he has caused to another, and if the creditor, or the injured person, brings as plaintiff an action against him before a civil court, the court will order an execution against the property of the defendant. This sanction differs from a fine which a criminal court may impose upon a delinquent. The property of which the delinquent is forcibly deprived is transferred under criminal law to the legal community, under civil law to the creditor or the injured person.

The differentiation of criminal and civil law and consequently of criminal and civil delicts is based on the difference between the two kinds of sanction. Delict and sanction are the two fundamental data of the law, which is a set of norms by which a coercive act, the sanction, is attached, as consequence, to a conduct, the delict, as a condition of the sanction.

3. *Legal Norm and Rule of Law: The "Ought"*

A norm prescribes or permits a certain human behavior. A set of norms which form for some reason or another a unit we call a normative order. The law is a normative order, and since legal norms provide for coercive acts as sanctions, the law is a coercive order.

The statements by which the science of law describes its object, the law, as a system of legal norms are statements to the effect that under certain conditions (among which the delict plays an essential part) a certain consequence, namely a sanction, ought to take place. These statements are called rules of law in contradistinction to legal norms, described by the rules of law. Legal norms are issued by legal authorities, rules of law are statements made by the legal science, which is not a legal authority and hence not competent to issue legal norms prescribing or permitting human behavior.

The connection established by a legal norm between the delict as condition and the sanction as consequence, is not a relation between cause and effect, such as is indicated in the statement: If a metallic body is heated, it expands. This statement is a so-called law of nature. By the laws of nature natural science describes its object, nature, just as legal science describes its object, the law, by rules of law. In the rule of law the connection between condition and consequence is characterized by the term "ought," in order to emphasize that the rule of law has not the meaning of a law of nature. It does not express the idea of a necessary or probable connection between one fact and another. Its meaning is not: if a delict occurs, a sanction will—necessarily or probably—take place; but: if a delict is committed, a sanction ought to be applied, even if it

The Nature of International Law

is actually not applied. By the formula "ought to be applied" nothing else is expressed but the idea that if the delict is committed the application of the sanction is legal. The statement that a sanction ought to be applied if a delict has been committed does not necessarily mean that a certain individual is legally obliged to apply a sanction. He may be only authorized to apply the sanction. Whether the application of the sanction provided for by the law is or is not the content of an obligation is a question different from the question as to the meaning of the connection between condition and consequence in the rule of law.

4. *The Delict*

The delict is usually characterized as a "violation" of the law. This is a figure of speech. Taken literally, "violation" means act of violence, i.e., exertion of physical force, which is possible only as directed against a being physically existent. It is its physical existence which is affected by such act. In this sense, the law as a norm providing that something ought to be done cannot be "violated." The specific "existence" of a norm consists in its validity; and the validity of a norm prescribing or permitting a definite conduct is not affected by a contrary conduct. If a definite conduct is prescribed or permitted, the possibility of a contrary conduct is of course presupposed. If theft were impossible, the norm "You shall not steal" would be meaningless. The delict is also described as "unlawful" or "illegal" behavior, which terms express the idea of a negation of the law. But the delict is neither a violation nor a negation of the law. It is conduct determined by the law as a condition of the sanction, likewise determined by the law. Only because a certain conduct is made by law the condition of a sanction is this conduct a delict or, what amounts to the same, is this behavior legally prohibited.

5. *Obligation (Duty) and Right*

If a conduct is the specific condition of a sanction, the contrary conduct is the content of a legal obligation. An individual is legally obliged to conduct himself in a definite way if a sanction is provided for the contrary conduct. The statement that I am legally obliged not to commit theft means that if I commit theft I ought to be punished; the statement that I am legally obliged to pay my debt means that if I do not pay my debt, a civil execution ought to be directed against my property. The subject of the legal obligation is the potential delinquent.

The concept of obligation (or duty) is usually opposed to the concept of right. The term "right" has many meanings. Thus, to have the right to behave in a certain manner may mean to be free to behave in this manner. To be legally free to behave in a certain manner may mean not to be under a legal obligation to behave in another manner. The term "right," however, may have not a mere negative but a positive significance. The statement that I have a right to behave in a certain manner may mean that others are obliged not to prevent me from behaving in this manner; and the statement that I have a right to claim that another individual behave in a certain manner may mean that he is obliged to behave in this manner. The right of an individual in this sense of the term is but the reflection of the obligation of another individual (or other individuals). Finally, the term "right" may designate the legal power conferred upon an individual to bring about a certain legal effect intended by that individual, especially the power to apply the sanction or to bring about directly or indirectly by a definite action the application of the sanction provided by the law, in case another individual does not fulfill his obligation.

In early law the execution of the sanction was decentralized, that is to say it was left to the individual whose interest was violated by the behavior of another individual which constituted the delict. This primitive legal technique is called the principle of self-help. It prevails in primitive law, which in case of murder authorizes the relatives of the murdered man to kill the murderer and his relatives. This is so-called blood revenge; and blood revenge is a sanction provided by primitive law. If a man did not pay his debt or did not repair a damage caused by him, the law authorized the creditor or injured party to take away, by force if necessary, some property of the debtor or the one responsible for the damage.

The Nature of International Law

This is the sanction provided by primitive law for a violation of the obligation to pay a debt or to repair a damage. Under such primitive law to have a right (in the specific sense of the term) means to be authorized by the law to execute a sanction. It is a characteristic of a technically more developed legal order that the execution of the sanction is centralized. This centralization consists in the establishment of a special organ, a tribunal, competent to ascertain in a definite procedure the fact that a delict has been committed, and to order the sanction provided for by the law; and in the establishment of a special executive organ competent to carry out the sanction ordered by the tribunal. To have under such a centralized legal order a right means to have the legal possibility of instituting a lawsuit, i.e., of putting in motion by an action brought before the competent tribunal the procedure which ultimately leads to the execution of the sanction. In this sense the creditor has a right to demand that the debtor shall pay his debt, or the owner of a thing has the right to demand that all the others refrain from interfering with his disposition of the thing.

6. *Responsibility: Individual and Collective*

Another legal concept is that of responsibility. Legal responsibility must be distinguished from legal obligation, especially from the obligation to repair an illegally caused damage. An individual is legally responsible for a delict if the sanction is directed against him. Thus, a man is responsible for a crime he has committed because and insofar as the law provides that he, i.e., the criminal, ought to be punished. A man is responsible for failure to repair a damage caused by him because and insofar as the law provides that a civil execution ought to be directed against his property. In these cases the delinquent, i.e., the individual who by his own behavior has committed the delict, is responsible for it. The subject of the obligation and the subject of the responsibility are identic. But it is possible that an individual other than the delinquent may be responsible for a delict. The law may provide that in case of a delict the sanction ought to be directed against an individual or individuals who have not committed the delict. If the sanction is to be directed against the delinquent, the individual is responsible for his own delict. In this case we speak of individual responsibility. If, however, the sanction is directed against an individual or individuals other than the delinquent, responsibility for a delict committed by others is established. The difference between obligation and responsibility manifests itself in the fact that an individual can be obliged only to behave in a certain way, i.e., to his own behavior, but that an individual cannot be obliged that another individual shall behave in a certain way, i.e., to the behavior of another. But an individual can be responsible not only for his own behavior but also for the behavior of another individual.

The individual responsible for a delict committed by another stands usually in a definite legal relation to the delinquent. The law may, for instance, provide that the father or husband is to be punished in case his child or his wife has committed a crime. The commander of an armed force occupying in time of war a city on enemy territory may order that the mayor of the city shall be executed if within the city illegitimate acts of warfare are committed against the occupying forces. All the members of a family are responsible for a delict committed by one of them if the sanction provided by the law may be directed against all of them. If individuals are responsible for a delict, not because they have committed it but because they belong to the group—family, tribe, or state—to which the delinquent belongs, we speak of collective responsibility. This is a special case of responsibility for a delict committed by another. Collective responsibility exists in case of blood revenge which is directed not only against the murderer but also against all the members of his family. Collective responsibility is established in the Ten Commandments where Yahweh threatens to punish the children and the children's children for the sins of their fathers. A certain relationship between the delinquent and other individuals justifies the identification of the delinquent with these individuals. This identification is at the basis of collective responsibility which prevails in primitive law; it is a manifestation of the collectivistic thinking and feeling so characteristic of primitive man, who does not consider himself as an individual essentially

The Nature of International Law

different from and independent of his fellow men but as an intrinsic part of his group. In modern national law individual responsibility generally prevails. Only exceptionally is collective responsibility established as, for instance, in case of corporations.

Responsibility for a delict should be distinguished from the obligation to repair the damage—material and moral—caused by the delict. Normally the delinquent, that is, the individual who by his own behavior has committed the delict, is obliged to repair the damage caused by the delict. But it is possible that the law imposes the obligation to repair the damage upon an individual other than the delinquent. This is, for instance, the case if the law obliges an employer to repair the damage caused by the negligence of his employee. Then it is usual to say that the employer is "responsible" for the damage caused by his employee. This terminology is misleading because it seems to imply the idea that the employer is responsible for the delict committed by another. However, the employer is not "responsible" for the damage; he is "obliged" to repair the damage; and he is responsible only for the failure to fulfill this obligation, that is to say, for his own delict, not for the delict of another, because if he does not repair the damage, a sanction ought to be directed against him. In this case, too, the sanction is directed against the delinquent. Legal responsibility is something different from legal obligation.

7. *Culpability and Absolute Responsibility*

Since law is a social order regulating the mutual behavior of men, a sanction is annexed to the conduct of an individual because of the harmful effect this conduct has, or may have, on other individuals. The harmful effect may be brought about by the delinquent intentionally and maliciously or only negligently; and it may be brought about without intention, malice, or negligence on the part of the delinquent, by mere accident. If the law annexes a sanction to a certain conduct only if the harmful effect of this conduct was intended or was brought about by negligence, we speak of responsibility based on fault (or culpability); if the law annexes a sanction to a certain conduct even if the harmful effect is brought about without intention or negligence on the part of the delinquent, we speak of absolute responsibility (or liability). In this latter case the fact that the injury inflicted by one individual upon another was not intended (with or without malice) nor caused by negligence (that is by omission of the care by which normally the harmful effect could be avoided) is no excuse.

The differentiation between responsibility based on fault (culpability) and absolute responsibility (liability) is characteristic of a relatively progressive legal order. It is unknown to primitive law, where, together with collective responsibility, absolute responsibility prevails. Collective responsibility is, by its very nature, absolute responsibility. For in the case of collective responsibility a sanction is directed against individuals who have not committed the delict. Since they have not committed the delict at all, they cannot have committed it intentionally, maliciously or negligently. A sanction is directed against them although there was no intention or malice or negligence on their side. Hence their responsibility is an absolute responsibility. Collective responsibility is always "absolute" with respect to the individual made responsible. However, it is possible that a legal order establishes responsibility of an individual (or individuals) for a delict committed by another only in case the delict has been committed by the other individual intentionally and maliciously or with culpable negligence. Then the responsibility established by the law is absolute with respect to the responsible individual (or individuals), but based on fault with respect to the individual who is the immediate delinquent. Such a situation is established, for instance, by a provision that a civil execution is to be directed against the property of a corporation—as the collective property of its members—in case a damage is caused intentionally or negligently by an organ of the corporation and no reparation made, but that no such sanction is to be applied in case the individual acting as an organ of the corporation has brought about the damage without intending it and has taken all the care by which normally such damage can be avoided. The responsibility of the corporation is the collective responsibility of its members;[1] and responsibility based on

---

[1] Cf. *infra*, p. 98ff.

The Nature of International Law

the fault of the immediate delinquent, but not on the fault of the responsible individual (or individuals), is of particular importance in connection with collective responsibility.

8. The Force Monopoly of the Community

The sanction as an act of coercion prescribed or permitted by the law is an act by which force is employed by one individual against another. Under national law the employment of force is a delict unless it is prescribed or permitted by the legal order; and, as a rule, it is prescribed or permitted by the law only as a sanction. If the behavior which constitutes the condition of the sanction is called "delict," this term has no moral connotation. It means only a definite behavior against which a sanction is provided for by the law.

It is characteristic of national law that it determines the conditions under which force may lawfully be employed. If employed under these conditions the employment of force is legal; it has, as a rule, the character of a sanction. If employed under other conditions it is illegal; it has the character of a delict. It is a characteristic feature of national law that the employment of force is, as a rule, either a sanction or a delict.[2]

In stipulating sanctions, the legal order authorizes a definite individual to perform the coercive act constituting the sanction. This individual, in carrying out the sanction, may be considered to act as an organ—centralized or decentralized—of the community constituted by the legal order. Hence the sanction may be considered to be an action of the community. That means that the act performed by an individual is imputed to the community. If a

---

[2] As an exception, the employment of force permitted by the law has not the character of a sanction in the usual sense of the term, as, for instance, in the case of forcible internment of insane individuals in an asylum or forcible isolation of individuals afflicted with a contagious disease. Forcible internment of citizens of an enemy state in time of war is a measure taken to prevent them from committing delicts against the state at war with their home state, and to that extent it may be interpreted as a sanction. The same interpretation may apply to the forcible internment in concentration camps in time of peace of politically suspected individuals.

social order provides that coercive acts shall be performed only under definite conditions, determined by it, and only by definite individuals, likewise determined by it, and if we consider these individuals as organs of the community constituted by the social order, we may say that the social order reserves the employment of force to the community. Such a social order establishes a force monopoly of the community.

The force monopoly of the community may be centralized or decentralized. It is centralized if the social order institutes, according to the principle of division of labor, special organs for the execution of the sanctions provided for by the order. This, as has been pointed out, is the case when a legal order institutes tribunals competent to ascertain in a procedure, determined by the law, whether a delict has been committed and who is responsible for it, and when the legal order institutes special organs to execute the sanctions ordered by the tribunals. The force monopoly of the community is decentralized if the principle of self-help prevails, that is to say, if the legal order leaves these functions to the individuals injured by the delict, as in the case of blood revenge. Although in this case the individuals appear to "take the law in their own hands," they may nevertheless be considered as acting as organs of the community. Even if the principle of self-help prevails, legal and illegal employment of force are to be distinguished. The relative of a murdered individual who takes revenge by killing the murderer or his relatives is not a murderer. The avenger does not violate the law; he executes the law and hence may be considered as an organ of the legal community constituted by the legal order. But he is not a special organ instituted according to the principle of division of labor, as a court or a sheriff is. If the principle of self-help prevails, i.e., if the law authorizes the individuals injured by the delict—and not special organs—to execute the sanction, the function of these individuals is determined by the legal order; they act in a manner authorized by the law. If they employ force, they enforce the law. Hence also in this case we may speak of a force monopoly of the community: for the conditions under which and the individuals through which force may be employed are determined by the legal order constituting the community. It is

The Nature of International Law

a characteristic feature of law to constitute a force monopoly of the legal community.

9. Self-help and Collective Security

Where the principle of self-help prevails, the legal order may authorize or even obligate subjects who are not the immediate victims of the delict to assist the victim in his lawful reaction against the delict, in his execution of the sanction. But the principle of self-help is eliminated if the legal order reserves the execution of the sanction to a special organ, that is, if the force monopoly of the community is centralized. If the members of the legal community are obliged—and not only authorized—to assist the victim of a delict in his legitimate reaction against the delict, that is to say, in the execution of the sanction, or if the execution of the sanction is reserved to a special organ of the community, we speak of collective security. Hence there are two stages in the development of collective security: the first is characterized by the fact that the principle of self-help still prevails, but the members of the community are legally obliged to assist the victim of a delict, especially the victim of an illegal employment of force, in his legal reaction against this delict, namely, in the execution of the sanction; the second is characterized by the fact that the execution of the sanction is reserved to a central organ of the community, and that means that a centralized force monopoly of the community is established.

It stands to reason that collective security is more effective if the force monopoly of the community is centralized than if it is decentralized. The most obvious defect of a decentralized force monopoly consists in the fact that there is no authority, different from and independent of the parties concerned, competent to ascertain in a concrete case that a delict has been committed. Consequently, if there is no agreement of the parties on this question, it remains doubtful whether the coercive act performed as a reaction against an alleged delict is a sanction or a delict. Another not less serious shortcoming of a decentralized force monopoly is that if the individual, or group of individuals, authorized by law to carry out the sanction is not more powerful than the delinquent and his group, the sanction cannot successfully be executed. In view of these facts, the concept of law is sometimes reserved for a coercive order which establishes a minimum of centralization by instituting tribunals and executive agencies. According to this view no true law exists as long as the principle of self-help prevails. The establishment of a relatively centralized system of collective security is supposed to be an essential prerequisite of the law.

This restriction of the concept of law is not accepted in this treatise. Here, a social order is considered as law even if it establishes only a decentralized force monopoly of the community constituted by the order, that is, if the principle of self-help still prevails. For centralization of the force monopoly of the community is the result of a slow and gradual evolution, within which the progress from a decentralized to a centralized coercive order —important as it may be—is not less decisive than the step which leads from a state of complete anarchy to a social order determining the conditions under which and the individual by whom force may be employed. Such an order establishes only a decentralized force monopoly of the community; it is a social order under which the principle of self-help prevails and hence a distinction is to be made between a legal and an illegal employment of force in the relations among men. This is the state of a primitive society in which blood revenge is a recognized institution established by custom. There is sufficient reason to characterize such a coercive order, based on the principle of self-help, as primitive law.

Moreover, even under the most centralized coercive order, the law of the state, the principle of self-help is not completely eliminated. It is preserved in the generally accepted institution of self-defense. Self-defense is a kind of self-help; it is legal employment of force by an individual against an illegal employment of force by another individual. In exercising self-defense an individual is authorized by the law to use force against the illegal aggressor. Under a primitive legal order which does not centralize the employment of force, the right of self-defense is implied in the principle of self-help. Under a legal order which establishes a

The Nature of International Law

centralized force monopoly, self-defense is the minimum of self-help, which is indispensable even within such a legal system.

10. Retribution and Prevention

A community, in the long run, is only possible if each individual respects certain interests—such as life, freedom, property, and other values—of everyone else, that is to say, if each refrains from forcibly interfering in this sphere of interests of the other. The social technique that we call "law" consists in inducing the individual to refrain from forcible interference in the sphere of interests of others by a specific means: namely, in case of such interference, the legal community itself reacts with a like interference in the sphere of interests of the individual responsible for the previous—the illegal—interference. Like for like. It is the idea of retribution which lies at the base of this social technique. Even if—in a relatively late stage of evolution—the purpose of the sanction is considered to be prevention and not mere retribution, only a change of ideology justifying the technique of the law takes place; the technique itself remains the same.

11. Law and Peace

By reserving the use of force to the community, that is, by determining the conditions under which certain individuals—and only these individuals—as organs of the legal community are authorized to interfere forcibly in the sphere of interests of those subjected to the legal order, the law guarantees peace. If peace is conceived as a state of absence of force, the law then provides only for relative, not for absolute, peace. The peace guaranteed by the law is not a state of complete absence of force, a state of anarchy. It is the state of a force monopoly, namely, the force monopoly of the legal community.

On the other hand, a definite sphere of interests of the individual is protected inasmuch as forcible interference in the sphere of interests of the individual is permitted only under definite conditions, and any other forcible interference in the sphere of interests of the individual is prohibited, or, in other terms, inasmuch as forcible interference in the sphere of interests of the individual is made a monopoly of the community. As long as the social order does not establish a force monopoly of the community, so long is there no sphere of interests of the individuals protected by the social order. In other words, there is no state of law which, in the sense developed here, is essentially a state of peace.

B. IS INTERNATIONAL LAW "LAW" IN THE TRUE SENSE OF THE TERM?

Assuming that the foregoing analysis is correct, it is possible to describe the law of a community, its legal order, by a system of sentences stating that under certain conditions a certain act of coercion ought to be performed. This hypothetical proposition is the basic form of a rule of law, the term "rule" being understood in a descriptive (not normative) sense.

1. Meaning of the Question

The question whether or not international law is law in the sense determined above is identical with the question whether or not the phenomena commonly called international law can be described by rules of law of the same kind as the rules by which national law may be described.

International law is true law if the coercive acts of states, the forcible interference of a state in the sphere of interests of another state, are, in principle, permitted only as a reaction against a delict, and accordingly the employment of force to any other end is forbidden; in other words, if the coercive act undertaken as a reaction against a delict can be interpreted as a reaction of the international legal community. International law is law in the same sense as national law, provided that it is, in principle, possible to interpret the employment of force directed by one state against another either as sanction or as delict.

The Nature of International Law

In speaking of international law, reference is made only to general or common international law, not to particular international law. General or common international law is customary law valid for all states belonging to the international community. (Customary law is law created by the habitual practice of the states.) Particular international law is valid for some states only, and comprises especially norms created by treaties valid only for the contracting parties.[3]

Hence our problem must be formulated as follows: Is there, according to general international law, such a thing as a sanction, i.e., a coercive act provided for as the consequence of a definite conduct of the state, a forcible interference in the normally protected sphere of interests of the state responsible for this conduct? This question implies the question as to whether there is according to general international law such a thing as a delict. For from previous statements it follows that, legally, conduct of a state can be considered a delict only if international law attaches to this conduct a sanction directed against a state responsible for this conduct.

2. *International Delicts*

It is a commonly accepted opinion that there exists in international law such a thing as a delict, that is, conduct of a state which is considered illegal, contrary to international law, and, therefore, a violation of international law. This follows from the fact that international law is regarded as a system of norms which prescribe or permit a certain conduct for states. If, e.g., a state, without a specific reason recognized by international law, invades territory of another state, or if a state fails to observe a treaty concluded with another state, its conduct is considered to be contrary to the international order in the same sense that the conduct of an individual who lies is considered contrary to the moral order. In this general sense, there is, without doubt, a delict in international law. But is there, in international law, such a thing as a delict in the specifically juristic sense? That is to say,

---

[3] Cf. *infra*, pp. 188ff.

is there a sanction, i.e., an enforcement action, provided for by international law to be directed against the state responsible for the delict, i.e., responsible for definite behavior, determined by international law as condition of the sanction?

3. International Sanctions

a. *Sanction and obligation of reparation.* By "sanction" in international law many writers mean the obligation to repair the moral and material damage caused by the delict. The reparation of the moral damage consists in a formal apology on the part of the delinquent state, and this apology may take the form of a ceremonial act, such as a salute to the flag of the wronged State, and the like. The reparation of the material damage consists in the re-establishment of the situation which would have existed if the illegal damage had not been caused; and, if this is not possible, in the payment of an adequate compensation. This obligation to make reparation may be called a substitute obligation, i.e., an obligation which arises when a state has failed to fulfill its main or primary obligation. The obligation to make reparation is substituted for the violated obligation.[4]

It is, however, possible that in a concrete case the obligation to make reparation, stipulated *in abstracto* by general international law, cannot come into existence. For an obligation to make reparation exists only if an international delict has been committed,

---

[4] In the *Case concerning the Factory at Chorzow* (Publications of the Permanent Court of International Justice, Series A, No. 17) the Court (1928) held that "it is a principle of international law, and even a general conception of law, that any breach of an engagement involves an obligation to make reparation" (p. 29). "The essential principle contained in the actual notion of an illegal act—a principle which seems to be established by international practice and in particular by the decisions of arbitral tribunals—is that reparation must, as far as possible, wipe out all the consequences of the illegal act and re-establish the situation which would in all probability, have existed if that act had not been committed. Restitution in kind, or, if this is not possible, payment of a sum corresponding to the value which a restitution in kind would bear; the award, if need be, of damages for loss sustained which would not be covered by restitution in kind or payment in place of it—such are the principles which should serve to determine the amount of compensation due for an act contrary to international law" (p. 47).

and there is, under general international law, no objective authority, especially no court, competent to ascertain the existence of a delict. This function is left by general international law to the states concerned. Consequently a state may consider itself to be under an obligation to make reparation only if it admits that it has committed a delict; that is to say, if there is an agreement of the states concerned in this respect, and such agreement might not be reached. Even if it has been reached, it does not suffice to establish the concrete obligation to make reparation. The state responsible for a delict is not obliged to comply with any unilateral demand for reparation made by the injured state. They must also come to an agreement concerning the content of the reparation to be made. As long as these agreements concerning the existence of the delict and the content of the reparation are not concluded, it is hardly possible to assume the existence of a concrete obligation to make reparation. Under national law, the situation is substantially different. No such agreements are necessary, for there are courts competent to ascertain the existence of the delict and to determine the content of the reparation to be made in case the parties concerned cannot reach agreement in these respects.

In view of the situation which exists under general international law, it is not excluded to assume that general international law does not impose upon the delinquent state the obligation to make reparation, and upon the injured state the obligation to try to get reparation from the state responsible for the delict before resorting to reprisals or war against the latter; but that general international law only provides that by an agreement concerning reparation of the moral and material damage caused by the delict, and by the fulfillment of the obligation established by this agreement the delinquent state can avoid the sanctions provided by general international law.

Even if it is admitted that under general international law the violation of an obligation automatically entails the substitute obligation to make reparation, this substitute obligation cannot be considered as having the character of a sanction. For a sanction is a coercive act, not an obligation.

By stipulating a sanction as consequence of a certain behavior, the law makes this behavior a delict, and thus establishes an obligation to the contrary behavior. Sanction and obligation are two different concepts. If by repairing the damage caused by a certain behavior the sanction stipulated as the consequence of this behavior can be avoided, the legal situation is correctly described by this statement: If somebody behaves in a certain way and if he does not repair the damage caused by his behavior, a coercive act, i.e., a sanction, ought to be executed. Then the sanction is conditioned by a delict composed of two acts: the behavior causing the damage and the nonreparation of the damage; and then the sanction may be considered as constituting a primary obligation to refrain from the behavior causing the damage and a substitute obligation to repair the damage in case of nonfulfillment of the primary obligation. But neither the one nor the other obligation is a sanction.

b. *International sanctions as enforcement measures.* Hence the decisive question as to the nature of international law may be formulated as follows: Does international law provide for coercive acts (enforcement actions) as the consequence of a certain conduct of states determined by international law; or, in other terms, does international law determine a certain conduct of states as the condition of certain enforcement actions, and thus make this conduct an international delict, the enforcement actions having the character of sanctions? Does international law provide for forcible interference into the normally protected sphere of interests of the state responsible for the delict? If such enforcement actions are provided for by international law, they can be taken only by the individual states as subjects of international law, not by special organs of the international community. For this legal community, constituted by general international law, being completely decentralized, has no special organs for the creation and application of the law. On account of its decentralization general international law has the character of a primitive law which is characterized by the fact that it does not establish special legislative, judicial, or administrative organs, but leaves the functions concerned to the individual subjects, members of the legal community. If general international law provides for coercive acts as sanctions, the

The Nature of International Law

states concerned are authorized to execute them or, as this aspect of the principle of self-help is usually characterized, to take the law in their own hands.[5]

4. Reprisals

An analysis of international relations shows that there are two different kinds of forcible interference in a state's sphere of interest which is normally protected by international law. The distinction rests upon the degree of forcible interference. Interference may in principle be limited or unlimited; that is, the enforcement action undertaken against a state may be restricted to the violation of certain interests of this state or it may affect all interests. A generally accepted opinion prevails as to the characterization of a limited interference in the sphere of interests of one state by another. Such an interference is considered as a delict in the sense of international law unless it has the character of a reprisal. It is permitted as a reprisal, and is not a delict insofar as it takes place as a reaction against a delict. The usual definition of reprisals is as follows: Reprisals are acts which, although normally illegal, are exceptionally permitted as reaction of one state against a violation of its right by another state. Typical

---

[5] In *The Queen v. Keyn* (Great Britain, Court for Crown Cases Reserved, 1876, 2 Law Reports, Exchequer Division 63) the Court stated: "Strictly speaking, international law is an inexact expression, and it is apt to mislead if its inexactness is not kept in mind. Law implies a law-giver, and a tribunal capable of enforcing it and coercing its transgressors. But there is no common law-giver to sovereign states; and no tribunal has the power to bind them by decrees or coerce them if they transgress." But in *The Prometheus* (Great Britain, Supreme Court of Hongkong, 1906, 2 Hongkong Law Reports 207, 225) the judge declared: "It was contended on behalf of the owners of the *Prometheus* that the term 'law' as applied to this recognized system of principles and rules known as international law is an inexact expression, that there is, in other words, no such thing as international law; that there can be no such law binding upon all nations inasmuch as there is no sanction for such law, that is to say that there is no means by which obedience to such law can be imposed upon any given nation refusing obedience thereto. I do not concur in that contention. In my opinion a law may be established and become international, that is to say binding upon all nations, by the agreement of such nations to be bound thereby, although it may be impossible to enforce obedience thereto by any given nation party to the agreement."

examples of reprisals against a state responsible for an international delict are the confiscation of property of the state or of its citizens, or nonfulfillment of treaty obligations in relation to that state. In wartime, reprisals may consist in nonobservance on the part of one belligerent of the rules respecting the means of warfare (e.g., the prohibition of the use of poison gas) as a reaction against a violation of these rules on the part of the other belligerent.

In the exercise of reprisals the use of armed force is not excluded. But if an enforcement action involves the use of armed force, it is difficult to distinguish in concrete cases between reprisals—as a limited interference—and the other type of enforcement action, namely, the unlimited interference in the sphere of interests of another state undertaken by armed force, which is called war.

It is a generally recognized principle that reprisals must be in proportion to the delict against which they are taken.[6] Hence there is nothing to prevent us from calling reprisals sanctions of international law. For reprisals are reactions against violations of international law, i.e., international delicts. General international

---

[6] The principles that reprisals are legal only as reaction against a violation of international law, and must be in proportion to the international delict, have been confirmed in *The Naulilaa Case* (Annual Digest of Public International Law Cases 1927–1928, Case No. 360). On October 19, 1914, when Germany was not yet at war with Portugal, a German official and two German officers of German South West Africa were killed by members of a Portuguese frontier post at Naulilaa. Two other Germans were wounded and interned. As a measure of reprisals, and at the order of the governor of German South West Africa, German forces attacked and destroyed a number of forts and posts in the frontier region of Portuguese territory. In addition, the German governor sent a military expedition in the direction of the fort of Naulilaa, whose garrison offered resistance but was finally forced to give up the fort and to retire. Portugal contended that the reprisals were unjustified and that Germany was responsible for the damage caused by the invasion. The Special Arbitral Tribunal, to which the case was submitted, found that the incident was entirely due to a misunderstanding caused largely by the fact that the Germans did not speak Portuguese and that the Portuguese officer who gave the order to fire believed himself to be in danger. The tribunal held that Germany was responsible, and stated that a necessary condition for the legitimate exercise of the right of reprisals is the violation of a rule of international law by the State against which the reprisals are directed; and that reprisals which are altogether out of proportion with the act which prompted them are excessive and therefore illegal.

The Nature of International Law

law confers upon each state the legal power of taking certain enforcement actions, which have the character of reprisals, i.e., of a limited interference in the sphere of interests of another state, in case certain interests of the former are violated by the latter. Thus international law makes these violations international delicts.

Not all interests of a state are protected in this way by general international law and hence have the character of rights. The conduct by which a state violates some interest of another state may not be a delict, that is to say, the state whose interest is violated may not be authorized to execute a sanction by taking an enforcement action against the state which has violated its interest; but it may react by a similar violation of an interest of the latter state. Such a reaction is called a retorsion. It is no sanction, for it is not an enforcement action—the employment of physical force in case of resistance not being permitted. Reprisals, however, are enforcement actions, insofar as in case of resistance the employment of physical force is permitted. Hence, the violation of interests of one state by another state against which reprisals —and that means in the last analysis employment of physical force—are not permitted is not an international delict.

The state which, authorized by international law, i.e., under the conditions determined by international law, resorts to reprisals may be considered to be acting as an organ of the international community constituted by international law. The enforcement action may be interpreted as an action of this community, its reaction against a violation of international law. But if a state under conditions other than those determined by international law takes the same enforcement action, it commits an international delict, because it is not authorized by the law to take such action.

5. War: Its Concept

Is such interpretation also possible with reference to war? Can an enforcement action involving the use of armed force and constituting an unlimited interference in the sphere of interest of a state by another state be construed either as a delict, i.e., as the condition of a sanction, or as a sanction? This is the question as to the legal meaning of war according to general international law. Is it possible to say that, according to international law, war is only permitted as a sanction, and any war which has not the character of a sanction is forbidden by international law, and thus constitutes a delict?

a. *War: A bilateral or a unilateral action?* Before answering this question it is necessary to determine the concept of war. In this respect there is no unanimity among the writers on international law. Some writers, following the authority of Grotius,[7] define war as a specific status; others, as a specific action. The status the former have in mind, is the so-called state of war. That a state is in a "state of war" in relation to another state means that the rules of international law concerning war, i.e., the rules stipulating obligations and rights of belligerents and neutrals, are applicable. Such a state of war is brought about by an act of war, that is to say, by an enforcement action involving the use of armed force. But some writers maintain that a state of war is brought about also by a mere declaration of war, that is, the formal declaration of the intention to resort to war, i.e., to use armed force, even if this intention is actually not, or not yet, carried into effect. They refer to the fact that during the First World War some Latin-American states declared war on the German Reich, after which a state of war was assumed to exist in the relation between these states and the German Reich, which status was terminated by peace treaties, although no use of armed force had taken place in their mutual relations. It may be that, according to general international law, a declaration of war has the effect that certain rules of international law concerning the obligations and rights of belligerents apply; for instance, the rules concerning the treatment of the citizens of one party staying in the territory of the other party, or the rules relating to the effect of war on treaties. But most of the rules concerning war cannot apply if no use of armed force takes place. If only some rules concerning war apply, no state of war in the full sense of the term exists, but only a status which is analogous or similar to a state of war. If this status is

---

[7] Grotius, *De jure belli ac pacis* (1625), Bk. I, Chap. I, sec. 2, par. 1: "War is the condition [status] of those contending by force, viewed simply as such."

The Nature of International Law

terminated by a treaty, this treaty is not a peace treaty in the true sense of the term. A state of war in the true and full sense of the term is brought about only by acts of war, that is to say, by the use of armed force; and only such a state may be, but need not necessarily be, terminated by a peace treaty. Consequently war is a specific action, not a status. From the point of view of international law, the most important fact is the resort to war, and that means resort to an action, not resort to a status. Some writers consider the intention to make war, the *animus belligerendi,* of the state or states involved in war as essential. *Animus belligerendi* means the intention to wage war. But this can be only the intention to perform acts of war, that is to say, to use armed force, with all the consequences international law attaches to the use of armed force.

Most of the writers define war as a contest between two or more states through their armed forces. If this definition is accepted, a unilateral enforcement action involving the use of armed force, directed by one state against another state which does not react by a similar enforcement action, cannot be considered as "war," and hence the norms of international law concerning war do not apply to such a unilateral enforcement action. It is, however, doubtful whether such a definition of war can be maintained. It is generally admitted that a unilateral enforcement action involving the use of armed force constitutes "war" if preceded by a declaration of war on the part of the state performing the enforcement action or answered by the state against which this action is directed by a declaration that it considers the action to be an act of war. The question as to whether war is essentially a bilateral action should not be confused with the question as to whether it is necessary, and who is competent, to ascertain that in a concrete case war exists. Like any fact to which international law attaches certain consequences, the fact "war" must be ascertained by the competent authorities. As long as no objective authority is established, it is for the states concerned to ascertain the existence of the fact "war" in the sense of international law. Hence it depends on these states to decide whether there is or is not war in their mutual relations. But a state attacked by another state may declare itself to be at war with the aggressor without resorting itself to a counterwar, and without the aggressor having formally declared war. Hence the existence of war does not depend on the existence of a counterwar.[8]

b. *War and counterwar.* The distinction between war and counterwar is indispensable if it is to be possible to qualify a war as illegal or legal, as delict or sanction. The war waged by one state against another may be illegal, whereas the war by which the other state reacts against the former may be legal; and vice versa. If there are rules of international law prohibiting war, imposing upon the states the legal obligation not to resort to war, there must be a sanction provided for in case a state resorts to war in violation of this obligation. If there are no collective sanctions established to be taken by an international organization, the only effective sanction is war, that is to say, counterwar as reaction against an illegal war. The counterwar may be resorted to by the state against which the illegal war has been directed—the immediate victim of an illegal war—and by a third state assisting the victim in its reaction against the delict. If the two actions —war and counterwar—are not differentiated, the situation can be characterized only by the statement that "the war" is simultaneously illegal and legal, a delict and a sanction, which implies a contradiction in terms. War and counterwar are in the same reciprocal relation as murder and capital punishment. Nobody maintains that murder exists only if capital punishment is actually executed. The rules of international law by which "war" is for-

---

[8] In the case *The Nayade* (Great Britain, High Court of Admiralty, 1802, 165 The English Reports 602–603) the question arose whether Portugal, an ally of Great Britain, was at war with France. The Court stated that "there was a wish on the part of Portugal not to consider herself as being at war with France," but declared that "it is by no means necessary that both countries should declare war. Whatever might be the prostration and submissive demeanour on one side, if France was unwilling to accept that submission, and persisted in attacking Portugal, it was sufficient."

In *The Eliza Ann* (Great Britain, High Court of Admiralty, 1813, 1 Dodson 244) the Court stated: "A declaration of war by one country only is not, as has been represented, a mere challenge, to be accepted or refused at pleasure by the other. It proves the existence of actual hostilities on one side at least, and puts the other party also into a state of war, though he may, perhaps, think proper to act on the defensive only."

bidden, and, accordingly, a "delict," refer only to the action of one state, not to the counteraction of the other. This is usually expressed by the statement that only a war of aggression, that is, the war on the part of the state which is the first to commit a hostile act of force, is forbidden, not the war waged by the state defending itself against the aggressor.

c. *War within the meaning of the Covenant of the League of Nations, the Kellogg-Briand Pact, and the Charter of the United Nations.* Article 16 of the Covenant of the League of Nations[9] provided for sanctions in case a member should "resort to war in disregard of its covenants" against another member. The delict conditioning the sanction was committed even if the attacked member did not resort to a counterwar; and it might omit doing so and rely on the action of the other members obliged by the Covenant to take enforcement measures against the delinquent state.

The Kellogg-Briand Pact[10] forbids war as an instrument of national policy. But as instrument of national policy only the employment of force by the state violating the pact, not the counteraction against this state, can be characterized.

It is highly significant that in the provision of the Charter of the United Nations by which war is prohibited (Article 2, paragraph 4), the term "war" does not appear at all. The Charter imposes upon the members the obligation to refrain from the use of force in their international relations. War is forbidden as a use of force by one state against another state, without any regard to the attitude of the latter. War must be considered as an employment of force directed by one state against another without regard to the counteraction of the latter not only when war is a delict, but also when war is a sanction. This is of particular importance in case war is a collective enforcement action involving the use of armed force, taken by an international organization as a reaction against a violation of international law. By calling such an action a "police action," we cannot deprive it of its character as war. The enforcement action involving the use of armed force to be

---

[9] Cf. *infra*, pp. 39ff.
[10] Cf. *infra*, pp. 42ff.

taken under the Charter of the United Nations by the Security Council[11] may have the character of war, regardless of whether or not it is answered by a counterwar on the part of the state against which it is directed.

د. *War of aggression and war of defense.* If a war has the legal character of a sanction, the question arises whether the counterwar is legal. Under national law, resistance against the use of force which has the character of a sanction is forbidden and constitutes a delict to which an additional sanction is attached. Under general international law, resistance by force against legitimate reprisals is certainly illegal and may be answered by additional reprisals or by war, as a sanction. If war as a sanction is resorted to against a violation of international law which violation is not constituted by a war resorted to against the state executing the sanction, the sanction has the character of a war of aggression (within the meaning of the definition given above) and the counterwar the character of a war of defense. As an exercise of the right of self-defense, such a counterwar seems to be legal and appears to be neither a delict nor a sanction. However, the right of self-defense must be considered as being restricted to defense against illegal aggression.[12] Not every war of aggression is illegal, and not every war of defense is legal. The frequent identification of "war of aggression" and "illegal war" is untenable. Under the Kellogg-Briand Pact, any of the states that are contracting parties to the pact may resort to war against another contracting party which has violated the pact by resorting to war against any of the contracting states. Hence, under the pact, a state may resort to war against another state although the latter has not attacked the former.

In this case a war of aggression is legal, and a war of defense illegal. Since the right of self-defense must be interpreted to be restricted to defense against an illegal aggression, counterwar as a reaction against a war which has the character of a sanction is always a delict. No additional sanction is practically possible against such a delict; nor is it necessary in order to qualify the

---

[11] Cf. *infra*, pp. 46ff.
[12] Cf. *infra*, p. 58f.

The Nature of International Law

counterwar as a delict, since a sanction is already in operation. Counterwar against an enforcement action involving or not involving the use of armed force taken by the Security Council under the Charter of the United Nations is certainly an illegal use of force within the meaning of Article 2, paragraph 4, of the Charter.[13] An enforcement action involving the use of armed force taken by the United Nations is not an "armed attack" within the meaning of Article 51 of the Charter, even if this enforcement action is taken by the Security Council against a state which did not resort to war. Hence the right of self-defense stipulated by Article 51 does not comprise a counterwar against a legitimate war undertaken as an enforcement action by the United Nations.

e. *Concept of "war" replaced by concept of "use of armed force."* If war is to be considered as a delict or as a sanction, then war cannot be defined as a bilateral action, but as an enforcement action involving the use of armed force. And if every use of force in the relations among states is forbidden, the question as to whether a use of force has the character of war is of secondary importance. But international jurisprudence cannot dispose of the concept of war as long as important rules of international law refer to "war," such as the rules regulating the conduct of war. Since not every enforcement action involving the use of armed force is "war" in the specific sense of international law, the question then arises under what conditions such action is war.

f. *Purpose of war.* This question usually is answered by inserting into the definition of war a reference to its purpose: to overpower the opponent and to impose upon him the conditions of peace. Since this purpose must be implied in the intention of the belligerents, both parties must have such intention. But it is hardly possible to deny that the attacked state may have only the intention to defend itself, without overpowering the aggressor, so that the war may end without a victory of one over the other. Even writers who characterize war by its purpose of the overpowering of one belligerent by the other, do not and cannot deny that, e.g., in maritime war a belligerent may limit itself to mere coast defense and that war—true war within the meaning of international law—

---

[13] Cf. *infra*, p. 45.

may be waged with the intention of exhausting the enemy, not of reaching victory over him. There are wars in which there is no victor and no vanquished.

The above-mentioned definition is problematical also because a war may be terminated without a peace treaty. The conclusion of the peace treaty, insofar as the treaty stipulates more than the termination of the state of war, is beyond the action of war.[14] Hence the intention of imposing the conditions of peace upon the opponent should not be inserted into the definition of war. The only difference between an enforcement action involving the use of armed force which has the character of war and other enforcement actions of a similar kind consists in the degree of the forcible interference in the sphere of interests of one state constituted by the action of the other. War is, in principle, an enforcement action involving the use of armed force performed by one state against another, constituting as it does an unlimited interference in the sphere of interests of the other state.

g. *International war and internal (civil) war.* It is assumed to be an essential characteristic of war that it is an action directed by a state (or a community of states) against another state (or a community of states). If one of the two parties is not a state in the sense of international law (or a community of states, such as the United Nations), the enforcement action, even if involving the use of armed force, is not a war in the sense of international law on either side. Hence a civil war, the fight of a revolutionary group against the legitimate government, is not an international war. There is an exception to the rule that war can exist only in the relation among states: If in a civil war the insurgents are recognized as a belligerent power.[15]

If a state, with its armed forces, assists another state, and that implies, assists the government of another state, in its fight against insurgents not recognized as a belligerent power, the enforcement action of the assisting state has the same character as that of the assisted state. It is participation in a civil war on the side of the legitimate government of the assisted state. This is an internal

---

[14] Cf. *infra*, pp. 67ff.
[15] Cf. *infra*, pp. 291ff.

The Nature of International Law

affair of this state, its reaction against a violation of its law, i.e., against an illegal use of force. Since participation of a state in a civil war within another state on the side of the legitimate government is legally possible only with the express or tacit consent of that state, the enforcement action of the assisting state is, in the last analysis, an action of the assisted state, because authorized by its government.

6. War: Its Legal Interpretation

a. *War not forbidden by general international law.* As to the legal character of war, two diametrically opposed views are advocated. According to one opinion, war under general international law is neither a delict nor a sanction. Any state that is not expressly bound by a special treaty to refrain from warring upon another state, or to resort to war only under definite conditions, may proceed to war against any other state on any ground without violating international law. According to this opinion, therefore, war does not constitute a delict. As the action of a state which is called war is not forbidden by general international law, it is to this extent permitted.

A certain restriction seems to be established by the rule, maintained by many writers on international law, that the states are obliged not to resort to war without a previous dispute and an attempt to settle it by negotiation. Since the rule concerned provides nothing with respect to the extent of the negotiations, the restriction is of little importance. A war resorted to after any kind of negotiation, without regard to the question as to whether it is or is not a reaction against a wrong suffered, is, according to this opinion, not a delict. Nor does war constitute a sanction; for there is in general international law no special provision which authorizes the state to resort to war. War is not set up by general international law as a specific reaction against illegal conduct of a state.

b. *The* bellum justum *doctrine.* The opposite opinion, however, holds that according to general international law war is forbidden in principle. War is permitted only as a reaction against an illegal act, a delict, that is to say, as a reaction against a definite conduct of states, determined by international law and permitted only when directed against the state responsible for this conduct, i.e., the delict. War is permitted as a reaction against an international delict not only to the immediate victim of the delict, but also to states which come to its assistance. Like reprisals, war has to be a sanction if it is not to be characterized as a delict. This is the theory of *bellum justum*—just[16] war.

(1) HISTORY OF THE DOCTRINE. The idea that war is an illegal act, a delict, if it is not a sanction, i.e., a reaction against a delict, is by no means an achievement of modern civilization. It is to be found under the most primitive conditions. It is unequivocally expressed even in the relationship between hostile groups within primitive society. In his article entitled "Primitive Law," Radcliffe-Brown writes: "The waging of war is in some communities, as among the Australian hordes, normally an act of retaliation, carried out by one group against another that is held responsible for an injury suffered, and the procedure is regulated by a recognized body of customs, which is equivalent to the international law of modern nations."[17] In general, this is typical of all wars among primitive peoples. Since international law is a primitive law it is quite natural that the principle of *bellum justum* has been conserved in this legal order.

It is therefore hardly astounding that one encounters the idea of just war in the interstate law of the ancient Greeks. "No war was undertaken without the belligerents alleging a definite cause considered by them as a valid and sufficient justification therefor."[18] As to the Romans, Cicero,[19] expressing the generally prevailing public opinion, states that only such wars could be considered legal actions as were undertaken either for reasons of defense or for reasons of vengeance: "Illa injusta bella sunt quae sunt sine causa suscepta, nam extra ulciscendi aut propulsandorum hostium causam bellum geri justum nullum potest." ("Wars undertaken without reason are unjust wars, for, except for the purpose of

---

[16] The term "just" meaning "legal" in the sense of positive international law.

[17] *Encyclopaedia of the Social Sciences* (1933), IX, 203.

[18] Coleman Phillipson, *The International Law and Custom of Ancient Greece and Rome* (1911), II, 179.

[19] Cicero *De republica* xxiii.

avenging or repulsing an enemy, no just war can be waged.")[20] Augustine (354–430) and Isidore of Seville (c. 570–636) are influenced in their theory of "'just war" by Cicero. From the writings of these authors the theory of "just war" is taken over by Thomas Aquinas (1224–1274). It became the dominating doctrine of the Middle Ages, only to be absorbed by the natural-law theories of the sixteenth, seventeenth, and eighteenth centuries. Grotius (1583–1645) in particular expounds the view that "no other just cause for undertaking war can there be excepting injury received."[21] And Vattel, one of the most representative writers on international law in the eighteenth century, speaking of the right to make war as "the right to use force," maintains that such right exists under international law as the natural law, as the law of nature applied to states only if it is needed for the defense and preservation of rights. Hence he defines war as "that state in which we prosecute our rights by force."[22] The idea that every war must have a just cause, and that in the last analysis this just cause can only be a wrong suffered, remains predominant until the end of the eighteenth century, but disappears almost entirely from the theories of positive international law during the nineteenth century, although it had still some influence on public opinion and on the diplomatic phraseology of the governments. Only after the close of the First World War was this doctrine of "just war" again taken up by certain authors.[23]

(2) OBJECTIONS AGAINST THE DOCTRINE. The objections put forward against the view that the *bellum justum* principle is part of general international law should not be underestimated. As long as no objective authority is established competent to decide whether the war to which one state resorts against another is legal or illegal, the application of the principle is indeed highly problematical. Still more serious is the argument that war can be successfully resorted to as sanction only if waged by a state which is more

---

[20] Cf. William Ballis, *The Legal Position of War* (1937), pp. 27ff.

[21] Grotius, Bk. ii, Chap. I, sec. 1, par. 4.

[22] Emerich de Vattel, *Le Droit des Gens, ou Principes de la loi naturelle appliqués à la conduite et aux affaires des nations et des souverains* (1758), Bk. iii, Chap. I, par. 1, 3. In defining war as a "state," Vattel follows Grotius.

[23] Cf. Leo Strisower, *Der Krieg und die Voelkerrechtsordnung* (1919).

powerful than its opponent. But, on the other hand, the fact must not be ignored that both arguments apply also to reprisals, and that it is nevertheless generally recognized that these enforcement actions are permitted by general international law only as reactions against an international delict, i.e., as sanctions. It would be more than paradoxical to assume that under international law a limited interference in the sphere of interests of a state is legally forbidden, and permitted only as a reaction against an international delict, i.e., as a reprisal, whereas an unlimited interference in the sphere of interests of a state, namely war, is not legally forbidden and hence is neither a delict nor a sanction. The obvious insufficiency of reprisals and war as sanctions of international law is the consequence of the complete decentralization of the community constituted by this law, which, precisely because of this decentralization, and especially because of the lack of a centralized executive power, has the typical character of a primitive law. If reprisals and war—typical measures of self-help—are not considered as legal sanctions because a minimum of centralization is considered to be an essential element of the law, the social order we call general international law cannot be regarded as law in the true sense of the term.

There is, however, one argument brought forth against the *bellum justum* doctrine which must be decidedly rejected. It is the argument that the function of war is not only to enforce the existing law but also to modify this law, to adapt it to changing circumstances; that the absence of a legislative power able to perform this function against recalcitrant states has the effect of preserving the *status quo* even if it is highly unsatisfactory. War, according to this view, is the dynamic force which may accomplish the result we expect in vain from a peaceful change brought about by agreement. War plays, in the realm of international law, the same role as revolution in the realm of national law. This comparison is utterly wrong. Revolution is a conflict between the subjects of a national community and its government; war is the conflict between two or more subjects of the international community. In contradistinction to revolutions, wars are waged not with the intention and for the purpose of changing the objective law, that is, the general norms of the legal order, but to realize subjective interests, to defend

The Nature of International Law

or destroy, and to acquire rights under the general norms of the unchanged objective law. It is true that the norms concerning the conduct of war may be changed as an unintentional effect of a long-established practice actually observed by the belligerents in their warfare. But the changes, if any, which have resulted from the last wars with regard to the rules of warfare can hardly justify war as a lawmaking factor. Apart from the law of war, war as such cannot change, and never has changed, general international law as a set of objective norms regulating the peaceful relations between states. Only the peace treaties could have such effect. As far as peace treaties between two belligerents are concerned, only a series of such treaties can change the objective law, provided they establish a new general principle which thus becomes a norm of customary international law. But, as a matter of fact, the overwhelming majority of the peace treaties had no such effect. Of the multilateral peace treaties, especially the treaties by which the First and Second World Wars have been terminated, it can hardly be said that they have changed general international law, and certainly not that they have changed this law in a progressive sense. The Charter of the United Nations, which claims to be general international law, and as such constitutes a change of this law, is not a peace treaty; and the fact that it was concluded during a war by belligerents united only against common enemies has proved to be so fateful to its effectiveness that all the intended changes became illusory.

It is further true that by war and especially by a peace treaty terminating a war, the legal relation between the belligerents, their subjective rights and duties, may be changed, but only on the basis of the pre-existent norms of general international law. However, a change of the *status quo* in the mutual relations of some states is not prevented by the absence of an international legislative organ, and a change brought about by a peace treaty may be highly problematical. For peace treaties are normally imposed by victorious upon vanquished states, and the change of the *status quo* they bring about may correspond to the existing—but rather transitory—power situation. That change hardly corresponds to an idea of justice, even if by justice nothing more is understood than an order which guarantees a durable peace. And even if it were true that war has the function of changing the objective law of nations, and not only the subjective rights and duties of the respective belligerents, the question still remains whether the sacrifices involved in this barbarous procedure are in any reasonable proportion to its effect.

c. *The* bellum justum *principle in positive international law.* (1) ARTICLE 231 OF THE PEACE TREATY OF VERSAILLES. In spite of the fact that most of the writers on international law prior to the First World War rejected the doctrine of a just war, and advocated the view that under general international law a state does not commit a delict by resorting to war—for any reason whatever—against any other state, one of the most important provisions of the Peace Treaty of Versailles, by which this war with Germany was terminated, presupposes this doctrine. The treaty imposed upon Germany and her allies the obligation to make reparation, not the obligation to pay a war indemnity, because President Wilson in his Fourteen Points had declared that no war indemnity should be extorted from the vanquished states. The obligation to make reparation, as pointed out, presupposes a violation of international law.

Article 231, the first article of Part VIII of this treaty, under the heading "Reparation," runs as follows: "The Allied and Associated Governments affirm and Germany accepts the responsibility of Germany and her allies for causing all the loss and damage to which the Allied and Associated Governments and their nations have been subjected as a consequence of the war imposed upon them by the aggression of Germany and her allies." This article justifies the reparation imposed on Germany by maintaining that Germany and her allies were responsible for an act of aggression. This means that Article 231 characterizes this aggression as an illegal act, as a delict. The article does not refer to the violation by Germany and her allies of particular treaties prohibiting war, such as the treaties guaranteeing the neutrality of Belgium and Luxemburg. The delict for which Germany and her allies are made responsible is "aggression" in general, i.e., resort to war in violation of general international law, which would be impossible if the authors of the peace treaty had shared the opinion that every state had a right to resort to war for any reason against any other state.

The Nature of International Law 39

Had the aggression which Germany admitted not been considered "illegal," no agreement concerning "reparation" would have been possible. The aggression of Germany and her allies was considered illegal because the war to which they resorted in 1914 was considered to have been a war "imposed" upon the Allied and Associated Governments. This can mean only that Germany and her allies resorted to war without sufficient reason, that is, without themselves having been wronged by the Allied and Associated Powers or by any one of them.

The question as to whether the *bellum justum* principle is part of general international law has lost a great deal of its importance since under the impact of the two world wars the employment of armed force in international relations has been forbidden by three treaties to which almost all the states of the world were contracting parties: the Covenant of the League of Nations (first part of the peace treaties with Germany, Austria, Hungary, Bulgaria), 1919; the Treaty for the Renunciation of War (Pact of Paris or Kellogg-Briand Pact), 1928; and the Charter of the United Nations, 1945.

(2) THE COVENANT OF THE LEAGUE OF NATIONS. The Covenant of the League of Nations did not prohibit resort to war under all circumstances. Self-help in the relationship among members of the League was not absolutely excluded. According to Articles 12 and 15, the members were obliged to submit their disputes either to an international tribunal or to the Council. Submission to an international tribunal presupposed agreement of the parties to the dispute. The members were obliged to carry out the decision of the tribunal and not to resort to war against a member of the League which complied therewith. War against a state which in violation of its obligation did not comply with the decision of the tribunal was not excluded (Articles 12 and 13). In case agreement to submit the dispute to a tribunal could not be reached, each party was entitled to submit the case to the Council, which was authorized to proceed at the request of one party to the dispute, no agreement for this purpose being necessary. The Council was first to endeavor "to effect a settlement of the dispute" by bringing about an agreement between the parties. If, however, the dispute

could not be settled in this way, the Council was bound to settle the dispute by making a recommendation to the parties. But only a recommendation unanimously agreed to by the members of the Council other than the representatives of the parties to the dispute gave the recommendation of the Council a legal effect. This effect consisted in the prohibition of war against the party which complied with the recommendation. War against the party which did not comply with the recommendation was not excluded. Neither was war excluded in case none of the parties complied with the recommendation of the Council. In case no unanimous recommendation could be reached by the Council, war was expressly permitted by the Covenant, but only "for the maintenance of right and justice" (Article 15, paragraph 7). If by this formula the maintenance of international law (proclaimed in the Preamble of the Covenant) was to be understood, and if the principle that war was permitted only for the purpose of maintaining international law applied to all cases where war was not forbidden (or expressly permitted), the Covenant could be considered to be in conformity with the *bellum justum* doctrine as presented above. Finally, war was not—or at least, not expressly—forbidden in case the dispute arose out of a matter of domestic jurisdiction. In this respect Article 15, paragraph 8, provided: "If the dispute between the parties is claimed by one of them, and is found by the Council, to arise out of a matter which by international law is solely within the domestic jurisdiction of that party, the Council shall so report, and shall make no recommendation as to its settlement." In all cases in which war was not forbidden the parties were obliged not to resort to war until three months after the decision of the international tribunal or the report or recommendation of the Council (Article 12, paragraph 1).

The fact that the Covenant restricted the principle of self-help only to a small extent is to be explained by the fact that it established only a minimum of collective security. According to Article 16, paragraph 1, the members were obliged to subject a member which in violation of the Covenant resorted to war, to economic sanctions, namely, "the severance of all trade or financial relations, the prohibition of all intercourse between their nationals and the

The Nature of International Law

nationals of the covenant-breaking State, and the prevention of all financial, commercial or personal intercourse between the nationals of the covenant-breaking State and the nationals of any other State, whether a Member of the League or not." In order to justify this obligation the Covenant provided that a member which resorted to war in disregard of the Covenant "shall *ipso facto* be deemed to have committed an act of war against all other Members of the League." This statement is nothing but a legal fiction which, in itself, does not add anything to the obligation to resort to the sanctions determined in Article 16, paragraph 1. In addition to this obligation the members were, under Article 16, paragraph 3, obliged to "mutually support one another in the financial and economic measures which are taken under this Article, in order to minimize the loss and inconvenience resulting from the above measures," and to "mutually support one another in resisting any special measures aimed at one of their number by the covenant-breaking State." As to military sanctions under Article 16, paragraph 2, the members were under no obligation. They were only authorized to take enforcement measures involving the use of their armed forces. The Council was not competent to interfere with economic sanctions. As to the military sanctions, the Council had only the power "to recommend to the several Governments concerned what effective military, naval or air force the Members of the League shall severally contribute to the armed forces to be used to protect the covenants of the League." According to Article 16, paragraph 3, the members were obliged to "take the necessary steps to afford passage through their territory to the forces of any of the Members of the League which are cooperating to protect the covenants of the League." The collective security established by the Covenant was almost completely decentralized. The decisive question as to whether a member had resorted to war in disregard of the Covenant was to be answered by each of the other members for itself. In carrying out the enforcement actions determined in Article 16 the members of the League were under no control of the Council or any other organ of the League. The recommendations made by the Council under Article 16, paragraph 2, had no binding force. The economic and military sanctions determined in Article 16, paragraphs 1–3, were directed only against violations of the Covenant by an illegal use of armed force, i.e., by resort to war, not against other international delicts committed by a member.

(3) THE KELLOGG-BRIAND PACT. The Treaty for the Renunciation of War, usually called the Kellogg-Briand Pact,[24] signed at Paris on August 27, 1928, stipulates: "[The High Contracting Parties] Convinced that all changes in their relations with one another should be sought only by pacific means and be the result of a peaceful and orderly process, and that any signatory power which shall hereafter seek to promote its national interests by resort to war should be denied the benefits furnished by this treaty . . . have agreed upon the following articles: ARTICLE I. The High Contracting Parties solemnly declare in the names of their respective peoples that they condemn recourse to war for the solution of international controversies, and renounce it as an instrument of national policy in their relations with one another. ARTICLE II. The High Contracting Parties agree that the settlement or solution of all disputes or conflicts of whatever nature or of whatever origin they may be, which may arise among them, shall never be sought except by pacific means." The prohibition of war established by the Kellogg-Briand Pact goes far beyond that established by the Covenant of the League of Nations. There are only two kinds of war which are not expressly forbidden: (1) a war which is not an instrument of national policy, and (2)—according to the Preamble —a war against a state which, in violation of its obligation under the pact, has resorted to war. Under this category falls not only a counterwar against a war of aggression, that is to say, a war waged in exercise of self-defense but also a war resorted to as reaction against the violation of the pact, by states which are not the victims of such violation. As to the first category—war which is not an instrument of national policy—two interpretations are possible. According to one, a war may be considered not to be an instrument of national policy only if it is an enforcement action involving the use of armed force taken in conformity with an international agreement for

---

[24] Aristide Briand was Foreign Minister of France; Frank B. Kellogg, Secretary of State of the United States of America.

The Nature of International Law 43

the purpose of collective security, as, for instance, a war resorted to by a member of the League of Nations as a military sanction in accordance with Article 16, paragraph 2 of the Covenant. If this interpretation is accepted, a war resorted to by one state against another, outside the system of collective security organized by an international agreement, is to be considered as an instrument of national policy and hence forbidden by the pact, except the case referred to in the Preamble. Consequently, the use of armed force against an international delict which does not consist in the employment of armed force is excluded. If, e.g., in a dispute decided by an international tribunal, one party, in violation of its obligation, fails to comply with the decision of the tribunal, the other party is not allowed under the pact to enforce the decision by the employment of armed force. If interpreted in this way, the pact constitutes a deterioration of the situation which exists under the Covenant and general international law, both of which allow in such case self-help by the use of armed force. Hence another interpretation of the formula "war as an instrument of national policy" is desirable.

In prohibiting war it must not be overlooked that war is not necessarily an international delict, but—as a reaction against a delict—a sanction; that war is the ultimate sanction of general international law and that it should not be abolished without being replaced by an organized collective enforcement action involving the use of armed force. Excluding war as a means of self-help without providing for an effective collective sanction has the undesirable effect of favoring states which violate international law without resorting to war. This effect of the pact may be avoided if the latter is interpreted not to exclude war as an instrument of international policy. Thus a war which is a reaction against a violation of international law, and that means a war waged for the maintenance of international law, is considered an instrument of international and hence not of national policy. It is reasonable to restrict self-help against violations of the law only insofar as self-help is replaced by effective collective security. Whatever interpretation of the phrase "instrument of national policy" is accepted, the Kellogg-Briand Pact is in complete conformity with the *bellum justum* principle, since it permits war only as a reaction against a violation of international law (though not against every violation of international law).[25]

By the Covenant as well as by the Kellogg-Briand Pact, only war—not other enforcement actions short of war, especially reprisals—was forbidden. A strict obligation to settle all disputes by peaceful means excludes, it is true, not only war but also reprisals to be taken by one party to the dispute against another party. But neither the Covenant nor the Kellogg-Briand Pact stipulated such an obligation. The Kellogg-Briand Pact, in Article II, imposes upon the contracting parties only the obligation to *seek* the settlement of their dispute by pacific means. This obligation may be fulfilled without reaching a settlement. Then war, but not reprisals, is forbidden by the pact.

7. *War (Use of Force) under the Charter of the United Nations*

a. *Centralization of the force monopoly.* In this respect the Charter of the United Nations (signed at San Francisco on June 26, 1945) constitutes a remarkable progress. It imposes upon the members of the Organization a strict obligation to settle their disputes by peaceful means and to refrain in their international relations not only from the use of any kind of force, including war as well as reprisals, but also from the threat of force. Article 2, paragraph 3, of the Charter provides: "All Members shall settle their international disputes by peaceful means in such a manner that inter-

---

[25] In *Macintosh v. United States* (Annual Digest 1929–1930, Case No. 137) the United States Circuit Court of Appeals (1930) reversed an order of the district court, by which a petition for naturalization was refused because the petitioner declared he could take the required oath of allegiance to the Government only with the reservation of the right to decide whether he would take up arms in defense of the country, not promising in advance to go to war regardless of the merits of the war. The circuit court of appeals justified its decision *inter alia* by the statement: "There is a distinction between a morally justified and an unjustified war, as recognized in international law. . . . Such recognition was given in the recent Kellogg Pact . . ." The Supreme Court reversed the decree of the circuit court of appeals and affirmed the decree of the district court.

national peace and security, and justice, are not endangered." This obligation is specified by other provisions of the Charter, especially by those of Chapter VI (Articles 33-38) by which certain procedures for the settlement of disputes and the adjustment of situations not having the character of disputes are established.[26] Article 2, paragraph 4, provides: "All Members shall refrain in their international relations from the threat or use of force against the territorial integrity or political independence of any state, or in any other manner inconsistent with the Purposes of the United Nations." The Charter reserves the use of force to a central organ of the United Nations, the Security Council. The collective security established by the Charter is characterized by a centralized force monopoly of the Organization. This force monopoly is first proclaimed in the Preamble by the statement that "armed force shall not be used, save in the common interest"; then in Article 1, paragraph 1, in the provision that the first "Purpose" of the United Nations is "to maintain international peace and security, and to that end: to take effective collective measures for the prevention and removal of threats to the peace, and for the suppression of acts of aggression or other breaches of the peace." Since under Article 2, paragraph 4, the members are obliged to refrain from the use of force in any manner "inconsistent with the Purposes of the United Nations," any use of force which has not the character of a "collective" measure is forbidden by the Charter (if it is not expressly permitted as an exception to the rule of Article 2, paragraph 4, by other provisions of the Charter). Article 24 expressly confers upon the Security Council the competence to exercise the force monopoly of the Organization, by providing that "in order to ensure prompt and effective action by the United Nations, its Members confer on the Security Council primary responsibility for the maintenance of international peace and security." Article 25 imposes upon the members the obligation "to accept and carry out the decisions of the Security Council in accordance with the present Charter," and Article 2, paragraph 5, provides: "All Members shall give the United Nations every assistance in any action it takes in accordance with the present Charter, and shall refrain

---

[26] Cf. *infra,* pp. 370ff.

from giving assistance to any state against which the United Nations is taking preventive or enforcement action."

b. *Enforcement measures.* The "prompt and effective action by the United Nations," referred to in Article 24, is specified in Chapter VII (Articles 39–50), which bears the title "Action with respect to Threats to the Peace, Breaches of the Peace, and Acts of Aggression." This action is an "enforcement action," and enforcement action can be taken by the Security Council only under the condition that there exists a "threat to the peace, breach of the peace, or act of aggression." The existence of this fact is to be determined by the Security Council. When the Council has determined the existence of a threat to or a breach of the peace, it may either make recommendations which it deems appropriate, or take one of the enforcement actions specified in Articles 41 and 42. This is provided for in Article 39, which runs as follows: "The Security Council shall determine the existence of any threat to the peace, breach of the peace, or act of aggression and shall make recommendations, or decide what measures shall be taken in accordance with Articles 41 and 42, to maintain or restore international peace and security."

Before making the recommendations or taking the measures referred to in Article 39, the Security Council may recommend to the parties certain "provisional measures." In this respect Article 40 provides: "In order to prevent an aggravation of the situation, the Security Council may, before making the recommendations or deciding upon the measures provided for in Article 39, call upon the parties concerned to comply with such provisional measures as it deems necessary or desirable. Such provisional measures shall be without prejudice to the rights, claims, or position of the parties concerned. The Security Council shall duly take account of failure to comply with such provisional measures."

As to the enforcement measures to be taken by the Council, two categories are to be distinguished: enforcement measures not involving the use of armed force, and enforcement measures involving the use of armed force. The enforcement measures not involving the use of armed force have the technical character of reprisals. They are determined in Article 41, which runs as follows: "The

Security Council may decide what measures not involving the use of armed force are to be employed to give effect to its decisions, and it may call upon the Members of the United Nations to apply such measures. These may include complete or partial interruption of economic relations and of rail, sea, air, postal, telegraphic, radio, and other means of communication, and the severance of diplomatic relations."

The enforcement measures involving the use of armed force have technically the character of war. In this respect Article 42 provides: "Should the Security Council consider that measures provided for in Article 41 would be inadequate or have proved to be inadequate, it may take such action by air, sea, or land forces as may be necessary to maintain or restore international peace and security. Such action may include demonstrations, blockade, and other operations by air, sea, or land forces of Members of the United Nations."

According to the intention of the Charter, measures involving the use of armed force should be taken only if measures not involving the use of armed force are considered to be inadequate or actually are inadequate. A special kind of military enforcement measure is regulated by Article 45, which runs as follows: "In order to enable the United Nations to take urgent military measures, Members shall hold immediately available national air-force contingents for combined international enforcement action. The strength and degree of readiness of these contingents and plans for their combined action shall be determined, within the limits laid down in the special agreement or agreements referred to in Article 43, by the Security Council with the assistance of the Military Staff Committee."

The difficult problem of placing at the disposal of the Security Council the necessary armed forces is solved by Article 43: "1. All Members of the United Nations, in order to contribute to the maintenance of international peace and security, undertake to make available to the Security Council, on its call and in accordance with a special agreement or agreements, armed forces, assistance, and facilities, including rights of passage, necessary for the purpose of maintaining international peace and security. 2. Such agreement or agreements shall govern the numbers and types of forces, their degree of readiness and general location, and the nature of the facilities and assistance to be provided. 3. The agreement or agreements shall be negotiated as soon as possible on the initiative of the Security Council. They shall be concluded between the Security Council and Members or between the Security Council and groups of Members and shall be subject to ratification by the signatory states in accordance with their respective constitutional processes."

It is of importance to note that the agreements referred to in this article do not establish the obligation of the members to place at the disposal of the Council parts of their own armed forces, but deal only with the manner in which this obligation is to be fulfilled. The obligation itself is unconditionally established by Article 43, paragraph 1, first sentence. The agreements refer only to the matters determined in Article 43, paragraph 2. It is of further importance to note that these agreements are treaties to be concluded by the United Nations, represented by the Security Council, on the one hand, and the members or groups of members, on the other hand. An obligation to conclude a treaty is technically not possible. Hence there is no legal obligation of the members to conclude the agreements referred to in Article 43, paragraph 2. However, the obligation of the members to place at the disposal of the Security Council part of their armed forces is worthless as long as the agreements in question are not in force.

The enforcement action to be taken by the Security Council is a collective action of the Organization, carried out by its members. In this respect Article 48 provides: "1. The action required to carry out the decisions of the Security Council for the maintenance of international peace and security shall be taken by all the Members of the United Nations or by some of them, as the Security Council may determine. 2. Such decisions shall be carried out by the Members of the United Nations directly and through their action in the appropriate international agencies of which they are members."

The members are not only obliged to carry out the decisions of the Council relating to the enforcement action, but also to assist one another in carrying out that obligation. Article 49 provides in this respect: "The Members of the United Nations shall join in

The Nature of International Law

affording mutual assistance in carrying out the measures decided upon by the Security Council."

The member whose armed forces are to be used in the enforcement action is entitled to participate in the respective decision of the Council. Article 44 provides: "When the Security Council has decided to use force it shall, before calling upon a Member not represented on it to provide armed forces in fulfillment of the obligations assumed under Article 43, invite that Member, if the Member so desires, to participate in the decisions of the Security Council concerning the employment of contingents of that Member's armed forces." The right of the member to participate in the decision does not exclude the possibility of being outvoted by the majority vote taken according to Article 27.

The Security Council, in taking enforcement action involving the use of armed force, is assisted by an auxiliary organ, the Military Staff Committee. In this respect the Charter provides: "ARTICLE 46. Plans for the application of armed force shall be made by the Security Council with the assistance of the Military Staff Committee. ARTICLE 47. 1. There shall be established a Military Staff Committee to advise and assist the Security Council on all questions relating to the Security Council's military requirements for the maintenance of international peace and security, the employment and command of forces placed at its disposal, the regulation of armaments, and possible disarmament. 2. The Military Staff Committee shall consist of the Chiefs of Staff of the permanent members of the Security Council or their representatives. Any Member of the United Nations not permanently represented on the Committee shall be invited by the Committee to be associated with it when the efficient discharge of the Committee's responsibilities requires the participation of that Member in its work. 3. The Military Staff Committee shall be responsible under the Security Council for the strategic direction of any armed forces placed at the disposal of the Security Council. Questions relating to the command of such forces shall be worked out subsequently. 4. The Military Staff Committee, with the authorization of the Security Council and after consultation with appropriate regional agencies, may establish regional subcommittees."

According to paragraph 1 of Article 47, the Security Council may be considered to be the commander in chief of the armed forces placed at its disposal. A collegiate organ is an instrument not quite appropriate for commanding armed forces. The Council may, in accordance with Article 29, appoint, as a subsidiary organ, an individual commander in chief. The armed forces of the United Nations, it is true, are composed of contingents placed by the members at the disposal of the Security Council. But they are under the unified command to be exercised either directly by the Security Council or by a commander in chief appointed by the Council.[27]

---

[27] In the case of the war in Korea the Security Council adopted, on June 25, 1950, a resolution (UN Doc. S/1501) in which it notes "with grave concern the armed attack upon the Republic of Korea by forces from North Korea" and "determines that this action constitutes a breach of the peace." This part of the resolution is based on Article 39 of the Charter. Then the Security Council "1. calls for the immediate cessation of hostilities; and calls upon the authorities of North Korea to withdraw forthwith their armed forces to the thirty-eighth parallel; 2. requests the United Nations Commission on Korea (a) to communicate its fully considered recommendations on the situation with the least possible delay; (b) to observe the withdrawal of the North Korean forces to the thirty-eighth parallel; and (c) to keep the Security Council informed on the execution of this resolution; 3. calls upon all Members to render every assistance to the United Nations in the execution of this resolution and to refrain from giving assistance to the North Korean authorities." The calls sub 1 are probably made under Article 40 and have the character of "provisional measures." The call sub 3 reminds the members of the United Nations of their obligation under Article 2, paragraph 5, of the Charter. On June 27, 1950, the Security Council adopted a resolution (UN Doc. S/1511) in which it "recommends that the Members of the United Nations furnish such assistance to the Republic of Korea as may be necessary to repel the armed attack and to restore international peace and security in the area." By this resolution the Security Council recommended to the members to use force if they considered it necessary to repel the armed attack by the North Korean forces and to restore peace. Such a recommendation is certainly covered by the wording of Article 39. But it is doubtful whether such a recommendation is in conformity with the spirit of Article 39, which provides that enforcement measures by the United Nations can be taken only in accordance with Article 41 or 42. The recommendation to the members to use armed force to assist the Republic of Korea in its fight against the forces from North Korea cannot be—as the wording of the resolution seems to indicate—a recommendation to exercise the right of collective self-defense. For, in accordance with Article 51 of the Charter, the members can exercise this right only "until the Security Council has taken the measures necessary to maintain international peace and security." These measures the Security Council actually took by its resolutions of June 25 and June 27. On July 7, 1950, the Security

The Nature of International Law

The provisions of the Charter concerning enforcement measures to be taken by the Security Council for the maintenance or restoration of international peace and security are practically inapplicable, partly because until now it was not possible to put into force the special agreements referred to in Article 43, and partly because of lack of unanimity of the permanent members of the Security Council, required for decisions of the Council under Articles 39, 41, and 42 of the Charter. This situation led to the resolution of the General Assembly called "Uniting for Peace," adopted on November 3, 1950. This resolution is based on an interpretation of the Charter according to which the force monopoly of the United Nations may be exercised not only by the Security Council but also by the General Assembly. According to this interpretation, the Charter confers on the General Assembly a secondary responsibility for the maintenance of international peace and security through prompt and effective action, and, consequently, the power to initiate, in case of a threat to the peace, breach of the peace, or act of aggression, the existence of which is to be determined by the General Assembly, an enforcement action, especially—in case of a breach of the peace or act of aggression—an enforcement action involving the use of armed force, by recommendations made to the members of the United Nations. The power of the General Assembly to make such recommendations is derived from Article 10 of the Charter, which provides: "The General Assembly may discuss any questions or any matters within the scope of the present Charter or relating to the powers and functions of any organs provided for in the present Charter, and, except as provided in Article 12, may make recommendations to the Members of the

Council adopted a resolution (UN Doc. S/1588) in which it "3. recommends that all Members providing military forces and other assistance pursuant to the aforesaid Security Council resolutions make such forces and other assistance available to a unified command under the United States; 4. requests the United States to designate the commander of such forces; 5. authorizes the unified command at its discretion to use the United Nations flag in the course of operations against North Korean forces concurrently with the flags of the various nations participating; 6. requests the United States to provide the Security Council with reports as appropriate on the course of action taken under the unified command." The recommendation sub 3, the requests sub 4 and 6, and the authorization sub 5 are probably all based on Article 39.

United Nations or to the Security Council or to both on any such questions or matters."

It is assumed that the only restriction of the power of the General Assembly to make recommendations is the one stipulated in Article 12, that the General Assembly shall not make recommendations on disputes or situations while the Security Council is dealing with these matters. Since Article 10 does not restrict the content of recommendations made by the General Assembly on questions within the scope of the Charter, the General Assembly may recommend to members the use of armed force. The provision of Article 11, paragraph 2, that the General Assembly shall refer to the Security Council "any such question on which action is necessary . . . either before or after discussion," is not considered as constituting a restriction of the General Assembly's power established by Article 10. The most important provisions of the resolution "Uniting for Peace" are:

1. "If the Security Council, because of lack of unanimity of the permanent members, fails to exercise its primary responsibility for the maintenance of international peace and security in any case where there appears to be a threat to the peace, breach of the peace, or act of aggression, the General Assembly shall consider the matter immediately with a view to making appropriate recommendations to Members for collective measures, including in the case of a breach of the peace or act of aggression the use of armed force when necessary to maintain or restore international peace and security"; 2. "[The General Assembly] recommends to the States Members of the United Nations that each Member maintain within its national armed forces elements so trained, organized and equipped that they could promptly be made available, in accordance with its constitutional processes, for service as a United Nations unit or units, upon recommendation by the Security Council or the General Assembly, without prejudice to the use of such elements in exercise of the right of individual or collective self-defense recognized in Article 51 of the Charter"; 3. "[Then General Assembly] establishes a Peace Observation Commission which, for the calendar years 1951 and 1952, shall be composed of 14 Members . . . and which could observe and report on the situation in any area

The Nature of International Law

where there exists international tension the continuance of which is likely to endanger the maintenance of international peace and security"; 4. "[The General Assembly] establishes a Collective Measures Committee consisting of 14 Members . . . and directs the Committee, in consultation with the Secretary-General and with such Member States as the Committee finds appropriate, to study and make a report to the Security Council and the General Assembly, not later than September 1, 1951, on methods . . . which might be used to maintain and strengthen international peace and security in accordance with the Purposes and Principles of the Charter, taking account of collective self-defense and regional arrangements (Articles 51 and 52 of the Charter)."[28]

c. *Difference between the Charter and the Covenant.* The decisive differences between the system of collective security established under the Covenant and that established under the Charter are as follows:

1. Competent to decide whether the condition of an enforcement action exists in a concrete case are, under the Charter, organs of the United Nations, the Security Council, and—according to the resolution of the General Assembly "Uniting for Peace"—also the General Assembly; under the Covenant, each member of the League of Nations.

2. Competent to take an enforcement action are, under the Charter, the Security Council by decisions binding upon the members, and—according to the resolution of the General Assembly "Uniting

---

[28] In application of the resolution "Uniting for Peace" the General Assembly adopted on February 1, 1951, with respect to the intervention of the communist Government of China in the war in Korea, a resolution the most important content of which is as follows: "The General Assembly . . . *finds* that the Central People's Government of the People's Republic of China, by giving direct aid and assistance to those who were already committing aggression in Korea and by engaging in hostilities against United Nations forces there, has itself engaged in aggression in Korea; *calls upon* the Central People's Government of the People's Republic of China to cause its forces and nationals in Korea to cease hostilities against the United Nations forces and to withdraw from Korea; *affirms* the determination of the United Nations to continue its action in Korea to meet the aggression; *calls upon* all states and authorities to continue to lend every assistance to the United Nations action in Korea; *calls upon* all states and authorities to refrain from giving any assistance to the aggressors in Korea . . ."

for Peace"—also the General Assembly by recommendations to the members; under the Covenant, each member of the League, being obliged to take enforcement action not involving the use of armed force (economic sanctions) and being authorized to take enforcement action involving the use of armed force (military sanctions). The Council was competent only in case of an enforcement action involving the use of armed force (military sanction) to make recommendations concerning this action.

3. Under the Charter, the Organization is to have a definite armed force at its disposal and under its command; this was not the case under the Covenant. The whole procedure of taking enforcement action, and hence the system of collective security, is centralized under the Charter, but it was almost completely decentralized under the Covenant.

4. The enforcement actions provided for by the Covenant— economic and military measures—had the character of sanctions. They were to be taken only in case the Covenant had been violated by a member resorting illegally to war, and were to be directed only against the delinquent member. Collective enforcement action under Chapter VII of the Charter may be taken by the Security Council in case of a threat to or breach of the peace, not only against a member of the United Nations but against any state (Article 39). Conduct of a state which the Security Council under Article 39 of the Charter declares to be a threat to or breach of the peace does not necessarily constitute a violation of the obligation stipulated in Article 2, paragraph 4: to refrain from the threat or use of force. The Security Council may consider the conduct of a state which is neither a threat of force nor a use of force, as a threat to or breach of the peace. If the enforcement actions to be taken by the Security Council under Article 39 are to be considered as sanctions, the Charter must be interpreted to impose upon the members not only the obligation to refrain from the threat or use of force, an obligation directly formulated in Article 2, paragraph 4, but the obligation to refrain from any conduct which the Security Council may consider to be a threat to or breach of the peace—stipulated indirectly in Article 39, which obligation goes far beyond the one stipulated in Article 2, paragraph 4.

The Nature of International Law

According to the resolution of the General Assembly "Uniting for Peace," enforcement action in conformity with a recommendation of the General Assembly may also be taken in case of a threat to or breach of the peace and not only against members, but against any state. In order to consider such action as a sanction, it must be assumed that the members of the United Nations are obliged to refrain from any conduct which either the Security Council or the General Assembly may consider as a threat to or breach of the peace.

According to the wording of Article 39, the Security Council may take an enforcement action not only against states but also against groups of individuals which have not the character of states, e.g., a people living on a stateless territory, or a community not recognized as a state by the United Nations, or insurgents not recognized as belligerent power. The United Nations, through the Security Council, may intervene in a civil war within a state if the Security Council considers this civil war as a threat to international peace.[29]

5. One of the most important differences between the Charter and the Covenant is that actually an enforcement action under Article 39 cannot be directed against a member that has a permanent seat in the Security Council, or a State that is protected by a permanent member of the Security Council, since a decision of the Security Council on an enforcement action requires, according to Article 27, a majority of seven members including the concurring

---

[29] In the case of Korea the Security Council recommended to the members to take enforcement action involving the use of armed force, against "forces from North Korea" or the "authorities of North Korea," which the Security Council did not consider to be the government of a state. This implies that the war between North Korea and South Korea was a civil war within the "Republic of Korea," which the Security Council assumed to be under the legitimate government of the South Korean authorities. Then the "armed attack" upon the Republic of Korea by forces from North Korea could not be—as the Security Council determined—a "breach of the peace," that is to say, a breach of international peace. For international peace is a relation between two or more states. It could only be a breach of internal peace and as such could be considered by the Security Council only as a threat to international peace, which, in addition to a "breach of the peace" (including "act of aggression") are the conditions under which enforcement measures can be taken under Article 39 "to maintain or restore *international* peace and security."

votes of the permanent members (veto right).³⁰ The complete decentralization of the enforcement action under the Covenant had the advantage that this undesirable consequence of the veto right was avoided. This is also the effect of the resolution "Uniting for Peace," according to which enforcement actions recommended by the General Assembly may be directed against a permanent member of the Security Council, since the principle of unanimity of the members having permanent seats in the Security Council does not apply in the voting procedure of the General Assembly.

d. *Sanctions other than enforcement measures under Article 39.* Other sanctions are provided by the Charter in Articles 5 and 6. Article 5 provides: "A Member of the United Nations against which preventive or enforcement action has been taken by the Security Council may be suspended from the exercise of the rights and privileges of membership by the General Assembly upon the recommendation of the Security Council. The exercise of these rights and privileges may be restored by the Security Council." By "preventive action" probably the "provisional measures" referred to in Article 40 are meant. Article 6 provides: "A Member of the United Nations which has persistently violated the Principles contained in the present Charter may be expelled from the Organization by the General Assembly upon the recommendation of the Security Council."

Whereas the Covenant had no provision analogous to that of Article 5 of the Charter, expulsion of a member was provided for by paragraph 4 of Article 16 of the Covenant. According to this provision the member to be expelled was excluded from voting in the Council competent to take the decision concerned. This is not the case under Article 6 of the Charter.

A special sanction is stipulated for violation of the financial obligations of the members. Article 17, paragraph 2, provides that "the expenses of the Organization shall be borne by the Members as apportioned by the General Assembly." Article 19 stipulates: "A Member of the United Nations which is in arrears in the payment of its financial contributions to the Organization shall have no vote in the General Assembly if the amount of its arrears equals

---

³⁰ Cf. *infra*, pp. 155, 180.

The Nature of International Law

or exceeds the amount of the contributions due from it for the preceding two full years. The General Assembly may, nevertheless, permit such a Member to vote if it is satisfied that the failure to pay is due to conditions beyond the control of the Member."

Suspension from the exercise of the right of voting in the General Assembly does not imply the suspension of the right of voting in the Security Council or in any other agency of the United Nations in case the member is represented not only in the General Assembly but also in the Security Council or in any other agency of the United Nations.

Also, Article 102 of the Charter may be interpreted to provide for a special sanction: "1. Every treaty and every international agreement entered into by any Member of the United Nations after the present Charter comes into force shall as soon as possible be registered with the Secretariat and published by it. 2. No party to any such treaty or international agreement which has not been registered in accordance with the provisions of paragraph 1 of this Article may invoke that treaty or agreement before any organ of the United Nations." The analogous provision of the Covenant is Article 18: "Every treaty or international engagement entered into hereafter by any Member of the League shall be forthwith registered with the Secretariat and shall as soon as possible be published by it. No such treaty or international engagement shall be binding until so registered."

The difference between Article 102 of the Charter and Article 18 of the Covenant is that under the Covenant the effect of non-registration of a treaty was intended to be complete invalidation of the treaty, which effect, with respect to treaties concluded by members with nonmembers, was not compatible with general international law. Under the Charter, on the other hand, non-registration of a treaty has only the effect of a relative invalidation: a nonregistered treaty is invalid only within the legal realm of the United Nations.

The Charter provides for sanctions against certain, but not against all, violations of international law. There may be delicts under general international law against which no sanctions can be applied in accordance with the Charter, even if Article 39 and the resolution of the General Assembly "Uniting for Peace" are interpreted to mean that any conduct of a state which may be considered by the Security Council or the General Assembly as a threat to or breach of the peace is a delict, and the enforcement action taken by the Security Council or in conformity with the recommendation of the General Assembly is a sanction. Nonfulfillment of a treaty obligation, e.g., may not be considered by the Security Council or by the General Assembly as a threat to or breach of the peace, and hence not as a delict under the Charter, but it is a delict under general international law. However, it is a delict under general international law only because general international law authorizes the contracting party whose interest is violated by the nonfulfillment of the treaty to resort to reprisals or war against the other contracting party responsible for the nonfulfillment. The Charter in Article 2, paragraph 4, prohibits the members from resorting to reprisals or war, that is to say, the Charter abolishes the sanctions of general international law, insofar as these sanctions are to be taken by individual members, by reserving the use of force to the Organization. But the Charter does not provide for collective sanctions to be taken by the Organization against every conduct of a state which, under general international law, is an international delict. This is no improvement of general international law; and if a legal obligation to behave in a certain way is assumed to exist only if a sanction is provided as a reaction against the contrary behavior, the Charter has the undesirable effect of depriving of their legal character all obligations established by general international law which are not at the same time obligations under the Charter.

e. *Individual and collective self-defense.* The centralization of the force monopoly established by the Charter is restricted by the right of the members to use force (a) in the exercise of the right of self-defense (Article 51) and (b) against former enemy states (Articles 107 and 53, paragraph 1).

The right of self-defense is sometimes presented as the application of a much wider right, that of self-preservation. According to a doctrine advocated by some writers, a state may, in the exercise of this right of self-preservation, act contrary to any norm of inter-

The Nature of International Law

national law, and thus violate any right of another state, if such action is necessary for its own preservation, that is to say, if otherwise the state cannot protect itself against an actual or threatened violation of vital interests.[31] Under such circumstances a state may especially invade the territory of another state and perform there coercive acts. That the state against which the action is directed has actually violated or threatened to violate a right of the state acting in self-preservation is not required. It is, however, hardly possible to prove the existence of such a right of self-preservation as being established by general international law. Only as a reaction against a violation of its own right by the conduct of another state may a state violate the otherwise legally protected interests of this state by resorting to reprisals or war. This restriction, however, exists with respect to resorting to war only if the principle of *bellum justum* is presupposed as part of positive international law. It is not consistent to reject this principle, to maintain that war, the possible violation of almost all the rights of the state, is not forbidden, and at the same time to maintain that the violation of the rights of another state is permitted only in the exercise of the right of self-preservation. Nor is it consistent to maintain, as some writers do, that a state has the right to violate the rights of others if such violation is necessary for its own preservation, and at the same time to admit that the action taken in the exercise of the right of self-preservation, although not prohibited by international law and consequently no delict, remains nevertheless a "violation" and requires reparation. If the action is not prohibited, it cannot be a violation in the legal sense of this term, "violation" being identical with "delict"; and if the state exercising the so-called right of self-preservation is obliged to repair the damage caused by its action, this action must be a

---

[31] In the case of *The Caroline* the Secretary of State of the United States of America declared: "Undoubtedly it is just, that, while it is admitted that exceptions to the rules of international law, especially the principle of the territorial integrity of States growing out of the great law of self-defense do exist, those exceptions should be confined to cases in which the necessity of that self-defense is instant, overwhelming, and leaving no choice of means, and no moment for deliberation." (Cf. John Bassett Moore, *A Digest of International Law* (1906), II, 412.)

delict, because only an illegally caused damage entails the obligation of reparation. If the exercise of the so-called right of self-preservation is a delict, there can be no "right" of self-preservation. What is meant by the "right" of a state to violate in case of necessity the rights of another state is probably only that such a violation of the rights of another state is morally excusable.

There can be no doubt on the other hand, that a right of self-defense exists under general international law. It is the right of a state to protect itself by the use of force against an illegal attack. If resort to war is prohibited by general or particular international law, the illegal attack may, but need not, consist in an act of war. Then the attacked state exercises self-defense by resorting to counterwar. The illegal attack may be the action of individuals not acting as organs of another state, but operating from the territory of another state. Then the attacked state exercises its right of self-defense by using force against these individuals on the territory of the other state only if the latter has violated its obligation to take the measures to prevent or repress the illegal attack. For the employment of force on the territory of another state is equivalent to the employment of force against the other state; and this is permitted only as a reaction against a violation of international law, that is, in this case, as a reprisal. Under general international law the right of self-defense, as the right to use force against an illegal use of force, is implied in the principle of self-help. An express provision permitting self-defense is necessary only within a legal order which generally prohibits the use of force on the part of the members of the legal community constituted by this order. Hence the Covenant of the League of Nations and the Kellogg-Briand Pact did not and need not contain such a provision. Under the Covenant, which did not prohibit reprisals and prohibited war only under definite conditions, self-defense exercised by counterwar against an illegal war was not among these conditions. Under the Kellogg-Briand Pact, which likewise did not prohibit reprisals, self-defense by counterwar against an illegal war was included in the clause of the preamble permitting war against a violator of the pact. However, the Charter of the United Nations, which establishes a centralized force monopoly of the

The Nature of International Law

Organization, must stipulate this right and actually does so in Article 51 which provides: "Nothing in the present Charter shall impair the inherent right of individual or collective self-defense if an armed attack occurs against a Member of the United Nations, until the Security Council has taken the measures necessary to maintain international peace and security. Measures taken by Members in the exercise of this right of self-defense shall be immediately reported to the Security Council and shall not in any way affect the authority and responsibility of the Security Council under the present Charter to take at any time such action as it deems necessary in order to maintain or restore international peace and security." This provision restricts the right of self-defense to the case of an "armed attack against a Member of the United Nations," and to the time until the Security Council intervenes. It extends this right by authorizing so-called collective self-defense, that is, the right of the members to assist an attacked member.

The Charter does not define the concept of "armed attack." Its interpretation is left to the states involved in the conflict, until the Security Council intervenes. It is, then, for this organ of the United Nations to decide whether an armed attack has occurred and which state is responsible for it, and to determine the specific measures necessary to restore peace. The Charter does not bind the Security Council to take enforcement action against the aggressor. The Council may take any measure which it considers necessary to restore peace. According to the wording of Article 51, the right of collective self-defense exists only in case of an armed attack against a member. Hence it is doubtful whether members, without violating their obligation under Article 2, paragraph 4, may assist a nonmember victim of an armed attack. This question is of particular importance in case of a treaty by which members assume the obligation to assist nonmembers, contracting parties to the treaty, in their defense against an armed attack. Such a treaty is the North Atlantic Defense Treaty signed at Washington on April 4, 1949, to which ten members and two nonmembers (Portugal and Italy) are contracting parties. Other treaties organizing collective self-defense are the Inter-American Treaty of Reciprocal

Assistance signed at Rio de Janeiro on September 2, 1947, the Treaty of Economic, Social and Cultural Collaboration and Collective Self-Defense signed at Brussels on March 17, 1948, and the Treaty signed by the United States, Australia, and New Zealand at San Francisco on September 1, 1951.

f. *Action against former enemy states.* As to actions against former enemy states, Article 107 provides: "Nothing in the present Charter shall invalidate or preclude action, in relation to any State which during the Second World War has been an enemy of any signatory to the present Charter, taken or authorized as a result of that war by the Governments having responsibility for such action."

Article 52 authorizes the members to enter into regional arrangements "for dealing with such matters relating to the maintenance of international peace and security as are appropriate for regional action," provided that such arrangements are "consistent with the Purposes and Principles of the United Nations." Article 53 provides that under regional arrangements no enforcement action shall be taken without the authorization of the Security Council, "with the exception of measures against any enemy State, as defined in paragraph 2 of this Article, provided for pursuant to Article 107 or in regional arrangements directed against renewal of aggressive policy on the part of any such State, until such time as the Organization may, on request of the Governments concerned, be charged with the responsibility for preventing further aggression by such a State." In paragraph 2 of Article 52 the term "enemy State" is defined as "any State which during the Second World War has been an enemy of any signatory of the present Charter." Since Article 51 establishing the right of collective self-defense provides that nothing in the Charter shall impair this right (which implies the right of taking enforcement action without the authorization of the Security Council), it may be assumed that under a regional arrangement enforcement action may be taken not only under the conditions expressly determined in Article 53, paragraph 1, but also in the exercise of the right of collective self-defense.

g. *Nonintervention in matters of "domestic jurisdiction."* An important limitation on the functions of the United Nations,

The Nature of International Law

though not a restriction of its force monopoly, is established by Article 2, paragraph 7, which stipulates: "Nothing contained in the present Charter shall authorize the United Nations to intervene in matters which are essentially within the domestic jurisdiction of any State or shall require the Members to submit such matters to settlement under the present Charter; but this principle shall not prejudice the application of enforcement measures under Chapter VII." In the first words the Charter prohibits the Organization from intervening in matters of domestic jurisdiction "of any State," not only of members. Then the Charter restricts the obligation of the members to settle their disputes by peaceful means by releasing them from the obligation to submit disputes arising out of such matters to settlement under the Charter, which probably means to settlement by the peaceful means provided for in Chapter VI of the Charter. But it does not mean that the members are authorized to settle such a dispute by the employment of force. For in the last part of Article 2, paragraph 7, enforcement measures taken by the Organization under Chapter VII are excluded from the principle of nonintervention. That means that the Security Council may take enforcement action, if the Council, under Article 39, determines the existence of a threat to or breach of the peace. This may mean that the members, although not obliged to settle by peaceful means a dispute arising out of a matter which is essentially within the domestic jurisdiction of one of the parties to the dispute, are not allowed to settle it by the threat or use of force because a threat or use of force may always be considered by the Security Council to be a threat to or breach of the peace. The centralized force monopoly of the Organization is not affected by Article 2, paragraph 7.[32]

The restricted principle of nonintervention established by Article 2, paragraph 7, is not identical with the so-called fundamental right of the states which is the reflection of the duty of nonintervention imposed upon the states by general international law (see *infra*, p. 157). The "intervention" prohibited by international law is usually defined as dictatorial interference by a state in the

---
[32] As to the meaning of "domestic jurisdiction," cf. *infra*, pp. 191ff.

affairs of another state. A "dictatorial" interference is an interference by the threat or use of force. Article 2, paragraph 7, does not prohibit such intervention on the part of the individual states —this prohibition is implied in Article 2, paragraph 4—but any kind of interference, also nondictatorial interference, on the part of the Organization. It is evident that general international law does not prohibit intervention under all circumstances: forcible interference in the sphere of interests of another state is permitted as reaction against a violation of international law. The writers who maintain the existence of a fundamental duty of nonintervention admit that intervention is permitted by general international law only under certain circumstances. An analysis of the reasons for which a state, according to this doctrine, may have a right of intervention against another state shows that intervention, as dictatorial interference by one state in the affairs of another state, is permitted only as reaction of the former against a violation of its right by the latter. Such a doctrine is possible only if the *bellum justum* principle is recognized. For it is incompatible with the view that war, the most radical dictatorial interference in the affairs of another state, is not forbidden by general international law. If threat to the peace and breach of the peace are to be considered as violations of the law of the United Nations, the intervention of the Security Council permitted by Article 2, paragraph 7, is in conformity with the general principle concerning intervention established by international law.

8. *War: Regulation of Its Conduct*

International law not only determines under what conditions resort to war is forbidden as a delict or permitted as a sanction, but regulates also the conduct of war regardless of whether the war is legal or illegal. The delict committed by resorting to war in violation of a rule prohibiting war, and the delict committed by violating the rules regulating the conduct of war must be distinguished. The latter delict may be committed in a legal as well as in an illegal war. Whereas the sanctions against a violation of the rules prohibiting war are a counterwar resorted to by the

The Nature of International Law 65

attacked state, and reprisals or war resorted to by other states in conformity with treaties concluded for this purpose, the sanctions against violations of the rules regulating the conduct of war can be only reprisals taken by a state already at war with the state responsible for such violations of the law. The rules regulating the conduct of war are rules of general customary or of particular contractual international law. In the latter case they are binding only upon the contracting states. The treaties concerned, concluded only by some and not by all of the states of the world, frequently contain rules formulating old general customary law. The binding force of some of these treaties is restricted by the so-called general participation clause according to which the provisions of the treaty shall apply only if all belligerents are parties to the treaty. One treaty (the Proctocol of 1925, concerning the use in war of asphyxiating, poisonous, and other gases) has been signed by some states with the reservation that the provisions of the treaty shall cease to be binding in relation to any belligerent whose armed forces, or the armed forces of whose allies, do not respect them.

The most important treaties regulating the conduct of war are as follows:

The Convention (III) relative to the opening of hostilities, signed at The Hague, October 18, 1907; the Convention (IV) respecting the laws and customs of war on land, signed at The Hague, October 18, 1907; the Declaration (IV. 3) concerning expanding bullets, signed at The Hague, July 29, 1899; the Declaration (IV, 2) concerning asphyxiating gases, signed at The Hague, July 29, 1899; the Protocol prohibiting the use in war of asphyxiating, poisonous, or other gases, and of bacteriological methods of warfare, opened for signature at Geneva, June 17, 1925; the Declaration of Paris of April 16, 1856, respecting warfare on sea; the Convention (VII) relating to the conversion of merchant ships into warships, signed at The Hague, October 18, 1907; the Convention (VIII) relative to the laying of automatic submarine contact mines, signed at The Hague, October 18, 1907; the Convention (IX) concerning bombardment by naval forces in time of war, signed at The Hague, October 18, 1907; the

Convention (XI) relative to certain restrictions with regard to the exercise of the right of capture in naval war, signed at The Hague, October 18, 1907; the Protocol concerning the use of submarines against merchant vessels, signed at London, November 6, 1936; the Declaration (XIV) prohibiting the discharge of projectiles and explosives from balloons, signed at The Hague, October 18, 1907; the Convention concerning the treatment of sick and wounded and of prisoners of war, signed at Geneva, July 29, 1929; the Convention (X), signed at The Hague, October 18, 1907, for the adaptation to maritime warfare of the principles of the Geneva Convention of August 22, 1864 for the amelioration of the condition of soldiers wounded in armies in the field (replaced with respect to warfare on land by the Convention of July 29, 1929); the Convention (V) respecting the rights and duties of neutral powers and persons in case of war on land, signed at The Hague, October 18, 1907; the Convention (XIII) concerning the rights and duties of neutral powers in naval war, signed at The Hague, October 18, 1907.[33]

On August 12, 1949, at Geneva, the representatives of the overwhelming majority of the states of the world signed the Final Act of a conference for the protection of war victims, to which four conventions were attached relating to: (1) the amelioration of the condition of wounded and sick members of armed forces in the field; (2) the amelioration of the condition of wounded and sick, and shipwrecked members of the armed forces at sea; (3) the treatment of prisoners of war; (4) the protection of civilian persons in war. Article 2 of each convention contains the following provisions: "The present Convention shall apply to all cases of declared war or of any other armed conflict which may arise between two or more of the High Contracting Parties, even if the state of war is not recognized by any of them.[34]—The Convention shall also apply to all cases of partial or total occupation of the territory of a High Contracting Party, even if the said

---

[33] Subsequent references to these conventions are usually by Roman numeral, as Convention IV.

[34] In quoted matter the dash, as used here, indicates a paragraph in the source.

The Nature of International Law

occupation meets with no armed resistance.—Although one of the Powers may not be a party to the present Convention, the Powers who are parties thereto shall remain bound by the Convention in relation to the said Power, if the latter accepts and applies the provisions thereof." It is important to note that the first of the three provisions extends the application of the Convention beyond the case of "war," in the usual sense of the word, to all kinds of "armed conflicts"; and that according to the third provision, the conventions are, conditionally, treaties in favor of third States —the states not contracting parties to the treaties. The condition that the noncontracting power "accepts and applies" the provisions of the conventions does not mean that that power has become a contracting party. To determine whether this condition is fulfilled is left to each contracting party.

The most important rules of international law regulating the conduct of war are as follows:

a. *The beginning and the end of war.* Article 1 of Convention III relative to the opening of hostilities provides that hostilities between states must not commence without previous and explicit warning in the form either of a declaration of war, giving reasons, or of an ultimatum, i.e., a final proposition terminating negotiations with conditional declaration of war. It is doubtful whether this provision, as is often assumed, is only the codification of a rule of general customary law; it certainly has not been respected in many cases.

The end of war is the beginning of peace. Usually the belligerents conclude a peace treaty which contains a clause to the effect that there shall be peace, or that the state of peace is established, or that the state of war is terminated in the relation between the belligerents. This clause implies that the contracting parties assume the obligation to abstain from further acts of war.[35] After the treaty has come into force, acts of war directed by one party against the other are considered to be illegal, a violation of the

---

[35] This obligation is expressly formulated, e.g., in Article I of the Peace Treaty of Lausanne, signed by Italy and Turkey on October 18, 1912. "Immediately after the signing of the present treaty the two governments pledge themselves to take the necessary measures to bring about immediate and simultaneous cessation of hostilities."

peace treaty. If the government of one belligerent, in violation of the peace treaty, continued to perform acts of war,[36] the war would not be terminated. Hence, it is not—as usually assumed—by the peace treaty,[37] it is by carrying out the obligation stipulated in the peace treaty that the belligerents terminate the war. Without a peace treaty being concluded, the Congress of the United States passed a resolution, approved by the President on July 2, 1921, to the effect that "the state of war declared to exist between the Imperial German Government and the United States of America by the joint resolution of Congress approved April 6, 1917, is hereby declared at an end." This was the ascertainment of the fact that the war between the two states was terminated. The treaty between the United States and Germany signed afterward, on August 25,

---

[36] This is different from the case where only parts of the armed forces of one belligerent, ignoring the fact that a peace treaty has come into force, commit an act of war. In this latter case only reparation of the wrong must be made. This principle was applied in *The John* (2 Dodson, 336 [1818]). The peace treaty signed at Ghent on December 24, 1814, by Great Britain and the United States of America provided that immediately after the ratification of the treaty orders should be sent out to the forces on either side to cease from further hostilities; and, further, that all vessels captured by either party after the times specified by the treaty should be restored. The *John,* an American vessel, was captured by a British man-of-war after the expiry of the period agreed upon, both captor and prize being in ignorance of the fact that peace had been concluded. Soon afterward the *John* was lost. A joint commission before which the American Government brought a claim for indemnity on behalf of the owners of the vessel decided the case in favor of an indemnity. Cf. Pitt Cobbett, *Leading Cases on International Law* (1924), II, 344.

[37] In the case of *Kotzias v. Tyser* (England, High Court of Justice, King's Bench Division, January 13, 1920; Annual Digest 1919–1922, Case No. 307) the plaintiff based his claim on a policy of insurance effected with the defendant on November 2, 1918, whereby the latter agreed to pay to the plaintiff a certain sum of money "in the event of peace between Great Britain and Germany not being concluded on or before the thirtieth day of June one thousand nine hundred and nineteen." The Court held that peace had not been concluded on or before June 30, 1919, and the plaintiff was therefore entitled to recover the sum insured by the policy, *inter alia* upon grounds of a principle of general international law, formulated by the Court as follows: "The authorities show that, in the absence of any specific statutory or contractual provision to the contrary, the general rule of international law is that as between civilized Powers who have been at war, peace is not concluded until a treaty of peace is finally binding upon the belligerents, and that that stage is not reached until ratifications of the treaty of peace have been exchanged between them."

The Nature of International Law

1921, was not a peace treaty in the specific sense of the term, that is to say, a treaty concluded for the purpose of terminating the war, but a treaty concluded "to restore friendly relations existing between the two nations prior to the outbreak of war." On December 31, 1946, the President of the United States proclaimed "the cessation of hostilities of World War II," and in a statement explaining the proclamation he said that the action did not have "the effect of terminating the state of war itself." But by a joint resolution of Congress, approved by the President on October 19, 1951, "the state of war" declared to exist between the United States and Germany by the joint resolution of Congress approved on December 11, 1941, was declared terminated. There are cases where it is impossible to conclude a peace treaty; for instance, when one belligerent as an effect of the war ceases to exist, either because its territory has been annexed by the other belligerent or because it has been dismembered and new states have been established on its territory. Besides, it is doubtful whether a contractual obligation to abstain from further acts of armed force is appropriate with respect to a war which is interpreted to be a sanction or a delict. The practice of concluding peace treaties for the purpose of terminating a war presupposes the view that the war is essentially a bilateral action and in itself neither a delict nor a sanction. A state cannot assume, by a treaty, the obligation to abstain from continuing to wage war if waging war is a delict. This obligation is already established by the rule of law prohibiting the war. And an obligation to terminate a war which has the character of a sanction is—at the least—superfluous, since, as a sanction, the war is to be terminated as soon as it has fulfilled its purpose. The practice of terminating war by a peace treaty is especially problematical in case war is a collective sanction directed by an international organization, in conformity with its constitution, against a delinquent state. Then the peace treaty would have to be concluded by the organization on the one hand and the delinquent state on the other. In concluding a treaty the contracting parties are on an equal footing. No such legal situation exists in the relation between the delinquent and the authority deciding and executing the sanction. This, of course, holds true only with respect to the specific function of a peace treaty: the obligation to refrain from further acts of war, not with respect to other obligations usually imposed by peace treaties on the contracting parties.

b. *The individuals against whom the destructive acts of war may be directed.* War is an enforcement action carried out through the armed forces of one state against another state. This action consists in the forcible deprivation of life, health, personal freedom, and property of human beings. The tendency to restrict the destructive effects of war led to the principle that individuals who do not directly or indirectly belong to the armed forces of the state against which the war is directed shall not be killed, wounded, or made prisoners, and that they shall not be deprived of their property, except under certain conditions. But it must be admitted that since the First World War the distinction between individuals who belong and those who do not belong to the armed forces of a state has become problematical. As to the distinction between individuals who belong directly to the armed forces insofar as they participate in the destructive operations (killing, wounding, taking prisoners, destroying property)—the so-called combatant members of the armed forces—and individuals who belong only indirectly to the armed forces, insofar as they do not participate in the destructive operations, such as chaplains, physicians, nurses, and the like—the so-called noncombatant members of the armed forces—it is a rule of general customary law that the latter must not be killed or wounded. They may be made prisoners of war, with the exception of persons whose function it is to take care of the wounded and sick. If these persons fall into the hands of the enemy, they must not be retained as prisoners of war but must be returned to the opponent as soon as possible. Even a combatant must not be killed or wounded if he has laid down his arms or, having no longer means of defense, has surrendered. It is forbidden to declare that no quarter will be given. The belligerent in whose power the prisoners of war are is obliged to release them and to repatriate them as soon as the war is terminated. These are rules of customary general international law, now also formulated in the

The Nature of International Law 71

Hague Convention of 1907 respecting the laws and customs of war on land and in the Geneva Convention of 1929 concerning the treatment of sick and wounded.[38]

c. *The means of destruction.* The rules of international law regulating the conduct of war restrict not only the category of individuals against whom the destructive acts of war may be directed but also the means of destruction. It is a rule of customary general international law, codified in Articles 23(a), (b), and (e) of the Regulations of the Hague Convention respecting

---

[38] The Geneva Convention of 1949 for the protection of civilian persons in time of war provides: "ARTICLE 32. The High Contracting Parties specifically agree that each of them is prohibited from taking any measure of such character as to cause the physical suffering, or extermination of protected persons in their hands. This prohibition applies not only to murder, torture, corporal punishment, mutilation and medical or scientific experiments not necessitated by the medical treatment of a protected person, but also to any other measures of brutality whether applied by civilian or military agents. ARTICLE 33. No protected person may be punished for an offence he or she has not personally committed. Collective penalties and likewise all measures of intimidation or terrorism are prohibited. Pillage is prohibited. Reprisals against protected persons and their property are prohibited. ARTICLE 34. The taking of hostages is prohibited."

Of particular importance is Article 3, which applies to civil war: "In the case of armed conflict not of an international character occurring in the territory of one of the High Contracting Parties, each party to the conflict shall be bound to apply, as a minimum, the following provisions: (1) Persons taking no active part in the hostilities, including members of armed forces who have laid down their arms and those placed *hors de combat* by sickness, wounds, detention, or any other cause, shall in all circumstances be treated humanely, without any adverse distinction founded on race, colour, religion or faith, sex, birth or wealth, or any other similar criteria. To this end, the following acts are and shall remain prohibited at any time and in any place whatsoever with respect to the above-mentioned persons: (a) violence to life and person, in particular murder of all kinds, mutilation, cruel treatment and torture; (b) taking of hostages; (c) outrages upon personal dignity, in particular humiliating and degrading treatment; (d) the passing of sentences and the carrying out of executions without previous judgment pronounced by a regularly constituted court, affording all the judicial guarantees which are recognized as indispensable by civilized peoples. (2) The wounded and sick shall be collected and cared for.—An impartial humanitarian body, such as the International Committee of the Red Cross, may offer its services to the Parties to the conflict.—The Parties to the conflict should further endeavour to bring into force, by means of special agreements, all or part of the other provisions of the present Convention.—The application of the preceding provisions shall not affect the legal status of the Parties to the conflict."

the laws and customs of war on land, that the employment of poison or poisoned weapons and of arms, projectiles, or material calculated to cause unnecessary suffering and to kill or wound treacherously individuals belonging to the hostile nation or army, is forbidden.

By various treaties the use of explosive or expanding bullets and projectiles diffusing asphyxiating or deleterious gases, and the launching of projectiles or explosives from balloons or other kind of aerial vessels has been forbidden. But these treaties have been ratified only by some and not by all of the states, and the prohibitions referring to air warfare were never respected.

In conformity with general international law applicable to any kind of warfare, Convention IV of 1907 stipulates with respect to warfare on land:

"ARTICLE 25. The attack or bombardment, by whatever means, of towns, villages, dwellings, or buildings which are undefended is prohibited. ARTICLE 26. The officer in command of an attacking force must, before commencing a bombardment, except in cases of assault, do all in his power to warn the authorities. ARTICLE 27. In sieges and bombardments all necessary steps must be taken to spare, as far as possible, buildings dedicated to religion, art, science, or charitable purposes, historic monuments, hospitals, and places where the sick and wounded are collected, provided they are not being used at the time for military purposes.—It is the duty of the besieged to indicate the presence of such buildings or places by distinctive and visible signs, which shall be notified to the enemy beforehand. ARTICLE 28. The pillage of a town or place, even when taken by assault, is prohibited."

Similar provisions are stipulated by the Hague Convention concerning bombardment by naval forces in time of war. The rules laid down in Articles 25, 26, and 27 of Convention IV were not respected in the air warfare of the two world wars. It may be doubted whether they are still to be considered as valid.

As to the destruction of enemy property, a rule of general international law, stipulated also in Article 23(g) of the Regulations of Convention IV provides that it is forbidden to destroy private or public enemy property unless such destruction be imperatively

The Nature of International Law

demanded by the necessities of war. As to the appropriation of enemy property, a distinction must be made between enemy property on the own territory of a belligerent, and enemy property on the territory of the enemy invaded by the belligerent. There is a rule of general international law forbidding the belligerents to confiscate private enemy property on their own territory and to annul debts due to enemy subjects. But there is no rule of general international law prohibiting a belligerent from confiscating certain public property of the enemy on the former's territory.

d. *Belligerent occupation.* It is a rule of general international law that by mere occupation of enemy territory in the course of war the occupied territory does not become territory of the occupying belligerent, or—as it is usually formulated—the occupying belligerent power does not acquire sovereignty over this territory, which remains territory of the state against which the war is directed. The occupying belligerent is obliged to administer the territory in a way determined by international law. The rules concerned are formulated in Articles 42–56 of the Regulations attached to Convention IV. According to Article 42, the territory is considered occupied when and insofar as it is actually placed under the authority of the hostile army. According to Article 43, the occupying state "shall take all the measures in his power to restore, and ensure, as far as possible, public order and safety, while respecting, unless absolutely prevented, the laws in force in the country." The occupying power may change the existing—substantive as well as procedural—law of the occupied territory only insofar as such change is necessary for the safety of its armed forces.[39] The occupying power is expressly forbidden "to force

---

[39] During the belligerent occupation of Belgium in the First World War by Germany the German governor-general issued, on August 8, 1918, an order prohibiting the sale of vegetables before they had been gathered. In *Bochart v. Committee of Supplies of Corneux* (Annual Digest 1919–1922, Case No. 327) the Belgian Court of Appeal of Liége, on February 28, 1920, held that a contract concluded in violation of this order was void. It stated that the occupying power acted in the place of the legitimate authority which for the time being had been ousted, and in conformity with the provisions of Article 43 of the Hague Convention. But, in *De Brabant and Gosselin v. T. and A. Florent* (Annual Digest 1919–1922, Case No. 328) the Court of Appeal of Brussels, on July 22, 1920, held that the German order of August 8, 1918, was not made

the inhabitants of territory occupied by it to furnish information about the army of the other belligerent, or about its means of defense" (Article 44), and "to compel the inhabitants of occupied territory to swear allegiance to the hostile Power" (Article 45). "Family honor and rights, the lives of persons, and private property, as well as religious convictions and practice, must be respected" (Article 46).

As to enemy property on the occupied territory, Article 46 provides that "private property cannot be confiscated." Article 47 of the Regulations prohibits pillage. But Article 53, paragraph 2, of the Regulations stipulates: "An army of occupation can only take possession of cash, funds, and realizable securities which are strictly the property of the State, depots of arms, means of

---

with a view to assuring public order and security, but to starving the population. It went beyond the powers given to the occupant by Article 43 of the Hague Convention; it never had the force of law and cannot therefore avoid an agreement properly concluded by the parties. In *Mathot v. Longué* (Annual Digest 1919–1922, Case No. 329) the Court of Appeal of Liége, on February 19, 1921, went as far as to state that the orders of the occupying power are not laws, but simply commands of the military authority of the occupant; that it is logically and legally inadmissible to say that "Article 43 of the Hague Convention conferred upon the occupying Power a positive right to legislate; . . . that all that was intended . . . was to restrict the abuse of force by the occupant and not to give him or recognize him as possessing any authority in the sphere of law."

In *Adriaenssens v. Ministère Public* (Annual Digest 1919–1922, Case No. 332) the Belgian Police Court of Antwerp (1919) held that the decision of a judge appointed by the occupying power was null and void. The court stated that the occupying power had no right to interfere in the judicial business of the country. Having only a temporary power over the country, it could not confer upon a judge appointed by itself the security of tenure required by the constitution. Accordingly, H. Q. (the judge appointed by the occupying power) could not be regarded as a regularly appointed Belgian magistrate, seeing that the occupying power had excused the citizens whom it appointed to public offices from taking the political oath required by the Belgian Law of June 18, 1869. But in the *Carinthia (Removal of Judges) Case* (Annual Digest 1919–1922, Case No. 333) the Austrian Supreme Court in Civil Matters (1919) held that the decision of a district court, the president of which had been removed during the belligerent occupation of Carinthia by the occupying troops of Yugoslavia and replaced by a judge appointed by them, was valid. The Austrian Supreme Court stated that, according to Article 43 of the Hague Convention respecting the laws and customs of war on land, the occupant is entitled to take steps for the maintenance of public order and security.

The Nature of International Law

transport, stores and supplies, and, generally, all movable property belonging to the State which may be used for military operations. All appliances, whether on land, at sea, or in the air, adapted for the transmission of news, or for the transport of persons or things, exclusive of cases governed by naval law, depots of arms, and, generally, all kinds of munitions of war, may be seized, even if they belong to private individuals, but must be restored and compensation fixed when peace is made." Public immovable property of the enemy cannot be appropriated as long as the occupant belligerent power has not extended its sovereignty over the occupied territory. Article 55 of the Regulations of Convention IV, in conformity with general international law provides: "The occupying State shall be regarded only as administrator and usufructuary of public buildings, real estate, forests, and agricultural estates belonging to the hostile State, and situated in the occupied country. It must safeguard the capital of these properties, and administer them in accordance with the rules of usufruct." And Article 56 provides: "The property of municipalities, that of institutions dedicated to religion, charity and education, the arts and sciences, even when State property, shall be treated as private property. All seizure of, destruction or wilful damage done to institutions of this character, historic monuments, works of art and science, is forbidden, and should be made the subject of legal proceedings."

The principle that enemy territory occupied by a belligerent in course of war remains the territory of the state against which the war is directed, can apply only as long as this community still exists as a state within the meaning of international law. This is hardly the case if, after occupation of the whole territory of an enemy state, its armed forces are completely defeated so that no further resistance is possible and its national government is abolished by the victorious state. Then the vanquished community is deprived of one of the essential elements of a state in the sense of international law: an effective and independent government, and hence has lost its character as a state. If the territory is not to be considered a stateless territory, it must be considered to be under the sovereignty of the occupant belligerent, which—in such a case—ceases to be restricted by the rules concerning belligerent occupation. This was the case with the territory of the German Reich occupied in the Second World War after the complete defeat and surrender of its armed forces. In view of the fact that the last national government of the German Reich was abolished, it may be assumed that this state ceased to exist as a subject of international law. If a belligerent state ceases legally to exist as an effect of the defeat, as, e.g., the Austro-Hungarian Monarchy in the First World War, or the German Reich in the Second World War, no peace treaty or any other treaty can be concluded with this state for the purpose of transferring the territory concerned, or parts of it, to the victorious or any other state.[40]

---

[40] In *Rex v. Bottrill, ex parte Kuechenmeister* (1947 Law Reports, King's Bench Division 41), at the hearing of the application of C. W. Kuechenmeister, a German national interned as an alien enemy in a British camp for a writ of habeas corpus, before the divisional court a certificate dated April 2, 1946, from the British Secretary of State for Foreign Affairs was produced by the Attorney General. It stated "(1) That under paragraph 5 of the preamble to the declaration, dated June 5, 1945, of the unconditional surrender of Germany, the governments of the United Kingdom, the United States of America, the Union of Soviet Socialist Republics and France assumed 'supreme authority with respect to Germany, including all the powers possessed by the German government, the High Command and any State, municipal or local government or authority. The assumption, for the purposes stated above, of the said authority and powers does not effect the annexation of Germany.' (2) That in consequence of this declaration Germany still exists as a State and German nationality as a nationality, but the Allied Control Commission are the agency through which the Government of Germany is carried on. (3) No treaty of peace or declaration of the Allied Powers having been made terminating the state of war with Germany, His Majesty is still in a state of war with Germany, although, as provided in the declaration of surrender, all active hostilities have ceased." The divisional court held "that the certificate was conclusive as to the matters it purported to certify; the applicant remained in consequence an alien enemy notwithstanding the unconditional surrender of Germany; and that as an alien enemy interned in this country he could not apply for a writ of habeas corpus." In his appeal the applicant's counsel submitted that the applicant was not an alien enemy. He stated that "the central German Government of Germany was . . . displaced, and its place completely taken by a government composed of the four United Nations. War predicates at least one other State against which the war is waged, and the declaration of Berlin ended Germany, for the time being, as a separate State. In support of that proposition he argued that a sovereign State which has no sovereign government is a contradiction in terms; and that, even if such a State be possible in international law, a State which has no national government cannot wage a war or be at

The Nature of International Law

On the territory of the abolished state a new state or some new states may be established. This was the case with the territory of the defeated Austro-Hungarian Monarchy, which was the territory of two united states. On this territory the Czechoslovakian and the Austrian Republics, and part of Poland have been established. This is also the case with the territory of the German Reich on which two new states came into existence: the western German state, called the Federal Republic of Germany; and the eastern German State, called the German Democratic Republic. But the new state or the new states, which have not been at war with the victorious state, cannot conclude a peace treaty and are not entitled to dispose of other territory but their own. That the Austrian Republic was forced to conclude a peace treaty with the Allied and Associated Powers, although this new state was not at war with the states which by their victory brought the Austro-Hungarian Monarchy to dismemberment, and that the Austrian Republic was forced to dispose in this treaty of territory of the disappeared state which never was territory of the Austrian Republic, was based on the fiction that the Austrian Republic was identical with the Austrian Monarchy. In the case of the German Reich, the governments of the occupant powers maintained the fiction that it continued to exist even after the abolishment of its last national government, and on the basis of this fiction it was assumed that the territory of the German Reich occupied by the four victorious powers was not under their sovereignty, but remained under the sovereignty of the German Reich. But the administration of the occupied territory was in no way in conformity with the rules concerning belligerent occupation.

e. *Warfare on sea.* There are special rules of international law which apply only to warfare on sea. The most important of these rules are as follows: The armed forces engaged in warfare on sea consist chiefly of men-of-war. Only men-of-war may perform acts of

---

war." But the Court held that "the Certificate of the Secretary of State for Foreign Affairs, which says in terms that we are still at war with Germany, is binding at least in our municipal law, and therefore on all the King's courts.... In our municipal law, whether it differs from international law or not, a state of war can continue, and the war with Germany is continuing, in spite of the fact that Germany thus ceased to have any independent central government...."

war and exercise the right of capture in maritime warfare. They must be distinguishable by external marks, such as a special flag, from merchant vessels. Merchant ships may be converted into warships under conditions determined by the Convention VII. They must be "placed under the direct authority, immediate control, and responsibility of the Power whose flag they fly," and they "must bear the external marks which distinguish the war-ships of their nationality. The commander must be in the service of the State and duly commissioned by the competent authorities. His name must figure on the list of the officers of the fighting fleet. The crew must be subject to military discipline. Every merchant ship converted into a war-ship must observe in its operations the laws and customs of war. A belligerent who converts a merchant ship into a war-ship must, as soon as possible, announce such conversion in the list of war-ships." Merchant ships not converted into warships may be armed for the purpose of defending themselves against attack. Privateering, that is, the formerly observed practice of commissioning private vessels through letters of marque to perform acts of war on sea and especially to capture enemy merchant vessels, is now forbidden by the Declaration of Paris of 1856. By Convention VIII of 1907 the laying of automatic submarine contact mines is restricted, and by Convention IX of 1907 the bombardment by naval forces of undefended ports, towns, villages, dwellings, or buildings is forbidden (Article 1). Excepted by Article 2 are "military works, military or naval establishments, depots of arms or war *matériel*, workshops or plant which could be utilized for the needs of the hostile fleet or army, and the ships of war in the harbor." Article 5 provides: "In bombardments by naval forces all the necessary measures must be taken by the commander to spare as far as possible sacred edifices, buildings used for artistic, scientific, or charitable purposes, historic monuments, hospitals, and places where the sick or wounded are collected, on the understanding that they are not used at the same time for military purposes."

Whereas private enemy property in warfare on land is in principle safe from appropriation, in warfare on sea private enemy vessels and private enemy goods thereon or on the public ships

The Nature of International Law

of the enemy may be seized and appropriated. According to a rule of general international law, the nationality of a ship is determined by the flag under which it legitimately sails. Hence in time of war a ship is to be considered as a neutral and not as an enemy ship only if it legitimately sails under the flag of a neutral state. The men-of-war of the belligerents have the right to visit and to search merchant vessels in order to ascertain the real nationality of the ship. Enemy goods on a neutral ship must not be seized (neutral flag covers enemy goods) with the exception of contraband of war,[41] a rule expressly stipulated by the Declaration of Paris of 1856. Contraband of war are goods the transport of which to the enemy is forbidden by either belligerent in conformity with general international law. The appropriation of a private enemy vessel and private enemy goods thereon, in contradistinction to captured public enemy vessels, is not possible without a decision enacted to this effect by a prize court of the capturing belligerent. Prize courts are national courts of the belligerents having jurisdiction to adjudicate upon capture at sea in time of war. Their establishment is provided for by general international law, and the national law which they apply must be in conformity with the rules of international law regulating capture at sea. Convention XI (Articles 5 and 6) provides: "When an enemy merchant ship is captured by a belligerent, such of its crew as are nationals of a neutral State are not made prisoners of war. The same rule applies in the case of the captain and officers likewise nationals of a neutral State, if they promise formally in writing not to serve on an enemy ship while the war lasts. The captain, officers, and members of the crew, when nationals of the enemy State, are not made prisoners of war, on condition that they make a formal promise in writing, not to undertake, while hostilities last, any service connected with the operations of the war." This Convention contains the general participation clause.

Destruction of the enemy merchant vessel before adjudication by a prize court is permitted in case the vessel offers resistance against search and seizure, or in case of necessity. But before destroying the vessel the captor must remove the persons on board

---

[41] Cf. *infra*, p. 128.

(crew and passengers) and the ship's papers; and submit the case to a prize court to decide whether capture and destruction were legal. These rules of general international law apply also to submarines. The treaty signed by the United States, Great Britain, France, Italy, and Japan in London on April 22, 1930, and the Protocol signed in London on November 6, 1936, and adhered to by other states, expressly stipulates: "In their action with regard to merchant ships, submarines must conform to the rules of international law to which surface vessels are subjected."[42]

Exceptionally, neutral ships and neutral goods may be seized and appropriated by the belligerents under the following circumstances: (a) In case a neutral merchant ship resists visit or search

---

[42] Cf. the famous case *The Lusitania* (United States, District Court, Southern District of New York, 1918, 251 Federal Reporter 715). During the First World War, on May 1, 1915, the British passenger-carrying merchantman *Lusitania* sailed from New York, bound for Liverpool, with 1,257 passengers and a crew of 702, making a total of 1,959 souls on board, men, women, and children. At approximately 2:10 on the afternoon of May 7, 1915, weather clear and sea smooth, without warning, the vessel was torpedoed and went down by the head in about 18 minutes, with an ultimate tragic loss of life of 1,195. Numerous suits having been begun against the Cunard Steamship Company, Limited, the owner of the vessel, proceeding was brought by the steamship company, as petitioner, to obtain an adjudication as to liability, and to limit petitioner's liability to its interest in the vessel and her pending freight. The court stated *inter alia:* "There is, of course, no doubt as to the right to make prize of an enemy ship on the high seas, and, under certain conditions, to destroy her, and equally no doubt of the obligation to safeguard the lives of all persons aboard whether passengers or crew. . . ." The court referred to section 116 of the German Prize Code, in force at the date of the *Lusitania's* destruction, which provided: "Before proceeding to a destruction of the vessel, the safety of all persons on board, and, so far as possible, their effects, is to be provided for, and all ship's papers and other evidentary material, which, according to the views of the persons at interest, is of value for the formulation of the judgment of the Prize Court, are to be taken over by the commander." The court held: "Thus, when the *Lusitania* sailed from New York, her owner and master were justified in believing that, whatever else had theretofore happened, this simple, humane, and universally accepted principle would not be violated. . . . The fault, therefore, must be laid upon those who are responsible for the sinking of the vessel, in the legal as well as moral sense. It is therefore not the Cunard Line, petitioner, which must be held liable for the loss of life and property. The cause of the sinking of the *Lusitania* was the illegal act of the Imperial German government, acting through its instrument, the submarine commander, and violating a cherished and humane rule observed, until this war, by even the bitterest antagonists. . . ."

The Nature of International Law

it may be captured, and the ship, after adjudication by a prize court, confiscated. Whether the cargo is also liable to confiscation is disputed. (b) In case of breach of blockade by a neutral merchant ship the latter may be captured and after adjudication by a prize court confiscated. Whether and to what extent the cargo also is liable to confiscation is disputed. Blockade is the shutting up by warships of the enemy's coast or part of it so as to prevent ingress and egress of ships and aircraft. According to the Declaration of Paris of 1856 the blockade must be effective in order to have the legal consequence just mentioned.[43] (c) In case a neutral merchant ship carries contraband of war, the latter may be confiscated after adjudication by a prize court. Whether the ship and the innocent part of its cargo is also liable to confiscation is disputed. (d) In case of so-called unneutral service, i.e., in case a neutral merchant ship carries certain persons such as members of the armed forces of the enemy, agents of the army, and the like, or dispatches for the enemy, the ship may be captured and after adjudication by a prize court, confiscated. Also, according to the practice of some states, that part of the cargo which belongs to the owner of the ship may be confiscated.

f. *Air warfare.* There are no valid rules of general international law applicable to air warfare which are not applicable to other kinds of warfare. Thus, the principles of immunity of noncombatants as well as the prohibition of the bombardment of undefended places apply—according to the original intention—certainly also to air warfare. But it is doubtful whether they have not become obsolete by the practice of the belligerents during the two world wars.

g. *Neutrality under general international law.* A belligerent is under international obligations not only toward the state with which it is at war but also toward the neutral states; and the neutral states are under international obligations toward the belligerents.

---

[43] In the case *Geipel v. Smith* (7 Law Reports, Queen's Bench Division 404) the British Court of Queen's Bench (1872) stated with respect to blockade: "It is a restraint, provided the blockade is effective; and in the eye of the law a blockade is effective if the enemies' ships are in such number and position as to render the running of the blockade a matter of danger, although some vessels may succeed in getting through."

A state is neutral in relation to states involved in a war. The state is neutral as long as it does not take part in this war.

It is usual to characterize the attitude which a neutral state is obliged to adopt toward the belligerents as impartiality. This attitude consists in the fulfillment of specific obligations established by general international law and codified in Conventions V and XIII of 1907. The most important of these obligations[44] are the obligation of the neutral state to refrain from giving assistance to one of the belligerents as may be detrimental to the other; the obligation to refrain from inflicting injuries on one of the belligerents as may benefit the other; and the obligation to refrain from granting any facilities whatever for military operations of the belligerents; but not the obligation to prohibit its own nationals from supplying belligerents with such facilities,[45] yet the obligation to prevent the fitting out or arming of any vessel within its jurisdiction which it has reason to believe is intended to cruise, or engage in hostile operations against either belligerent, and to prevent the departure from its jurisdiction of any vessel intended to cruise, or engage in hostile operations, which had been adapted entirely or partly within its jurisdiction for use in war;[46] the obligation to

---

[44] As to the formulation of these obligations, cf. L. Oppenheim, *International Law*, 6th ed., edited by H. Lauterpacht (1944) Vol II., §§ 293ff.

[45] In *Pearson v. Parson* (United States, Circuit Court, Eastern District of Louisiana, 1901, 108 Federal Reporter 461) the court stated: "The principle that neutral citizens may lawfully sell to belligerents has long since been settled in this country by the highest judicial authority. In the case of *The Santissima Trinidad,* 7 Wheat. 340, Mr. Justice Story, as the organ of the Supreme Court [1822], said: "There is nothing in our laws or in the law of nations that forbids our citizens from sending armed vessels, as well as munitions of war, to foreign ports for sale. It is a commercial adventure which no nation is bound to prohibit, and which only exposes the persons engaged in it to the penalty of confiscation.' See, also, the case of *The Bermuda* [1865] 3 Wall. 551. . . ." Cf. also *Pearson v. Allis Chalmers Company* (United States, Circuit Court, Milwaukee County, Wisconsin, 1915; 11 *American Journal of International Law* [1917] 883).

[46] In *The Alabama Claims* (United States-Great Britain, Claims Arbitration, 1872, 4 Papers Relating to the Treaty of Washington of 1871 [42d Cong., 3d Sess., Ex. Doc. 1]) an arbitral tribunal was established by a treaty entered into by the United States and Great Britain, on May 8, 1871, to decide a dispute which had arisen out of acts committed by several vessels constructed in England for the Confederate Navy to be used in the Civil War. Article VI of the treaty provided: "In deciding the matters submitted to the Arbitrators, they shall be

The Nature of International Law

prevent the belligerents from making use of its neutral territory and its resources for military purposes during the war;[47] and the obligation to prevent each belligerent from interfering with the neutral's legitimate intercourse with the other belligerent. The

---

governed by the following three rules, which are agreed upon by the High Contracting Parties as rules to be taken as applicable to the case, and by such principles of international law not inconsistent therewith as the Arbitrators shall determine to have been applicable to the case.

"Rules: A neutral government is bound

"First, to use due diligence to prevent the fitting out, arming or equipping, within its jurisdiction, of any vessel which it has reasonable ground to believe is intended to cruise or to carry on war against a Power with which it is at peace; and also to use like diligence to prevent the departure from its jurisdiction of any vessel intended to cruise or carry on war as above, such vessel having been specially adapted, in whole or in part, within its jurisdiction, to warlike use.

"Secondly, not to permit or suffer either belligerent to make use of its ports or waters as the base of naval operations against the other, or for the purpose of the renewal or augmentation of military supplies or arms, or the recruitment of men.

"Thirdly, to exercise due diligence in its own ports and waters, and, as to all persons within its judisdiction, to prevent any violation of the foregoing obligations and duties.

"Her Britannic Majesty has commanded her High Commissioners and Plenipotentiaries to declare that Her Majesty's Government cannot assent to the foregoing rules as a statement of principles of international law which were in force at the time when the claims mentioned in Article I arose, but that Her Majesty's Government in order to evince its desire of strengthening the friendly relations between the two countries and of making satisfactory provision for the future, agrees that in deciding the questions between the two countries arising out of those claims, the Arbitrators should assume that Her Majesty's Government had undertaken to act upon the principles set forth in these rules.

"And the High Contracting Parties agree to observe these rules as between themselves in future, and to bring them to the knowledge of other maritime Powers, and to invite them to accede to them."

[47] Articles 21 and 22 of Convention XIII provide: "ARTICLE 21. A prize may only be brought into a neutral port on account of unseaworthiness, stress of weather, or want of fuel or provisions. It must leave as soon as the circumstances which justified its entry are at an end. If it does not, the neutral Power must order it to leave at once; should it fail to obey, the neutral Power must employ the means at its disposal to release it with its officers and crew and to intern the prize crew. ARTICLE 22. A neutral Power must, similarly, release a prize brought into one of its ports under circumstances other than those referred to in Article 21."

The Steamship Appam (United States, Supreme Court, 1917, 243 U.S. 124), a British cargo and passenger steamship, was captured during the First World War by the German cruiser *Moewe* and brought by a prize crew into a port

most important obligations of the belligerent are the obligation to refrain from making use of neutral territory for military purposes and from interfering with the legitimate intercourse of the neutral states with the other belligerents and the obligation to refrain from appropriating neutral goods on enemy ships, with the exception of contraband. As pointed out, belligerents have the right to appropriate neutral merchant ships for breach of blockade and to appropriate contraband on a neutral vessel.

Most of the writers on international law maintain that under general international law there is no obligation of the states to be and to remain neutral in a war between other states. The lack of such obligation is not inconsistent with the obligation of a state to adopt an attitude of impartiality toward the belligerents in a war in which the state is not involved, as long as it is not involved, provided that under general international law a state may resort to war against any other state for any reason whatever. By resorting to war against one of the belligerents the neutral state does not violate the obligations it has as a neutral state; it simply terminates its status of neutrality. On the other hand, violation of the obligations which a neutral state has toward the belligerents is not identical with ending the status of neutrality, which is terminated only by the outbreak of war between the neutral state and a belligerent. However, the statement that under general international law there is no obligation to be or to remain neutral is not quite correct, if the *bellum justum* principle is assumed to be part of positive international law. According to this principle, not only

---

of the United States, at that time a neutral Power. By order of the American Government the crew and the passengers of the ship were liberated, and the prize crew was interned. A suit brought by the owners of the *Appam* to recover possession of the vessel and a suit brought by the master of the *Appam* to recover possession of the cargo were decided in favor of the libellants. In its opinion the Supreme Court stated *inter alia:* "It was not the purpose to bring the vessel here within the privileges universally recognized in international law, i.e., for necessary fuel or provisions, or because of stress of weather or necessity of repairs, and to leave as soon as the cause of such entry was satisfied or removed . . . She [the *Appam*] . . . was sent into the American port with the intention of being kept there indefinitely . . . We cannot avoid the conclusion that in thus making use of an American port there was a clear breach of the neutral rights of this government, as recognized under the principles of international law governing the obligations of neutrals . . ."

The Nature of International Law

the state whose right has been violated by another state is authorized to resort to war against the delinquent state, but also other states may, in assisting the violated state, resort to war against the delinquent state. But they are not obliged to resort to war against the delinquent state, even if this state is guilty of having resorted to an illegal war. Hence they may or may not remain neutral. But they are obliged not to resort to war against the belligerent whose war is legal. In other words, third states may take part in a war on the side of the belligerent waging a legal war, but they must not take part in a war on the side of a belligerent waging an illegal war. If they choose not to resort to war against the delinquent belligerent, if they remain neutral, they are under the obligation of impartiality. That means that they are not allowed to take measures short of war exclusively against the delinquent state. Being allowed to resort to war against the belligerent guilty of having resorted to an illegal war, but not being allowed to take measures short of war against this state, seems to be not consistent. But, if it is assumed that according to the *bellum justum* principle the states are not only permitted to resort to war against the belligerent guilty of having resorted to an illegal war but also to take measures short of war against this belligerent, then the fundamental principle of the institution of neutrality—the obligation of impartiality—would be incompatible with the *bellum justum* doctrine.

h. *Neutrality under the Covenant.* It stands to reason that a state, by an international agreement may assume the obligation to remain neutral in a definite war or in all wars. In the latter case one speaks of a permanent neutrality or of neutralization of a state. For the time being only the Swiss Confederation is such a neutralized state (declaration signed on March 20, 1815, by Great Britain, Austria, France, Portugal, Prussia, Spain, Sweden, and Russia, and acceded to by Switzerland on May 27, 1815). Likewise a state may assume by an international agreement the obligation not to remain neutral, that is to say the obligation to resort to war on the side of a belligerent; but if the *bellum justum* principle is supposed to be positive law, a state may assume only the obligation to participate in a war on the side of a belligerent waging a legal war. Another question is whether a state may assume by a treaty the obligation to perform, in case of a war between other states, certain acts short of war inconsistent with the obligations of a neutral state. Such a treaty obligation is established by Article 16 of the Covenant of the League of Nations. Paragraph 1 of this article obliges the members of the League to take certain economic sanctions against a member which in violation of the Covenant resorted to war against another member. These economic sanctions which a member is obliged to take, even if it does not itself resort to war against the delinquent state (not being obliged to take the military sanctions referred to in paragraph 2), are inconsistent with the obligation it has as a neutral state under general international law. This is particularly the case with respect to the obligation stipulated by paragraph 3 of Article 16—to take the necessary steps to afford passage through their territory to the forces of any of the members of the League which resort to war against the delinquent member.

Article 16, paragraph 1, of the Covenant provides that, should a member of the League resort to war in violation of the Covenant, "it shall *ipso facto* be deemed to have committed an act of war against all other Members of the League," which implies that all other members of the League are to be considered as being in a state of war with the violator of the Covenant and, consequently, as not neutral. But this provision is a legal fiction, since the members against which the delinquent member did not resort to war are actually not in a state of war and are not obliged to resort to war against the delinquent state; and as long as they do not resort to war against the delinquent member, they are neutral. It is true that the Assembly of the League of Nations, by a resolution adopted on October 4, 1921, interpreted the above-quoted provision of Article 16, paragraph 1, to mean that "the unilateral action of the defaulting State cannot create a state of war; it merely entitles the other Members of the League to resort to acts of war or declare themselves in a state of war with the Covenant-breaking State. . . ." But this interpretation is hardly compatible with the wording of Article 16, paragraph 1.

i. *Neutrality under the Kellogg-Briand Pact*. The Kellogg-Briand Pact is a multilateral treaty imposing upon the contracting states

The Nature of International Law

the obligation to refrain from waging war as an instrument of national policy. As a multilateral treaty, it may be interpreted to confer upon each contracting party the right to demand that all the other parties fulfill their obligation under the treaty, so that if one party does not fulfill its obligation, it violates a right of the other parties. Under general international law a state may resort to reprisals as a reaction against a violation of its right. Consequently, if a state in violation of the Kellogg-Briand Pact resorts to war against another state that is a party to the pact, any other party may not only resort to war (according to a provision of the preamble) but also may, without resorting to war, take measures short of war as reprisals against the violator of the pact. Thus the obligation of a neutral state, that is a state not involved in the war between other states, to adopt an attitude of strict impartiality toward the belligerents is not valid in the relationship among the parties to the pact in case of a war waged as an instrument of national policy.

j. *Neutrality under the Charter.* In case of a war between members of the United Nations, the members which are not involved in such a war, and that means are neutral, are permitted by the Charter to assist the belligerent who is the victim of an "armed attack," but not the belligerent who is guilty of this armed attack. This is implied in the provision of Article 51 that nothing in the Charter shall impair the "right of individual and collective self-defense if an armed attack occurs against a Member of the United Nations, until the Security Council has taken the measures necessary to maintain international peace and security." This provision may be interpreted to mean that the neutral members of the United Nations are authorized by the Charter to resort not only to war but also to enforcement actions not involving the use of armed force against the state guilty of an armed attack, but that they are not allowed to resort to enforcement actions, involving or not involving the use of armed force, against the victim of an armed attack resorting to a counterwar. If this interpretation is accepted, the rule of general international law imposing the obligation of impartiality upon neutral states is superseded by the Charter. The same is true with respect to Article 2, paragraph 5, of the Charter if applied in case of war between two members. This provision imposes upon the other members the obligation to give the Organization every assistance in any action it takes against the one and in favor of the other belligerent, and the obligation to refrain from giving assistance to the belligerent against which the Organization is taking preventive or enforcment action. If the action which the Organization, under Article 39 or Article 51, takes against a member involved in a war and the assistance which the members not involved in this war are obliged to give the Organization in its action under Article 2, paragraph 5, are measures not involving the use of armed force, the neutral members are supposed not to adopt an attitude of impartiality toward the belligerents. Under Articles 39 and 51, the Security Council may take an enforcement action involving the use of armed force against a member guilty of a threat to or breach of the peace. If the member against which this action is directed offers armed resistance, there is a war of the United Nations against a member and a counterwar of the member against the United Nations. In this war are actually involved on the part of the Organization only those members through the armed forces of which the action of the Security Council is carried out in conformity with Article 48 of the Charter. This article provides that the action required to carry out the decisions of the Security Council adopted under Article 39 "shall be taken by all the Members of the United Nations or by some of them, as the Security Council may determine." Hence in a war between the Organization and a member, many members may be neutral, provided that it is not assumed that in such a case all the members of the United Nations are in a state of war with the member against which the Organization takes an enforcement action involving the use of armed force. Such assumption is, as pointed out, a legal fiction. In contradistinction to the Covenant, the Charter does not contain a formula maintaining this fiction. If Article 2, paragraph 5, applies in such a case and the members not involved in that war are to assist the Organization by taking measures short of war against the member at which the enforcement action of the Organization is directed, the obligation of impartiality, imposed by general international law upon neutral states, is superseded by the Charter.

The Nature of International Law

If it is assumed that under the Kellogg-Briand Pact reprisals against a violator of the pact, the fulfillment of the obligations stipulated by Article 16, paragraphs 1 and 3 of the Covenant, and Article 2, paragraph 5 of the Charter, as well as the exercise of the right of collective self-defense by the taking of measures short of war against the aggressor under Article 51 of the Charter, that all these actions do not constitute a violation of the obligations of neutral states established by general international law, it must also be assumed that the norms of general international law concerning these obligations are only *jus dispositivum* ("yielding law"), not *jus cogens* ("cogent law"),[48] that is to say, that they may be repealed by treaty provisions in the relation among the contracting parties.

Insofar as the above-quoted provisions of Article 2, paragraph 5, Article 39, and Article 51 of the Charter, in virtue of Article 2, paragraph 6, apply also to nonmember states, their validity may be doubted, except if it is assumed that the Charter—in spite of being a treaty to which not all the states are contracting parties—has the character of general international law.[49] Under this assumption the legal institute of neutrality has to be considered as abolished. To the extent that the distinction between war as delict and war as sanction is sustained, and collective security is established within a universal organization, the fundamental principle of the legal institution of neutrality—indiscriminative impartiality toward the belligerents on the part of states not actually involved in a war between other states—cannot be maintained.

---

[48] Cf. *infra*, p. 344.
[49] Cf. *infra*, p. 347.

II.
THE SPHERES OF VALIDITY
OF INTERNATIONAL LAW

A. THE SPHERES OF VALIDITY OF A LEGAL ORDER

International law is a normative order, and a normative order is a system of valid norms. Legal norms regulate human behavior, and human behavior takes place in time and space. Consequently, legal norms have relation to time and space. They are valid for a certain time and for a certain space (territory). Hence we speak of a temporal and a territorial sphere of validity of legal norms or a legal order. To determine how men ought to behave, the law must determine when and where they ought to behave in the determined way. The human behavior regulated by legal norms consists of a personal and a material element: the personal element is the individual who ought to behave in a certain way; the material element is the behavior, that is to say, the acts which the individual ought to perform or from the performance of which he ought to refrain. Hence we speak of a personal and a material sphere of validity of legal norms. The material sphere refers to the subject matters regulated by the legal norms. Norms may differ not only with respect to the territory, or the time, or the persons for whom they are valid, but also with respect to the subject matters they regulate. There are norms regulating economic life and norms regulating religious life; norms regulating agriculture, and norms regulating education.

In describing a legal order we must distinguish its territorial, temporal, personal, and material sphere of validity.°

The decisive question for all these spheres of validity is whether they are limited or unlimited. If it is supposed that a certain order is the supreme order, that there is no other order higher than that order, it must be concluded that its spheres of validity are unlimited. For only a norm can establish a limitation of the territorial, personal, material, or temporal sphere of validity of another norm; and norms which limit the spheres of validity of a certain normative order must belong either to this order, thus limiting its own spheres of validity, or to an order superior to this order.

The normative order traditionally called international law does not contain norms limiting its spheres of validity; and insofar as this normative order is considered as a supreme legal order which is not under any other legal order, the validity of the international legal order cannot be limited in any direction. This is exactly what distinguishes the international legal order from a national legal order, which, if this term is taken in its specific sense, on the contrary is generally considered to be limited if not with respect to all, so certainly with respect to its territorial, temporal, and personal spheres of validity. That a national legal order, the law of one state, is valid only for the territory of this state, and not everywhere; that it is valid only for certain individuals, the citizens of the state and the foreigners staying in the territory of the state, and not for the whole of mankind; that it is not valid eternally but becomes valid and ceases to be valid at a certain point of time—these will hardly be denied. If these limitations of the spheres of validity of the national legal order have a legal character, they must be established by a legal order, and if the national legal order does not itself limit its spheres of validity, only a legal order superior to the national legal order can have this effect. There is no other legal order that can be considered as superior to the national legal orders but the international legal order. And, indeed, it is possible to find in the international legal order the norms by which the spheres of validity of the national legal orders are limited. This limitation of the spheres of validity of the national legal orders is an essential function of the international legal order. For, only insofar as the international legal order fulfills this function, the legal coexistence of several states, that is to say, the simultaneous validity of several national legal orders, becomes possible.

B. THE TERRITORIAL AND TEMPORAL SPHERES OF VALIDITY OF INTERNATIONAL LAW

It is easy to understand that the international legal order possesses an unlimited validity in time and space. The notion of the sphere of validity has a purely potential meaning. To say that the

Spheres of Validity of International Law

international legal order is universally valid does not imply that it is effective everywhere and all the time, but only that if a fact to which the international legal order attaches one of its specific consequences occurs anywhere, this consequence likewise ought to occur. This means that no legal norm exists which claims to exclude the validity of international law anywhere. That there may actually be places where the facts, determined by international law, do not occur at a particular moment is without importance. One might argue that, since international law is valid only for states, it does not apply to territories where there is no state. However, a state may be born there at any moment, and the birth of states is regulated by international law. War, as delict or sanction determined by international law, can also be waged in a territory which is the territory of no state, and thus the norms of international law concerning the conduct of war likewise apply to those territories. The occupation of stateless territory, too, is regulated by international law.

The same is true of the temporal sphere of validity. The norms of general international law claim permanent validity without any legal norm limiting this claim. No positive norm restricting the temporal validity of general international law exists. It is vain to object that international law has appeared in the course of time, that formerly there were periods when international law did not yet exist. This is without importance, for the norms of international law can also have retroactive effect. There is no rule of general international law prohibiting the establishment—especially by treaties—of norms with retroactive force.

This does not mean, of course, that all the norms of international law are permanently valid. There can be no doubt that, in the course of time, general international law has undergone certain changes, that norms of general international law which were valid at an earlier time have ceased to be valid or have been modified. A legal relation implying duties of one state and corresponding rights of another state is to be judged by that international law under which the legal relation has been established,[1] provided that there

---

[1] The principles regulating the temporal sphere of validity of legal norms by which previous legal norms have been modified or abolished are sometimes

is no sufficient reason to assume that the new international law has retroactive force. Certain norms of particular international law—contractual norms—often are intended to be valid only for a certain time or until their abrogation by another contractual norm. But this limitation does not hold for the norm of general international law which is the legal basis of all treaties, namely, the norm *pacta sunt servanda* ("treaties must be observed").

C. THE PERSONAL SPHERE OF VALIDITY OF INTERNATIONAL LAW: THE SUBJECTS OF INTERNATIONAL LAW

1. *Juristic Persons as Subjects of Law*

To examine the personal sphere of validity of international law is to ask who are the subjects whose conduct is regulated by international law. We shall show that in this respect, too, the validity of international law knows no limits.

---

called "intertemporal law." This term has been used in the *Island of Palmas Case.* (Tribunal of the Permanent Court of Arbitration, 1928, published in 22 *American Journal of International Law* [1928] 867.) This was a dispute between the United States of America and the Netherlands, concerning the territorial sovereignty over the Island of Palmas. The question was whether the earlier rule of international law that territory may be acquired by discovery, or the later rule that acquisition of territory requires effective occupation, was to be applied in this case. The arbitrator declared in his opinion: "It is admitted by both sides that international law underwent profound modifications between the end of the Middle-Ages and the end of the 19th century, as regards the rights of discovery and acquisition of uninhabited regions or regions inhabited by savages or semi-civilised peoples. Both Parties are also agreed that a juridical fact must be appreciated in the light of the law contemporary with it, and not of the law in force at the time when a dispute in regard to it arises or falls to be settled. . . . As regards the question which of different legal systems prevailing at successive periods is to be applied in a particular case (the so-called intertemporal law), a distinction must be made between the creation of rights and the existence of rights. The same principle which subjects the act creative of a right to the law in force at the time the right arises, demands that the existence of the right, in other words its continued manifestation, shall follow the conditions required by the evolution of law. . . . For these reasons, discovery alone, without any subsequent act, cannot at the present time suffice to prove sovereignty over the Island of Palmas. . . ."

Spheres of Validity of International Law

It is, however, desirable to draw attention at once to a restriction resulting from the nature of law. Law is essentially the regulation of human conduct. The regulation of the mutual conduct of men is the meaning of all law. Law is a social category. Like all law, international law, too, is a regulation of human conduct. It is to men that the norms of international law apply; it is against men that they provide sanctions; it is to men that they entrust the competence of creating the norms of the order. If international law lays down duties, responsibilities, and rights (it must do so if it is a legal order), these duties, responsibilities, and rights can have only human conduct for content. For a duty which would not be the duty of a man to behave in a certain way would not be a legal duty; a responsibility which would not consist in a sanction executed by men and directed against men would not be a legal responsibility. Similarly, a right which would not consist of a power, competence, or capacity which must manifest itself by some human action would not be a legal right. If duty, responsibility, and right do not refer to the conduct of men, duty, responsibility, and right would be only empty formulas, meaningless words.

Thus law can impose duties and responsibilities or confer rights only upon human individuals. But it is said that law obligates and authorizes not only individuals, but also juristic persons, and that especially international law obligates and authorizes not individuals but juristic persons by obligating and authorizing states. This is the traditional theory: Only states, states as juristic persons, are the subjects of international law. Or, in other terms: International law imposes duties and responsibilities and confers rights upon states only, and not upon individuals, human beings. This doctrine is untenable. The subjects of international law, too, are individuals. The statement that the subjects of international law are states as juristic persons does not mean that the subjects of international law are not individuals; it means that individuals are subjects of international law in a specific way, in another than the ordinary way in which individuals are subjects of national law.

The juristic person as an entity different from the so-called natural or physical person, the human individual, is an auxiliary concept of juristic thinking, an instrument of legal theory, the purpose of which is to simplify the description of legal phenomena. A juristic person is not a reality of positive law or of nature. When it is said that a juristic person—a corporation, for instance—has a duty (obligation) or a right, this means that there exists a duty or a right which has the conduct of an individual for its content, but that this individual has the duty or the right in his capacity as a member or organ of the corporation. Since the individual has the duty or the right in his capacity as a member or organ of the corporation, we say that it is the corporation, as a juristic person, which has the duty or the right. We refer, we impute, the duty or the right to the corporation, because the individual who is the true subject of the duty or the right has the duty or the right in his capacity as a member or organ of the corporation. The corporation is conceived of as an acting person. This person is nothing but the personification of the special order constituting the corporation. The special order constituting a corporation is the statute or so-called bylaws of the corporation. The statute or bylaws are the rules organizing the corporation; they determine the members and the organs of the corporation and the relationship between the members and the organs. Duties and rights of a corporation are duties and rights of individuals in their capacity as members or organs of the corporation. The statement that a corporation has certain duties and certain rights does not mean that the duties and rights in question are duties and rights of a juristic person and consequently not the duties and rights of individuals. On the contrary, they are duties and rights of individuals, but of individuals in their capacity as members or organs of the corporation. Consequently, if it is asked "Who is the subject of a certain legal order?"—meaning to whom do the norms of this legal order apply, whose conduct does this order regulate by imposing duties or conferring rights?—one must never reply that the subjects are not "individuals," but only "juristic persons." Because even if one ought to reply that the subjects of the legal order are juristic persons, individuals would not thereby be excluded. On the contrary, individuals would necessarily be involved as subjects to whom the norms of this legal order apply.

There certainly is an important difference between duties and rights of a juristic person, that is to say, duties and rights which individuals have in their capacity as organs or members of a community represented as a juristic person, and duties and rights which individuals have independently of their belonging to such a community. The difference consists in the fact that the individuals whose conduct forms the content of the duties and rights of the juristic person, are determined only indirectly by the national legal order under which the juristic person exists, whereas the individuals whose conduct forms the content of the duties and rights of so-called physical persons are directly determined by the national legal order. The national legal order leaves it to the special legal orders, constituting the legal communities represented as juristic persons, to determine the individuals who, as organs or members of this community, have to fulfill these duties or exercise these rights. The fulfillment of the duties and the exercise of the rights of the community by the individuals belonging as organs and members to the community are regulated by the statute constituting the community. Hence it may be said that the duties and rights of a juristic person are collective duties and rights of individuals, in contradistinction to individual duties and rights, duties and rights individuals have independently of their belonging to a community represented as a juristic person.

As to the responsibility of a juristic person, it is nothing but the collective responsibility of the individuals belonging to the community represented as a juristic person. A juristic person is responsible for a civil or criminal delict if the sanction is to be directed against the juristic person. But to direct a civil or criminal sanction against a juristic person can mean nothing else but to direct a civil or criminal sanction against individuals in their capacity as organs or members of the community represented as a juristic person. Responsibility of a juristic person for a civil delict means that a civil execution is to be directed against the property of the juristic person, which is the collective property of the members of the community represented as a juristic person. Responsibility of a juristic person for a criminal delict means that the punishment provided for the delict is to be inflicted upon individuals, not because they have committed the delict, but because they belong as members or organs to the community represented as a juristic person.

All this must be taken into consideration in order to judge the traditional doctrine that only states and not individuals can be subjects of international law, i.e., subjects of the duties, responsibilities, and rights established by the international legal order.

2. The State as Subject of International Law

a. *The state as a centralized legal order.* If we say that international law regulates the mutual behavior of states, we consider the state as an acting person. The state is, of course, not a natural or physical person, not a man or a superman. It is a so-called juristic person, or, what amounts to the same, a corporation. As a juristic person the state is the personification of a social order, constituting the community we call "state." If we try to characterize the phenomenon "state" without using a personification, we have no other possibility than to say that the state is a social order, or the community constituted by this order; and if we examine this order, we find that it is a coercive order, an order providing coercive acts as sanctions. The state is usually called a political organization, and organization means order. The "political" element consists just in the coercive character of this organization or order. It is the fact that the social order we call state is a coercive order, an order providing for coercive acts as sanctions. Since the sanctions provided by this order are socially organized sanctions, not transcendental sanctions, the coercive order or political organization we call state, or, in other terms, the state as a social order, can be no other than a legal order. The state as a juristic person is the personification of a legal order constituting a legal community. This community is constituted only by this legal order. The individuals who belong to this community are united, they form a social unit by being subjected to the same legal order. What they have in common is the legal order regulating their mutual behavior. The state as a community is not a biological, psychological, or sociological unit; it is, as a legal community, a specifically juristic unit.

But not every legal order constituting a legal community is a state. Neither the primitive legal order constituting a primitive legal community nor the international legal order constituting the inter-

Spheres of Validity of International Law

national legal community is a state. What is the difference? The difference between a legal order or legal community we call a state and a primitive legal order or the international legal order we refuse to call a state appears in the degree of centralization. The state is a relatively centralized legal order (or community).

Centralization is a very complex phenomenon.[2] In this connection only one side of the phenomenon is of interest. We speak of centralization, of a centralized legal order, if the norms of this order are created and applied, and especially if the sanctions are executed, by special organs functioning according to the principle of division of labor. Consequently the organs creating and applying the legal order, and especially the organs executing the sanctions, are different from and more or less independent of the individuals subject to the order. Even the primitive legal order or, what amounts to the same thing, the primitive legal community, has organs, but not organs functioning according to the principle of the division of labor—no central organs. Every individual when injured by another individual is authorized to apply the law, to execute the sanction provided by the legal order. By the establishment of central organs, especially by the centralization of the use of force, by the centralization of the execution of the sanctions, the primitive legal community becomes a state.

It is just in the degree of this centralization that the legal community of the primitives—the prestatal legal community—as well as the international or superstatal legal community is distinguished from the community we call "state." As pointed out,[3] there is no reason for restricting the concept of law to the coercive order constituting the state, that is, to a relatively centralized coercive order, allowing the law of a state only to count as "law" in the true sense. The different degrees of centralization that find expression in the content of an order are the basis of no such essential difference as to justify distinguishing one coercive order from another as law from nonlaw, solely according to the degree of its centralization.

A distinction much more significant than the degree of centralization is the monopolization of the use of force. Between an order

---

[2] Cf. Hans Kelsen, *General Theory of Law and State* (1949), pp. 303ff.
[3] Cf. *supra*, pp. 3ff., 16.

that reserves to the community the use of force and one that does not, there exists a much greater difference than between two coercive orders both of which monopolize the use of force, but one of which is centralized and the other decentralized. If international law can be counted as an order which monopolizes the use of force—and such, as we have seen, is the case—then it is similar to national law in a decisive point. If one refrains from calling international law true "law" just because it is not centralized to the same degree as national law, not only the creation of its norms but their application as well being decentralized, a distinction of technical significance is made; but this distinction is not an essential one.

b. *The relationship of superiority and inferiority.* It is on this basis that an argument is to be judged that is put forth perhaps the most often and the most successfully against the legal nature of international law. The thought, formulated differently by different authorities, yet in its essence always the same, may be put as follows: So-called international law cannot be classed as "law" in the same sense as national law (regarded as law par excellence) because an important difference exists between the two systems of norms. This difference lies in the fact that behind national law—true law—stands the state. It is the state that, as the highest authority, as "sovereign" power superior to its subjects, sets up the law for the ordering of the conduct of these, its subjects. This presupposes that the state is not only a normative authority, but at the same time is an effective power, strong enough to put through, against opposition, the law it has established, strong enough to "enforce the law," as one says. In such a supreme authority or sovereign power, traditional theory sees the specific "political" element. Traditional theory calls a society in which such an authority or sovereign power exists a "political" society, or a state; and considers the relationship of the individuals to this authority as essential to national law. It is a relationship of superiority and inferiority. Hence, according to this view, law is an order whose guarantor or creator—sometimes the expression "source" is also used—is the state, a political supreme authority or power which constitutes the relationship of superiority and inferiority. So-called international law, however, exhibits no such authority or sovereign power. Behind international law there is no political authority guaranteeing this order, standing above its subjects, the states. Here there is no relationship of political superiority and inferiority between the states and a super-state. Here all the subjects are themselves sovereign entities and as such are on a footing of equality one with the other. Just for this reason so-called international law cannot be classed as "true" law; at best it can be considered only as "positive international morality," as John Austin,[4] who lent the weight of his great authority to this whole line of reasoning, puts it.

This view stands and falls with the statement that international law does not constitute a relationship of superiority and inferiority as does national law, but a relationship of equality. It is therefore necessary to establish the actual meaning of the figurative expression "superiority and inferiority." What does it mean to say that someone or something in relation to someone or something else is inferior (subordinate), that the other is superior? In the social sphere it can mean only a specific normative relationship, a relationship that is constituted by a normative order, a system of obligating and authorizing norms. That one individual is inferior to another, and hence that the latter is superior to the former, means that the one is obliged by the social order to obey the commands of the other, and that the latter is authorized by the order to command the former. Hence the relationship of superiority and inferiority exists really not between the individuals themselves but between the individuals on the one hand, and the order regulating their conduct on the other. It is the order that in the last instance commands the one to obey the other; it is the order which he obeys when he carries out the commands of the individual who is empowered by the order to issue commands. And the authority of this individual is in the last analysis only the authority of the normative order, an authority delegated to the individual by that order.

As far as the relationship of individuals among themselves is concerned, they are always on an equal footing, since they are all

---

[4] John Austin, *Lectures on Jurisprudence* (1885), I, 173.

subject to the order superior to them because this order regulates their mutual conduct. They are all obligated and authorized by the order; and if the order is a legal order, they are legal subjects, irrespective of what the substance of their duties and rights may be. He upon whom the legal order confers the right to issue commands, i.e., legal norms, is not less subjected to the legal order than he upon whom the legal order imposes the duty to obey these commands. Superiority and inferiority, as must be emphasized again and again, are only figurative expressions. They signify a normative bond, the relationship of the individual to the normative order.

For a relationship of superiority and inferiority to exist, it is a matter of indifference how the norms are created that enjoin the individuals to certain conduct, whether by custom, by decree of an assemblage of the people, by enactment of parliament, or by the act of an autocrat. These are only different degrees of centralization or decentralization of the process by which the norms are created. Certainly, individuals are more clearly aware of the relationship of superiority and inferiority; it is more obvious, more tangible, so to say, if the norms by which they are bound are created by a definite person; it is most clear and most tangible if they are created by a single individual, an autocrat, that is, in the case of the greatest centralization of the process of creation of the law. But even in this case, the individuals are not actually subordinated to the individual from whom the norm emanates, but to the order that delegates the authority to this man; not to the lawmaker, but to the law; to the law on account of which the lawmaker is a lawmaker; to the constitution which has granted him competence to issue laws. *Non sub homine sed sub lege* ("Not under man but under the law") is a well-known principle of democracy. It is a principle of any legal order.

If the relationship of superiority and inferiority is understood in this normative sense, then there is, in this point, no difference between national and international law—if the latter has any validity as a system of norms regulating the mutual relations of states. For, if international law obligates states to certain conduct in any manner whatsoever—even if only in the way in which morals obligate individuals—then, states, and that means individuals as organs of the states, are just as subordinated to international law as are individuals to the national legal order; and just the same relationship of superiority and inferiority exists in the realm of international law as in the realm of national law. In the realm of general international law that does not institute special organs for the creation of law this relationship of superiority and inferiority is not so easily apparent. But when two or more states by treaty set up a court to decide their disputes, the relationship between this international court and the states in question is just the same relationship of superiority and inferiority as the relationship between a national court and the individuals that are subject to its jurisdiction; the parties to the dispute are obliged by the legal order to carry out the decision of the court, to conduct themselves as the court directs. They are bound by a general norm of the legal order establishing the court to obey the individual norm issuing from the court. And the fact of being bound by a norm presumed to be valid is the meaning of superiority and inferiority.

c. *The state as power.* In traditional political theory the state is characterized as endowed with "power." One speaks of the "power of the state" as of an essential element of the state. In diplomatic language the state is called a "power"; great powers are distinguished from small powers. It is the power of the state which is imagined as behind the law, it is by its power that the state enforces the law, guarantees "its" law. But what is power, in general, and the power of the state in particular?

It stands to reason that power as a social concept is here in question; not power as natural phenomenon, such as electric power and the like. The statement that a man has power over another man seems to mean that a man is able to induce another man or other men to behave as he desires. But this is merely a natural relation, the relation between cause and effect, and as such not essentially different from the relationship which exists when a man masters an animal or fells a tree. Such a relation is not a social relation, even when actually existing between two men. It is "social" only if it is regulated by a norm. Power as a specific social phenomenon comes into consideration only within the framework of a social order regulating the mutual behavior of men. If we speak of the power of the state as a power which an individual exercises over other individuals, we mean the power an individual, authorized by the state as a social order, exercises over other individuals. The power of the individual concerned is the authority conferred upon him by the social order. But by the power of the state, or the state as power, we mean the power of the social order, not the power of definite individuals under this order.

The statement that a social order has "power" means that it is effective, and that means that it is by and large obeyed and applied. The power of a social order is its efficacy.

If one speaks of the power of the state, one probably thinks first of prisons and the electric chair, guns and cannon; and if one is a believer in the materialistic interpretation of history, of the bank accounts of the employers and of their factories. One should not forget, however, that all these are inanimate objects which, in order to be instruments of power, must be put to use by men; and men put these instruments to use for one purpose or another if they are instigated to do so by other individuals through commands, that is, through norms. The phenomenon of power appears here in that these commands are executed, in that the norms regulating the use of prisons and electric chairs, guns and cannon, bank accounts and factories, are actually obeyed and applied. Power is not prisons and electric chairs, guns and cannon, bank accounts and factories; power is not a substance, not a thing different from the social order, hidden somewhere behind the order. Social power is only the efficacy of an order regulating the mutual conduct of individuals. Behind every social order that we regard as valid is power, for we regard a social order as valid only if it is to a certain extent effective, that is to say, if this order is by and large obeyed and applied.

But, one might object, it is the essential characteristic of law that the power behind it is the state. This statement is misleading. For the state itself is nothing but an order, an organized power, or, what amounts to the same, an organization. The statement that the state is a "power" means nothing else but that this social order is effective. As a power, the state is the efficacy of a legal order, and as an order or organization it is this legal order itself, or, when imaged as a personal being—the personification of this order.

d. *The state as a point of imputation.* We can convince ourselves quite empirically and in a comparatively simple fashion that the state is, indeed, a social order and, as an order, actually only the national legal order; as a person, only the personification of this order; as a power, only the efficacy of this order. For, how does the state, in itself invisible and intangible, manifest itself in actual social life? In the acts of individuals which we regard as acts of state. Not every individual can perform an act of state, and not every act of an individual able to perform an act of state is such an act. What, then, is the criterion? Wherein can we distinguish human activity characterized as acts of state from human activities that are not acts of state? This is the decisive question that leads to the nature of the state.

If we say that the act of a certain individual is an act of state, we attribute this act to another person than the acting individual, to another person, so to speak, behind the individual. To attribute an act performed by an individual to a "person" different from the acting individual is possible only if we presuppose a normative order regulating the conduct of individuals in general, and determining in particular the acts of the individual in question. An act performed by an individual can be attributed to the state as an acting person, this act can be characterized as an act of state only if it conforms in a specific way to the social order we presuppose as valid. That we attribute this act to the state means only that we refer this act to the unity of the order determining it. When we say that the state punishes the criminal, although actually it is always an individual who performs this act called punishment of a criminal, we are only expressing figuratively the fact that provision is made for punishment of a criminal in a norm of the legal order, that the individual performing the punishment executes the legal order. To regard the state as a person who acts is only to personify the order that we presuppose as valid when we interpret certain acts of individuals as acts of state. But we presuppose validity of such an order, we use such an order as a scheme of interpretation, only if this order is sufficiently effective. This efficacy of the national legal order is the "power" of the state.

It is a fact of experience that a coercive order, such as the legal order, gains in efficacy if it is centralized; if it establishes for its creation and application special organs functioning according to the principle of division of labor. The efficacy of a coercive order is especially intensified by centralizing the execution of the sanctions, by establishing central executive organs. When some writers say that international law is not law, because law is an order behind which is the state, an order which the state creates, guarantees, and so on, this means—to formulate the idea stripped of all personification and figurative language—that the international order is not sufficiently centralized to be called law. Such a statement presupposes that the idea of law is identified with a relatively centralized coercive order. This identification, however, implies an inadmissible narrowing of the concept of law. Even a completely decentralized coercive order, as the social order of a primitive society, or the order regulating the mutual behavior of the states, is law; but the community constituted by such a legal order is not a state.

e. *The sovereignty of the state.* As pointed out, many writers maintain that the relationship which exists between the state and international law differs essentially from the relationship which exists between individuals and national law, because the state as subject of international law is "sovereign," whereas the individual as subject of national law is not "sovereign."[5] Whatever may be understood by this word of many meanings, and however much the definitions of this concept may differ from one another, most of them agree on one point: the thing characterized as "sovereign," whether it be an order, a community, an organ, or a power, must be regarded as the highest, above which there can be no higher, authority limiting the function of the sovereign entity, binding the sovereign. Sovereignty in its original sense means "highest authority."

If one assumes that the state, as the authority or source of its law, is sovereign or, more correctly put, if one assumes that the

---

[5] As to the doctrine of sovereignty, cf. *infra,* pp. 438ff.

national legal order is the highest authority, then no other order can be conceived to exist above the state or above the legal order of the state, binding upon the state or the individuals representing it. The inevitable consequence of the assumption that the state as a legal order is sovereign in the original sense of this term is that international law cannot be considered as a legal order superior to the national legal orders; that, if it exists at all, it can be considered only as part of the national legal order; and that international law is part of the national law of a state if this state has recognized international law as binding upon it. This view, advocated by many writers, will be discussed in another connection.[6] But even if international law is not considered as a legal order superior to the national legal orders, if it is conceived of as a part of the respective national legal order, the state, as an acting person—and that means the individuals in their capacity as organs of the state—must be considered as subjected to international law, since they must be considered as subjected to their national law. Only as a normative order, not as an acting person, can the state be "sovereign" in the true sense of the term. For the state as an acting person means an individual human being acting as organ of the state, and this individual is, precisely in his capacity as organ of the state, subjected to the legal order. He is an organ of the state only insofar as his acts can be attributed to the state, and his acts can be attributed to the state only insofar as they are determined in a specific way by the legal order constituting the state. Even if international law is considered as part of national law, the state as a person must be considered to be subjected to international—as part of national—law. Hence international law must be considered as superior to the state as a subject of obligations and rights; a relationship of superiority and inferiority between international law and the state as a person cannot be denied.

If it is assumed that such a relationship can be established only by a "power," then the same power is to be found behind international law that is supposed to be behind national law. For this "power" is—as pointed out—nothing but the efficacy of the

---

[6] Cf. *infra*, pp. 435ff.

normative order. Whether international law is considered to be a legal order superior to the national legal orders, or part of these orders, it is to be considered as a valid order only if it is by and large effective. If the norms of international law had no efficacy, if they were not, by and large, obeyed and applied, it would not be possible to conceive of international law as a valid order. If, however, as is actually the case, international law is considered as an effective normative order, then there is behind international law—just as there is behind national law—a "power." If international law is considered to be part of national law, it is the state, the community established by the national legal order, which—according to the traditional doctrine—is the power behind this law. If international law is considered to be a legal order superior to the national legal orders, then it is the international community constituted by international law which is behind this law, in exactly the same sense as the state is behind the national law. And this international legal community can be called the bearer, guarantor, or source of international law in just the same sense as the state can be called the bearer, guarantor, or source of national law. One should never forget that these are only figurative expressions, personifications, that have no independent meaning. If one resolves them, the dualism of law and state disappears, and it is no longer possible to deny to international law the character of law on the ground that behind international law there is no "state."

f. *The state a community subjected only to international law.* If we assume that the state is legally subjected to international law as to a legal order superior to the national legal order, the state, that is to say, the national legal order, cannot be sovereign, i.e., the supreme legal authority. But it is an essential characteristic of this national legal order, or its personification, i.e., the state as a juristic person or corporation, that it is subjected *only* to the international legal order and not to another national legal order. That means that a community, in order to be a state in the sense of international law, must be independent of other states. But it does not mean that a state in the sense of international law must be independent of international communities. All the states are

Spheres of Validity of International Law 111

members of the international community constituted by general international law, and hence subjected to that law; and a state may, without losing its character as a state, be a member of an international community constituted by particular international law, i.e., by a treaty to which the state is a contracting party. In this case the state is subjected not only to general but also to particular international law, since it is under the law of this particular international community, that is to say, under the law created by the treaty constituting the international community, and under the law created by the organs of the international community in conformity with its constituent treaty. But a state loses its quality as a state if the law created by the treaty assumes the character of national law because of the centralization of the community constituted by the treaty, as is the case of a treaty by which a federal state is established.[7] In this case national law is created by an act of international law. The doctrine advocated by some writers[8] that national law cannot have its origin in a procedure of international law is not correct.

By a treaty concluded by two states, one of them may be placed under the so-called protectorate or "suzerainty" of the other. By this treaty one state is in certain respects, namely, in respect to foreign affairs, placed under the national law of the other. The foreign affairs of the two states are so centralized that the organ of one state has the power to handle also the foreign affairs of the other state, under the law of the former. Hence the state placed under protectorate loses its quality as a state in the sense of international law because it ceases to be subjected only to international law, being subjected to the national law of the state exercising the protectorate.[9]

---

[7] Cf. *infra*, pp. 168ff.

[8] E.g., W. W. Willoughby, *The Fundamental Concepts of Public Law* (1924), p. 284.

[9] Examples of protectorates are San Marino, under the protectorate of Italy; Tunis and Morocco, under the protectorate of France; the Federated Malay States and other (not federated) States of the Malay Peninsula, under the protectorate of Great Britain. The agreement concluded by Great Britain and the State of Perlis, a nonfederated Malay State, on April 28, 1930, contains the following provision: "His Highness the Rajah of Perlis

A state may even be governed by an international community. This is the case if an organ of an international community is at the same time the government of a state which is not a member of this community, as the Security Council regarding the Free Territory of Trieste, in conformity with a Statute annexed to the Peace Treaty with Italy (the statute is not yet in force). This is not a democratic form of government since the government of such a state is not, directly or indirectly, appointed by the people of that state, but the community in question is a state in the sense of international law because it is not dependent on the governments of other states or, what amounts to the same, is not subjected to other national legal orders. But if a territory, together with its population—as that of Germany after its defeat in the Second World War—is governed by a body the members of which are appointed by the governments of other states and are under the legal obligation to comply with the instructions given them by their own governments, the territory and population in question cannot be considered as elements of a state, different from the states exercising legal control over that territory and population. Whatever the legal status of such a territory and population may be, it is not that of a "sovereign" state, i.e., a community subjected only to international law.

g. *External and internal, divided sovereignty.* Some writers distinguish the external sovereignty referring to the relation of the state to other states, from the internal sovereignty referring to the relation of the state to its subjects. But the one cannot be separated from the other; and if a state is subjected to another state with respect to its international relations, it is not "sovereign" even if its legislative, administrative, and judicial power is not restricted otherwise.[10]

---

shall have no political dealings with any foreign Power or potentate except through the medium of His Britannic Majesty's representative."

[10] In *Duff Development Co., Ltd. v. Government of Kelantan* (Great Britain, House of Lords, 1924 Law Reports, A.C. 797) the British Government declared that Kelantan was a sovereign State in the Malay Peninsula in spite of the fact that there was an agreement between Great Britain and Kelantan, dated October 22, 1910, according to which Kelantan should have no relations with any foreign power except through the King of

Spheres of Validity of International Law

Although sovereignty is essentially a quality, the quality of the state as a normative order, the term is frequently used to designate a certain quality of state power or the state power as a whole. In this connection "power" means legal power, and that means the competence or jurisdiction of the state. If by sovereignty an unrestricted power is meant, it is certainly incompatible with international law, which, by imposing obligations upon the state, restricts its power. The degree of this restriction is very different according to the treaties entered into by the state concerned. Then the question arises of how far such restriction of power may go without depriving the community of its quality of a state. The only reliable criterion is that the state is not subjected to the national law of another state. If a state by a treaty entered into with another state submits in any respect whatever to the national law of the other—or any other—state, it ceases to be subjected only to international law and hence ceases to be a state in the sense of international law. The typical case is a treaty by which several states establish a federal state of which they become so-called component states. Since the effect of the treaty containing the federal constitution is that the contracting states submit to the national law of the federal state, they lose their quality as states in the sense of international law. The doctrine that they remain "sovereign" states—the sovereignty being divided between the component states and the federation—is based on the idea that sovereignty is a quantity of state power and hence divisible. However, it is not the sovereignty which is divided, and which as a quality is not divisible; it is the state power or, more exactly formulated, it is the competence of the state which—in a federal state—is divided between a central organ and several local organs.

To avoid misunderstandings, it is advisable not to use the ambiguous term "sovereignty" at all in relation to the state. Since sovereignty originally means an absolute quality, relative sover-

---

Great Britain. The agreement provided also that "nothing in this agreement shall affect the administrative authority now held by the Rajah of Kelantan." In the House of Lords Viscount Finlay stated: "While there are extensive limitations upon its [Kelantan's] independence, the enclosed documents do not negative the view that there is quite enough independence left to support the claim to sovereignty."

eignty—whether it means not a supreme but the one next to the supreme authority, or only internal not also external sovereignty, or not total but divided sovereignty—is a contradiction in terms. There is in the English language no specific term to express the idea that the state, as the national legal order, is subordinated only to the international legal order. (The German term "Voelkerrechtsunmittelbarkeit" is not translatable.) It is by this direct relation to international law that we may differentiate the state as a juristic person or corporation, and the corporations within the state: the latter are subject to the national legal order, to the law of the state within which they are established. The state as a juristic person is the personification of a relatively centralized legal order, inferior only to international law. This is the nature of the state as subject of international law.

3. *The Subjects of Obligation and Responsibility in International Law*

The traditional doctrine that only states, not individuals, are the subjects of international law means that the personal sphere of validity of the international legal order is limited. According to this doctrine, the norms of international law can impose obligations and responsibilities and confer rights only upon states, not upon individuals. This limitation of the personal sphere of validity constitutes, according to that doctrine, an essential characteristic of international law. This doctrine is incorrect. The subjects of international law are—like the subjects of national law—individual human beings. States as juristic persons are subjects of international law in the same way as corporations as juristic persons are subjects of national law. The statement that states as juristic persons are subjects of international law does not mean that individuals are not the subjects of the obligations, responsibilities, and rights established by that law. It only means that individual human beings are indirectly and collectively, in their capacity as organs or members of the state, subjects of the obligations, responsibilities, and rights presented as obligations, responsibilities, and rights of the state. Besides, human beings are also directly and

Spheres of Validity of International Law

individually subjects of obligations, responsibilities, and rights established by international law.

a. *The state as subject of international obligations.* That international law imposes an obligation upon a state means that the individual who by his conduct may fulfill or violate the obligation is not directly determined by the norms of international law, but that the latter leaves the determination of this individual to national law. More exactly, the international legal order delegates the determination of this individual to the national legal order. For example, the rule that the state is obligated to respect the territorial integrity of other states and hence not to invade with its armed forces or parts of them the territory of another state, means that the individual who under the constitution of the state is competent to dispose of the armed forces of the state—e.g., the Head of State as commander in chief—is obligated by international law to refrain from ordering the armed forces or parts of them to invade the territory of another state. That the state is obligated by an international convention to introduce an eight-hour workday means that the organs (legislative and executive) which, according to the constitution of the state, are competent to regulate the matter in question, are bound by international law to perform the acts necessary for the establishment of a regime according to which employees must not work more than eight hours a day.

If the competent organs of the state do not fulfill the obligations established by international law, the state commits an international delict for which international law provides a sanction. But the sanctions stipulated by this law—and this is the second characteristic element of the phenomenon we call "obligation of the state by international law"—war or reprisals, are not directed against the organs whose function it was to fulfill the obligations of international law and who have not done so. The sanctions affect neither the individual who as Head of State, in violation of international law, has ordered the armed forces of the state or parts of them to invade the territory of another state, nor the members of the government who, in violation of the treaty, have failed to submit a bill to the individuals forming the parliament, nor the parliament itself which has not voted the law concerning the eight-hour workday, and so on. The sanctions—war or reprisals—directly or indirectly affect the people of the state, i.e., the individuals belonging to the state, and in case of war especially the individuals belonging to the armed forces of the state. The human beings against whom the sanctions are to be directed are not determined individually, as is the case when the law provides that the sanction is to be directed against that individual who, by his own behavior, has committed the delict. International law determines only a group of individuals against whom the sanctions may be directed: in case of reprisals, the subjects of the state responsible for the delict; in case of war, the members of its armed forces. That means that international law establishes collective responsibility for the violation of the obligations imposed upon the states. Hence the statement that international law imposes obligations upon states, or that states as juristic persons are the subjects of the obligations stipulated by international law, means (1) international law imposes obligations upon individuals in their capacity as organs of the state; individuals in their capacity as organs of the state are the subjects of the international obligations. But international law determines only indirectly these individuals who, by their own behavior, ought to fulfill the obligations stipulated by international law and who may commit the international delict imputed to the state; international law delegates the determination of these individuals to national law. And (2) international law, by providing for reprisals or war as sanctions, establishes collective responsibility of the subjects of the state or of the members of the armed forces for violations of international law.

b. *The state as subject of international responsibility.* (1) RE-SPONSIBILITY OF THE STATE: COLLECTIVE RESPONSIBILITY. This collective responsibility is the "responsibility of the state" under general international law. It is a responsibility constituted by the specific sanctions of international law—reprisals and war—different from the responsibility established by national law, which as a rule is individual responsibility and which, according to the nature of the sanctions—civil execution or punishment—is either civil or criminal responsibility. The responsibility of the state established by gen-

Spheres of Validity of International Law

eral international law is neither civil nor criminal responsibility. There is no differentiation of civil and criminal law within international law. The international responsibility of a state for nonpayment of debts based on international law is not different from its responsibility for the violation of any other international obligation. Even if an international delict—as, for instance, resort to an illegal war—is sometimes called a "crime," the collective responsibility of the state for such delict is not a criminal responsibility, because reprisals and war have not the specific character of punishment.[11]

(2) "ACT OF STATE." The responsibility of the state under general international law is responsibility for violations of international law committed by conduct which may be interpreted as conduct of the state, that is to say, the conduct of an individual human being, imputable to the state. Such conduct is usually called "act of state" (comprising actions as well as omission of actions prescribed by international law). The individual whose act is imputable to the state acts as an organ of the state. It is the national legal order, the law of the state, which determines under what conditions an individual acts as an organ of the state; and, as pointed out, the international legal order delegates to the national legal orders the determination of the individuals who in their capacity as organs of the state have to perform the acts prescribed or authorized by international law, that is, the individuals who have to fulfill the obligations imposed and to exercise the rights conferred by international law upon the state.

The question as to whether an act performed by a human being is an act of state, that is to say, may be imputed to the state, must be answered on the basis of the national legal order, the law of the state whose act is in question. An act the performance of which is not prescribed or permitted by the law of a state cannot be imputed to the state, i.e., interpreted as an act of the state. But such an act may, according to international law, have the same legal effects as an act imputable to the state, especially if the act is performed by an individual who, as an organ of the state, is competent under the law of the state to represent the state in

---

[11] Cf. *supra,* pp. 23ff., 33ff.

relation to other states, such as the Head of State. Thus, for instance, according to some writers, a treaty is concluded by a state if it is concluded by the Head of State, even if the constitution of the state confers the power to conclude treaties not, or not exclusively, upon the Head of State, but on the parliament, or on the Head of State together with the parliament. A declaration of war made by the Head of State may be considered as fulfillment of the state's obligation under the Hague Convention III, although according to the constitution of the state concerned, the parliament, not the Head of State, is competent to declare war. In these cases it might be assumed that the individuals competent to exercise the right of the state or to fulfill the obligation of the state are directly determined by international law, at least insofar as not only national law but also international law may determine the individuals competent to act as organs of the state, that is, to perform acts of state. If this interpretation is accepted, the question as to whether an act performed by an individual human being is an act of state is to be answered in principle on the basis of the national law of the respective states, but exceptionally on the basis of international law if the act performed by the individual concerned has, according to international law, the same effect as the same act performed by an individual authorized or obliged by the national law to perform the act.

Traditional doctrine defines as acts of state within the meaning of international law only those acts which are performed by the government (comprising the Head of State and the cabinet) or at the command or with the authorization of the government;[12]

---

[12] In *Buron v. Denman* (Great Britain, Court of Exchequer, 1848, 2 Exchequer Division 167) the court held that an act performed by a naval commander, although not performed at the command or with the authorization of the government, was to be considered as an act of state, because subsequently ratified by the government. "The principal question is, whether the conduct of the defendant . . . can be justified as an act of state done by authority of the Crown. It is not contended that there was any previous authority. . . . Therefore the justification of the defendant depends upon the subsequent ratification of his acts. A well-known maxim of the law between private individuals is, *Omnis ratihabitio retrotrahitur et mandato aequiparatur*. . . . Therefore, generally speaking, between subject and subject, a subsequent ratification of an act done as agent is equal to a prior

not acts performed by organs of the state which are not under the authority of the government, such as the parliament or the courts, which, according to the constitution of modern states, are independent of the government. There can be no doubt that international law may be violated by a legislative or judicial act performed by a parliament or by a court within its competence. But those who refuse to interpret such violation of international law as an "act of state" and hence as an "international delinquency," that is to say, as an international delict imputable to the state, admit that if it is not possible to reach an agreement between the state whose parliament or court has violated the international law and the state whose interest is violated, the latter state is authorized to resort to reprisals or war. But this is exactly the same situation which exists in case of a violation of international law committed by an act performed by the government or at the command or with the authorization of the government. In this case as well as in the case of its responsibility for acts of its legislative or judicial organs, the state is responsible for its own acts. There is no sufficient reason to exclude from the concept of "act of state" the acts performed by the legislative and judicial organs of the states.

(3) DIRECT AND INDIRECT RESPONSIBILITY OF THE STATE. Some writers maintain that the state is responsible not only for violations of international law committed by its own acts (so-called "international delinquencies"), but also for certain violations of international law committed by acts not imputable to the state according to its own (or to international) law; in other terms, that the state is responsible also for acts performed by other persons than the state itself. Such acts may be performed by organs of the state not competent to perform the acts concerned, or by private individuals. Responsibility of the state for acts imputable

---

authority. . . . you have to take it as the direction of the court, that if the Crown, with knowledge of what has been done, ratified the defendant's act by the Secretaries of State or the Lords of the Admiralty, this action cannot be maintained. In the documents which have been read there is ample evidence of ratification . . . if this act, by adoption, becomes the act of the Crown, the seizure of the slaves and goods by the defendant is a seizure by the Crown, and an act of state for which the defendant is irresponsible, and, therefore, entitled to a verdict on the plea of 'Not Guilty'."

to the state is called "direct" or "original"; responsibility of the state for acts not imputable to the state, "indirect" or "vicarious" responsibility. However, by so-called indirect or vicarious responsibility, not a responsibility in the true sense of the term but a specific obligation of the state is understood—the obligation to repair a wrong; and that means the moral and material damage caused by a violation of international law not imputable to the state.[13] The obligation to repair the wrong inflicted upon the other state may consist in repealing the act or in disowning it if it has the external appearance of an act of state; in expressing regret or apologizing to the wronged state; in punishing the individual who has performed the act; in paying compensation for the material damage caused by the act. The extent of this obligation of reparation may differ in different cases, and requires agreement between the two states concerned.[14] Under general international law the state is obliged to prevent certain acts of private persons injurious to other states,[15]

---

[13] In the *Thomas Y. Youmans Case* (Annual Digest 1925–1926, Case No. 162) three American subjects were killed at the hands of a mob in the state of Michoacán, Mexico, following a dispute over wages with a Mexican worker. Previous to the murder the mayor of the town, being unable to quiet the mob, ordered a lieutenant of the state forces to proceed with troops to quell the riot and to put an end to the attack upon the Americans. The troops, on arriving at the scene of the riot, instead of dispersing the mob, opened fire on the house in which the Americans took refuge and killed one of them. The other two American subjects were then forced to leave the house, and as they did so they were killed by the troops and the mob. No adequate steps were subsequently taken to mete out punishment to the guilty. Some of the soldiers were arrested but not sentenced. Seventeen of the arrested escaped, some of them after they had been set at liberty on bail. The United States and Mexico General Claims Commission (1926) held that a government is responsible for wrongful acts of soldiers even when acting in disobedience of rules laid down by superior authority, when it is clear that at the time of the commission of those acts the soldiers were on duty and under the immediate supervision and in the presence of a commanding superior. Inflicting personal injuries or wanton destruction or looting on the part of soldiers cannot always be regarded as purely private acts. Freedom from responsibility in case of a state organ acting outside the scope of its competence does not mean that a government is never responsible for a wrongful act committed by its officials. Further, that Mexico was also responsible for not having taken proper steps to apprehend and to punish the persons involved in the crime.

[14] Cf. *supra*, pp. 20f.

[15] Cf. *infra*, p. 126.

Spheres of Validity of International Law 121

and, if it is not possible to prevent them, to punish the delinquents and to force them to repair the material damage caused by the injurious act. This obligation, too, is sometimes presented as indirect or vicarious responsibility of the state, that is to say, as responsibility of the state for violations of international law not committed by its own acts.[16] But in all the cases of so-called indirect or vicarious responsibility, the state is responsible only for its own conduct; for the state makes itself responsible in the true sense of the term, and that means that the state is liable to a sanction only if it does not fulfill by its own conduct the obligation to prevent or repair the wrong committed by acts not imputable to the state; that is to say, the state is responsible only for

---

[16] Cf. the *Laura M. B. Janes Case* (United States and Mexico, General Claims Commission, 1926, Annual Digest 1925–1926, Case No. 158). An American citizen was killed on the territory of Mexico. The evidence showed that the action taken by the Mexican authorities was inefficient and dilatory. Eight years after the murder had been committed the murderer had not been apprehended. The commission held that Mexico was liable in damages. There had taken place such a failure on the part of the Mexican authorities to take prompt and efficient action to apprehend the murderer as to warrant an award of indemnity. The basis of the responsibility of the state, however, is here not complicity with the perpetrator by condoning or ratifying through executive inaction the criminal act, but solely the specific fact of denial of justice, namely, the failure to fulfill the state's own international duty to prosecute and punish the offender.

In *United States (Rosa Gelbtrunk Claim) v. Salvador* (United States and Salvador, Claims Arbitration, 1902; U.S. Foreign Relations, 1902, p. 877) the arbitral tribunal rejected a claim for compensation of damages caused in the course of a revolution in Salvador, 1898. In its opinion the tribunal stated: "A citizen or subject of one nation who, in the pursuit of commercial enterprise, carries on trade within the territory and under the protection of the sovereignty of a nation other than his own is to be considered as having cast in his lot with the subjects or citizens of the State in which he resides and carries on business . . . . The State to which he owes national allegiance has no right to claim for him as against the nation in which he is resident any other or different treatment in case of loss by war—either foreign or civil —revolution, insurrection, or other internal disturbance caused by organized military force or by soldiers, than that which the latter country metes out to its own subjects or citizens. . . . It is, however, not to be assumed that this rule would apply in a case of mob violence which might, if due diligence had been used, have been prevented by civil authorities alone or by such authorities aided by an available military force. In such case of spoliation by a mob, especially where the disorder has arisen in hostility to foreigners, a different rule may prevail."

its own delict. If, however, it is assumed that the obligation to repair the wrong is not the automatic consequence of a violation of international law but the result of an agreement concerning the reparation, and if it is further assumed that in case no such agreement between the states concerned is reached the injured state is authorized by general international law to resort to reprisals or war against the other state, then this state may be considered to be responsible for a delict not imputable to it. Then, responsibility of a state for a delict committed by other persons exists in case the delict is committed by an incompetent organ of the state, that is, an organ acting without authorization of its government, or by private individuals performing on the territory of the state acts injurious to another state.

(4) ABSOLUTE RESPONSIBILITY OF THE STATE. The question as to whether the international responsibility of the state has the character of absolute responsibility (liability), or responsibility based on fault (culpability), is much discussed. Since the international responsibility of the state has the character of collective responsibility, the answer to this question depends on whether it refers to the individuals collectively responsible for the violation of international law committed by the conduct of a state organ, or to the individual who in his capacity as organ of the state has, by his conduct, violated international law.[17] As pointed out, collective responsibility is always absolute responsibility since it cannot be based on the fault of the responsible individuals, that is, the individuals against whom the sanctions are directed. But these individuals may be made responsible only if the delict has been committed intentionally or negligently by the immediate delinquent. Then their responsibility is based, not on their own, but on the delinquent's fault.

A delict of the state is always the conduct of an individual acting as an organ of the state. Hence the question whether the international responsibility of the state is absolute responsibility or culpability may also be formulated as the question whether the fault of the individual whose conduct is imputed to the state is an essential condition of the sanction provided by international law against the

[17] Cf. *supra*, pp. 107f., 117ff.

Spheres of Validity of International Law

state. Some writers maintain that an act of state injurious to another state, which objectively constitutes a violation of international law, is nevertheless not an international delinquency (and that means is not the condition of a sanction) if committed neither intentionally nor maliciously nor negligently. Other writers maintain, on the contrary, that within general international law absolute responsibility—at least in principle—prevails with respect to the individuals whose conduct constitutes the delict.[18] There are also decisions of international tribunals which may be interpreted in this way.[19] It is hardly possible to answer the question in a general way. There is no doubt that the state is responsible for violations of international law committed negligently by its organs. According to some writers, no sanction against the state is justified when it can be proved that the competent organs of the state have taken the necessary measures to avoid the violation of the right of the other state. But the state cannot escape responsibility by proving only that its organs did not intentionally and maliciously violate international law. If by "responsibility" is understood not only being liable to an enforcement action as sanction but also to be obliged to repair the wrong done, and if "responsibility based on fault" (culpability) is considered to comprise not only the case that the wrong has been committed intentionally and maliciously but also the case that the wrong has been committed negligently, the international responsibility of the state has, with respect to the individuals collectively responsible, the character of absolute responsibility, but with respect to the individuals whose conduct constitutes the international delict, in principle, the character of culpability. There are, however, cases where the state is responsible although no negligence on the part of its organ has taken place. Thus, for instance, according to Article 3 of the Hague

---

[18] Cf. *supra*, p. 19.

[19] In the case *The Jessie*, before the British-American Claims Arbitral Tribunal (1921), the United States was held responsible to Great Britain for an action of its officers performed neither with intention, malice, nor negligence. The tribunal declared: "Any government is responsible to other governments for errors in judgment of its officials purporting to act within the scope of their duties and vested with power to enforce their demands." Cf. British Yearbook of International Law (1938), p. 115.

Convention of 1907 respecting the laws and customs of war on land,[20] a belligerent state is "responsible" ("liable") for all violations of the Regulations laid down in that Convention, whether committed by its organs or by individuals belonging to its armed forces but not acting in their capacity as organs. That means that the belligerent state is obliged to pay compensation for the damage caused by a violation of the regulations, whether or not committed intentionally and maliciously or negligently.

c. *Individuals as subjects of international obligations and responsibilities.* The principle that under international law states are the subjects of the obligations and responsibilities established by that law is a rule which has important exceptions. The specific legal technique implied in this principle does not result from the essence, as an unchangeable nature, of international law. For there are, exceptionally, norms of international law which determine directly the individual who, by his own conduct, may commit or abstain from committing the international delict, norms of international law which establish individual responsibility by directing sanctions exclusively against the immediate delinquent or against another physical person individually and directly determined by international law. Consequently, these sanctions cannot have the character of war or reprisals, which, by their very nature, constitute collective responsibility. They have the same character as sanctions of national law.

(1) THE PROHIBITION OF PIRACY. This is, for example, the case of the norm of general international law which prohibits piracy. Piracy is usually defined as acts of violence committed on the high seas against persons or property by the crew of a private vessel with the intent to plunder. Piracy can be committed only by private persons, not by an act of state; hence not by the crew of a public vessel acting at the command or with the authorization of a government.[21] International law authorizes all states to seize

---

[20] Cf. *supra*, pp. 117ff.

[21] In *The Helena* (Great Britain, High Court of Admiralty, 1801, 4 C. Robinson's Reports 3) the Court decided that the capture of a British merchant vessel by an Algerine corsair (privateer) was not an act of piracy because Algiers being a State "the act of capture and condemnation was not a mere private act of depredation." Although Tunis, Tripoli, and Algiers were

Spheres of Validity of International Law

—through their public or private vessels—pirates on the open sea and to punish them, irrespective of their nationality, through their own courts. The punishment may be determined by national law.

The norm of general international law authorizing the states to punish pirates attaches to the fact "piracy," which it itself determines, a sanction individually directed against the person committing piracy. It prohibits piracy by obligating all individuals to refrain therefrom. The individuals are not obligated in a way different from the way they are obligated by norms of national law. As the norm forbidding piracy is a norm of international law, it is individuals who are immediate subjects of international law, subjects of an international obligation. The act of coercion, the sanction, is directed against the pirate who violates his obligation under international law. It is not directed against a state—in particular not against the state of which the pirate is a citizen—in the way in which reprisals or war is directed against a state, i.e., directed against the people of this state. In case of piracy, individual, and not collective, responsibility for a violation of international law takes place. The sanction, executed by the organs of a definite state, is applied here in execution of a norm of international law. For, in the absence of this norm it would be contrary to international law to perform acts of sovereignty, especially acts of coercion, against or on board foreign ships.[22] The principle of the freedom of the seas, a very important principle of international law, consists precisely of this rule forbidding every act of coercion against or affecting foreign ships on the high seas. The rule author-

---

formerly considered as pirate states, "they have long acquired the character of established governments"; hence "they cannot properly be esteemed pirates, but enemies . . . . Although their notions of justice, to be observed between nations, differ from those which we entertain, we do not, on that account, venture to call in question their public acts." In excluding acts of state from the rule concerning piracy, the Court applied the principle that no state has jurisdiction over the acts of another state. Cf. *infra*, pp. 235ff.

In *Re Piracy Jure Gentium* (Annual Digest 1933–1934, Case No. 89) the Judicial Committee of the Privy Council (1934) held: "Actual robbery is not an essential element in the crime of piracy *jure gentium*. A frustrated attempt to commit a piratical robbery is equally piracy *jure gentium*."

[22] Cf. *infra*, pp. 224f.

izing the states to seize and punish pirates on the high seas is a restriction of the rule concerning the freedom of the seas, and as the latter is a rule of general international law, the former must likewise be a rule of general international law. The penalty to be inflicted upon the pirate, it is true, is not directly determined by international law, which leaves the determination of the punishment to national law. But in determining the penalty for piracy by its criminal law and in inflicting a penalty upon the pirate through its own court, the state executes international law; it acts as organ of the international community constituted by general international law, just as the individual committing piracy violates an obligation directly imposed upon him, and not upon his state or any other state, by international law, which makes this individual, and not a state, responsible for the delict.

(2) ILLEGAL USE OF FLAG. Under general international law every vessel must sail under the flag of a state; but international law leaves it to the national law of the state to determine the conditions under which a vessel is allowed to sail under the flag of that state. All states are authorized to seize through their warships ships which illegitimately sail under their flags and to confiscate the ship by decision of their own courts, as a penalty for abuse of flag. That means that the owner of the ship and the master of the ship are directly obliged by international law not to commit the delict, and that the owner is made individually responsible for the delict.

(3) ACTS OF PRIVATE PERSONS INJURIOUS TO FOREIGN STATES. As pointed out, the states are obliged by general international law to prevent certain acts injurious to other states from being committed on their territories, and if prevention is not possible, to punish the delinquents and force them to repair the damage caused by the delict. Such injurious acts are, e.g., violation of the person of a Head of State staying on foreign territory, or of a diplomatic envoy; insult to a flag or another official emblem of a foreign state; attempts directed against the territorial integrity of a foreign state or intended to overthrow the legitimate government of another state. All these acts are violations of international law, which forbids such acts by obligating the states to punish the

Spheres of Validity of International Law

delinquents. In punishing the delinquents, the states, through their courts, execute international law, although they may at the same time execute their own national law, enacted in conformity with international law. Hence the obligation to forbear from committing these delicts is imposed in the first place by international and in the second place by national law, directly upon the individuals concerned. They are subjects of international obligations; and individual criminal responsibility is established for the violation of these obligations by general international law.

(4) THE CONVENTION FOR THE PROTECTION OF SUBMARINE TELEGRAPH CABLES. Another example showing the possibility of a direct obligation of individuals under international law, and the establishment of individual criminal as well as civil responsibility for violations of that law, is the International Convention for the Protection of Submarine Telegraph Cables (March 14, 1884). This convention provides (Article II): "The breaking or injury of a submarine cable, done willfully or through culpable negligence, and resulting in the total or partial interruption or embarrassment of telegraphic communication, shall be a punishable offense (but the punishment inflicted shall be no bar to a civil action for damages)." By this provision individual criminal responsibility for the delict determined in the convention is established. According to Article XII of the convention, the punishment shall be "fine or imprisonment or both." Civil responsibility is established by Article IV: "The owner of a cable who, by the laying or repairing of that cable, shall cause the breaking or injury of another cable, shall be required to pay the cost of the repairs which such breaking or injury shall have rendered necessary, but such payment shall not bar enforcement, if there be ground therefor, of Article II of this Convention." Article VIII stipulates: "(1) The courts competent to take cognizance of infractions of this Convention shall be those of the country to which the vessel on board of which the infraction has been committed belongs. (2) It is, moreover, understood that, in cases in which the provision contained in the foregoing paragraph cannot be carried out, the repression of violations of this Convention shall take place, in each of the contracting States, in the case of its subjects or citizens, in accordance with the general rule of penal com-

petence established by the special laws of those States, or by international treaties."

(5) BREACH OF BLOCKADE AND CARRIAGE OF CONTRABAND. The rules of general international law concerning breach of blockade and carriage of contraband impose various obligations upon individuals and establish individual responsibility for the violation of these obligations. By authorizing the belligerents to seize neutral vessels and to confiscate them through decisions of their prize courts for breach of blockade, general international law imposes upon the owners and masters of neutral vessels—not upon the neutral state—the obligation to refrain from committing this delict and makes the owner of the vessel individually responsible for the delict, which is characterized by some writers as a "criminal act." By authorizing the belligerents to prohibit the carriage of contraband and to confiscate the contraband cargo through decision of their prize courts, general international law imposes upon the owners and masters of neutral vessels, not upon the neutral state, the obligation to refrain from carriage of contraband, and makes the owner of the contraband cargo individually responsible for this delict.

(6) WAR CRIMES. Violations of the rules of warfare are called war crimes. General international law obligates the states to punish their own war criminals, and authorizes any belligerent state to punish the prisoners of war in its power for having violated the rules of warfare prior to capture. Hence general international law imposes upon individuals, as private persons, the obligation to refrain from committing war crimes, and establishes individual criminal responsibility for the commission of such crimes by private persons. Article 3 of Convention IV provides: "A belligerent party which violates the provisions of the said Regulations [annexed to the convention] shall, if the case demands, be liable to pay compensation. It shall be responsible for all acts committed by persons forming part of its armed forces." The first sentence means that a belligerent party is obliged to pay compensation for violations of the regulations committed by an act of state; the second sentence refers also to violations of the regulations committed by private persons.

Spheres of Validity of International Law

That the belligerent party is "responsible" means that it is obliged to pay compensation for the damage caused by these acts.

(7) ACTS OF ILLEGITIMATE WARFARE. General international law authorizes a belligerent power occupying enemy territory to punish persons for acts of illegitimate warfare, that is to say, for acts committed in war by private individuals against the armed forces of the enemy. Individuals who do not belong to the armed forces of a belligerent are not allowed to take up arms against the enemy; if they do so, they commit a violation of international law, which obligates them to refrain from committing this delict and makes them individually responsible for it by authorizing the belligerent against which the delict is directed to punish them. They are direct subjects of international obligations and international responsibilities.

(8) ESPIONAGE. The same is true with respect to espionage. According to Article 29 of the Regulations of Convention IV, "a person can only be considered a spy when, acting clandestinely or on false pretences, he obtains or endeavors to obtain information in the zone of operations of a belligerent, with the intention of communicating it to the hostile party." General international law authorizes the state against which acts of espionage have been committed to punish the perpetrator as a criminal, even if the acts concerned have been committed at the command or with the authorization of the enemy government, i.e., as acts of state. In contradistinction to other war crimes, the states in whose interest espionage is committed are not obliged to prevent and to punish acts of this nature. The state which employs spies in its own interest is not responsible for these acts. The individual, however, who commits these acts may, according to international law, be punished by the injured state. In this case, general international law establishes only the individual responsibility of the perpetrator.[23]

---

[23] Cf. Ex parte Quirin et al. (Annual Digest 1941–1942, Case No. 168). The facts in this case were: In June, 1942, after the declaration of war between the United States and the German Reich, eight members of the German armed forces had been landed on the coast of the United States in coastal defense zones. They brought with them explosives, fuses, and incendiary and timing devices, and immediately after landing, buried their uniforms and

Most of the writers on international law, under the influence of the doctrine that only states, and not individuals, are subjects of international law, maintain that international law, as a law between states, does not and cannot forbid individuals from performing or refraining from performing a certain act. To maintain that international law does not forbid certain acts, although inter-

---

the materials mentioned and proceeded in civilian dress to various points in the United States. All had received instructions from the German High Command to destroy war industries, railroad centers, bridges, power plants, and other war facilities in the United States in return for regular salary payments from the German Government. On June 27, 1942, they were arrested in civilian clothing in New York or Chicago by the Federal Bureau of Investigation. In this case the United States Supreme Court (1942) stated: "By universal agreement and practice, the law of war draws a distinction between the armed forces and the peaceful populations of belligerent nations and also between those who are lawful and unlawful combatants. Lawful combatants are subject to capture and detention as prisoners of war by opposing military forces. Unlawful combatants are likewise subject to capture and detention, but in addition they are subject to trial and punishment by military tribunals for acts which render their belligerency unlawful. The spy who secretly and without uniform passes the military lines of a belligerent in time of war, seeking to gather military information and communicate it to the enemy, or an enemy combatant who without uniform comes secretly through the lines for the purpose of waging war by destruction of life or property, are familiar examples of belligerents who are generally deemed not to be entitled to the status of prisoners of war, but to be offenders against the law of war subject to trial and punishment by military tribunals . . . . By a long course of practical administrative construction by its military authorities, our Government has likewise recognized that those who during time of war pass surreptitiously from enemy territory into our own, discarding their uniforms upon entry, for the commission of hostile acts involving destruction of life and property, have the status of unlawful combatants punishable as such by military commission. This precept of the law of war has been so recognized in practice both here and abroad, and has so generally been accepted as valid by authorities on international law, that we think it must be regarded as a rule or principle of the law of war recognized by this Government by its enactment of the Fifteenth Article of War." The Court held that the charge "on which petitioners are detained for trial by the Military Commission, alleged an offense which the President is authorized to order tried by military commission; that his Order convening the Commission was a lawful order and that the Commission was lawfully constituted; that the petitioners were held in lawful custody and did not show cause for their discharge." Subsequent to the decision of the Supreme Court, six of the accused persons were sentenced by a military tribunal to death, one was sentenced to life imprisonment, and one to thirty years' imprisonment.

national law authorizes the punishment of these acts, is not consistent. If there is a rule of general international law authorizing states to punish individuals for having performed certain acts determined by international law, then international law forbids these acts, exactly in the same way that national law forbids theft and murder by authorizing the state to punish thieves and murderers.

(9) OBLIGATION TO WARN AUTHORITIES CONCERNED BEFORE BOMBARDMENT. A particular situation exists under the provisions of Article 26 of the Regulations of Convention IV and Article 6 of Convention IX, concerning bombardment by naval forces in time of war. These provisions impose upon the commander of the attacking forces, that is to say, on a particular organ of the belligerent state, the obligation to warn the authorities of the attacked place before commencing a bombardment. Article 5 of Convention IX imposes upon the commander the obligation to spare in a bombardment certain buildings. The analogous provision of the Regulations of Convention IV imposes this obligation on the belligerent state, not on a particular organ.[24] In the first case a rule of international law establishes the obligation of a definite individual; but not his individual responsibility when he omits the warning at the command or with the authorization of his government, that is to say, if his omission is imputable to the state. Responsible for a violation of this obligation by an act of state is the belligerent state, against which in such a case the other belligerent may resort to reprisals, constituting collective responsibility. If, however, the commander violates his international obligation on his own initiative, he is individually responsible to his state, and if in the power of the enemy, to that state for having committed a war crime.

d. *Individual responsibility for acts of state.* Violation of the rules regulating the conduct of war (war crimes) must be distinguished from violation of the rules prohibiting resort to war.

---

[24] Article 27 of the Regulations provides: "In sieges and bombardments all necessary steps must be taken to spare, as far as possible, buildings dedicated to religion, art, science, or charitable purposes . . . ." Article 5 of Convention IX stipulates: "In bombardments by naval forces all the necessary measures must be taken by the commander to spare as far as possible sacred edifices, buildings used for artistic, scientific, or charitable purposes . . . ."

Whereas the latter can be committed only by acts of state, the former may be also committed by private persons. General international law does not establish individual responsibility for illegal resort to war, nor for war crimes committed as acts of state. Such responsibility may be, and actually has been, established by international agreements creating particular international law.

(1) ARTICLE 227 OF THE PEACE TREATY OF VERSAILLES. Article 227 of the Treaty of Versailles—an article which was never executed—stipulated that ex-Emperor William II should be brought before an international criminal court "for a supreme offense against international morality and the sanctity of treaties." By the "offense" was meant in the first place the violation of Germany's obligation to respect the neutrality of Belgium and Luxemburg, guaranteed by Germany. Article 227 stipulated further: "If the accused is recognized to be guilty, it will be the duty of this tribunal to fix the punishment which it considers should be imposed." This norm of conventional international law was based on the presumption that an individual, determined by this norm, had in his capacity as head of the German Reich violated international morality and international law, and it provided that an international tribunal should inflict a penalty, to be determined by the tribunal itself, on this individual. The provision of the Treaty of Versailles made the norms of international morality—by delegation or adoption for this particular case—legal norms by attaching a penal sanction to a violation of the rules of international morality. In addition it attached to the violation of certain treaties an individual penalty. Hence Article 227 made an individual responsible for a violation of rules of international law which he committed in his capacity as organ of a state. By so doing, the conventional norm of this article imposed criminal responsibility for violations of international law upon an individual, with retroactive effect. For the norms of international law, the violation of which Article 227 of the Treaty of Versailles declared to be punishable infractions, did not establish any individual responsibility. The violations of law for which William II was made responsible had the character of acts of state. The norms of international law, the violation of which the Treaty of Versailles declared as individually punishable, established the

responsibility only of the state, and that means collective not individual responsibility. The norms of international morality to which Article 227 refers were not yet norms of international law at the time the offenses were committed for which Article 227 stipulated a sanction.

In the case of William II, individual criminal responsibility for acts of state was established with the consent of the state for whose acts individual criminal responsibility was to be established. Germany ratified the Peace Treaty of Versailles and thus gave its consent to the provision of Article 227. This consent was essential. For there exists a rule of general international law that no state has criminal or civil jurisdiction (i.e., jurisdiction exercised by its criminal or civil courts) over the acts of another state without the consent of the latter.[25]

(2) THE LONDON AGREEMENT OF 1945 FOR THE PROSECUTION OF WAR CRIMINALS. Another treaty by which individual criminal responsibility for violations of international law by acts of state was established is the agreement signed on August 8, 1945, at London, for the Prosecution of European Axis War Criminals. This treaty was concluded, as stated in its Preamble, by the Government of the United Kingdom of Great Britain and Northern Ireland, the Government of the United States of America, the Provisional Government of the French Republic, and the Government of the Union of Soviet Socialist Republics for the prosecution and punishment of the major war criminals of the European Axis. In the Preamble, the contracting parties, called in the text of the treaty "the signatories," declare that they are "acting in the interest of all the United Nations." This statement, however, would have been legally correct if all the other United Nations had adhered to the treaty. This was possible, since Article 5 provides that "any Government of the United Nations may adhere to this agreement by notice given through the diplomatic channel to the Government of the United Kingdom, who shall inform the other signatories and adhering Governments of each such adherence." However, some, not all governments of the United Nations adhered to the London Agreement. As far as the parties to the treaty of August 8, 1945, are con-

---

[25] Cf. *infra,* pp. 235ff.

cerned, there exists a striking difference between this treaty and the Treaty of Versailles. The latter has been ratified by Germany, that is, by the state whose organ was to be tried and thus was made responsible for acts of his state by the international court to be established by the treaty. Hence the provision of the Treaty of Versailles establishing the criminal responsibility of the German Emperor for violations of international law committed in his capacity as organ of the German Reich was in conformity with the rule of general international law that no state has jurisdiction over the acts of another state without the consent of the latter.[26] The European Axis Powers, however, are not contracting parties to the London Agreement, concluded for the prosecution of their organs and subjects made individually responsible for illegal acts of their states.

Article 1 of the London Agreement instituted "an International Military Tribunal for the trial of war criminals whose offenses have no particular geographical location, whether they be accused individually or in their capacity as members of organizations or groups or in both capacities." According to Article 2, "The constitution, jurisdiction and functions of the International Military Tribunal shall be those set out in the Charter annexed to this Agreement, which Charter shall form an integral part of this Agreement." According to Article 2 of the said Charter, the International Military Tribunal consisted of four members, each with an alternate. One member and one alternate were appointed by each of the signatories. According to Article 14 of this Charter, each signatory appointed a chief prosecutor for the investigation of the charges against and the prosecution of major war criminals.

Article 6 of the Charter stipulated: "The Tribunal established by the agreement referred to in Article 2 hereof for the trial and punishment of the major war criminals of the European Axis countries shall have the power to try and punish persons who, acting in the interests of the European Axis countries, whether as individuals or as members of organizations, committed any of the following crimes. The following acts, or any of them, are crimes coming within the jurisdiction of the Tribunal for which there shall be

---

[26] Cf. *infra*, pp. 235ff.

Spheres of Validity of International Law 135

individual responsibility: (A) Crimes against peace. Namely, planning, preparation, initiation or waging of a war of aggression, or a war in violation of international treaties, agreements or assurances, or participation in a common plan or conspiracy for the accomplishment of any of the foregoing. (B) War Crimes. Namely, violations of the laws or customs of war. Such violations shall include, but not be limited to, murder, ill-treatment or deportation to slave labor or for any other purpose of civilian population of, or in, occupied territory, murder or ill-treatment of prisoners of war or persons on the seas, killing of hostages, plunder of public or private property, wanton destruction of cities, towns or villages or devastation not justified by military necessity. (C) Crimes against humanity. Namely, murder, extermination, enslavement, deportation, and other inhumane acts committed against any civilian population, before or during the war; or persecutions on political, racial or religious grounds in execution of, or in connection with, any crime within the jurisdiction of the Tribunal, whether or not in violation of the domestic law of the country where perpetrated. Leaders, organizers, instigators and accomplices participating in the formulation or execution of a common plan or conspiracy to commit any of the foregoing crimes are responsible for all acts performed by any persons in execution of such plan."

Prior to the London Agreement the only "crime against peace" was an illegal resort to war, that is, resort to war in violation of general international law, provided that the *bellum justum* principle is supposed to be part of positive international law, and resort to war in violation of an international agreement, such as the Covenant of the League of Nations, the Kellogg-Briand Pact, a neutralization treaty, or a so-called nonaggression pact by which two or more states assume the obligation not to attack one another. "Planning," "preparation," and "initiation" of war, as well as "participation in a common plan or conspiracy for the accomplishment of any of the foregoing," mentioned in clause (A) of Article 6, are new international delicts. The same is true with respect of most acts mentioned in clause (C) as "crimes against humanity."

Articles 7 and 8 establish individual responsibility for acts of state. Article 7 provides: "The official position of defendants, whether as heads of state or responsible officials in Government departments, shall not be considered as freeing them from responsibility or mitigating punishment." Article 8: "The fact that the defendant acted pursuant to order of his Government, or of a superior, shall not free him from responsibility, but may be considered in mitigation of punishment if the Tribunal determines that justice so requires." Article 8 covers not only acts of state but also acts not imputable to the state. Under the two articles an individual may be punished for having committed one of the crimes determined in the Charter of the London Agreement, whether the act has or has not the character of an act of state and whether or not the act has been committed in execution of an order having or not having the character of an act of state. From the point of view of general international law, the difference between an act performed at superior command and an act performed on the own initiative of the acting individual is irrelevant. Only the question whether the act is or is not an act of state is decisive. An act performed at superior command may or may not be an act of state. It is not an act of state if the command is not an act of state. The responsibility for acts performed at superior command is a specific problem of criminal law, not of international law.[27]

---

[27] In the case of *The Llandovery Castle* (Germany, Reichsgericht, 1921; Annual Digest 1923–1924, Case No. 235) two subordinate officers of a German submarine were accused of having fired on the lifeboats of the British hospital ship *The Llandovery Castle*, sunk by the German submarine during the First World War, and thus having killed the people who were in the boats. The accused defended themselves by arguing that they acted at the command of their superior officer. The court held that the act of firing on the boats, with the killing of the people who were in them, constituted homicide according to Article 212 of the Penal Code and that "the firing on the boats was an offence against the law of nations." The court held further that the defense of superior orders could not be admitted in the present case. According to paragraph 2 of Article 47 of the German Military Penal Code the subordinate obeying an order involving a violation of the law is liable to punishment if it is known to him that the order of the superior is contrary to law. "This applies in the case of the accused. It is certainly to be urged in favor of the military subordinates, that they are under no obligation to question the order of their superior officer, and they can count upon its legality. But no such confidence can be held to exist if such an order is universally known to everybody, including the accused, to be without any doubt whatever against the law. This

Spheres of Validity of International Law

According to Article 27 of the Charter of the London Agreement, the tribunal had the right "to impose upon a defendant, on conviction, death or such other punishment as shall be determined by it to be just."

Insofar as the London Agreement establishes individual criminal responsibility for violations of international law committed by acts of state, for which, at the time these violations were committed, only collective responsibility existed; and insofar as the London Agreement establishes individual criminal responsibility for acts which, at the time they were committed, did not constitute any violation of existing national or international law (but only of rules of morality), the London Agreement has the character of retroactive criminal law (*ex post facto* law).

General international law does not prohibit—as do some state constitutions—the enactment of legal rules with retroactive force. The London Agreement is in this respect not at variance with general international law. But the view that this agreement in establishing individual criminal responsibility for the crimes against peace, determined in Article 6 (A) of its Charter, does not have retroactive force because such individual criminal responsibility had already been established by the Kellogg-Briand Pact, has no

---

happens only in rare and exceptional cases. But this case was precisely one of them, for in the present instance it was perfectly clear to the accused that killing defenseless people in the life boats could be nothing else but a breach of the law."

In the trials of war criminals conducted by the military tribunals of the Allied and Associated Powers in connection with the Second World War, the plea of superior command has been raised by the defense more frequently than any other. (Cf. *Law Reports of Trials of War Criminals*, Selected and prepared by the United Nations War Crimes Commission [1949] XV, 157ff.) In the practice of these tribunals the test was "whether an order, *illegal* under international law, on which an accused had acted was or must be presumed to have been known to him to be so illegal, or was obviously so illegal ('illegal on its face' to use the term employed by the Tribunal in the *High Command Trial*) or should have been recognized by him as being so illegal. The *general upshot* of a large number of decisions, and of the advice of Judge Advocates to British or Commonwealth courts, is that, if the order comes within one or more of these categories, then the accused cannot rely upon the plea of superior orders."

basis, either in the wording of this pact or in the intention of the contracting parties.[28]

Principles similar to those established by the London Agreement

---

[28] Cf. Judgment of the International Military Tribunal for the Trial of *German Major War Criminals.* (Presented by the Secretary of State for Foreign Affairs to Parliament by Command of His Majesty, Cmd. 6964, London [1946], pp. 39–40 and "International Military Tribunal [Nuremberg] Judgment and Sentences, October 1, 1946," 41 *American Journal of International Law* [1947] 218f.) "In the opinion of the Tribunal, the solemn renunciation of war as an instrument of national policy necessarily involves the proposition that such a war is illegal in international law; and that those who plan and wage such a war, with its inevitable and terrible consequences, are committing a crime in so doing. . . . But it is argued that the Pact does not expressly enact that such wars are crimes, or set up courts to try those who make such wars. To that extent the same is true with regard to the laws of war contained in the Hague Convention. The Hague Convention of 1907 prohibited resort to certain methods of waging war. These included the inhumane treatment of prisoners, the employment of poisoned weapons, the improper use of flags of truce, and similar matters. Many of these prohibitions had been enforced long before the dates of the Convention; but since 1907 they have certainly been crimes, punishable as offenses against the laws of war; yet the Hague Convention nowhere designates such practices as criminal, nor is any sentence prescribed, nor any mention made of a court to try and punish offenders. For many years past, however, military tribunals have tried and punished individuals guilty of violating the rules of land warfare laid down by this Convention. In the opinion of the Tribunal, those who wage aggressive war are doing that which is equally illegal, and of much greater moment than a breach of one of the rules of the Hague Convention." To support the view that an illegal war is, within the meaning of the Kellogg-Briand Pact, an international "crime," the judgment refers to various international documents, such as the Geneva Protocol of 1924 for the Pacific Settlement of International Disputes, and others, which, indeed, contain statements to that effect. But these statements did not establish individual criminal responsibility of members of a government for having resorted to an illegal war. Such responsibility can be established only by a legal norm providing for the punishment of the individuals concerned. The jurisdiction of the military tribunals to which the judgment of the International Military Tribunal refers was totally different from the jurisdiction conferred by the London Agreement upon the International Military Tribunal. The military tribunals which, prior to the judgment of Nuremberg, punished war criminals applied positive national criminal law, the law of the state which had transformed the rules of the Hague Convention—rules regulating the conduct of war—into its own criminal law. Prior to the London Agreement, no state had transformed the rules of international law prohibiting resort to war—different from the rules of warfare—into national criminal law; and no military tribunal had tried and punished individuals for having resorted to an internationally illegal war.

Spheres of Validity of International Law

are stipulated in the Charter of the International Tribunal for the Far East, approved by the Supreme Commander of the Allied Forces on January 19, 1946, on the basis of the Japanese Instrument of Surrender, signed on September 2, 1945.

4. The Subjects of Rights in International Law

a. *States as subjects of international rights.* General international law, as a primitive law,[29] confers a right upon a state by authorizing the state, that is to say, individuals as organs of the state, to resort to war or reprisals against the state which has violated certain interests of the former state, protected by international law. That a state has an international right means that a certain individual or certain individuals, whose determination is left to the law of the state, have under international law the power to bring about by their action as organs of the state the execution of the sanctions provided by general international law against the state responsible for the violation of the law. Also, the ascertainment of the violation of the law is left to the states concerned. If it is not possible to reach an agreement with respect to this question, it is for each state to decide it for itself. This is the consequence of the complete decentralization of general international law which does not institute courts with compulsory jurisdiction. A state can have a right in the sense of a legal capacity to bring about a judicial decision by which the violation of the law is ascertained, only insofar as an international tribunal exists. An international tribunal can be established only by a treaty concluded by the states which are willing to submit their disputes to the tribunal.

A national tribunal objectively ascertains the violation of a legal obligation and orders the sanction to be executed by special organs. In the absence of an internationally organized executive power, the international tribunals must limit themselves to ascertaining the violation of an international obligation and to ordering reparation for the illegally caused damage. The international tribunal has no power to enforce its decision, that is to say, to order a sanction to be executed by a special organ against the state which refuses

---

[29] Cf. *supra*, pp. 22, 36.

to comply with the decision of the tribunal, as is the case under national law. Under general international law the enforcement of the judicial decision, that is to say, the execution of the sanction is left to the state whose legal interest is injured by the nonexecution of the decision of the international tribunal. In this case the statement that a state has an international right in relation to another state means that a certain individual or certain individuals in their capacity as organs of the state have the legal capacity to bring the disputed case before an international tribunal, and that the state, i.e., certain individuals as organs of that State, is authorized to execute the sanctions provided by international law against the other state if the latter does not comply with the decision of the tribunal.

b. *Individuals as subjects of international rights.* Can individuals, not as organs of state but as private persons, have international rights in relation to states or to other private persons? International law, especially a treaty, confers rights on individuals by authorizing private persons to bring a lawsuit against a state before a national or an international tribunal. In that case the tribunal may ascertain the violation of the law, i.e., the rights of the private person (the plaintiff) on the part of the state (the defendant), and order reparation. If the state is obliged by the treaty to comply with the decision of the tribunal, noncompliance may be considered as a violation of the treaty, with the consequences such a delict has under general international law: enforcement action on the part of the other contracting parties against the delinquent state.

(1) THE CONVENTION CONCERNING AN INTERNATIONAL PRIZE COURT. An example of treaties conferring rights on private persons by authorizing them to invoke an international tribunal is the abortive Hague Convention (XII)—which was never ratified—concerning the establishment of an International Prize Court. According to Article 4 of this convention, an appeal from the decisions of national prize courts could have been brought before the International Prize Court, not only by the neutral state whose own property or that of its nationals was injuriously affected by the decision of the national prize court, but also by private individuals injured by the decisions of the national prize courts. According to Article 8,

Spheres of Validity of International Law

the International Prize Court could have pronounced the capture of the vessel to be null. In this case, "the Court shall order restitution of the vessel or cargo, and shall fix, if there is occasion, the amount of the damages. If the vessel or cargo have been sold or destroyed, the Court shall determine the compensation to be given to the owner on this account." As to the execution of the decisions of the International Prize Court, the convention only provides in Article 9: "The contracting Powers undertake to submit in good faith to the decisions of the International Prize Court and to carry them out with the least possible delay."

(2) ARTICLES 297 AND 304 OF THE TREATY OF VERSAILLES. Another example is offered by Article 297 of the Treaty of Versailles. The nationals of the Allied and Associated Powers—individuals—could bring actions against Germany before mixed arbitral tribunals instituted in conformity with Article 304 of the treaty. These private individuals were authorized to claim the rights they had to payment of damages which Germany's application of extraordinary war measures may have caused them. The provision of Article 304(b) of the Treaty of Versailles is particularly interesting. According to its terms, arbitral tribunals were competent to settle disputes arising out of contracts concluded previous to the Treaty of Versailles between citizens of the Allied and Associated Powers and German nationals. It was a question of litigations between private individuals for whom the competence of the German tribunals was put aside in favor of an international tribunal. In this case, too, an international agreement conferred upon private individuals the quality of parties before an international tribunal, and thus the quality of subjects of international law. This remains true even when the arbitral tribunal settled the dispute in conformity with the national law of one of the parties. The decision of the arbitral tribunal, in virtue of Article 304(g), was to be executed against a private person by the state to which the private person belonged.[30]

---

[30] In *Sigwald, Charles v. Germany* (Annual Digest 1925–1926, Case No. 255) the French-German Mixed Arbitral Tribunal (1926) held that the right granted under Article 297(e) was an individual right belonging to subjects of the Allied Powers, which might be put forward directly against Germany without the interposition of the French Government; and that, as the Treaty of Ver-

(3) THE GERMANO-POLISH CONVENTION CONCERNING UPPER SILESIA. Another example of rights of individuals under international law is furnished by the Germano-Polish Convention regarding Upper Silesia, signed at Geneva, May 15, 1922. Article 5 of this convention authorized private persons to bring a suit before an international court against the state which had violated certain interests of these individuals protected by the convention. Since the interested parties were, in this case, private persons, the convention attributed rights to individuals as private persons by conferring on them the power to appeal to an international tribunal even against their own state.[31]

---

sailles came into force after the Agreement of November 15, 1919, an express exception to Article 297(e) was necessary in order to deprive an individual of any rights accruing to him under it.

In the case of *Civilian War Claimants Association, Ltd. v. The King* (Annual Digest 1931–1932, Case No. 118) the question arose whether the provision of Article 232 of the Peace Treaty of Versailles imposing upon Germany the obligation to "make compensation for all damage done to the civilian population of the Allied and Associated Powers and their property," established rights of the private persons concerned. In the British House of Lords (1931) Lord Atkin said: ". . . when the Crown is negotiating with another Sovereign a treaty, it is inconsistent with its sovereign position that it should be acting as agent for the nationals of the sovereign State, unless indeed the Crown chooses expressly to declare that it is acting as agent. There is nothing, so far as I know, to prevent the Crown acting as agent or trustee if it chooses deliberately to do so. In the circumstances of this case there appears to me to be nothing which indicates that the Crown expressly assumed the position of agent or trustee, and I think the circumstances negative the idea that the Crown ever did intend to occupy that position and negative any circumstance from which the law might impose upon it the position either of agent or trustee." In this statement the question as to whether a treaty establishes rights of private persons is dealt with from the point of view of the doctrine that a treaty concluded by the government is a legal transaction, and that consequently private persons can acquire rights under the treaty only if the government in concluding the treaty acts as an agent for these persons. But a treaty is not only a legal transaction establishing subjective duties and rights on the basis of objective law, but also a procedure by which objective law is created. Hence the government in concluding a treaty need not act as agent for private persons, in order to establish rights of these persons. The government in concluding a treaty may be considered as acting in its capacity of an authority creating objective law. Then the only question is whether by this law rights of private persons are established. With reference to Article 232 of the Peace Treaty of Versailles this question may be answered in the negative.

[31] In *Steiner and Gross v. Polish State* (Annual Digest 1927–1928, Case No. 188) a Polish and a Czechoslovak citizen brought action against the Polish State

(4) HUMAN RIGHTS IN THE CHARTER OF THE UNITED NATIONS. If "rights" are to be conferred on individuals by an international agreement, the latter must impose upon the states parties to the agreement the obligation to recognize the jurisdiction of a tribunal to which the individuals have access in case of a violation of the rights on the part of the state, as well as the obligation to comply with the decision of the tribunal. It may be a national or an international tribunal;[32] but the rights are guaranteed more effectively

---

before the Upper Silesian Arbitral Tribunal on the basis of the German-Polish Convention of May 15, 1922. The Polish government contended that the convention did not confer upon Polish nationals a right of action against the Polish State; that it was a general principle of international law that an individual could not invoke an international authority against his own state; that this principle ought to be applied in regard to the interpretation of the convention; that any interpretation to the contrary would place the state against which such right was accorded in a position worse than that of states under the regime of capitulations and that the tribunal therefore had no jurisdiction. The tribunal (1928) held that the Polish contention must be rejected and that the tribunal had jurisdiction. The convention conferred in unequivocal terms jurisdiction upon the tribunal irrespective of the nationality of the claimants, and, the terms of the convention being clear, it was unnecessary to add to it a limitation which did not appear from its wording. There was an additional reason for not introducing any such limitation, seeing that the guiding principle of this part of the convention was the respect of private rights and the preservation of the economic unity of Upper Silesia, and that no one of these considerations was compatible with the exclusion of any category of claims for the sole reason of the nationality of the claimant.

[32] A treaty conferring upon individuals a right of action before national courts was the convention concluded on November 9, 1920, between Poland and the Free City of Danzig, concerning the railways within the territory of Danzig. In *Menge v. Polish Railway Administration* (Annual Digest 1925–1926, Case No. 258) the High Court of Danzig (1925) held *inter alia:* In order to give effect to the apparent purpose of a treaty and to the implied intention of the parties, the court will construe the provisions of a treaty regulating private rights of individuals in such a manner as to recognize claims grounded directly in the treaty and put forward by private persons without interposition on the part of their state.

Another treaty of this kind was the so-called *Beamtenabkommen*, a convention concluded on October 22, 1921, by Danzig and Poland, regulating questions relating to the employment of officials, employees, and workmen of the Danzig railways. The Permanent Court of International Justice (1928) in an advisory opinion (Publications of the Permanent Court of International Justice, Series B, No. 15) stated: "It may be readily admitted that, according to a well established principle of international law, the *Beamtenabkommen*, being an international agreement, cannot, as such, create direct rights and obligations for private indi-

when the states are subjected to an international tribunal. Without subjecting the state to the jurisdiction of a tribunal, no "rights" of individuals in relation to the state are established. The Charter of the United Nations, in the Preamble and in Article 1, paragraph 3; Article 13, paragraph 1(b); Article 55(c); and Article 62, paragraph 2, proclaims the principle of respect for fundamental human rights. But it is hardly possible to interpret these provisions as constituting legal obligations of the members to treat their subjects in conformity with this principle.[33] Nor has the Universal Declara-

viduals. But it cannot be disputed that the very object of an international agreement, according to the intention of the contracting Parties, may be the adoption by the Parties of some definite rules creating individual rights and obligations and enforceable by the national courts. That there is such an intention in the present case can be established by reference to the terms of the *Beamtenabkommen*. The fact that the various provisions were put in the form of an *Abkommen* [agreement] is corroborative, but not conclusive evidence as to the character and legal effects of the instrument. The intention of the Parties, which is to be ascertained from the contents of the Agreement, taking into consideration the manner in which the Agreement has been applied, is decisive. This principle of interpretation should be applied by the Court in the present case.–The wording and general tenor of the *Beamtenabkommen* show that its provisions are directly applicable as between the officials and the Administration."

[33] However, in *Re Drummond Wren* (Annual Digest 1943–1945, Case No. 50) the High Court of Ontario, Canada (1945), held that a restrictive covenant attached to certain lands, which read as follows: "Land not to be sold to Jews, or to persons of objectionable nationality," was void and of noneffect. In the justification of its decision the court referred *inter alia* to the Charter of the United Nations: "It is a well recognized rule that courts may look at various Dominion and Provincial Acts and public law as an aid in determining principles relative to public policy. . . . First and of profound significance is the recent San Francisco Charter, to which Canada was a signatory, and which the Dominion Parliament has now ratified." In this connection the Court quotes the Preamble and Articles 1 and 55.

In the case *Sei Fujii v. State of California* (Advance California Appellate Reports, May 5, 1950, p. 154) the State District Court of Appeals held on April 24, 1950: (1) The Charter of the United Nations (59 Stats. 1035ff.; U.S. Code Cong. Service, 79th Cong. 1945, p. 964) has become the supreme law of the land in accordance with the United States Constitution, Article VI, clause 2; (2) The Alien Property Initiative Act of 1920 (Stats. 1921, p. lxxxiii; Deering's Gen. Laws, Act 261) limiting ownership and use of property by aliens ineligible for citizenship to such rights only as they may have by virtue of treaties existing at the date of its enactment between this country and that of which such aliens were subjects or citizens, is in direct conflict with the terms and purposes of the Charter of the United Nations, is incompatible with Article

Spheres of Validity of International Law

tion of Human Rights, approved by the General Assembly of the United Nations on December 10, 1948, the character of an international agreement binding upon the members of the United Nations. The resolution by which the General Assembly adopted the Declaration has only the character of a recommendation. The Preamble states: "The General Assembly, Proclaims this Universal Declaration of Human Rights as a common standard of achievement for all peoples and all nations, to the end that every individual and every organ of society, keeping this Declaration constantly in mind, shall strive by teaching and education to promote respect for these rights and freedoms and by progressive measures, national and international, to secure their universal and effective recognition and observance, both among the peoples of Member States themselves and among the peoples of territories under their jurisdiction." Article 8 of the Declaration states: "Everyone has the right to an effective remedy by the competent national tribunals for acts violating the fundamental rights granted him by the constitution or by law." No international tribunal is suggested.[34]

Rights of individuals not only may be established but also may be abolished by a treaty. Since the state under general international

---

17 of the Declaration of Human Rights enacted by the General Assembly of the United Nations (December 10, 1948), and hence is invalid.

[34] The rights formulated in the Declaration are:

"Art. 1. All human beings are born free and equal in dignity and rights. They are endowed with reason and conscience and should act towards one another in a spirit of brotherhood.

"Art. 2. Everyone is entitled to all the rights and freedoms set forth in this Declaration, without distinction of any kind, such as race, colour, sex, language, religion, political or other opinion, national or social origin, property, birth or other status. Furthermore, no distinction shall be made on the basis of the political, jurisdictional or international status of the country or territory to which a person belongs, whether it be independent, trust, non-self-governing or under any other limitation of sovereignty.

"Art. 3. Everyone has the right to life, liberty and the security of person.

"Art. 4. No one shall be held in slavery or servitude; slavery and the slave trade shall be prohibited in all their forms.

"Art. 5. No one shall be subjected to torture or to cruel, inhuman or degrading treatment or punishment.

"Art. 6. Everyone has the right to recognition everywhere as a person before the law.

"Art. 7. All are equal before the law and are entitled without any discrimination to equal protection of the law. All are entitled to equal protection against

law has lawmaking power with respect to its nationals, it may, in a treaty concluded with another state, dispose of the rights, especially of the property rights of its nationals. Thus, the German

---

any discrimination in violation of this Declaration and against any incitement to such discrimination.

"ART. 8. Everyone has the right to an effective remedy by the competent national tribunals for acts violating the fundamental rights granted him by the constitution or by law.

"ART. 9. No one shall be subjected to arbitrary arrest, detention or exile.

"ART. 10. Everyone is entitled in full equality to a fair and public hearing by an independent and impartial tribunal, in the determination of his rights and obligations and of any criminal charge against him.

"ART. 11. (1) Everyone charged with a penal offence has the right to be presumed innocent until proved guilty according to law in a public trial at which he has had all the guarantees necessary for his defence. (2) No one shall be held guilty of any penal offense on account of any act or ommission which did not constitute a penal offense, under national or international law, at the time when it was committed. Nor shall a heavier penalty be imposed than the one that was applicable at the time the penal offence was committed.

"ART. 12. No one shall be subjected to arbitrary interference with his privacy, family, home or correspondence, nor to attacks upon his honour and reputation. Everyone has the right to the protection of the law against such interference or attacks.

"ART. 13. (1) Everyone has the right to freedom of movement and residence within the borders of each state. (2) Everyone has the right to leave any country, including his own, and to return to his country.

"ART. 14. (1) Everyone has the right to seek and to enjoy in other countries asylum from persecution. (2) This right may not be invoked in the case of prosecutions genuinely arising from nonpolitical crimes or from acts contrary to the purposes and principles of the United Nations.

"ART. 15. (1) Everyone has the right to a nationality. (2) No one shall be arbitrarily deprived of his nationality nor denied the right to change his nationality.

"ART. 16. (1) Men and women of full age, without any limitation due to race, nationality or religion, have the right to marry and to found a family. They are entitled to equal rights as to marriage, during marriage and at its dissolution. (2) Marriage shall be entered into only with the free and full consent of the intending spouses. (3) The family is the natural and fundamental group unit of society and is entitled to protection by society and the State.

"ART. 17. (1) Everyone has the right to own property alone as well as in association with others. (2) No one shall be arbitrarily deprived of his property.

"ART. 18. Everyone has the right to freedom of thought, conscience and religion; this right includes freedom to change his religion or belief, and freedom, either alone or in community with others and in public or private, to manifest his religion or belief in teaching, practice, worship and observance.

"ART. 19. Everyone has the right to freedom of opinion and expression; this

Spheres of Validity of International Law 147

Government in the Peace Treaty of Versailles (Part VIII, Annex III) "on behalf of themselves and so to bind all other persons interested" ceded to the Allied and Associated Governments all German

right includes freedom to hold opinions without interference and to seek, receive and impart information and ideas through any media and regardless of frontiers.

"ART. 20. (1) Everyone has the right to freedom of peaceful assembly and association. (2) No one may be compelled to belong to an association.

"ART. 21. (1) Everyone has the right to take part in the Government of his country, directly or through freely chosen representatives. (2) Everyone has the right of equal access to public service in his country. (3) The will of the people shall be the basis of the authority of government; this will shall be expressed in periodic and genuine elections which shall be by universal and equal suffrage and shall be held by secret vote or by equivalent free voting procedures.

"ART. 22. Everyone, as a member of society, has the right to social security and is entitled to realization, through national effort and international cooperation and in accordance with the organization and resources of each State, of the economic, social, and cultural rights indispensable for his dignity and the free development of his personality.

"ART. 23. (1) Everyone has the right to work, to free choice of employment, to just and favorable conditions of work and to protection against unemployment. (2) Everyone, without any discrimination, has the right to equal pay for equal work. (3) Everyone who works has the right to just and favorable remuneration insuring for himself and his family an existence worthy of human dignity, and supplemented, if necessary, by other means of social protection. (4) Everyone has the right to form and to join trade unions for the protection of his interests.

"ART. 24. Everyone has the right to rest and leisure, including reasonable limitation of working hours and periodic holidays with pay.

"ART. 25. (1) Everyone has the right to a standard of living adequate for the health and well-being of himself and of his family, including food, clothing, housing, and medical care and necessary social services, and the right to security in the event of unemployment, sickness, disability, widowhood, old age or other lack of livelihood in circumstances beyond his control. (2) Motherhood and childhood are entitled to special care and assistance. All children, whether born in or out of wedlock, shall enjoy the same social protection.

"ART. 26. (1) Everyone has the right to education. Education shall be free, at least in the elementary and fundamental stages. Elementary education shall be compulsory. Technical and professional education shall be made generally available and higher education shall be equally accessible to all on the basis of merit. (2) Education shall be directed to the full development of the human personality and to the strengthening of respect for human rights and fundamental freedoms. It shall promote understanding, tolerance and friendship among all nations, racial or religious groups, and shall further the activities of the United Nations for the maintenance of peace. (3) Parents have a prior right to choose the kind of education that shall be given to their children.

"ART. 27. (1) Everyone has the right freely to participate in the cultural

merchants ships of 1,600 tons gross and upwards.[35] In the Peace Treaty with Italy signed February 10, 1947 (Article 76), Italy waived "all claims of any description against the Allied and Associated Powers on behalf of the Italian Government or Italian nationals arising directly out of the war or out of actions taken because of the existence of a state of war . . . ."

5. The So-Called Fundamental Rights of the State

According to a view prevailing in the eighteenth and nineteenth centuries and maintained even today by some writers, every state has—in its capacity as a member of the family of nations—some

life of the community, to enjoy the arts and to share in scientific advancement and its benefits. (2) Everyone has the right to the protection of the moral and material interests resulting from any scientific, literary or artistic production of which he is the author.

"ART. 28. Everyone is entitled to a social and international order in which the rights and freedoms set forth in this Declaration can be fully realized.

"ART. 29. (1) Everyone has duties to the community in which alone the free and full development of his personality is possible. (2) In the exercise of his rights and freedoms, everyone shall be subject only to such limitations as are determined by law solely for the purpose of securing due recognition and respect for the rights and freedoms of others and of meeting the just requirements of morality, public order and the general welfare in a democratic society. (3) These rights and freedoms may in no case be exercised contrary to the purposes and principles of the United Nations.

"ART. 30. Nothing in this Declaration may be interpreted as implying for any State, group, or person any right to engage in any activity or to perform any act aimed at the destruction of any of the rights and freedoms set forth herein."

The representatives of Belgium, Denmark, France, the German Federal Republic, Iceland, Ireland, Italy, Luxembourg, the Netherlands, Norway, the Saar, Turkey, and the United Kingdom of Great Britain and Northern Ireland signed at Rome, on November 4, 1950, the text of a Convention for the protection of human rights and fundamental freedoms. According to Article 19, a European Court of Human Rights shall be established. But the persons whose rights or freedom, guaranteed in the Convention, are violated cannot bring a case before the court which, according to Article 48, is open only to the states contracting parties to the Convention and to a European Commission of Human Rights, the members of which are, according to Article 21, to be elected by a Committee of Ministers. (Cf. 45 *American Journal of International Law*, April, 1951, Supplement, 24 ff.)

[35] In the case *The Blonde*, the British Privy Council (1922 Law Reports, 1 A.C. 313, 335, 337) said: "There can be no doubt that Germany was com-

fundamental rights. These rights are not stipulated by general customary international law or by international agreements, as the other rights and duties of the states are, but originate in the nature of the state or of the international community. The norms constituting these fundamental rights of the state are supposed to be the ultimate basis and source of positive international law and, consequently, to have a greater obligatory force than the rules of positive international law created by custom and treaties.

a. *The natural-law doctrine as basis of the "fundamental rights of the state."* The idea of fundamental rights of the state deducible from the nature of the state or the international community is the application of the doctrine of natural law to the relationship between states. According to the natural-law doctrine,[36] the individual has—independent of any positive legal order—some rights which can be deduced directly from nature in general, and in particular from nature as created by God; so that the rights in question appear as stipulated by the will of God. The nature from which these rights are deduced is mostly considered to be the nature of man himself, in particular his reason; consequently one speaks of inborn or inherent rights, in contradistinction to rights conferred upon man by a positive legal order. Sometimes it is the nature of man's relation to other men, the nature of society, which is considered to be the true source of these fundamental rights of man. These rights are, according to most of the followers of the natural-law doctrine, freedom, equality, property, self-preservation.

An unbiased analysis of the natural-law doctrine shows that it is impossible to deduce from "nature" any rights. For the right of an individual presupposes the duty of another individual, and nature, that is, a complex of facts determined by the laws of causality, does not impose duties and therefore does not confer rights upon men or other beings. Cognition of nature is cognition of facts in their causal connection. From the statement that something "is"—and according to the principle of causality necessarily must

---

petent, on behalf of those nationals who were German subjects within the operation of the Treaty, to make cessions which would bind them and effect a transfer of their rights of property, as if the cession had been made personally by the owner concerned."

[36] Cf. *infra*, pp. 241, 310f., 315f.

or probably will be—never follows that something "ought" to be, that it is the duty or right of somebody to behave in a certain way. It is impossible to proceed from the sphere of the "is" on the way of a logical conclusion to the sphere of the "ought." Duties and rights presuppose the existence of a normative order, a system of norms prescribing or permitting a certain behavior of men, and this normative order can be established only by acts of human beings. Only human beings are capable of creating norms, that is, rules obligating and authorizing men. Insofar as human actions are supposed to be brought about by a psychic phenomenon called "will," norms are considered to be created by acts of will. The human will creating norms may manifest itself in acts consciously directed at the creation of norms, namely, in commands, in legislative acts, and the like; or in custom, that is, the habitual or usual course of acting accompanied by the conviction that men ought to act in this way. Nature has no "will." The conception of a nature endowed with will—and this conception is implied in the conception of a nature as legislative authority—a nature imposing duties and conferring rights is rather an animistic myth than a scientific interpretation of facts. Acts of will of superhuman personal beings, however, lie beyond human science, in particular beyond legal science.

Rights are always stipulated by a normative order established by acts of human beings, that is, by a positive system of morality or by positive law. If "natural" rights are maintained, we have to distinguish two different possibilities: either these rights are really stipulated by a positive order; then the statement that these rights are "natural" or "fundamental," i.e., that they are deduced from nature, is, in itself, scientifically incorrect and meaningless, but has the political function of justifying the stipulation of these rights; or the rights characterized as "natural" or "fundamental" are not stipulated by a positive order; then the statement has the character of a postulate, directed at the legislator, to stipulate such rights; and the postulate may be realized—in the field of law—either by constitutional reform or by revolution.

b. *The fundamental rights as principles presupposed by international law.* The clear distinction between positive duties and rights and mere ideologies or political postulates is of the greatest

Spheres of Validity of International Law 151

importance for a scientific presentation of the law. It is only another version of the old natural-law doctrine when a writer tries to maintain the theory of fundamental rights of the state by arguing in the following way: it is necessary to distinguish in any legal order the rights stipulated by this order from the legal principles presupposed by this legal order. The so-called fundamental rights of the states are legal principles which are the conditions on which an international law is possible at all, the legal principles on which the positive international law is built up. We can find out these principles by an analysis of the nature of international law. In other terms, the fundamental rights of the state can be deduced from the nature of international law. This is the same idea as expressed by the above-mentioned statement that the fundamental rights of the states are the ultimate basis or source of positive international law and have therefore a greater obligatory force than the rules of positive international law.

This version of the natural-law doctrine is logically just as impossible as is the classical version of that doctrine. Legal principles can never be presupposed by a legal order; they can only be created in conformity with this order. For they are "legal" only because and insofar as they are established on the basis of a positive legal order. The only principle which may and must be presupposed is the fundamental principle determining the first constitution of the legal order, "constitution" meaning the rules determining the methods by which the law is to be created. These methods are custom, legislation, treaties.[37] Certainly the creation of substantive law is not a creation out of nothing. Legislation as well as custom is directed by some general principles. But these principles are moral or political principles, and not legal principles, and consequently cannot impose legal duties or confer legal rights upon men or states as long as these principles are not stipulated by legislation, custom, or treaties. As legal principles they are not the source or basis of the legal order by which they are stipulated; on the contrary, the positive legal order is their basis or source. Hence they have no greater obligatory force than the other norms stipulated by the positive legal order, unless the positive legal order itself grants

---

[37] Cf. *infra*, pp. 303ff.

them a greater obligatory force by making their abolishment or modification more difficult. This is impossible if the legal order—as general international law—has the character of customary law, if the rules of this order acquire as well as lose their validity by custom.

c. *The fundamental rights deduced from the personality of the state.* The so-called fundamental rights of the states are rights of the states only insofar as they are stipulated by general international law, which has the character of customary law. This is the only doctrine which can be maintained from the point of view of legal positivism. But even writers who, in principle, accept this view fall back to the natural-law doctrine by trying to deduce the fundamental rights of the state from the nature of the state as an international personality. However, "international personality of the state" means only that general international law imposes duties and confers rights upon states (and that means, upon individuals as organs of the states). The state is an international personality because it is a subject of international duties and rights. This statement says nothing about the content of these duties and rights. The concept of legal personality is a thoroughly formal concept. Hence it is impossible to deduce from the fact that the state is an international personality some definite rights of the state, such as the right of legal equality, the right of respect (or dignity), the right of independence (or sovereignty), the right of existence (or self-preservation), the right of nonintervention on the part of other states, the right of jurisdiction. These are the rights which are usually presented as "fundamental" rights of the state.

The idea of deriving these rights from the international personality of the state presupposes the assumption that the state exists as a personality, that is, as a subject of rights, prior to its entering the international community, and that it enters voluntarily the international community, and only under the condition that it retains these rights, especially the right of equality and the right of independence (sovereignty). Since entering the international community implies submission to international law, and this implies a certain restriction of the natural freedom, i.e., the sovereignty, of the state, the state is supposed to enter the international com-

Spheres of Validity of International Law 153

munity, that is to say, to consent to this restriction of its sovereignty, only under the condition that the other states accept the same restriction of their sovereignty. An essential element of this view is the idea that the international community, or the legal order constituting this community, i.e., general international law, is based on the common consent of the states, or, which amounts to the same, on a contract of the members of this community. This doctrine, widespread among writers on international law, has exactly the same character as the natural-law doctrine concerning the basis of the state or what amounts to the same, of the reason of validity of the national legal order. According to this theory, men are in their state of nature free and equal. The state, the national legal order, comes into existence by the fact that the free and equal individuals assent to an agreement concerning a social order regulating their mutual behavior. Every individual restricts voluntarily his freedom in the interest of all the other individuals, on the condition that the others restrict their freedom in the same way. This is the so-called social contract. Such an event, however, has never taken place. Social order is not the result of a contract entered into by the individuals to be bound by the social order; it is the result of force and custom. And the individual is bound by the social order not because he gives his consent to the social order. He is bound without and even against his will. He is born into a community, and is, from the very moment of his birth, subjected to the social order constituting this community. Hence the doctrine of the social contract is a fiction, the purpose of which is not to explain the origin of the state, or, what amounts to the same, the existence of the national legal order, but to justify this fact, that is to say, to justify the fact that the individuals are bound by a legal order imposing duties and conferring rights upon them. This justification presupposes that equality and freedom are the highest values. If men are by their very nature equal and free, they can be bound only by a social order based on their consent, that is to say, established by a contract voluntarily entered into by those who are to be bound by it.

d. *The common consent of the states as basis of international law.* But actually men are by their nature neither free nor equal; and even if they were free and equal by their nature, they are, by law, bound to behave in a certain way, without their consent.

The theory of a common consent of the states voluntarily entering the international community, as the basis of this community or of the international law constituting this community, rests on the same fiction. The states are bound by general international law without and even against their will. Thus, for instance, a new state, as soon as it comes into existence, has all the rights and all the duties stipulated by general international law, without any act of recognition of general international law on the part of this state being necessary. It may be assumed that international law becomes applicable to a newly established community when the latter is recognized as a state by the other states. Such recognition implies the ascertainment that the community fulfills the requirements of a state in the sense of international law.[38] Among these requirements, however, is not the condition that the new state submit to existing international law.[39] Just as the individual does not submit voluntarily to the law of the state which is binding upon him without and even against his will, a state does not submit voluntarily to international law, which is binding upon it whether it does recognize international law or does not recognize it. No state can withdraw from the international community or, what amounts to the same, from the international law constituting this community; and as long as it is not a member of this community, that is to say, as long as international law does not apply to it, it is not a "state"; it is legally nonexistent. When the so-called fundamental rights of the state are presented as derived from the nature of the international community or from the nature or personality of the state, they are, in truth, presupposed as established by a kind of natural international law conferring these rights upon the national community prior to its entering the international community, at a time when the national community exists in a "state of nature" analogous to that state of nature in which the individual—according to the natural-law doctrine—exists prior to his entering the national com-

---

[38] Cf. *infra*, pp. 264ff.

[39] As to the doctrine that international law must be recognized by the state in order to be binding on it, cf. *infra*, pp. 313, 432ff.

munity, the state. In the theory of national law this fiction was abandoned long ago; in the theory of international law it is still—consciously or unconsciously—maintained, especially regarding the most important of the fundamental rights, the right of equality and the right of sovereignty.

e. *Equality and sovereignty as fundamental rights of the state.* However, equality and sovereignty are not rights with which the state is endowed when it enters the international community. The states are legally equal insofar as general international law treats them in this way, i.e., insofar as general international law imposes upon all of them the same duties and confers upon all of them the same rights. This, however, is evidently not the case. Littoral states have under general international law duties and rights which inland states have not,[40] just as men have under national law other duties and rights than women. Legal inequality of states is not incompatible with a legal regulation of interstate relations. As a matter of fact, there are treaties by which privileges are conferred upon some of the contracting states, and are not conferred upon the others, which do not lose their quality as states by such treatment. The Charter of the United Nations confers upon five great powers the privilege of the so-called veto right, without violating the principle of equality allegedly established by general international law. And in spite of the legal inequality of the states under the Charter, the latter proclaims in its Article 2, paragraph 1: "The Organization is based on the principle of the sovereign equality of all its Members." It is evidently not equality in the law, but equality before the law, which is meant by the right of equality attributed by jurisprudence to individuals as well as to states, in spite of the fact that men as well as states are actually not equal. But there are differences which the law does and differences which the law does not recognize as relevant. Equality before the law means that the law-applying organs, in applying the law, must not make a difference which is not recognized by the law, that the law shall be applied as the law intends to be applied. Equality before the law means application of the law in conformity with the law, lawfulness, legality. It is a postulate directed at the law-applying organs, not

---

[40] Cf. *infra*, pp. 219ff.

a "right" of the subjects. Sometimes certain principles of positive international law, such as the principle of unanimity (in contradistinction to the principle of the majority vote) and especially the principle that treaties are binding only upon the contracting states, or the principle that no state has jurisdiction over another state, are presented as consequences of the "right of equality." Insofar as these principles prevail, equality of the states in the law may be assumed. But these principles are valid only with important restrictions, as will be shown in another connection.[41]

There is no, and there cannot be, a fundamental right of sovereignty of the states, if this term is taken in its original sense—of supreme authority.[42] As subjects of international rights the states are subjected to international law, even if international law is considered to be part of national law. Hence, the states as subjects of rights are as little "sovereign" as the individual is "sovereign" under national law. The authority of international law or, what amounts to the same, the authority of the international community is established above the states, just as the authority of the national community, the state, is established above the individuals. If the so-called sovereignty of the state is considered as compatible with international law, it can mean only, as pointed out, that a state in the sense of international law is legally subjected only to international law—customary general or conventional particular international law—and not to the national law of another state. If by "sovereignty" is meant that a community, in order to be a state, must be subordinated only to international law, and not to the national law of another state, sovereignty may be considered as an essential quality of the state. Since the state as a national community is constituted by a national legal order, it is more correct to formulate the principle concerned by the statement that a coercive order constitutes a state in the sense of international law if it is subordinated only to international law.

To present the principle that a community is a state or, what amounts to the same, is "sovereign" in the sense of international law, if it is subjected only to international law, as a "right" of

---

[41] Cf. *infra*, pp. 345ff.
[42] Cf. *supra*, pp. 438ff.

Spheres of Validity of International Law

sovereignty, is hardly correct. Sovereignty in this sense is not the right of a state, for it is a condition under which a community is a state and has the rights of a state under international law. The idea that sovereignty is a "right" of the state may be—and actually is—misused to prevent the establishment of certain international institutions considered to be incompatible with this "right", as for instance, the establishment by a treaty of an international tribunal having jurisdiction in matters of human rights, or having compulsory jurisdiction in all disputes arising among the states that are contracting parties to the treaty. A state may refuse to conclude such a treaty, but it cannot justify its attitude by its "right" of sovereignty. From the right of sovereignty one has deduced the legal power of a state to withdraw by a unilateral act from an international community, in spite of the fact that the treaty constituting this community does not confer upon the members such a right.[43] But no such power can be deduced from the alleged "right" of sovereignty.

International law imposes upon the states the obligation to respect certain interests of the other states. The violation of certain interests of a state thus protected by international law, especially the violation of its territorial integrity, is usually characterized as violation of its right of sovereignty. But there is no essential difference between this and any other illegal interference in the legally protected sphere of interests of a state by another state; and the international delicts concerned may be described without the use of the misleading term "sovereignty."

f. *Other fundamental rights.* The question whether and to what extent the other so-called fundamental rights exist, such as the right to existence, the right to respect, the right to nonintervention on the part of other states, the right of jurisdiction, cannot be answered by the fictitious presupposition that the state, by entering the international community, retains these rights, but only by an analysis of positive international law.[44]

---

[43] Cf. *infra,* pp. 356ff., 445f.

[44] As to the right of self-preservation, cf. *supra,* pp. 58f., 157, the right to nonintervention, *supra,* pp. 63f.

The International Law Commission, established by the General Assembly of the United Nations (123d meeting on November 21, 1947) has prepared a

6. Communities Not Having the Character of States as Subjects of International Law

Not only states and individuals, but also communities which have not the character of states, are subjects of international law.

Draft Declaration on the Rights and Duties of States to be adopted by the General Assembly. The Declaration contains the following provisions:

"ART. 1. Every State has the right to independence and hence to exercise freely, without dictation by any other State, all its legal powers, including the choice of its own form of government.

"ART. 2. Every State has the right to exercise jurisdiction over its territory and over all persons and things therein, subject to the immunities recognized by international law.

"ART. 3. Every State has the duty to refrain from intervention in the internal or external affairs of any other State.

"ART. 4. Every State has the duty to refrain from fomenting civil strife in the territory of another State, and to prevent the organization within its territory of activities calculated to foment such civil strife.

"ART. 5. Every State has the right to equality in law with every other State.

"ART. 6. Every State has the duty to treat all persons under its jurisdiction with respect for human rights and fundamental freedoms, without distinction as to race, sex, language, or religion.

"ART. 7. Every State has the duty to ensure that conditions prevailing in its territory do not menace international peace and order.

"ART. 8. Every State has the duty to settle its disputes with other States by peaceful means in such a manner that international peace and security, and justice, are not endangered.

"ART. 9. Every State has the duty to refrain from resorting to war as an instrument of national policy, and to refrain from the threat or use of force against the territorial integrity or political independence of another State, or in any other manner inconsistent with international law and order.

"ART. 10. Every State has the duty to refrain from giving assistance to any State which is acting in violation of Article 9, or against which the United Nations is taking preventive or enforcement action.

"ART. 11. Every State has the duty to refrain from recognizing any territorial acquisition by another State acting in violation of Article 9.

"ART. 12. Every State has the right of individual or collective self-defense against armed attack.

"ART. 13. Every State has the duty to carry out in good faith its obligations arising from treaties and other sources of international law, and it may not invoke provisions in its constitution or its laws as an excuse for failure to perform this duty.

"ART. 14. Every State has the duty to conduct its relations with other States in accordance with international law and with the principle that the sovereignty of each State is subject to the supremacy of international law."

These may be communities of individuals or communities of states.

a. *Communities of individuals.* (1) THE CHURCH. A community of individuals which, although not having the character of a state, is a subject of international law, is the Roman Catholic Church represented by the Pope, the so-called Holy See. It is generally recognized that the Pope as Head of the Church may conclude with states certain treaties, especially for the purpose of regulating ecclesiastical matters. The latter treaties, called concordats, have a legal character, for they impose obligations and confer rights upon the contracting parties. The obligations and rights established by these treaties are international obligations and rights, and their violation is an international delict. The treaties concluded by the Church with the states have their reason of validity not in any national law. For national law, as the law of one state, cannot impose obligations or confer rights upon the Pope as Head of the Church, or what amounts to the same, upon the Catholic Church as such, since the Church is a community the legal existence of which extends beyond the sphere of validity of any national legal order. The Church is an order constituting a community which comprises the Catholics of the whole world. Only the norm of general international law concerning treaties can confer upon these agreements, especially upon the concordats, a law-creating effect. As a subject of international law, the Church has the right of legation, that is to say, to send and receive diplomatic envoys who enjoy the privileges granted by general international law to such persons. However, there are differences between the Catholic Church and a state as subjects of international law, especially as concerns the sanctions to be executed by and against them. The Catholic Church cannot wage war, nor can war be waged against the Church. Only reprisals by which one encroaches on the legal rights of the other are possible.

The concordats concluded with the Roman Catholic Church must be distinguished from the treaty by which the State of the Vatican City has been established, and the treaties concluded with this state.

The State of the Vatican City has been created by a treaty, concluded on February 11, 1929, between Italy and the Holy See, the so-called Lateran Treaty. In this treaty Italy "recognizes the full ownership, exclusive dominion, and sovereign authority and jurisdiction of the Holy See over the Vatican," i.e., a certain territory within Rome. That means that Italy gave up a part of its territory for the purpose of a new state being established on it. This territory does not exceed one hundred acres; nevertheless it is the territory of a state. Its population does not reach seven hundred and is composed almost exclusively of individuals residing therein by virtue of their office. Nevertheless it is the population of a state. Since the Pope is the government, all the elements of a state in the sense of international law are existent. Italy recognized in this treaty the State of the Vatican City under the sovereignty of the Supreme Pontiff (Article 26). Article 24 of the treaty contains the declaration that the Holy See, that is, the Pope as the head of the new state, does not desire to take and shall not take part in temporal rivalries between other states and in international conferences concerned with such matters "save and except in the event of such parties making a mutual appeal to the pacific mission of the Holy See, the latter reserving in any event the right of exercising its moral and spiritual power." Accordingly, the same article provides that the Vatican City shall in all circumstances be considered as neutral and inviolable territory. By this treaty, concluded between the Roman Catholic Church and Italy, some international duties are imposed and some international rights are conferred upon the new state. This state is a juristic person different from the Roman Catholic Church. The Head of the Church is at the same time the Head of the State of the Vatican City. There exists a personal union between the Church and this state. But the State of the Vatican City, limited to a certain territory, must not be identified with the Church, which is tied to no limited territory. That means the territorial sphere of validity of the State of the Vatican City is limited, as every state territory is, whereas the territorial sphere of validity of the Roman Catholic Church is not limited. The Church, however, is not outside space, as is sometimes stated. The social order we call the Catholic Church has a territorial sphere of validity as any normative order regulating human behavior has.

Spheres of Validity of International Law

Only, this territorial sphere of validity, the legal existence of the Catholic Church in space, is not limited.

(2) STATELIKE COMMUNITIES. (a) Insurgents recognized as belligerent power. There are statelike communities which do not fulfill all the requirements of a state in the sense of international law but nevertheless are considered to be subjects of international obligations and rights. Such a community is established by the fact that in a civil war the insurgents gain effective control over a part of the territory and the population of the state within which the civil war takes place. If the insurgents are recognized as a belligerent power, the rules of general international law concerning the conduct of war and neutrality apply to their relations with other states. Hence they are subjects of international law, although the effective control which the government of the insurgents exercises over a certain territory and its population is not yet definitely stabilized because the civil war is still going on. The conditions under which the recognition of insurgents as a belligerent power is possible will be discussed in Part III of this treatise.[45]

(b) Protectorates. Another case of a statelike community which may be a subject of international law is a state which, by a treaty concluded with another state, submits to a protectorate exercised by the latter. The protectorate, as pointed out,[46] consists in the fact that the protector state is competent to manage, through its own organs, and that means, in conformity with its own constitution, all or the most important international affairs of the protected community. The effect of a protectorate treaty is that a body politic under protectorate is partly subjected to the national legal order of another state and not exclusively to the international legal order, and hence has lost that independence which is an essential element of a state in the sense of international law. It is a statelike community, not a full state. If it has conferred upon the protector state only part of its competence in international matters, there remain between the protected body politic and other states relations which are not within the sphere of the pro-

---

[45] Cf. *infra*, pp. 201ff.
[46] Cf. *supra*, p. 111.

tectorate; hence the statelike community under protectorate has international obligations and rights independently of the protector state. In this case the protected community has a restricted international personality. If, however, a state confers upon another state its whole competence in international affairs, then it disappears completely from the sphere of international relations and cannot be considered as a subject of international law. The international personality of the protected community is, so to speak, completely absorbed by the protector state, which alone is a subject of international law.[47]

(c) *Mandated and trust territories not subjects of international law.* According to Article 75 of the Charter of the United Nations an "international trusteeship system" is established under the authority of the United Nations "for the administration and supervision of such territories as may be placed thereunder by subsequent individual agreements." The trusteeship system was intended to replace the mandate system established in Article 22 of the Covenant of the League of Nations, which runs as follows:

"1. To those colonies and territories which as a consequence of the late war have ceased to be under the sovereignty of the States which formerly governed them and which are inhabited by peoples not yet able to stand by themselves under the strenuous conditions of the modern world, there should be applied the principle that

---

[47] In the case of *H. C. van Hoogstraten v. Low Lum Seng* (Federated Malay States, Supreme Court, 1939; Annual Digest 1938–1940, Case No. 16) the question arose whether the Federated Malay States, under the protectorate of Great Britain, were at war with Germany. The Court held that the Federated Malay States were at war with Germany: "Seeing that the Suzerain or Protecting Power has, and alone has, the power to place the Protected State at war or at peace, it is clear I must examine the acts of the Protecting Power and if such examination does not clearly answer the question, then the source of information to which I must address myself is to the Executive Government where lies the power to make war or not to make war, and in the present instance that means the British Government whose representative is the High Commissioner." The court then referred to the official gazettes containing a number of declarations by the British high commissioner and concluded: "These acts of the High Commissioner which are the acts of the Suzerain or Protecting Power are clear and unequivocal. They place the Federated Malay States at war with Germany. It therefore follows that all German nationals are alien enemies."

Spheres of Validity of International Law

the well-being and development of such peoples form a sacred trust of civilization and that securities for the performance of this trust should be embodied in this Covenant. 2. The best method of giving practical effect to this principle is that the tutelage of such peoples should be intrusted to advanced nations, who by reason of their resources, their experience or their geographical position can best undertake this responsibility, and who are willing to accept it, and that this tutelage should be exercised by them as Mandatories on behalf of the League. 3. The character of the mandate must differ according to the stage of the development of the people, the geographical situation of the territory, its economic conditions and other similar circumstances. 4. Certain communities formerly belonging to the Turkish Empire have reached a stage of development where their existence as independent nations can be provisionally recognized subject to the rendering of administrative advice and assistance by a Mandatory until such time as they are able to stand alone. The wishes of these communities must be a principal consideration in the selection of the Mandatory. 5. Other peoples, especially those of Central Africa, are at such a stage that the Mandatory must be responsible for the administration of the territory under conditions which will guarantee freedom of conscience and religion, subject only to the maintenance of public order and morals, the prohibition of abuses such as the slave trade, the arms traffic and the liquor traffic, and the prevention of the establishment of fortifications or military and naval bases and of military training of the natives for other than police purposes and the defense of territory, and will also secure equal opportunities for the trade and commerce of other Members of the League. 6. There are territories, such as Southwest Africa and certain of the South Pacific islands, which, owing to the sparseness of their population, or their small size, or their remoteness from the centers of civilization, or their geographical contiguity to the territory of the Mandatory, and other circumstances, can be best administered under the laws of the Mandatory as integral portions of its territory, subject to the safeguards above mentioned in the interests of the indigenous population. 7. In every case of mandate, the Mandatory shall render to the Council an annual report in reference to the territory committed to its charge. 8. The degree of authority, control, or administration to be exercised by the Mandatory shall, if not previously agreed upon by the Members of the League, be explicitly defined in each case by the Council. 9. A permanent Commission shall be constituted to receive and examine the annual reports of the Mandatories and to advise the Council on all matters relating to the observance of the mandates." With the dissolution of the League of Nations, which implies the termination of the validity of the Covenant, the legal basis of the mandate system, and hence the mandate system itself, has ceased to exist.[48]

The basic objectives of the trusteeship system, laid down in Article 76 of the Charter, are: "a. to further international peace and security; b. to promote the political, economic, social, and educational advancement of the inhabitants of the trust territories, and their progressive development towards self-government or independence as may be appropriate to the particular circumstances of each territory and its peoples and the freely expressed wishes of the peoples concerned, and as may be provided by

---

[48] The essential element of the legal status established by a "mandate" consists in the supervision to be exercised by the League of Nations, represented by the Council. Together with the legal existence of the League, the function of supervision was terminated. If there is no supervision to be exercised by the League, there is no mandate, which, according to Article 22 of the Covenant, had to be exercised "on behalf of the League." In its resolution of April 18, 1946 (by which the League was dissolved), the Assembly expressly declared that "on the termination of the League's existence its functions with respect to the mandated territories will come to an end." However, the International Court of Justice, in its advisory opinion of July 11, 1950, on the *International status of South-West Africa* (International Court of Justice, Reports, 1950, p. 128), declared that although the League's functions came to an end, the mandates themselves did not come to an end, and that consequently "South-West Africa is a territory under the international Mandate assumed by the Union of South Africa on December 17th 1920." The Court declared further that the supervisory functions are to be exercised by the United Nations; although the territory of South-West Africa was not placed under the trusteeship system of the United Nations and although the Court stated "that the provisions of Chapter XII of the Charter 'International Trusteeship System' do not impose on the Union of South Africa a legal obligation to place the Territory under the Trusteeship System."

Spheres of Validity of International Law

the terms of each trusteeship agreement; c. to encourage respect for human rights and for fundamental freedoms for all without distinction as to race, sex, language, or religion, and to encourage recognition of the interdependence of the peoples of the world; and d. to ensure equal treatment in social, economic, and commercial matters for all Members of the United Nations and their nationals, and also equal treatment for the latter in the administration of justice, without prejudice to the attainment of the foregoing objectives and subject to the provisions of Article 80."

Article 80 provides: "Except as may be agreed upon in individual trusteeship agreements, made under Articles 77, 79, and 81, placing each territory under the trusteeship system, and until such agreements have been concluded, nothing in this Chapter shall be construed in or of itself to alter in any manner the rights whatsoever of any states or any peoples or the terms of existing international instruments to which Members of the United Nations may respectively be parties."

According to Articles 79, 83, and 85, the terms of trusteeship for each territory to be placed under the trusteeship system shall be agreed upon by "the states directly concerned" and shall be approved by the General Assembly or, if the trust territory is designated in the agreement as a strategic area, by the Security Council. That the agreement must be approved by an organ of the United Nations means that the United Nations on the one hand, and the states directly concerned on the other hand, must be contracting parties to the trusteeship agreement. The Charter does not define the concept of "states directly concerned." It only stipulates that in case a territory formerly held under mandate in conformity with the Covenant of the League of Nations is to be placed under the trusteeship system, the mandatory power, if a member of the United Nations, is included in "the states directly concerned." Some, not all, of the former mandate territories have been placed under trusteeship by the states which, in conformity with the Covenant of the League of Nations, had been the mandatory powers.[49] The former Japanese-mandated

---

[49] The following former mandated territories have been placed under the trusteeship system: by Great Britain: British Togoland, British Cameroons,

islands were placed under trusteeship by an agreement in which the United States of America was designated as the administering authority. This procedure is in conformity with general international law only if it is supposed that the mandatory powers, after the dissolution of the League, which implied the termination of the mandate system, and the United States after the surrender of Japan, extended their sovereignty over the respective territories.[50] Otherwise they were not entitled to dispose of these territories. Under Article 81 of the Charter not only members but also a nonmember state may be designated in the trusteeship agreement as the administering authority. At its 316th Plenary Meeting, the General Assembly approved a trusteeship agreement for Somaliland, a former Italian colony. In this agreement Italy, not a member of the United Nations, is designated as administering authority.

In the trusteeship agreements no other functions are conferred upon the United Nations than those indicated in the Charter. These functions are, with respect to nonstrategic areas, to "consider reports submitted by the administering authority; accept petitions and examine them in consultation with the administering authority; provide for periodic visits to the respective trust territories at

---

Tanganyika; by the Commonwealth of Australia: New Guinea; by France: French Togoland, French Cameroons; by Belgium: Ruanda-Urundi; by New Zealand: Western Samoa; by Australia, New Zealand, and the United Kingdom: Nauru; by the United States of America: the former Japanese-mandated islands. The Union of South Africa refused to place the former mandated territory of South-West Africa under the trusteeship system (cf. *supra*, p. 164n.).

[50] In Article 2 (d) of the Peace Treaty with Japan, signed at San Francisco on September 8, 1951, "Japan renounces all right, title and claim in connection with the League of Nations Mandate System, and accepts the action of the United Nations Security Council of April 2, 1947, extending the trusteeship system to the Pacific Islands formerly under mandate to Japan." Article 3 of the peace treaty reads as follows: "Japan will concur in any proposal of the United States to the United Nations to place under its trusteeship system, with the United States as the sole administering authority, Nansei Shoto south of 29° north latitude (including the Ryukyu Islands and the Daito Islands), Nanpo Shoto south of Sofu Gan (including the Bonin Islands, Rosario Island and the Volcano Islands) and Parece Vela and Marcus Island. Pending the making of such a proposal and affirmative action thereon, the United States will have the right to exercise all and any powers of administration, legislation and jurisdiction over the territory and inhabitants of these islands, including their territorial waters."

Spheres of Validity of International Law

times agreed upon with the administering authority" (Article 87); and to approve alterations or amendments of the trusteeship agreements (Article 85). These functions are to be exercised by the General Assembly and, under its authority, by the Trusteeship Council. With respect to the strategic areas, the Charter only provides in Article 83: "1. All functions of the United Nations relating to strategic areas, including the approval of the terms of the trusteeship agreements and of their alteration or amendment, shall be exercised by the Security Council. 2. The basic objectives set forth in Article 76 shall be applicable to the people of each strategic area. 3. The Security Council shall, subject to the provisions of the trusteeship agreements and without prejudice to security considerations, avail itself of the assistance of the Trusteeship Council to perform those functions of the United Nations under the trusteeship system relating to political, economic, social, and educational matters in the strategic areas."

Whereas the mandated territories, according to Article 22 of the Covenant, were to be administered by the Mandatories as a "tutelage" "on behalf of the League," and hence could be considered as placed under the sovereignty of the League of Nations, the legal status of the trust territories can hardly be interpreted in an analogous way. The Charter does not provide that these territories shall be administered "on behalf" of the United Nations and the powers to be conferred upon the Organization in conformity with the Charter—and actually conferred upon it by the existing trusteeship agreements—are so restricted that there is no reason to assume that the territorial sovereignty over the trust territories is vested in the United Nations. The actually existing trust territories are under the territorial sovereignty of the states which, in the exercise of their right to dispose of these territories, placed them under trusteeship by agreements entered into with the United Nations, and have become administering authorities within the meaning of Article 81.[51] Hence the trust

---
[51] Article 5 of the Trusteeship Agreement for British Togoland runs as follows: ". . . the Administering Authority shall have full powers of legislation, administration and jurisdiction in the Territory, and shall administer it in accordance with his own laws as an integral part of his territory with such modification as may be required by local conditions and subject to the provisions of the

territories are not subjects of international law. The Charter does not preclude a trusteeship agreement by which the sovereignty over the trust territory is conferred upon the United Nations itself. According to Article 81, the Organization may even be made the administering authority. But none of the existing trusteeship agreements has conferred upon the Organization the sovereignty over the trust territory or the function of administering authority.

b. *Communities of states.* (1) FEDERAL STATE. The protectorate treaty constitutes the community of a state and of a statelike body politic. This community is characterized by a partial or total centralization of the foreign affairs of the two members of this community, of which only one is a full state in the sense of international law. For it is centralization of the administration of the foreign affairs when the foreign affairs of two political bodies are administered by one and the same organ, and not by two organs different from and independent of each other. If the centralization of the administration of foreign affairs is complete, international law ceases to be applicable to the relations between the protector state and the protected body politic. The community constituted by the protectorate treaty is international only with regard to its creation by an international agreement entered into by two states, but not with regard to its structure. From the point of view of international law, a protectorate with total centralization of foreign affairs is an internal matter of the protector state, which alone appears in international relations. If the centralization is only partial, so that the body politic under protectorate retains a certain competence in foreign affairs, both members are subjects of international law; but the international community constituted by the protectorate treaty is not a subject of international law.[52]

United Nations Charter and of this Agreement . . . ." Although the formula "as an integral part of his territory" does not appear in all trusteeship agreements, it correctly expresses the legal status of all trust territories in relation to the administering authorities.

[52] The so-called Protectorate of Bohemia and Moravia established by an agreement concluded on March 15, 1939, by the German Reich and the Czechoslovak Republic is not a true protectorate. By this agreement the Czechoslovak Republic conferred upon the Government of the German Reich not only the

Spheres of Validity of International Law

Centralization of the administration of foreign affairs of two or more states may also be achieved by a treaty of the states concerned conferring the administration of their foreign affairs not upon an organ of one of them, but upon an organ of the community com-

---

power to conduct the foreign affairs of the Republic but other powers which are far beyond the power which a protector state has in relation to the protected community. In the agreement, the President of the Czechoslovak Republic "placed the destiny of the Czech people and country with confidence in the hands of the Fuehrer of the German Reich. The Fuehrer accepted this declaration and expressed his determination to take the Czech people under the protection of the German Reich and to guarantee to it an autonomous development of its national life in accordance with its particular characteristics." That means that the Czechoslovak Republic conferred upon the German Reich all the legal power the Republic had under international law, whereas the Reich assumed only the obligation to grant autonomy to the Czech people. The agreement of March 15, 1939, means the incorporation of the territory and population of the Czechoslovak Republic into the German Reich, and hence the end of the existence of the former. A decree which the German Government, on the basis of the agreement, issued unilaterally on March 16, 1939, contains, among others, the following provisions:

The territories of the former Czecho-Slovak State occupied by the German troops in March, 1939, belong henceforth to the territory of the Great German Reich, and enter under its protection as the "Protectorate of Bohemia and Moravia." In so far as the defense of the Reich demands it, the Fuehrer and Reich Chancellor will make for the individual portions of these territories dispositions which may diverge from this rule. (Art. I.) The Protectorate of Bohemia and Moravia is autonomous and administers itself. It exercises its sovereign rights which fall to it within the framework of the Protectorate in accordance with the political, military, and economic needs of the Reich. These sovereign rights it exercises through its own organs and its own authorities, with its own officials. (Art. III.) The head of the autonomous administration of the Protectorate of Bohemia and Moravia enjoys the protection and the rights of the head of a state. The head of the Protectorate must have the confidence of the Fuehrer and Reich Chancellor for the discharge of his office. (Art. IV.) As the guardian of Reich interests, the Fuehrer and Chancellor appoints a "Reich Protector in Bohemia and Moravia." His seat of authority is Prague. As the representative of the Fuehrer and Reich Chancellor, and as the plenipotentiary of the Reich Government, the Reich Protector has the task of ensuring that the lines of policy laid down by the Fuehrer and Reich Chancellor are observed. Membership of the Government of the Protectorate is subject to confirmation by the Reich Protector. This confirmation can be withdrawn. The Reich Protector is authorized to inform himself about all measures taken by the Government of the Protectorate and to give advice. He can object to measures which are calculated to injure the Reich, and when there is danger of delay can himself issue decrees necessary in the common interest. The promulgation of laws, decrees, and other legal enactments as well as the execution of admin-

posed of the contracting states, the constitution of the community being stipulated by that treaty. The community constituted by such a treaty has the character of a state, and the constitution the character of national law when not only the administration of foreign affairs but also other functions of the contracting states are conferred upon organs of the new community; that is to say, when the degree of centralization established by the constituting treaty is that characteristic of a state. This is the way by which a federal state may be established. By concluding such a treaty and submitting to the federal constitution, the contracting states lose their character as states in the sense of international law. They become so-called component states of the federal state provided that they retain, at least partly, the functions typical of a state: legislation, administration, and judiciary, the competence regarding these functions being divided between the federation and its members. The centralization in the field of foreign affairs may not be complete; the component states may have some competence left in this respect, for instance, the power to conclude treaties with third states in certain fields. Then they may be considered as subjects of international law, with a restricted personality. But since the component states have this competence in accordance with the federal constitution, the organs of the

---

istrative measures and valid judicial decisions, is to be stopped when the Reich Protector objects to them. (Art. V.) The foreign affairs of the Protectorate, and in particular, the protection of its subjects abroad, are taken over by the Reich. The Reich will direct foreign affairs in such a way as to correspond to the common interest. The Protectorate will have a representative accredited to the Reich Government with the official designation of "Minister" (*Gesandter*). (Art. VI.) The Reich provides for the military protection of the Protectorate. In carrying out this protection the Reich keeps garrisons and military establishments in the Protectorate. For the maintenance of internal security and order the Protectorate can set up its own bodies. Their organization, strength, number and armament are determined by the Reich Government. (Art. VII.) Insofar as the common interest demands it, the Reich can promulgate legal enactments applicable to the Protectorate. Insofar as there is a common need for it, the Reich can take administrative branches into its own administration and set up the requisite Reich authorities for them. The Reich Government can take measures necessary for the maintenance of security and order. (Art. XI.)

In view of the far-reaching restrictions of the autonomy granted to the Czech people, there were of course no "sovereign" rights left to the autonomous administration, in spite of the use of that term in Article III of the decree.

component states, in concluding treaties within the competence conferred upon them by the federal constitution, may also be considered as indirect organs of the federal state; hence the international person concluding these treaties may be considered to be the federal state acting, in certain respects, through a component state.

(2) REAL UNION. It is usual to represent "real unions" and "personal unions" as separate types of state unions. Both are associations of two monarchies in which the head of the one state is at the same time the head of the other. But whereas in case of a real union the identity of the Head of State is based on a constitution valid for both states, and hence permanent, the identity is merely accidental and hence transitory in case of a personal union. The real union has a character not very different from that of a federal state if according to the constitution certain competences of the two monarchies, such as the foreign affairs and military matters, are completely or partly centralized and administered by the monarch in cooperation with other central organs, such as a minister of foreign affairs, a minister of war, and the like. The Austro-Hungarian Monarchy, which was dissolved as an effect of the First World War, was such a real union. If the centralization of the international affairs is total—as was the case with the Austro-Hungarian Monarchy—only the real union as such, and neither of the two united states is a subject of international law. The so-called personal union is not a subject of international law; only the states united by the common monarch are.

(3) CONFEDERATION OF STATES. In a federal state the competence or legal power of the total state is distributed between a central government and some local governments. Hence the structure of a federal state is characterized by the fact that the total state is composed of a central body, the federation, and some local bodies, the component states. The federation and the component states are all partial communities; they form together the total community, the federal state. Each of these partial communities has its own legislative and executive organs; and also sometimes its own judicial organs. But the organs of the federation are at the same time organs of the total community, the federal state. For this reason the fed-

eration is usually not distinguished, as a partial community, from the federal state, as the total community.

It is because of the degree of its centralization that the total community is a national, not an international, community—a state, and not a mere union of states. Also international communities which, because of the degree of their decentralization, have not the character of a state may have special organs different from the organs of the member states. Since every treaty concluded by two or more states constitutes an international community (as long as international law remains applicable to the relations among the members of the community), two kinds of international communities must be distinguished: organized and not organized international communities. An organized international community is constituted by a treaty which institutes special organs of the international community for the pursuance of the purposes for which the community has been established. This community is an "international" community; it has not the character of a state. The legal order laid down in the constituent treaty has the character of international not of national law if the centralization does not reach that degree which is characteristic of a state. An organized international community is an international organization. In contradistinction to a federal state, it is a confederation of states. German terminology, which distinguishes between *Bundesstaat* ("federal state") and *Staatenbund* ("confederation of states") is more precise.

It is usual to reserve the term "confederation" of states or "confederated states" to certain historical organizations of states, such as the German Confederation (*der Deutsche Bund*, 1815–1866), the Swiss Confederation, and the United States of America before the two latter confederations became federal states (the United States in 1787, the Swiss Confederation in 1848). But there is no essential difference between these confederations of states and other organized communities of states (international organizations) which are not so centralized as to form a federal state. The members of a confederation of states (an organized community of states or an international organization) have unrestricted competence in foreign affairs, although they may be under certain

Spheres of Validity of International Law 173

obligations with respect to their international relations, imposed upon them by the constituent treaty. If this treaty confers upon the international community the power to conclude, through its organs, for its specific purposes, international agreements with member states or nonmember states, the organization as such is a subject of international law.

To be a subject of international law means to be subjected to international law. If an international community of states is a subject of international law, it has certain obligations and rights established by general international law as well as the obligations and rights established by its constituent treaty and the treaties it has concluded. The obligations and rights which an organized international community of states (i.e., an international organization) has under general international law, or, what amounts to the same, the extent to which general international law is applicable to such an international community of states as subject of international law, depend on the powers conferred upon the international community, and that means, on the special organs of the community, by its constituent treaty. An international community which is a subject of international law is always under the obligation of general international law to respect the treaties concluded by it, because an international community is a subject of international law only if its constitution confers upon it at least the power to conclude treaties. If the international community is a subject of international law, it may exercise the right of active and passive legation, that is to say, it may send and receive diplomatic envoys. If its constitution confers upon the international community the power to govern, by a central organ, a definite territory (or, as it is usually formulated, confers on the international community sovereignty over a certain territory) different from the territories of the member states, then, and only then, the international community has the right that the integrity of that territory be respected. If the international community has under its constitution the power to dispose of its own armed force, different from the armed forces of the member states, and hence can wage war, then, and then only, the international community has all the obligations and rights which general international law establishes with respect to war. If an international organization has its own armed forces, it can resort to war as a sanction, i.e., as a reaction against a violation of its rights; and if it has no armed force of its own, it can apply reprisals. As to the possibility of directing these sanctions against an international community of states which is a subject of international law, reprisals can be directed against such a community insofar as it has rights, that is, legally protected interests, reprisals consisting in a violation of such rights. As to war as a sanction, it seems that it can be directed against an international community which is a subject of international law only as a counterwar against its armed forces (different from the armed forces of its members), or if the international community has a territory of its own, different from the territories of its members.

If the treaty constituting an international community confers upon organs of the community the power to adopt decisions legally binding upon the member states, or to take enforcement actions having the character of reprisals or war as reactions against violations of the constituent treaty or against other international delicts committed by member states, then the obligations and rights established by these decisions are international obligations and rights and the enforcement actions taken by the organization are international sanctions. The international organization competent to establish such obligations and rights and to apply such sanctions is to be considered, in this respect too, as a subject of international law.

c. *The League of Nations and the United Nations*. The two most important international organizations, established in the twentieth century in connection with the two world wars, are the League of Nations and the United Nations.

(1) THE LEAGUE OF NATIONS. The League of Nations was constituted by its Covenant, which formed Part I of the peace treaties concluded in 1919–1920 with Germany at Versailles, with Austria at St. Germain, with Hungary at Trianon, and with Bulgaria at Neuilly. The main purpose was the maintenance of international peace. But the League of Nations was not able to prevent the Second World War, which led to the dissolution of this organization in 1946. According to Article 1 of the Covenant, the original mem-

Spheres of Validity of International Law

bers of the League were the signatories named in an Annex to the Covenant. These were the Allied and Associated Powers which had been at war with the four states just mentioned. But the United States of America, though a "signatory" and therefore, according to the wording of Article 1, an original member, did not become a member of the League of Nations because it did not ratify the peace treaties. Original members were also some neutral states named in the Annex and invited to accede to the Covenant by a unilateral declaration deposited with the Secretariat of the League within two months of the coming into force of the Covenant. Admission of subsequent members could be effected by decisions of the Assembly, made by a two-thirds majority of the members. Any member could withdraw from the League, after two years' notice (Article 1, paragraph 3), or immediately in case of an amendment to the Covenant not consented to by the member (Article 26, paragraph 2).

The main organs of the League were the Assembly and the Council. The Assembly consisted of the representatives of the members. Each member had one vote and not more than three representatives (Article 3). The Council, according to Article 4, consisted of representatives of the so-called Principal Allied and Associated Powers—namely, the United States, the British Empire, France, Italy, and Japan, which were permanent members of the Council—and the representatives of four other members selected by the Assembly. Since the United States did not ratify the peace treaties, it did not become a member of the Council, contrary to the wording of Article 4. With the approval of the majority of the Assembly, the Council could name additional members of the League whose representatives would always be members of the Council; the Council with like approval could increase the number of members of the League to be selected by the Assembly for representation on the Council (Article 4, paragraph 2). Any member of the League not represented on the Council was to be invited to send a representative to sit as a member at any meeting of the Council during the consideration of matters specially affecting the interests of that member of the League (Article 4, paragraph 5). At meetings of the Council, each member of the

League represented on the Council had one vote, and not more than one representative (Article 4, paragraph 6). As to the voting procedure in the Assembly as well as in the Council, unanimity of the members represented at the meeting was required, except where otherwise expressly provided, concerning decisions on nonprocedural matters. Procedural matters could be decided by a majority of the members represented at the meeting (Article 5).

In case of decisions referring to a dispute, the votes of the parties to the dispute were not to be counted (Article 15, paragraphs 6 and 7). An analogous principle applied to a decision by which a member was to be expelled from the League (Article 16, paragraph 4).

The main functions of the League with respect to its purpose of maintaining the peace were the settlement of disputes and the enforcement actions to be taken against violations of the Covenant. The latter have been dealt with in Part I of this treatise;[53] the former will be discussed in Part III.

(2) THE UNITED NATIONS. The United Nations was established independently of peace treaties terminating the Second World War. It is constituted by the Charter of the United Nations, signed at San Francisco on June 26, 1945. Its main purpose is the same as that of the League of Nations—the maintenance of peace; its organization is very similar to that of its predecessor. As to the original membership, Article 3 provides: "The original Members of the United Nations shall be the states which, having participated in the United Nations Conference on International Organization at San Francisco, or having previously signed the Declaration by United Nations of January 1, 1942, sign the present Charter and ratify it in accordance with Article 110." Only Poland did not sign the Charter at San Francisco, but signed the Declaration by United Nations and hence was allowed to become an original member of the United Nations. With respect to subsequent membership, Article 4 stipulates: "1. Membership in the United Nations is open to all other peace-loving states which accept the obligations contained in the present Charter and, in the judgment of the Organization, are able and willing to carry out these

---

[53] Cf. *supra*, pp. 40ff.

Spheres of Validity of International Law

obligations. 2. The admission of any such state to membership in the United Nations will be effected by a decision of the General Assembly upon the recommendation of the Security Council."[54] By 1952 nine States have been admitted to membership in the United Nations, so that the Organization has sixty members.[55] In con-

---

[54] *Article 4, paragraph 1*, has been interpreted in the advisory opinion of the International Court of Justice of May 28, 1948, concerning *Admission to the United Nations* (Charter Article 4) as follows: "The Court, by nine votes to six, is of opinion that a Member of the United Nations which is called upon, in virtue of Article 4 of the Charter, to pronounce itself by its vote, either in the Security Council or in the General Assembly, on the admission of a State to membership in the United Nations, is not juridically entitled to make its consent to the admission dependent on conditions not expressly provided by paragraph 1 of the said Article; and that, in particular, a Member of the Organization cannot, while it recognizes the conditions set forth in that provision to be fulfilled by the State concerned, subject its affirmative vote to the additional condition that other States be admitted to membership in the United Nations together with that State." (International Court of Justice, Reports, 1948, p. 65.)

As to Article 4, paragraph 2, the International Court of Justice in its advisory opinion of March 3, 1950, concerning *Competence of Assembly regarding admission to the United Nations* stated: "The Court has no doubt as to the meaning of this text. It requires two things to effect admission: a 'recommendation' of the Security Council and a 'decision' of the General Assembly. It is in the nature of things that the recommendation should come before the decision. The word 'recommendation,' and the word 'upon' preceding it, imply the idea that the recommendation is the foundation of the decision to admit, and that the latter rests upon the recommendation. Both these acts are indispensable to form the judgment of the Organization to which the previous paragraph of Article 4 refers. The text under consideration means that the General Assembly can only decide to admit upon the recommendation of the Security Council; it determines the respective roles of the two organs whose combined action is required before admission can be effected: in other words, the recommendation of the Security Council is the condition precedent to the decision of the Assembly by which the admission is effected." (International Court of Justice, Reports, 1950, p. 4.)

[55] The following states are members of the United Nations: Afghanistan, Argentina, Australia, Belgium, Bolivia, Brazil, Burma, Byelorussian SSR, Canada, Chile, China, Colombia, Costa Rica, Cuba, Czechoslovakia, Denmark, Dominican Republic, Ecuador, Egypt, El Salvador, Ethiopia, France, Greece, Guatemala, Haiti, Honduras, Iceland, India, Indonesia, Iran, Iraq, Israel, Lebanon, Liberia, Luxembourg, Mexico, Netherlands, New Zealand, Nicaragua, Norway, Pakistan, Panama, Paraguay, Peru, Philippines, Poland, Saudi-Arabia, Sweden, Syria, Thailand, Turkey, Ukrainian SSR, Union of South Africa, USSR, United Kingdom, United States, Uruguay, Venezuela, Yemen, Yugoslavia.

tradistinction to the Covenant, the Charter does not contain provisions concerning withdrawal from the Organization. Hence withdrawal of a member cannot be based on the wording of the Charter. But according to an interpretation laid down in a resolution of Commission I of the San Francisco Conference, a member may withdraw from the Organization in case of "exceptional circumstances."[56]

The main organs of the United Nations are the General Assembly and the Security Council. As to the General Assembly, Article 9 provides: "1. The General Assembly shall consist of all the Members of the United Nations. 2. Each Member shall have not more than five representatives in the General Assembly." Article 18 stipulates: "1. Each member of the General Assembly shall have one vote. 2. Decisions of the General Assembly on important questions shall be made by a two-thirds majority of the members present and voting. These questions shall include: recommendations with respect to the maintenance of international peace and security, the election of the non-permanent members of the Security Council, the election of the members of the Economic and Social Council, the election of members of the Trusteeship Council in accordance with paragraph 1(c) of Article 86, the admission of new Members to the United Nations, the suspension of the rights and privileges of membership, the expulsion of Members, questions relating to the operation of the trusteeship system, and budgetary questions. 3. Decisions on other questions, including the determination of additional categories of questions to be decided by a two-thirds majority, shall be made by a majority of the members present and voting." Article 20 provides: "The General Assembly shall meet in regular annual sessions and in such special sessions as occasion may require. Special sessions shall be convoked by the Secretary-General at the request of the Security Council or of a majority of the Members of the United Nations." According to the Rules of Procedure of the General Assembly (amended by the resolution of the General Assembly of November 3, 1950, called "Uniting for Peace") emergency special sessions shall be convened within twenty-four hours of the receipt by the Secretary-General of a request for such a session

---

[56] Cf. *infra*, p. 338.

from the Security Council or of a request from the majority of the members of the United Nations.

As to the Security Council, Article 23 provides: "1. The Security Council shall consist of eleven Members of the United Nations. The Republic of China, France, the Union of Soviet Socialist Republics, the United Kingdom of Great Britain and Northern Ireland, and the United States of America shall be permanent members of the Security Council. The General Assembly shall elect six other Members of the United Nations to be non-permanent members of the Security Council, due regard being specially paid, in the first instance to the contribution of Members of the United Nations to the maintenance of international peace and security and to the other purposes of the Organization, and also to equitable geographical distribution. 2. The non-permanent members of the Security Council shall be elected for a term of two years. In the first election of the non-permanent members, however, three shall be chosen for a term of one year. A retiring member shall not be eligible for immediate re-election. 3. Each member of the Security Council shall have one representative." In contradistinction to the Covenant, the Charter does not allow an increase of the number of the permanent or nonpermanent members of the Security Council determined by the Charter. The Security Council, unlike the General Assembly, is in continuous function. Article 28, paragraph 1, stipulates: "1. The Security Council shall be so organized as to be able to function continuously. Each member of the Security Council shall for this purpose be represented at all times at the seat of the Organization." As to the voting procedure, Article 27 stipulates: "1. Each member of the Security Council shall have one vote. 2. Decisions of the Security Council on procedural matters shall be made by an affirmative vote of seven members. 3. Decisions of the Security Council on all other matters shall be made by an affirmative vote of seven members including the concurring votes of the permanent members; provided that, in decisions under Chapter VI, and under paragraph 3 of Article 52, a party to a dispute shall abstain from voting." The principle laid down in the last sentence of paragraph 3 applies only to disputes, not to other situations, and only to the decisions expressly referred to in this sentence, not to decisions taken under Chapter VII (Action with Respect to Threats to the Peace, Breaches of the Peace, and Acts of Aggression). It does not apply in the procedure of the General Assembly.

The most striking difference between the Covenant and the Charter consists in the fact that the latter accepts the majority-vote principle for the procedure in the two main bodies of the Organization. Unanimity must exist only among the five permanent members of the Security Council and only with respect to decisions on nonprocedural matters. This is the so-called veto right of the permanent members of the Security Council. No decision of this body on a nonprocedural matter can be taken against the vote of one permanent member.

As to the question whether the concurrent votes of all five permanent members are required for a decision on a nonprocedural matter, that is to say, whether abstention or absence from voting by a permanent member prevents a valid decision on such a matter, the wording of the English text of the Charter[57] allows an affirmative as well as a negative answer. The practice of the Security Council shows a tendency in favor of the second interpretation, so that a decision may be taken by the affirmative vote of seven members, including the concurring votes of its permanent members present and voting. The principle of unanimity of the permanent members of the Security Council applies also outside the procedure of the Security Council. According to Article 110, the Charter could come into force only upon the deposit of ratifications by the five states to which permanent seats in the Security Council were granted in the Charter, and by a majority of the other signatory states. According to Articles 108 and 109, an amendment to the Charter shall come into force when adopted by a vote of two thirds of the members of the General Assembly or of the members of a General Conference of the members of the United Nations, convoked for this

---

[57] Whereas the English text of Article 27, paragraph 3, reads: ". . . including the concurring votes of the permanent members," the French text reads: ". . . les voix de tous les membres permanents (the votes of *all* the permanent members)." The other texts of Article 27, paragraph 3, have the same wording as the French text. According to Article 111 of the Charter, all five texts (the Chinese, French, Russian, English, and Spanish texts) "are equally authentic."

Spheres of Validity of International Law

purpose, and ratified by two thirds of the members, including all the permanent members of the Security Council. Articles 108, 109, and 110—in contradistinction to the English text of Article 27, paragraph 3—provide the cooperation of all the five states which are permanent members of the Security Council.

States which are not members of the Security Council may participate under certain circumstances in the discussion of the Security Council. In this respect, Articles 31 and 32 come into consideration. Article 31: "Any Member of the United Nations which is not a member of the Security Council may participate, without vote, in the discussion of any question brought before the Security Council whenever the latter considers that the interests of that Member are specially affected." Article 32: "Any Member of the United Nations which is not a member of the Security Council or any state which is not a Member of the United Nations, if it is a party to a dispute under consideration by the Security Council, shall be invited to participate, without vote, in the discussion relating to the dispute. The Security Council shall lay down such conditions as it deems just for the participation of a state which is not a Member of the United Nations." There is one case where a member state which is not a member of the Security Council may participate in a decision of the Security Council. Article 44 provides: "When the Security Council has decided to use force it shall, before calling upon a Member not represented on it to provide armed forces in fulfillment of the obligations assumed under Article 43, invite that Member, if the Member so desires, to participate in the decisions of the Security Council concerning the employment of contingents of that Member's armed forces."

The main functions of the Security Council and the General Assembly with respect to the purpose of maintaining peace is the settlement of disputes and the taking of enforcement actions. As to the first-mentioned function, the two organs have concurring competences. This function will be analyzed in Part IV of this treatise.[58] As to the enforcement actions to be taken in case of a threat to or breach of the peace, the Security Council has, according to the

---
[58] Cf. *infra*, pp. 368ff.

intentions of the framers of the Charter, exclusive competence. But according to the resolution of the General Assembly of November 3, 1950, called "Uniting for Peace," the General Assembly may recommend to members the use of force, and in case of a breach of the peace or act of aggression, the use of armed force. This function has been discussed in Part I of this treatise.[59]

For the purpose of promoting economic and social cooperation under the authority of the General Assembly, the Charter has established the Economic and Social Council. Article 61 stipulates: "1. The Economic and Social Council shall consist of eighteen Members of the United Nations elected by the General Assembly. 2. Subject to the provisions of paragraph 3, six members of the Economic and Social Council shall be elected each year for a term of three years. A retiring member shall be eligible for immediate re-election. 3. At the first election, eighteen members of the Economic and Social Council shall be chosen. The term of office of six members so chosen shall expire at the end of one year, and of six other members at the end of two years, in accordance with arrangements made by the General Assembly. 4. Each member of the Economic and Social Council shall have one representative." For the purpose of supervising, under the authority of the General Assembly or of the Security Council, the administration of territories placed under the trusteeship system of the United Nations, the Trusteeship Council is established. Article 86 provides: "1. The Trusteeship Council shall consist of the following Members of the United Nations: a. those Members administering trust territories; b. such of those Members mentioned by name in Article 23 as are not administering trust territories; and c. as many other Members elected for three-year terms by the General Assembly as may be necessary to ensure that the total number of members of the Trusteeship Council is equally divided between those Members of the United Nations which administer trust territories and those which do not. 2. Each member of the Trusteeship Council shall designate one specially qualified person to represent it therein."

According to Article 97, a Secretary-General shall be appointed by the General Assembly upon the recommendation of the Security

---

[59] Cf. *supra*, pp. 46ff.

Council.[60] He shall be the chief administrative officer of the Organization. The Secretary-General shall act in that capacity in all meetings of the General Assembly, of the Security Council, of the Economic and Social Council, and of the Trusteeship Council, and shall perform such other functions as are entrusted to him by these organs. The Secretary-General shall make an annual report to the General Assembly on the work of the Organization (Articles 97, 98). The Secretary-General is assisted by the other members of the Secretariat, the staff of which is appointed by the Secretary-General under regulations established by the General Assembly (Article 101, paragraph 1).

Article 52 authorizes the members of the United Nations to enter into regional arrangements or to establish by such arrangements regional agencies for dealing with such matters relating to the maintenance of international peace and security as are appropriate for regional action, "provided that such arrangements or agencies and their activities are consistent with the purposes and principles of the United Nations" (Article 52, paragraph 1). Regional organizations may be considered to be indirect organs of the United Nations. The Security Council shall encourage the development of pacific settlement of local disputes through such regional arrangements or by such regional agencies (Article 52, paragraph 3) and shall,

---

[60] The term of the first Secretary-General expired on February 1, 1951. He was reappointed for a period of three years by a resolution of the General Assembly adopted on November 1, 1950, without a previous recommendation of the Security Council. The resolution reads as follows: "The General Assembly, having received communications from the President of the Security Council, dated 12 October and 25 October 1950, stating that the Security Council has been unable to agree on a recommendation to the General Assembly regarding the appointment of a Secretary-General, considering the necessity to ensure the uninterrupted exercise of the functions vested by the Charter in the office of the Secretary-General, considering that the Security Council recommended to the first regular session of the General Assembly the appointment of Mr. Trygve Lie as Secretary-General and that, on 1 February 1946, the General Assembly appointed Mr. Trygve Lie as Secretary-General for a five-year term, decides that the present Secretary-General shall be continued in office for a period of three years." A decision to the effect that "the present Secretary-General shall be continued in office for a period of three years" amounts to a reappointment of the first Secretary-General. The Charter makes no difference between appointment and reappointment. Cf. the advisory opinion of the International Court of Justice of March 3, 1950, quoted *supra*, p. 177.

where appropriate, utilize such regional arrangements or agencies for enforcement action under its authority (Article 53, paragraph 1).

The Charter authorizes the United Nations to enter into international agreements with members as well as with nonmembers, and with other international organizations. Such agreements are, e.g., the "special agreements" referred to in Article 43, to be concluded between the Security Council and members for the purpose of placing at the disposal of the Security Council contingents of the armed forces of the respective members; the conventions concerning the privileges and immunities to be granted by the members to the United Nations and its representatives and officials, referred to in Article 105; the trusteeship agreements entered into by the General Assembly or the Security Council with the states directly concerned in accordance with Articles 75, 79, 83, and 85; the agreements constituted by the acceptance on the part of nonmembers of the conditions laid down by the Security Council under Article 32 for the participation of nonmembers in the discussion of a dispute to which the nonmember state is a party; the agreements by which the specialized agencies are to be brought into relationship with the United Nations in accordance with Articles 57 and 63; and others. By conferring upon the United Nations the power to conclude treaties, the Charter bestows international personality on the Organization.[61]

---

[61] In its advisory opinion of April 11, 1949, concerning *Reparation for injuries suffered in the service of the United Nations* (International Court of Justice, Reports, 1949, p. 174) the International Court of Justice answered in the affirmative the question as to whether the United Nations possesses international personality. The Court said: "The Charter has not been content to make the Organization created by it merely a centre 'for harmonizing the actions of nations in the attainment of these common ends' (Article 1, paragraph 4). It has equipped that centre with organs, and has given it special tasks. It has defined the position of the Members in relation to the Organization by requiring them to give it every assistance in any action undertaken by it (Article 2, paragraph 5), and to accept and carry out the decisions of the Security Council; by authorizing the General Assembly to make recommendations to the Members; by giving the Organization legal capacity and privileges and immunities in the territory of each of its Members; and by providing for the conclusion of agreements between the Organization and its Members. Practice—in particular the conclusion of conventions to which the Organization is a party—has confirmed this character of the Organization, which occupies a position in certain respects in detachment from its Members, and which

d. *The International Labor Organization.* Other international organizations not constituted by the Charter but working in the economic, social, cultural, educational, health, and related fields, are to be—and some have been—brought into relationship with the United Nations through agreements entered into with the respective organizations by the United Nations represented by the Economic and Social Council. The agreements must be approved by the General Assembly. The Charter refers to these organizations as "specialized agencies" (Articles 57, 63). The most important among these specialized agencies brought into relationship with the United Nations is the International Labor Organization, originally established by Part XIII of the four peace treaties

---

is under a duty to remind them, if need be, of certain obligations. It must be added that the Organization is a political body, charged with political tasks of an important character, and covering a wide field, namely the maintenance of international peace and security, the development of friendly relations among nations, and the achievement of international co-operation in the solution of problems of an economic, social, cultural or humanitarian character (Article 1); and in dealing with its Members it employs political means. The 'Convention on the Privileges and Immunities of the United Nations' of 1946 creates rights and duties between each of the signatories and the Organization (see, in particular, Section 35). It is difficult to see how such a convention could operate except upon the international plane and as between parties possessing international personality.

"In the opinion of the Court, the Organization was intended to exercise and enjoy, and is in fact exercising and enjoying, functions and rights which can only be explained on the basis of the possession of a large measure of international personality and the capacity to operate upon an international plane. It is at present the supreme type of international organization, and it could not carry out the intentions of its founders if it was devoid of international personality. It must be acknowledged that its Members, by entrusting certain functions to it, with the attendant duties and responsibilities, have clothed it with the competence required to enable those functions to be effectively discharged.

"Accordingly, the Court has come to the conclusion that the Organization is an international person. That is not the same thing as saying that it is a State, which it certainly is not, or that its legal personality and rights and duties are the same as those of a State. Still less is it the same thing as saying that it is 'a super-State,' whatever that expression may mean. It does not even imply that all its rights and duties must be upon the international plane, any more than all the rights and duties of a State must be upon that plane. What it does mean is that it is a subject of international law and capable of possessing international rights and duties, and that it has capacity to maintain its rights by bringing international claims."

terminating the First World War, and linked to the League of Nations in certain ways. After the dissolution of the League, it continued to exist as an independent international organization. Even prior to the dissolution of the League, the articles of the peace treaties concerning the International Labor Organization were renumbered and, under the title "Constitution of the International Labor Organization," embodied in a separate instrument.

The purpose of the International Labor Organization is to promote international cooperation in the field of industry and labor. As long as the International Labor Organization was linked to the League of Nations, membership in the League carried with it membership in the Organization. Article 1, paragraphs 2–6, of the Constitution of the International Labor Organization now provides: "The Members of the International Labor Organization shall be the States which were Members of the Organization on 1 November 1945, and such other States as may become Members in pursuance of the provisions of paragraphs 3 and 4 of this article.—Any original Member of the United Nations and any State admitted to membership in the United Nations by a decision of the General Assembly in accordance with the provisions of the Charter may become a Member of the International Labor Organization by communicating to the Director-General of the International Labor Office its formal acceptance of the obligations of the Constitution of the International Labor Organization.—The General Conference of the International Labor Organization may also admit Members to the Organization by a vote concurred in by two thirds of the delegates attending the session, including two thirds of the Government delegates present and voting. Such admission shall take effect on the communication to the Director-General of the International Labor Office by the Government of the new Member of its formal acceptance of the obligations of the Constitution of the Organization.—No Member of the International Labor Organization may withdraw from the Organization without giving notice of its intention so to do to the Director-General of the International Labor Office. Such notice shall take effect two years after the date of its reception by the Director-General, subject to the Member having at that time fulfilled all

Spheres of Validity of International Law 187

financial obligations arising out of its membership. When a member has ratified any international labor Convention, such withdrawal shall not affect the continued validity for the period provided for in the Convention of all obligations arising thereunder or relating thereto.—In the event of any State having ceased to be a Member of the Organization, its re-admission to membership shall be governed by the provisions of paragraph 3 or paragraph 4 of this article as the case may be."

The main organs of the International Labor Organization are the General Conference, the Governing Body, and the International Labor Office. According to Article 3, paragraph 1, of the Constitution, the General Conference "shall be held from time to time as occasion may require, and at least once in every year. It shall be composed of four representatives of each of the Members, of whom two shall be Government delegates and the two others shall be delegates representing respectively the employers and the workpeople of each of the Members." Article 3, paragraph 5, obligates the member states to nominate nongovernment delegates chosen in agreement with the industrial organizations, if such organizations exist, which are most representative of employers or workpeople, as the case may be, in their respective countries. Whereas ordinarily only governments are represented on an organ of an international organization, and the method of appointing the representative is left to the discretion of the government concerned, the Constitution of the International Labor Organization—an international agreement—determines directly the way in which two of the four delegates of a member state are to be appointed, by requiring agreement on the part of industrial organizations. Consequently, not only the appointing governments or their states but also the industrial organizations may be considered to be represented on the General Conference. The Governing Body, in accordance with Article 7, shall consist of thirty-two persons: sixteen representing governments, eight representing the employers, and eight representing the workers. Of the sixteen persons representing governments, eight shall be appointed by the members which are of chief industrial importance, and eight shall be appointed by the members selected for that purpose by the government delegates to the Conference, excluding the delegates of the eight members mentioned above. The International Labor Office is headed by a Director-General who, according to Article 8, shall be appointed by the Governing Body, and, subject to the instructions of the Governing Body, shall be responsible for the efficient conduct of the International Labor Office and for such other duties as may be assigned to him. The staff of the International Labor Office shall be appointed by the Director-General under regulations approved by the Governing Body (Article 9).

7. *General and Particular International Law*

As pointed out, the personal sphere of validity of international law as such is not limited by any norm of a higher legal order. But the norms of the international legal order do not all have the same sphere of validity with regard to the persons upon whom they impose duties and confer rights. One is accustomed to distinguish general (or common) international law from particular international law. The term "general international law" designates the norms of international law which are valid for all the states of the world, whereas the term "particular international law" designates norms of international law valid only for certain states. General international law is, as a matter of fact, customary law. As treaties are in principle binding only upon the contracting parties, and as there is no treaty concluded by or adhered to by all the states of the world, there is only customary, not conventional general international law. The Charter of the United Nations, a treaty to which many, but not all, states are contracting parties, claims, it is true, to be binding—at least regarding some of its provisions—upon all the states and thus to have the character of general international law. This question will be discussed in Part IV of this treatise.[62] Particular international law is normally created by treaties; but it may also be created by a particular custom in the establishment of which only some states participate.

The statement that there are norms of international law which are valid for all states does not mean that these norms are actually

---

[62] Cf. *infra*, pp. 347f.

Spheres of Validity of International Law

binding upon all states; it means only that they are potentially binding upon all states, that is to say that they are binding upon any state if it fulfills the conditions under which they claim to be binding. Under general international law a littoral state has obligations and rights which, actually, an inland state has not, but which it will have as soon as it acquires territory with a sea coast. By defining general international law as law binding upon all the states we do not exclude the possibility that persons other than states are subjects of international law. As pointed out, certain norms, potentially valid for all states, authorizing or obligating states to inflict under certain conditions sanctions upon individuals, are binding also upon these individuals; certain norms, potentially valid for all states, are valid also for the Roman Catholic Church and certain statelike communities and confederations of states. Hence general international law may be defined as the norms of international law which are potentially valid for the entire international community.

Although the norms of particular international law are directly valid for only a limited number of states and not for all the subjects of the international community, these norms may constitute a legal situation which, as such, must be respected by all other states. There is for every state a legal obligation to respect the rights of other states acquired under international law. Thus the states are, e.g., obliged to respect the territorial integrity of other states, which means that the states are obliged to respect the right some other state has to a certain territory. The obligation of the states to respect the rights of other states acquired under international law is the consequence of the fact that the particular international law which constitutes the acquired right is always created on the basis of a rule of general international law. Hence particular international law is indirectly binding upon all the subjects of the international legal order. For example, State A concludes a treaty of cession with State B. In execution of this treaty, State A withdraws its organs from the ceded territory, and State B occupies the territory. In this way, the territory concerned becomes a part of the territory of State B. This legal situation, which consists in the fact that now the territory in question legally belongs to State B, is constituted by a treaty concluded between two states only, that is, by a norm of particular international law. But the particular conventional international law is created on the basis of the rule *pacta sunt servanda,* which is a rule of general (customary) international law. The legal fact that the ceded territory belongs to State B exists not only for the two states which are contracting parties to the treaty, but also for all the other states. All the other states are obligated to respect this new legal situation constituted by a norm of particular international law. This legal effect of the treaty manifests itself in that after the treaty has come into force no state except B can occupy the territory without violating the law. A treaty concluded between two states, creating particular law, has legal effects for all the other states.[63]

The principle that particular international law, valid directly for only some states, or the legal situation created by particular international law, must be respected also by all the other states which did not participate in the establishment of the law-creating fact does not preclude the other principle—that it is for each of the other states to decide whether the fact by which particular international law has been created actually exists. If, e.g., a state incorporates the territory of another state, a third state is obliged to respect the new legal situation only if it "recognizes" the incorporation, that is to say, if it, directly or indirectly, admits that the facts exist which, according to general international law, may bring about the territorial change.[64]

Hence there is no "particular" international law in an absolute sense of the term. International law is, like all law, general law, though the largest part of its norms has the character of particular law in a relative sense of the term.

D. THE MATERIAL SPHERE OF VALIDITY OF INTERNATIONAL LAW

Like the personal, territorial, and temporal, the material sphere of validity of international law is unlimited. The norms of inter-

---

[63] Cf. *infra,* p. 347.
[64] Cf. *infra,* pp. 267, 269f.

national law may therefore relate to any subject matter whatever, in particular to those matters which are usually regulated by national law.

1. *International and National (Domestic) Jurisdiction*

The problem of the material sphere of validity of international law may be presented as the question whether it is possible to draw a line between the material sphere of validity of international law and that of national law. It is the question whether there exist matters which, by their very nature, can be regulated only and exclusively by norms of international law, and matters which, by their very nature, can be regulated only and exclusively by norms of national law. That the law "regulates" a matter means—in this connection—that the law stipulates an obligation to behave in a certain way in respect to this matter. The norms of a legal order are general or individual norms. The most important individual norms are judicial or quasi-judicial decisions. That a matter can be regulated by international law means that this matter can be regulated by a rule of customary or conventional international law or by the decision of an international agency, especially an international tribunal. That a matter can be regulated only by national law means that in this matter an obligation to behave in a certain way can be stipulated only by the customary or statutory law of a state or by a decision of a court of this state, not by a decision of an international agency. Such matters are usually characterized as matters which, by their very nature, are solely or exclusively within the domestic jurisdiction of a state. That means that a regulation of these matters by a general or an individual norm of international law is excluded, and an exclusive competence (jurisdiction) of the state is established. However, there are no matters which, by their very nature, are reserved to regulation by national law and are not susceptible of regulation by international law. There exist no matters which, by their very nature, are solely (exclusively) within the domestic jurisdiction of a state, matters which, by their very nature, cannot be regulated by a general or individual norm of international law, that is to say, matters in which no obligation can be stipulated by a general or an individual norm of international law. International law may regulate all matters, even such as are normally regulated by national law only and hence considered as "domestic" matters; for example, constitutional questions such as the form of government, the acquisition and loss of nationality, labor problems, the whole domain of social policy, religious problems, immigration and tariff questions, problems of penal law and those of penal procedure, problems of civil law and civil procedure.

All these matters may be regulated by a norm of international law, and they are actually regulated by international law, for instance, when they are the object of an international agreement. By a treaty a state may assume the obligation to adopt or maintain a republican or a monarchical form of government, to naturalize citizens of another state only on certain conditions, to establish an eight-hour workday, to recognize religious freedom for its nationals, to allow immigration to the citizens of another state, to apply a special tariff to the importation of certain goods from a certain state, to conform certain rules of its criminal or civil law to a model agreed upon in an international convention, and so on. If a dispute arises out of such a matter, it may be settled by an international agency, especially by an international tribunal, provided that such an agency is established by a treaty. In all these cases matters which normally are regulated only and exclusively by norms of national law are then regulated by norms of international law, or at least, also by a norm of international law.

2. *Implementation of International Law by National Law*

The law may regulate a matter not only in a positive way by stipulating an obligation to behave in a certain way in respect to this matter, but also in a negative way, by refraining from stipulating an obligation in this matter. Then the persons subjected to the law are legally free to behave in this matter as they please. What is legally not forbidden is legally permitted. In this sense there is no matter that is not "regulated" by the law, be it national or international law. If there is no norm of international law by

Spheres of Validity of International Law

which an obligation is imposed upon a state in a certain matter, it is by international law that the state is free to behave as it pleases, that this matter is within its domestic jurisdiction.

Matters may positively be regulated by norms of international law and at the same time by norms of national law. The norm of international law may require implementation by norms of national law. For instance, a norm of general international law imposes upon the states the obligation to make a formal declaration of war before resorting to hostilities. The fulfillment of this obligation is not possible without a provision of the national law of the state concerned determining the organ competent to make a declaration of war. Another example of implementation of international law by national law is a treaty concerning extradition, imposing upon the contracting states only the obligation to issue statutes regulating extradition in conformity with the content of the treaty. In order to be applied by the organs of the state to the subjects of the state, the treaty must first be executed by a national statute enacted by the legislative organ of the state. But the treaty may impose upon the contracting states, not the obligation to enact a national extradition law of a certain content, but the obligation to extradite individuals determined in the treaty under conditions likewise determined in the treaty. That is to say, the extradition treaty may obligate not the legislative but the administrative or judicial organs of the contracting states. The extradition treaty can then be applied by the administrative or judicial organs of the contracting states without an implementation of international law by a legislative act of national law being necessary; but the administrative or judicial organs competent to apply the extradition treaty must be determined by national law. If the national legal order already contains norms regulating extradition, no further implementation of the norm of international law by a norm of national law is necessary. A norm of international law may obligate or authorize the states to punish individuals for having committed crimes determined by this norm, but may leave it to the states to determine the penalty, as, e.g., in the case of piracy. The norm of national law determining the penalty is an implementation of the norm of international law obligating or authorizing the states to punish certain individuals. A norm of international law may impose an obligation or confer a right upon a state and at the same time determine the organ of the state which has to fulfill the obligation or to exercise the right. A treaty may, for instance, provide that the criminal courts of the contracting states shall inflict upon individuals having committed a crime determined by the treaty a punishment likewise determined by the treaty. As a matter of fact, the national law always contains norms instituting criminal courts, and these norms of national law constitute the necessary implementation of the norm of international law. Some writers assume that a norm of general international law authorizes the heads of the states to conclude treaties. But it is for the national law to determine the individual who is to be considered as the head of the state. In this sense, all the norms of international law imposing obligations or conferring rights upon states require implementation by national law; for these international obligations can be fulfilled and these international rights exercised only by organs of the state, and these organs must be instituted by national law. But if the national law already contains the norms that make the application of international law possible, no further implementation is necessary. A norm of international law which is applicable by the organs of the states without further implementation by national law may be called a self-executing norm.

3. *Transformation of International Law into National Law*

Implementation of international law by national law must be distinguished from so-called transformation of international law into national law. Under the constitution of a state, the administrative and especially the judicial organs may be bound to apply only national law, that is to say, statutes enacted by the legislative organ or decrees issued by the competent executive organs. Then international law, even if it should not require implementation, can be applied by the administrative and judicial organs of the state only if "transformed" into a statute or decree, that is to say, if the content of the norm of international law has been made the content of a norm of national law. Such a transformation is not

Spheres of Validity of International Law

necessary from the point of view of international law.[65] A state is responsible for a violation of international law even if the only reason for this violation is that transformation into its national law, required by its constitution, has not taken place.[66] Transformation of international law into national law may be necessary from the point of view of national law only. But no transformation of a customary or a conventional norm of international law obligating or authorizing the state to perform a certain act of legislation is possible. By enacting the statute concerned, the state simply fulfills its international obligation or exercises its international right; it does not "transform" international into national law. Only norms of international law providing for administrative or judicial acts of the state need transformation; and this only if the administrative or judicial organs are bound by the constitution to apply solely national law. The written or the unwritten constitution of a state may contain the rule that international law is part of national law.[67]

---

[65] In its advisory opinion concerning *Jurisdiction of the Courts of Danzig*, the Permanent Court of International Justice (1928) declared that an international agreement "cannot, as such, create direct rights and obligations for private individuals. But it cannot be disputed that the very object of an international agreement, according to the intention of the contracting Parties, may be the adoption by the Parties of some definite rules creating individual rights and obligations and enforceable by the national courts." The Court came to the conclusion that in the concrete case an international agreement was "directly applicable" by the courts of Danzig. (Publications of the Permanent Court of International Justice, Series B, No. 15, pp. 17 f.)

[66] In its advisory opinion concerning *Treatment of Polish Nationals and Other Persons of Polish Origin or Speech in the Danzig Territory*, the Permanent Court of International Justice (1932) declared "that, while on the one hand, according to generally accepted principles, a State cannot rely, as against another State, on the provisions of the latter's Constitution, but only on international law and international obligations duly accepted, on the other hand and conversely, a State cannot adduce as against another State its own Constitution with a view to evading obligations incumbent upon it under international law or treaties in force." (Publications of the Permanent Court of International Justice, Series A/B, No. 44, p. 24.)

[67] In the Anglo-Saxon countries, the principle that international law is part of national law is recognized as a rule of common law. The Constitution of the Federal Republic of Germany (Bonn Constitution) provides in Article 25: "The general rules of international law shall form part of federal law. They shall take precedence over the laws and create rights and duties directly for the inhabitants of the federal territory."

This rule may be interpreted to constitute a general transformation of international law into national law. In this case no transformation of a particular norm of international law, especially no transformation of treaties, is necessary.[68]

4. Article 2, Paragraph 7, of the Charter of the United Nations

The incorrect assumption that there exist matters which, by their very nature, are solely (exclusively) within the domestic jurisdiction of a state and hence excluded from regulation by a general or individual norm of international law, that international law, by its very nature, is not able to stipulate obligations in such matters, is the background of an important provision of the Charter of the United Nations, which has already been noted in a previous connection.[69] It is the provision of Article 2, paragraph 7, according to which intervention on the part of the Organization "in matters which are essentially within the domestic jurisdiction of any state" is prohibited, with the exception of intervention by enforcement measures taken under Chapter VII, that is to say, by the Security Council after it has determined the existence of a threat to or breach of the peace. This provision has been taken over, with some alterations, from the Covenant of the League of Nations. Its Article 15, paragraph 8, runs as follows: "If the dispute between the parties is claimed by one of them, and is found by the Council, to arise out of a matter which by international law is solely within the domestic jurisdiction of that party, the Council shall so report, and shall make no recommendation as to its settlement." The authors of paragraph 8 started from the supposition that there exist matters which, by their very nature, are solely within the domestic jurisdiction of a state and hence excluded from regulation by international law. They considered especially immigration and tariff matters as being solely within the domestic jurisdiction of the states. Consequently, they came to the conclusion that if the dispute refers to such a matter, the Council of the League, an inter-

---

[68] As to transformation of treaties into national law, cf. *infra*, pp. 351ff.
[69] Cf. *supra*, p. 63.

national agency, shall not and cannot be competent to settle the dispute by a decision which has the character of an international legal act.[70]

However, since there are no matters which, by their very nature, are "solely within the domestic jurisdiction" of a state, the

---

[70] In *Tunis-Morocco Nationality Decrees* the Permanent Court of International Justice, 1923, interpreted Article 15, paragraph 8, of the Covenant as follows: "From one point of view, it might well be said that the jurisdiction of a State is exclusive within the limits fixed by international law—using this expression in its wider sense, that is to say, embracing both customary law and general as well as particular treaty law. But a careful scrutiny of paragraph 8 of Article 15 shows that it is not in this sense that exclusive jurisdiction is referred to in that paragraph. The words 'solely within the domestic jurisdiction' seem rather to contemplate certain matters which, though they may very closely concern the interests of more than one State, are not, in principle, regulated by international law. As regards such matters, each State is sole judge.

"The question whether a certain matter is or is not solely within the jurisdiction of a State is an essentially relative question; it depends upon the development of international relations. Thus, in the present state of international law, questions of nationality are, in the opinion of the Court, in principle within this reserved domain.

"For the purpose of the present opinion, it is enough to observe that it may well happen that, in a matter which, like that of nationality, is not, in principle, regulated by international law, the right of a State to use its discretion is nevertheless restricted by obligations which it may have undertaken towards other States. In such a case, jurisdiction which, in principle, belongs solely to the State, is limited by rules of international law. Article 15, paragraph 8, then ceases to apply as regards those States which are entitled to invoke such rules, and the dispute as to the question whether a State has or has not the right to take certain measures becomes in these circumstances a dispute of an international character and falls outside the scope of the exception contained in this paragraph. To hold that a State has not exclusive jurisdiction does not in any way prejudice the final decision as to whether that State has a right to adopt such measures." (Publications of the Permanent Court of International Justice, Series B, No. 4, pp. 23 f.)

This interpretation is highly problematical. Just as there are no matters which, by their very nature, are "solely" within the domestic jurisdiction of the states, there are no matters which by their very nature are "in principle" not regulated by international law. There is no "principle" according to which certain matters cannot or must not be regulated by international law. The Court admits that a matter which "in principle" is not regulated by international law may actually be regulated by international law when regulated by a treaty; and then ceases to be solely within the domestic jurisdiction of the state concerned. There are, as pointed out, even no matters which are actually not "regulated" by international law, if the term is taken not only

inevitable effect of an application of Article 15, paragraph 8, is in conflict with its wording. If there is a dispute between two states, that is to say, if one state claims a certain conduct of the other state and the other state rejects this claim, there are only two possibilities. Either there exists a norm of customary or conventional international law which imposes upon the defendant an obligation to conduct itself as the plaintiff claims; then the matter out of which the dispute arose is not within the domestic jurisdiction of the defendant. Or there is no such norm of customary or contractual international law; then the matter is within the domestic jurisdiction of the defendant. The matter is within the domestic jurisdiction not by its very nature, but because at that moment no norm of international law regulates the matter out of which the dispute arose by establishing an obligation of the states to conduct themselves with respect to this matter in a certain way. If a state is not obliged by international law to conduct itself in a certain way, it is, "by international law," free; it has under international law the right to conduct itself as it pleases; and no other state has the right to claim a certain conduct of the state which is not obliged to this conduct. Consequently, in the case before the Council the defendant is right when, referring to its domestic jurisdiction, it rejects the claim of the plaintiff, and the plaintiff is wrong in claiming a conduct to which the other is not obliged. If the Council finds that the matter is "solely within the domestic jurisdiction" of one of the conflicting states, the Council declares that this state is right and that the other state is wrong according to positive international law. That means that the Council actually decides the case, although according to Article 15, paragraph 8, the Council shall not even make a recommendation as to its settlement.

---

in its positive but also in its negative sense. There are only matters in respect to which there is no norm of customary or conventional international law by which an obligation is imposed upon a state to behave in a certain way in respect to a certain matter. Then, and only then, the matter is solely or exclusively—but not "essentially"—within the domestic jurisdiction of the state; meaning that the state is legally free to behave in this matter as it pleases. Article 15, paragraph 8, of the Covenant quite correctly speaks of a matter which "by international law" is solely within the domestic jurisdiction of the state.

Spheres of Validity of International Law

Article 2, paragraph 7, of the Charter differs from Article 15, paragraph 8, of the Covenant in the following points: (1) The prohibition to intervene is not restricted to intervention by the Security Council in disputes; it refers to any activity of all the organs of the Organization, with the exception of enforcement measures taken under Chapter VII. (2) The matters in which the Organization is prohibited from intervening are not characterized as being "by international law solely," but as being "essentially within the domestic jurisdiction of any state," without reference to international law. (3) Whereas according to Article 15, paragraph 8, of the Covenant the question as to whether a matter is solely within the domestic jurisdiction of a state is to be decided by the Council, Article 2, paragraph 7, does not confer upon the Security Council or any other organ of the United Nations the competence to decide this question. Consequently, the decision is left to the state concerned. If, however, the matter has been brought by one party before the Security Council or the General Assembly or the International Court of Justice and the other party rejects the jurisdiction of the international organ by claiming that the matter is essentially within its domestic jurisdiction, these organs of the United Nations, too, are competent to answer the question as to whether the matter is or is not essentially within the domestic jurisdiction of the state claiming this jurisdiction. Then the question arises as to whether the organ, in deciding the question, is bound by the statement of the party claiming the matter to be within its domestic jurisdiction. This question may be answered in the affirmative as well as in the negative. In the first case, any state may exclude the jurisdiction of the Organization in any case whatever, referring to its domestic jurisdiction. In the second case, the decision of the question as to whether the matter is essentially within the domestic jurisdiction of the state concerned is left to the discretion of the respective organ of the United Nations. Neither the one nor the other interpretation leads to a satisfactory result, because there are no matters which are "essentially" within the domestic jurisdiction of a state, just as there are no matters which by their very nature are "solely" within the domestic jurisdiction of a state. The replacement of the word "solely" by the word "essentially," together with the omission of any reference to "international law," has the consequence that even a matter which is regulated by international law, for instance, a matter with respect to which there exists an obligation imposed upon a state by a treaty, may be declared as being "essentially"—though not "solely" and not "by international law"—within the domestic jurisdiction of the state invoking its domestic jurisdiction—which is certainly a more than paradoxical result.[71]

The exclusion of matters of "domestic jurisdiction" from the intervention of an international organization is not justified even in case the question is disputed whether there exists a rule of international law imposing an obligation on one of the disputing states with respect to these matters. For if this question is disputed and if no agreement of the parties to the dispute can be reached, there is no other way to a pacific settlement of the dispute but by the decision of an international agency. In accordance with the second part of Article 2, paragraph 7, of the Charter, the United Nations may intervene in a matter of domestic jurisdiction by applying enforcement measures under Chapter VII. This is of particular importance in case of a civil war taking place within a state, whether a member or not of the United Nations. But such intervention is possible only if the Security Council under Article 39 of the Charter,

---

[71] In its advisory opinion of March 30, 1950, on the *Interpretation of Peace Treaties* (with Bulgaria, Hungary, and Rumania) the International Court of Justice stated with respect to the request made by the General Assembly for the advisory opinion of the Court: "The object of the Request . . . is directed solely to obtaining from the Court certain clarifications of a legal nature regarding the applicability of the procedure for the settlement of disputes by the Commissions provided for in the express terms of Article 36 of the Treaty with Bulgaria, Article 40 of the Treaty with Hungary and Article 38 of the Treaty with Romania. The interpretation of the terms of a treaty for this purpose could not be considered as a question essentially within the domestic jurisdiction of a State. It is a question of international law which, by its very nature, lies within the competence of the Court.—These considerations also suffice to dispose of the objection based on the principle of domestic jurisdiction and directed specifically against the competence of the Court, namely, that the Court, as an organ of the United Nations, is bound to observe the provisions of the Charter, including Article 2, paragraph 7." (International Court of Justice, Reports, 1950, p. 65.)

Spheres of Validity of International Law

has previously decided that the civil war constitutes a threat to the international peace.

5. Definition of International Law

If there are no matters which by their very nature are solely or essentially within the domestic jurisdiction of the states, that is to say, which can be regulated only by norms of national law and not by norms of international law, then all matters whatever can be regulated by international law. The material sphere of validity of the international legal order is unlimited. Consequently it is impossible to define the concept of international law by its object, i.e., by the matters to which its norms refer or which they regulate. It is impossible to define international law (as some writers do) as the system of norms regulating the external affairs of the states, i.e., the relations between states, in contradistinction to national law, which regulates the internal, i.e., the domestic affairs within a state. Every internal or domestic affair becomes an external affair, an affair between states, if it becomes the object of an international treaty. It is not correct to say that an affair may be regulated by international law because it is an external affair, and that an affair may be regulated by national law because it is an internal affair. On the contrary, an affair is an external affair, an affair between states, because it is regulated by international law, and it is an internal affair, an affair within one state, a "domestic" affair, because and as long as it is positively regulated only by national law.

If, nevertheless, one may define international law as an interstate law, it is because this definition does not refer to the specific object of international law, but to the procedure of its creation. This procedure is characterized by the fact that the norms of international law are created by the collaboration of two or more states. This is true for conventional as well as for customary international law. National law, however, insofar as it is created by acts of state at all, is created by acts of *one* state only. But there are norms of national law which are not created by acts of state, such as customary national law and the law created by legal transactions.

6. Exclusive International Jurisdiction

There are no matters which cannot be regulated by international law, but there are matters which can be regulated only by international law, and not by national law, i.e., the law of one state, the validity of which is limited to a certain territory and its population. The original tendency of international law, its primary function, so to speak, is to determine the territorial, personal, temporal, and material spheres of validity of the national legal orders and thus to coordinate them. Indeed, this is a function which international law alone can perform. National law, as the law of one state, as a legal order the validity of which is limited to a definite territory and the population living on this territory, cannot perform this function. We shall examine this function of international law in Part III.

Another matter which can be regulated only by international law and not by national law, insofar as it is conceived of as the law of one state, i.e., as a legal order the validity of which is limited to a certain territory and its population, is the creation and application of international law, especially the conclusion of treaties, the establishment of international tribunals, and the like.

International law more and more shows the trend to regulate matters which originally were positively regulated only by national law, the tendency to restrict more and more the so-called domestic jurisdiction of the states. For the matters of so-called domestic jurisdiction are more and more subjected to regulation by treaties. If they are at the same time regulated by norms of national law in conformity with the treaties concerned, we are confronted by a simultaneous competence of national and international law. We may characterize this phenomenon as the increasing inclination to internationalize the law, to determine the content of the norms of national law by international law, or to replace national by international law created by treaties.

III.

THE ESSENTIAL FUNCTION OF INTERNATIONAL LAW: THE DETERMINATION OF THE SPHERES OF VALIDITY OF THE NATIONAL LEGAL ORDERS (LEGAL EXISTENCE OF THE STATE) BY THE INTERNATIONAL LEGAL ORDER

THE preceding examinations of the spheres of validity of international law has shown that international law obligates and authorizes states by obligating and authorizing individuals as organs of the states, leaving the determination of these individuals to the national legal orders. Only exceptionally does international law obligate and authorize individuals directly. The norms of international law are mostly incomplete norms; they require completion by norms of national law. The international legal order presupposes the existence of the national legal orders. Without the latter, the former would be an inapplicable fragment of a legal order. Hence reference to national law is inherent in the meaning of the norms of international law. In this sense, the international legal order delegates to the national legal orders the completion of its own norms.

If we examine the norms of present international law with respect to the subject matters which they regulate, we can distinguish two different groups: (1) norms referring to matters that can be regulated in a positive way only by international law, and do not allow of such regulation through national law, conceived of as the law of one state, the validity of which is limited to a certain territory and its population. In these norms, the essential function of international law is manifested. (2) Norms referring to subject matters that can be regulated also by national law, and that actually are regulated only by national law insofar as customary or conventional international law does not regulate them in a positive way, that is to say, by establishing obligations with respect to these matters (as, for instance, norms concerning the acquisition and loss of citizenship). The latter are norms that are possibly norms of international law; the former are norms that are necessarily norms of international law.

When norms are classified as being necessarily norms of international law because they refer to subject matters that, by their very nature, cannot be regulated by national law, a certain assumption concerning the relationship between international and national law is presupposed. It is the assumption that international law is superior to national law. The meaning of this assumption, and of the opposite assumption that international law is not superior to national law but valid only as part of national law, will be discussed in the last part of this treatise.[1] But even if it is not assumed that international law is superior to national law, if it is assumed that international law is valid only as part of national law because international law is valid only if recognized by the state or, what amounts to the same, in the law of the state, it must be admitted that the state as subject of obligations, responsibilities, and rights is subjected to the law—be it international or "its own" national law.[2] If we conceive of the state as a social order, and that means, as a legal order, i.e., the national legal order, we must admit that the spheres of validity of this national legal order are determined by the international legal order, whether the international legal order is supposed to be superior to or part of the national legal order. If it is assumed that international law is valid only as part of national law, it is necessary to distinguish between the norms of a national legal order which are international law and norms of the national law which have not this character and thus are national law in a narrower and specific sense of the term (not comprising international law). Then it is the spheres of validity of the national law in this narrower sense which are determined by international law (as part of the national law in a wider sense of the term).

In examining the so-called elements of the state, we shall see that the sphere of existence of the states is delimited at least in a territorial and a personal respect. Each state can claim as "its territory" only a part of space, and as "its people" only a part of mankind. Interference by one state with the territorial or personal sphere of another state—for instance, performing an act of coercion on the territory of another state without its consent, or forcing the citizen of another state to do military service—is considered as forbidden, as a "violation" of the "right" of the other state. Closer examination shows that the existence of the state in time and the subject matters to be regulated by its law are also determined by a normative order. Such a normative delimitation of the existence of the state,

---

[1] Cf. *infra*, pp. 403ff.
[2] Cf. *infra*, p. 439.

or, what amounts to the same, the determination of the spheres of validity of national legal orders by an international normative order, is acknowledged even by those who deny the legal character of the international order. It is only this normative delimitation which renders it possible that the states can be considered as coexistent side by side as equal subjects, i.e., as equally subjected to an international order.

This delimitation is the specific function of international law. It is in fact by international law that the territorial and personal as well as the temporal and material spheres of validity of the national legal orders are determined. The norms regulating these subject matters are essentially and necessarily norms of international law.

A. DETERMINATION OF THE TERRITORIAL SPHERE OF VALIDITY OF THE NATIONAL LEGAL ORDER (TERRITORY OF THE STATE) BY INTERNATIONAL LAW

1. The Territory of the State as the Territorial Sphere of Validity of the National Legal Order

Traditional doctrine distinguishes three "elements" of the state: its territory, its people, and its power exercised by an independent and effective government. It is assumed to be of the essence of a state that it occupies a certain limited territory. The state, conceived of as a social unity, seems to imply a geographical unity as well: one state, one territory. A closer examination, however, shows that the unity of the state territory is in no way a natural geographic one. The territory of a state need not necessarily consist of one piece of land. Such kind of territory is named "integrate territory." The state territory may be "dismembered." Sometimes to one and the same state territory belong parts of space which are not physically contiguous but separated from each other by territories belonging to another state or to no state at all. To the territory of a state belong its colonies, from which it may be separated by the ocean, and also so-called "enclosures" that are completely surrounded by the territory of another state. These geographically disconnected areas form a unity only insofar as one and the same legal order is valid for all of them. The unity of the state territory, and therefore the territorial unity of the state, is a juristic and not a geographically natural unity. For the territory of a state is legally nothing but the territorial sphere of validity of the national legal order called a state.

Those normative orders that are designated as states are characterized precisely by the fact that their territorial spheres of validity are limited. This distinguishes them from other social orders, especially from international law, which claims to be valid everywhere, its territorial sphere of validity being unlimited.

The limitation of the sphere of validity of the coercive order called a state to a definite territory means that this order, the national legal order, must according to international law restrict—in principle—the performance of the coercive acts provided by it to that territory: the territory of the state. Actually, it is not impossible that a general or individual norm of the legal order of a certain state should prescribe that a coercive act shall be carried out within the territory of another state, and that an organ of the former state shall execute this norm. But should such a norm be enacted or executed by one state (without the consent of the other state), the enactment of the norm and its execution, that is, the performance of the coercive act within the territory of the other state, would be illegal. The legal order violated by these acts is international law. For it is positive international law that determines and thus delimits from one another the territorial spheres of validity of the various national legal orders. If their territorial spheres of validity were not legally delimited, if the states did not have fixed boundaries, the various national legal orders, and that means the many states, could not possibly coexist without conflicts.

This delimitation of the territorial spheres of validity of the national legal orders, the restriction of the legal existence of the state—at least in principle—to a space within its boundaries, has, as pointed out, a normative character. The territory of the state is not the area where the acts of the state, and especially the coercive

The Essential Function of International Law

acts, are actually carried out. By the fact that a single act of the state is carried out on a certain territory, this territory does not become the territory of the state whose organ has carried out the act. An act of the state may be carried out illegally on the territory of another state. The territory of the state is a space within which the acts of the state, and especially its coercive acts, are allowed by general international law to be carried out, a space within which the acts of a state may legally be performed.

But, as an exception, a state may legally perform acts, and especially coercive acts on the territory of another state. This is the case (1) if a state is authorized by particular international law, i.e., by a treaty concluded with the other state, to perform on this territory certain acts determined in the treaty; and (2) if a state in time of war occupies a part of the territory of the enemy. Then the occupying state is authorized by general international law to perform certain acts determined by that law on the occupied territory, which thereby does not become the territory of the occupying state. Hence we may define the territory of the state as that space within which a state is authorized by general international law to perform all acts provided for by its national law or, which amounts to the same, the space within which according to general international law the organs determined by a national legal order are authorized to execute this order. The international legal order determines how the validity of the national legal orders is restricted to a certain space and what are the boundaries of this space.

2. The Restriction of the Territorial Sphere of Validity of the National Legal Order

That the validity of the national legal order is restricted by the international legal order to a certain space, the so-called territory of the state, does not mean that the national legal order is authorized to regulate only the behavior of individuals which takes place within this space. The restriction refers in the first place to the coercive acts provided by the national legal order and the procedure leading to these acts.

The law regulates human behavior by attaching sanctions to the contrary behavior, to the delict. But the delict is—as pointed out—not the only condition of the sanction, e.g., in case of a typical civil delict a legal transaction, a contract, must have been concluded, the nonfulfillment of which constitutes the delict. According to a generally recognized rule of international law, all individuals staying on the territory of a state are subjected to the law of that state. Hence this law may, in principle, attach to delicts (together with other conditioning facts) sanctions to be inflicted upon the individuals staying on the territory of the state concerned wherever the delict and other conditioning facts have taken place, unless in this respect certain restrictions result from other rules of general international law. Such rules are the norms obligating the state to treat citizens of another state in a certain way. As to the place of the delict and the other conditioning facts to which the law of a state may attach sanctions, there exists a difference between the citizens of the state concerned and the citizens of another state. With regard to its own citizens, no restriction exists. Under the law of a state, sanctions may be inflicted upon the citizens of this state for delicts of any kind committed on foreign territory. But there are certain facts existing and certain acts performed outside the territory of a state which must not be made by the law of this state the conditions of a sanction if the delict is committed by the citizen of another state. Thus it would constitute a violation of international law if the law of a state imposed the obligation to pay a tax upon the citizen of another state, in other words, provided a sanction in case of nonpayment of the tax, e.g., for a real estate which the alien has on the territory of his own state; or if the law of one state attached punishment to an act which is no crime according to the law of another state, as, for instance, bigamy, in case the act is performed by a citizen of that state on its territory. Trial and punishment of the alien could be considered by his state as a violation of its right. But there is no clear rule determining these cases. There is especially no agreement among the writers on international law as to the jurisdiction of states over crimes committed by aliens abroad. Some advocate the view that the competence of the state to punish crimes committed outside its own territory is restricted

The Essential Function of International Law

to the punishment of its own citizens. But this view is not in conformity with the practice of the states. It may be assumed that a state has jurisdiction over crimes committed outside its territory by citizens of another state, at least (1) if the acts are performed in preparation of and in participation in common crimes committed or attempted to be committed in the state claiming jurisdiction; or (2) if by these acts subjects of the state claiming jurisdiction are injured; or (3) if these acts are directed against its own safety.[3]

---

[3] Cf. Oppenheim, op. cit., Vol. 1, § 147. In the case *A. K. Cutting* (Moore, Digest of International Law, II, 228 ff.) Mexican courts (1886) exercised criminal jurisdiction over an American citizen for having published in Texas an article by which he allegedly libeled a Mexican citizen. The paper was not published in Mexico. In spite of representations made by the Government of the United States the jurisdiction was sustained by the courts of Mexico and approved by the executive branch of the Mexican Government upon the authority of a Mexican statute which provided that "penal offenses committed in a foreign country . . . by a foreigner against Mexicans, may be punished in the Republic [Mexico] and according to its laws," subject to the condition "that the accused be in the Republic, whether he has come voluntarily or has been brought by extradition proceedings." But the treaty of extradition concluded in 1899 by the United States and Mexico provided in Article III that "each contracting party agrees not to assume jurisdiction in the punishment of crimes committed exclusively within the territory of the other."

In *The Lotus Case* (Publications of the Permanent Court of International Justice, Series A, No. 10) the Permanent Court of International Justice (1927) expressed the opinion that there is no rule of international law which prohibits a state from exercising jurisdiction over a foreigner in respect of an offense committed outside its territory. "Though it is true that in all systems of law the principle of the territorial character of criminal law is fundamental, it is equally true that all or nearly all these systems of law extend their action to offences committed outside the territory of the State which adopts them, and they do so in ways which vary from State to State. The territoriality of criminal law, therefore, is not an absolute principle of international law and by no means coincides with territorial sovereignty" (p. 20). But in a dissenting opinion a member of the Court stated that "a State cannot rightfully assume to punish foreigners for alleged infraction of laws to which they were not, at the time of the alleged offence, in any wise subject."

In the case *In re Bayot* (France, Court of Cassation, Criminal Chamber, 1923; Annual Digest 1923–1924, Case No. 54) Bayot, a Belgian subject, was charged with having, during the First World War, procured in Belgium metals and objects of all kinds for the German authorities, and with having assisted, for a substantial remuneration, German officers and policemen to discover articles which their owners were concealing. On these charges he

There is certainly no difference between citizens and aliens as to the exercise of the criminal jurisdiction of a state, especially the execution of the criminal sanction, which in all cases must take place on the territory of the state exercising its jurisdiction.

That the legal power of the state is limited to its own territory does not mean that no act of the state may legally be carried out outside this state's territory. The limitation refers in principle to coercive acts in the wider sense of the term, including also the preparation of coercive acts. But these acts must not be executed on the territory of another state without the latter's consent. Without such consent they constitute a violation of international law. But there are acts of state which may be performed on the territory of another state without asking for the consent of the latter. Thus, e.g., a Head of State, during his stay in a foreign state, may conclude treaties, promulgate laws, or appoint officials by putting his signature on the documents concerned, all without infringing upon the right of the state he is visiting. But he would violate international law if he were to have his police arrest one of his subjects on the territory of the state where he is a guest. It is, however, not possible to draw a clear line between acts of state which do and those which do not require the consent of the state on the territory of which they are performed.

3. *The Territory of the State in a Narrower and in a Wider Sense*

a. *The boundaries of the state: The principle of effectiveness.* Within the so-called territory of the state as the territorial sphere of validity of the national legal order, that is, within the space where a certain state is authorized by general international law to execute its national law, we have to distinguish the territory of

---

was arrested, prosecuted, and sentenced in France. The Court held that "even if the right to punish, which emanates from the sovereign power, does not extend in principle beyond territorial limits, a contrary rule obtains in the case provided for by Article 7 of the *Code d'Instruction criminelle* which, based on the right of legitimate defense, gives the French courts jurisdiction to take cognizance of crimes aimed at the security of the State committed outside French territory by a foreigner who has been arrested in France . . . ."

The Essential Function of International Law

the state in a narrower and in a wider sense. The territory of the state in a narrower sense is that space within which in principle one state only, the state to which the territory belongs, is entitled to exercise its legal power, and especially to carry out coercive acts, a space from which all the other states are excluded. It is the space for which, according to general international law, only one definite national legal order is authorized to prescribe coercive acts, the space within which only the coercive acts stipulated by this order may be executed. It is the space within the so-called boundaries of the state.

The boundaries of the state are determined according to the principle of effectiveness, which plays an important part in international law. The exclusive validity of a national legal order extends according to international law just as far as this order is firmly established, i.e., is, on the whole, effective; as far as the national legal order is permanently obeyed and applied.

Traditional theory distinguishes between "natural" and "artificial," i.e., legal boundaries; but the boundaries of a state have always a legal character, whether or not they coincide with such "natural" frontiers, as, e.g., a river or a mountain range. So-called natural boundaries consisting of water are of different kinds: rivers, lakes, landlocked seas, and a maritime belt.

b. *Acquisition of territory.* The boundaries of a state may be determined by a treaty. By such a treaty an existing boundary, established according to the principle of effectiveness, may be confirmed. But by a treaty also new boundaries may be established, for instance, by a treaty of cession. Such a treaty gives the state to which the territory has been ceded, the cessionary, a legal title against the ceding state. The former acquires by the treaty of cession the right to take possession of the ceded territory, that is, to extend to that area the validity and efficacy of its legal order. The ceded territory, however, does not cease to be part of the territory of the ceding state and does not become part of the cessionary's territory until the cessionary has actually taken possession of the ceded territory. If the ceding state, in violation of its treaty obligation, refuses to withdraw from the ceded territory, it commits an international delict, and the cessionary is authorized by general international law to take enforcement actions against the delinquent state; but the territory concerned remains the territory of the delinquent state, no territorial change taking place. The legal situation is about the same as that which exists under national law if the latter requires for the transfer of property, in addition to a contract of purchase, acquisition of effective possession.

A state may not only retain but also acquire territory by conduct which constitutes a violation of international law. This is admitted by many writers in case of so-called prescription, that is, in case a state is in undisturbed possession of a territory during a certain period of time. Such territory is considered to be legally the territory of the possessing state even if the effective possession has taken place by an illegal action. This, too, is an application of the principle of effectiveness.

Acquisition of territory by an illegal action may also take place in case of so-called subjugation. If a state in the course of a war occupies the enemy territory and defeats its opponent completely so that no further resistance on its part is possible, the victorious state may—after having firmly established its dominion over the conquered territory—incorporate it in its territory. An incorporation of territory which takes place without the consent of the legitimate owner is called annexation. The territory of a conquered state may be annexed by a victorious state with the intention of incorporating it permanently or with the intention of disposing of it sooner or later, for instance, by ceding it to a third state or by establishing a new state on it. Whatever the intention of the conqueror may be, the annexed territory legally becomes its own territory, even if the war waged by the victor against the vanquished was an illegal war and the annexation of the vanquished state an international delict. It is again the principle of effectiveness as a principle of international law under which this territorial change takes place.

The principle of effectiveness manifests itself with particular clearness in case a state acquires territory which belongs to no state (stateless territory) by occupation. Such occupation has the effect of the acquisition of territory only if it is effective, that is to say, if the state concerned takes the territory into real possession

The Essential Function of International Law

and establishes there some kind of administration. It is now generally recognized that mere discovery of a territory does not create a title. Some writers maintain that mere discovery gives an "inchoate" title, that means that during the time necessary to establish effective possession after the discovery of the territory, the other states are legally excluded from the occupation of the territory concerned.[4]

The principle of effectiveness prevails under general international law to a much greater extent than under national law, the law of a state. For, under a centralized coercive order a legal situation can be maintained and, when illegally changed, restored, by intervention of the executive power exercised by central organs of the legal community. This may be also the case within a centralized international community established by particular conventional international law, guaranteeing effectively the territorial integrity of the contracting states. Under general international law, the states are

---

[4] In the *Island of Palmas Arbitration* (22 *American Journal of International Law* [1928] 867 ff.) the arbitrator stated: "Titles of acquisition of territorial sovereignty in present-day international law are either based on an act of effective apprehension, such as occupation or conquest, or, like cession, presuppose that the ceding and the cessionary Power or at least one of them, have the faculty of effectively disposing of the ceded territory. In the same way natural accretion can only be conceived of as an accretion to a portion of territory where there exists an actual sovereignty capable of extending to a spot which falls within its sphere of activity. It seems therefore natural that an element which is essential for the constitution of sovereignty should not be lacking in its continuation. So true is this, that practice, as well as doctrine, recognizes—though under different legal formulae and with certain differences as to the conditions required—that the continuous and peaceful display of territorial sovereignty (peaceful in relation to other States) is as good as a title. The growing insistence with which international law, ever since the middle of the 18th century, has demanded that the occupation shall be effective would be inconceivable, if effectiveness were required only for the act of acquisition and not equally for the maintenance of the right. . . . The principle that continuous and peaceful display of the functions of State within a given region is a constituent element of territorial sovereignty is not only based on the conditions of the formation of independent States and their boundaries (as shown by the experience of political history) as well as on an international jurisprudence and doctrine widely accepted; this principle has further been recognized in more than one federal State, where a jurisdiction is established in order to apply, as need arises, rules of international law to the interstate relations of the State members." Cf. also the *Clipperton Island Arbitration, infra*, p. 225.

obliged to respect the territorial integrity of the other states; but a violation of this obligation does not exclude the change of the legal situation. The principle advocated by some writers—*ex injuria jus non oritur* ("a right cannot originate in an illegal act")—does not, or not without important exceptions, apply in international law.

c. *Territorial supremacy.* That the territory enclosed by the boundaries of a state legally belongs to this state or—as it is usually characterized—that it is under the territorial supremacy or sovereignty of this state means that all individuals staying on this territory are, in principle, subjected to the legal power of that state and only of that state. This is expressed in the rule *Qui in territorio meo est, etiam meus subditus est* ("If somebody is in my territory he is also subjected to me"). It does not mean that the territory is the property of the state. Property is the specific relation between an individual (or a group of individuals) and all the other individuals with respect to a thing. The essence of this relation is that the proprietor has the right to dispose of the thing, all the other individuals being obliged not to interfere with his disposition. This relationship is normally established by national law; it is a relationship among individuals under the national law. No such relationship is designated by the statement that a certain territory "belongs" to a certain state. "Territory of a state" is a figurative expression designating a certain quality of the national law—its territorial sphere of validity—not a relationship among individuals under the law. The territory of a state is not a thing; it is especially not the land or a piece of land; it is a space determined by international law. Property in land within this space may or may not be the property of the state as a juristic person. But a state may own land not only within its own space, that is the territorial sphere of validity of its own law or under its own territorial supremacy or sovereignty, but also within the territory of another state, i.e., under the territorial supremacy or sovereignty of another state.

The incorrect idea that the territory of the state is the property of the state has probably its origin in the fact that international law confers upon the state rights and upon the other states obligations, which show a certain analogy to the rights and obligations involved in property. All the states are obliged to respect the so-

The Essential Function of International Law 217

called territorial integrity of another state, which means that they are obliged to refrain from performing certain acts within that space which is the "territory" of another state. International law confers upon each state the right to dispose of its territory. Under international law, only the state within the boundaries of which a territory lies is entitled to dispose of this territory, which means that according to general international law, only organs of the national legal order have the power to enter into international legal transactions referring to the territory which is the territorial sphere of validity of that national legal order. These legal transactions have the effect that other states (or international communities) acquire the right to exercise certain, or even all, functions of a state within this space or a certain part of this space. In case a state confers upon another the right to exercise permanently all functions of a state within a part of the former's territory, including the right to transfer this right to others (to dispose of the territory), we speak of cession. A mere lease of territory is established if the right to perform all functions of a state within part of the territory of a state is conferred by this state upon another state only for a definite period of time and without the right to transfer this right to other states. Other international transactions with respect to the territory or parts of the territory of a state are treaties by which a territory (or part of it) is placed under the trusteeship system of the United Nations (or, formerly, under the mandate system of the League of Nations); treaties by which a state confers upon another state the right to erect fortifications or keep armed forces on its territory;[5] and the like.

---

[5] For instance, the treaty signed by the United States and Japan at San Francisco on September 8, 1951, which reads as follows: "ARTICLE I. Japan grants, and the United States of America accepts the right, upon the coming into force of the treaty of peace and of this treaty, to dispose United States land, air and sea forces in and about Japan. Such forces may be utilized to contribute to the maintenance of international peace and security in the Far East and to the security of Japan against armed attack from without, including assistance given at the express request of the Japanese Government to put down large-scale internal riots and disturbances in Japan, caused through instigation or intervention by an outside power or powers. ARTICLE II. During the exercise of the right referred to in Article I, Japan will not grant, without the prior consent of the United States of America, any bases or any rights,

d. *The "impenetrability" of the state.* The principle that the national legal order has exclusive validity for a certain territory, the territory of the state in the narrower sense, and that within this territory all individuals are subjected only and exclusively to this national legal order or to the coercive power of this state, is usually expressed by saying that only one state can exist on the same territory, or—borrowing a phrase from physics—that the state is "impenetrable." There are, however, exceptions to this principle. There are certain individuals staying on the territory of a state who, according to general international law, are not subjected to the legal and especially not to the coercive power of the state, individuals who enjoy the privilege of so-called exterritoriality. This problem will be discussed in connection with the personal sphere of validity of the national legal order,[6] which, too, is restricted by this privilege. Only the territorial sphere of validity of the national legal order is restricted, or, what amounts to the same, on the territory of one state another state is existent in case a state by a treaty confers upon another state the right to exercise certain functions, especially to perform coercive acts, on the former's territory, acts that otherwise would not be allowed under general international law. In wartime, a state is, even by general international law, permitted to undertake coercive acts on foreign territory that it occupies militarily (belligerent occupation).

Another exception is the so-called *condominium* exercised by two (or more) states over the same territory. The legal order valid for this territory is a common part of the legal orders of the states

---

powers or authority whatsoever, in or relating to bases or the right of garrison or of maneuver, or transit of ground, air or naval forces to any third power. ARTICLE III. The conditions which shall govern the disposition of armed forces of the United States of America in and about Japan shall be determined by administration agreements between the two Governments. ARTICLE IV. This treaty shall expire whenever in the opinion of the Governments of the United States of America and of Japan there shall have come into force such United Nations arrangements or such alternate individual or collective security dispositions as will satisfactorily provide for the maintenance by the United Nations or otherwise of international peace and security in the Japan area. ARTICLE V. This treaty shall be ratified by the United States of America and Japan and will come into force when instruments of ratification thereof have been exchanged by them at Washington."

[6] Cf. *infra*, pp. 228ff.

The Essential Function of International Law

exercising the condominium. The norms of this legal order are established by an agreement between the States exercising the condominium and applied by common organs of these states. The territory of the condominium is a common territory of these states, a common territorial sphere of validity of their national legal orders.

The federal state is sometimes referred to as a further exception: the territory of each component state, it is argued, is simultaneously part of the territory of the federal state. But the so-called component states of a federal state are not states in the sense of international law; and even when they have a limited right to conclude treaties, they never have the power to confer by such treaties territorial rights upon other states.

e. *The maritime belt.* The territory of the state in a narrower sense of the term, i.e., the territory within which in principle only one state is authorized to exercise its legal power, should be distinguished from areas where all states are permitted to exercise their legal power, to carry out coercive acts provided for by their national law, with certain restrictions. Such areas are the open sea (or high seas) and the territories which have the character of no-state's land because they do not legally belong to any particular state.

The open sea (high seas) is that part of the sea which lies beyond the territorial waters (or maritime belt). The territorial waters (the maritime belt) are that part of the sea adjacent to the coast of a state which is under the latter's effective control. That the territorial waters belong to the littoral state is a rule of international law, recognized even by Grotius, who maintained that "sovereignty over a part of the sea" is gained "by means of territory insofar as those who sail over the part of the sea along the coast may be constrained from the land."[7] Bynkershoek, in his treatise *De Dominio*

---

[7] Grotius, *De jure belli ac pacis* (1625), Bk. II, Chap. III, sec. 13. In the *Corfu Channel Case* the International Court of Justice (1949) (International Court of Justice, Reports, 1949, p. 4) gave judgment that "the People's Republic of Albania is responsible under international law for explosions which occurred on October 22nd, 1946, in Albanian waters, and for the damage and loss of human life that resulted therefrom." The Court assumed that "the laying of the minefield which caused the explosions on October 22nd, 1946, could not have been accomplished without the knowledge of the Albanian Government." The Court was of the opinion that Albania violated its obliga-

Maris[8] formulated the rule concerned in the frequently quoted sentence: *Terrae potestas finitur ubi finitur vis armorum* ("The dominion over the land ends where the power of arms ends"). He concluded that "the dominion of land over the sea extends as far as a cannon will carry." This was considered to be a distance of three miles measured from the low-water mark.[9] The three-mile rule was generally recognized during the nineteenth and at the beginning of the twentieth century only insofar as it determined a minimum distance. Many states claimed supremacy over a much wider area; and some writers advocated the doctrine that each state has the right to determine for itself the extent of its territorial waters. Nowadays, the three-mile rule is certainly obsolete. But the principle remains valid that the territorial waters do not extend beyond that part of the sea over which the littoral state can exercise effective control.[10]

---

tions to notify "for the benefit of shipping in general, the existence of a minefield in Albanian territorial waters" and to warn the approaching British warships of the imminent danger. The Court based Albania's responsibility on "every State's obligation not to allow knowingly its territory to be used for acts contrary to the rights of other States." Thus the Court declared the Albanian territorial waters as the territory of the Albanian State. Consequently the Court considered that a mine-sweeping operation carried out by British warships on November 12 and 13, 1946, "against the clearly expressed wish of the Albanian Government" as a violation of the sovereignty of Albania. The Court gave judgment that "by reason of the acts of the British Navy in Albanian waters in the course of the Operation of November 12th and 13th, 1946, the United Kingdom violated the sovereignty of the People's Republic of Albania, and that this declaration by the Court constitutes in itself appropriate satisfaction."

[8] Bynkershoek, *De dominio maris* (1702), Chap. II. The above-quoted sentence continues as follows: "for that is as far as we seem to have both command and possession. I am speaking, however, of our own times, in which we use those engines of war; otherwise I should have to say in general terms that the control from the land ends where the power of men's weapons ends; for it is this, as we have said, that guarantees possession."

[9] In the case of *The Anna* (5 C. Robinson's Reports 373) the British High Court of Admiralty (1805) held: "We all know that the rule of law on this subject is *terrae dominium finitur ubi finitur armorum vis*, and since the introduction of fire arms, that distance has usually been recognized to be about three miles from the shore."

[10] In *The Elida* (Germany, Imperial Supreme Prize Court, 1915; 1 Entscheidungen des Oberprisengerichts 9) the Swedish ship *Elida*, with a cargo of wood, was captured by a German torpedo boat within four miles

The Essential Function of International Law

The territorial waters are, as pointed out, part of the territory of the littoral state. But general international law imposes upon that state the obligation to permit in time of peace inoffensive passage of the merchantmen of all the other states. Whether and to what extent such an obligation exists with respect to men-of-war is disputed. Oppenheim, e.g., maintains that there is a rule obligating

---

of the Swedish coast, but outside the three-mile limit, because of alleged carriage of contraband. The prize court stated in its opinion: "It is true that a considerable number of States have extended by national law their territorial jurisdiction beyond the three-mile limit, either generally or with regard to certain legal rights. This particularly applies to Sweden and Norway, which extended their national waters to a distance of four miles. A number of other States even went much further in this respect. But a special international title, valid in relation to the German Empire, and therefore to be taken into account by the prize court, does not exist, for up to the present time the Swedish claim has been recognized only by the Norwegian Government. According to official information from the German Foreign Office, Germany especially in the course of the discussions concerning this matter which took place in 1874, did not accept Sweden's point of view but treated the question of national waters as an open one, while England insisted upon the three-mile limit. Similarly in 1897, when the Swedish Government addressed a communication to the German Legation at Stockholm concerning the fishery jurisdiction, the German Government restricted itself to raising no objection against Sweden's claim to a four-mile boundary for the fishery and the question of the neutralization of this marine area in case of war was not thereby affected.—Therefore, under these circumstances, the decision must rest upon the basis of the German Prize Regulations, which in No. 3a forbid the application of prize law within a zone of only three nautical miles from the low-water mark of neutral coasts." But the court denied the legality of the seizure because the cargo was no contraband.

In *Republic of Panama (Compañía de Navegación Nacional) v. United States of America* (United States-Panama, General Claims Commission, 1933, Hunt, Report of American and Panamanian Arbitration [1934], p. 812), the commission stated: "The general rule of the extension of sovereignty over the 3-mile zone is clearly established. Exceptions to the completeness of this sovereignty should be supported by clear authority. There is a clear preponderance of authority to the effect that this sovereignty is qualified by what is known as the right of innocent passage, and that this qualification forbids the sovereign actually to prohibit the innocent passage of alien merchant vessels through its territorial waters.—There is no clear preponderance of authority to the effect that such vessels when passing through territorial waters are exempt from civil arrest. In the absence of such authority, the Commission cannot say that a country may not, under the rules of international law, assert the right to arrest on civil process merchant ships passing through its territorial waters."

the littoral states to permit inoffensive passage of foreign men-of-war through such parts of the maritime belt as form part of the highways for international traffic.[11] Foreign merchantmen which cast anchor in the maritime belt of a state are under the jurisdiction of that state. Whether merchantmen which do not stay but merely pass through the maritime belt are under the jurisdiction of the littoral state is doubtful.[12] But it is generally recognized that men-of-war and other public vessels[13] are always exempt from this jurisdiction.

---

[11] Cf. Oppenheim, *l.c.* I, § 188.—In the *Corfu Channel Case* (cf. *supra*, p. 219) the International Court of Justice did not consider the general question "whether States under international law have a right to send warships in time of peace through territorial waters not included in a strait." But the Court declared: "It is, in the opinion of the Court, generally recognized and in accordance with international custom that States in time of peace have a right to send their warships through straits used for international navigation between two parts of the high seas without the previous authorization of a coastal State, provided that the passage is innocent. Unless otherwise prescribed in an international convention, there is no right for a coastal State to prohibit such passage through straits in time of peace."

[12] The Final Act of the Hague Conference on the Progressive Codification of International Law (1930) contains the following rules concerning criminal and civil jurisdiction over vessels passing through territorial waters: ARTICLE 8. A coastal State may not take any steps on board a foreign vessel passing through the territorial sea to arrest any person or to conduct any investigation by reason of any crime committed on board the vessel during its passage, save only in the following cases: (1) if the consequences of the crime extend beyond the vessel; or (2) if the crime is of a kind to disturb the peace of the country or the good order of the territorial sea; or (3) if the assistance of the local authorities has been requested by the captain of the vessel or by the consul of the country whose flag the vessel flies. ARTICLE 9. A coastal State may not arrest nor divert a foreign vessel passing through the territorial sea for the purpose of exercising civil jurisdiction in relation to a person on board the vessel. A coastal State may not levy execution against, or arrest the vessel for the purpose of any civil proceedings save only in respect of obligations or liabilities incurred by the vessel itself in the course of or for the purpose of its voyage through the waters of the coastal State."

[13] In *The Parlement Belge* (1819, 4 Law Reports, Probate Division 197 ff.) the British Court of Appeal held that "an unarmed packet [The Parlement Belge] belonging to the sovereign of a foreign state, and in the hands of officers commissioned by him, and employed in carrying mails, is not liable to be seized in a suit in rem to recover redress for a collision, and this immunity is not lost by reason of the packet's also carrying merchandize and passengers for hire,"

The Essential Function of International Law

Different from the territorial waters (or maritime belt) of a state are its national waters, the waters in its lakes, its canals, its rivers together with their mouths, and its ports and harbors. National waters belong legally to the territory of the state in the narrower sense of the term. With respect to its national waters, a state is not subjected to any restriction by general international law. But it should be noted that the territorial as well as the national waters of a state can be ceded only together with the adjacent land territory of which they are considered to be an accessory.

f. *The open sea.* The open sea (high seas) is an area where any state is entitled to undertake any action, that is to say, exercise its jurisdiction—especially its coercive power—on board its own ships, that is, on board the ships which legitimately sail under the flag of this state. The usual way to describe the legal situation of a vessel on the open sea is to say that it has to be considered as a floating part of its home state. That means that a vessel on the open sea is under the exclusive jurisdiction of the state under the flag of which it legitimately sails. Exclusive jurisdiction means that no other state but the flag state is entitled to exercise coercive power on board the ship which legitimately sails under its flag. That the ship is considered to be a floating part of its home state means further that the national law of the flag state may provide that anything which happens on the ship shall be considered as if it happened on the territory of the flag state, such as the birth of a child, a legal transaction, a crime, and the like.[14]

---

[14] In the case *Rex v. Gordon-Finlayson* (England, High Court, King's Bench Division; Annual Digest 1941–1942, Case No. 67) the question arose before a British court whether the provision of the British Army Act, 1881, that "a person subject to military law shall not be tried by court martial for treason, murder, manslaughter, treason-felony, or rape committed in the United Kingdom" was applicable to a case of murder committed by an officer of the British forces in a British ship on the high seas. The Court (1941) held that the alleged crime was not committed in the United Kingdom, as a British ship on the high seas was not part of the United Kingdom within the proviso to section 41 of the Army Act. The Court said: ". . . it is because it is necessary for some Court to have jurisdiction over a crime committed on a British ship that it was held, and has always been the law for a great many years, that there is jurisdiction in those circumstances, although the person has not committed the crime in England, to try him in the same way as if he had committed the crime in England, for the reason that he is

The jurisdiction which a state has on the open sea is restricted insofar as it is not allowed to be exercised on board or against foreign ships. Coercive acts especially, must not be performed by the crew of a vessel of one state on board or against a vessel of another state. But there are exceptions to this rule. Under certain circumstances, a state, acting through its men-of-war, can use force against vessels of other states on the open sea: (1) a littoral state is allowed to pursue into the open sea a foreign merchantman which has violated the law in its territorial waters and to seize it in order to bring it to trial; (2) each state is allowed to seize and bring to trial a foreign vessel illegally sailing under its flag; (3) a belligerent state is allowed to seize a neutral merchantman for breach of blockade or carriage of contraband in order to bring it to trial; (4) finally, all states, acting through their men-of-war or any other vessels sailing legitimately under their flag, are allowed to seize piratical vessels in order to bring pirates to punishment.

Apart from these exceptions, no state is permitted to use force against another state, and that means against the ship of another state, on the open sea. Hence no state can legally occupy a part of the open sea and reserve it for its exclusive use by preventing another state from establishing fisheries or laying telegraph or telephone cables, and the like. These rules constitute the so-called "freedom of the open sea," proclaimed by Hugo Grotius who maintained that the sea by its very nature cannot be the property of a state.[15] In modern theory of international law, the free-

---

alleged to have committed a crime upon a British ship, where all persons are under the aegis of the British flag, which carries with it the rights and privileges of a British subject and the liability to the British law."

[15] Hugo Grotius, *Mare Liberum* (1608) (English translation: *The Freedom of the Seas*. Carnegie Endowment for International Peace, 1916) chap. V: "Two conclusions may be drawn from what has thus far been said. The first is, that that which cannot be occupied, or which never has been occupied, cannot be the property of any one, because all property has arisen from occupation. The second is, that all that which has been so constituted by nature that although serving some one person it still suffices for the common use of all other persons, is today and ought in perpetuity to remain in the same condition as when it was first created by nature.... The air belongs to this class of things for two reasons. First, it is not susceptible of occupation; and second its common use is destined for all men. For the same reasons the sea is common to all, because it is so limitless that it cannot become a possession of any one,

The Essential Function of International Law

dom of the open sea is formulated on the principle that no part of the open sea can be subjected to the sovereignty of any state and hence cannot be incorporated into the territory of any state through occupation. That does not mean that States cannot exercise their "sovereignty" or legal power on the open sea. On the contrary, each state is authorized by general international law to do so, that is to say, to execute its own law and especially to perform coercive acts on the open sea, but only on board its own ships, and not—with certain exceptions—against the ships of other states. The open sea is the territory of all states, but it is not the exclusive territory of one state, not the exclusive territorial sphere of validity of one national legal order. It is a space where, so to speak, the territorial spheres of validity of the different national legal orders penetrate each other.

g. *No-state's land.* Territory which is the land of no state has a legal status similar to that of the open sea, insofar as on this territory every state may exercise its legal power in the same way as on its own territory, i.e., the territory within its own boundaries. But there exists an essential difference: no-state's land can be legally acquired by any state through effective occupation, that is to say, in accordance with the principle of effectiveness.[16]

---

and because it is adapted for the use of all, whether we consider it from the point of view of navigation or of fisheries."

[16] In the *Clipperton Island Arbitration* (France-Mexico, 1931; 26 *American Journal of International Law* [1932] 390) the King of Italy, as arbiter, decided that Clipperton Island belonged to France. In his opinion he stated: "There is ground to admit that, when in November, 1858, France proclaimed her sovereignty over Clipperton, that island was in the legal situation of *territorium nullius,* and, therefore, susceptible of occupation. The question remains whether France proceeded to an effective occupation, satisfying the conditions required by international law for the validity of this kind of territorial acquisition. . . . It is beyond doubt that by immemorial usage having the force of law, besides the *animus occupandi,* the actual, and not the nominal, taking of possession is a necessary condition of occupation. This taking of possession consists in the act, or series of acts, by which the occupying state reduces to its possession the territory in question and takes steps to exercise exclusive authority there. Strictly speaking, and in ordinary cases, that only takes place when the state establishes in the territory itself an organization capable of making its laws respected. But this step is, properly speaking, but a means of procedure to the taking of possession, and, therefore, is not identical with the latter. There may also be cases where it is

h. *Subsoil and air space.* The territory of a state is usually considered as a determinate portion of the earth's surface. This idea is incorrect. The territory of the state, as the territorial sphere of validity of the national legal order, is not a plane, but a space of three dimensions. The validity as well as the efficacy of the national legal order extends not only in width and length but also in depth and height. What traditional theory defines as "territory of the state"—that portion of the earth's surface delimited by the boundaries of the State—is only a visible plane formed by a transverse section of the state's three-dimensional space.

According to traditional doctrine, the space below this plane, as the territory of the state, belongs to that state and extends in principle until the center of the earth, being delimited only by the analogous space below the territories of the neighboring states, and, in the case of a littoral state, by the space below the open sea. The subsoil below the territorial waters of a state has the same legal status as the territory of the state in the narrower sense of the term. The same principle applies to the air space above the territory of a state which, according to the traditional doctrine, is unlimited. In conformity with this doctrine, Article 1 of the International Air Convention, concluded in 1919, declared that "every State has complete and exclusive sovereignty in the air space above its territory and territorial waters."[17] This doctrine ignores the principle of effectiveness. But is is hardly possible to maintain that under general international law the space below and above the territory of a state belongs to that state, irrespective of, and consequently also beyond, its effective control.

The air space above the open sea shares the legal status of the open sea; but the bed and the subsoil beneath the bed of the open sea has the legal status of no-state's land. It may be acquired

---

unnecessary to have recourse to this method. Thus, if a territory, by virtue of the fact that it was completely uninhabited, is, from the first moment when the occupying state makes its appearance there, at the absolute and undisputed disposition of that state, from that moment the taking of possession must be considered as accomplished, and the occupation is thereby completed."

[17] The Final Act of the International Civil Aviation Conference, December 7, 1944, did not affect the principle laid down in Article 1 of the International Air Convention of 1919.

through effective occupation. This is important with respect to tunnels, coal mines, and the like. But, an occupation of the bed or the subsoil beneath the bed of the open sea which would endanger the freedom of the open sea is illegal.

B. DETERMINATION OF THE PERSONAL SPHERE OF VALIDITY OF THE NATIONAL LEGAL ORDER (THE PEOPLE OF THE STATE) BY INTERNATIONAL LAW

1. *The People of the State as the Personal Sphere of Validity of the National Legal Order*

A second "element" of the state, according to traditional theory, is the people—usually defined as the human beings residing within the territory of the state. They are regarded as a unity. As the state has one territory only, so it has only one people; and as the unity of the territory is a juristic, not a natural one, so is the unity of the people. It is constituted by the unity of the legal order valid for the individuals regarded as the people of the state. Individuals of different races, languages, and religions very often actually form one "people," that is to say, the people of one state; and they can form one people, in spite of all these and other differences, because the people of the state are the individuals whose behavior is regulated by the national legal order; that is, the personal sphere of validity of this order.

Just as the territorial sphere of validity of the national legal order is limited, so is the personal sphere. An individual belongs to the people of a given state if he is included in the personal sphere of validity of its legal order. As every contemporary state comprises only a part of space, so it also comprises only a part of mankind. And as the territorial sphere of validity of the national legal order is determined by international law, so is its personal sphere.

How does international law determine the personal sphere of validity of the national legal order? Whose behavior is the national legal order authorized by international law to regulate? Or, in other terms, what individuals can the state subject to its legal power, and that means its coercive power, without violating international law and consequently the rights of other states?

According to general international law, the coercive acts provided by the national legal order may be directed only against individuals who are within the territory of the state, that is, within the space which international law determines as the territorial sphere of validity of the national legal order. The determination of the territory of a state by international law has been described in the previous chapter. International law determines the people of the state only indirectly, by determining the territory of the state. The former results from the latter.

2. Exterritoriality

A state can exercise its coercive power, in principle, against anybody within its territory. All the individuals staying within the territory of the state are subjected to its coercive power; that means that all the individuals staying within the territorial sphere of validity of a national legal order are subjected to this order with respect to the execution of the coercive acts provided by this order.[18] But this rule of international law is subject to exceptions. It is the international institution of so-called exterritoriality by which the above-mentioned rule is restricted.

a. *Exterritoriality as restriction of the personal sphere of validity of the national legal order.* According to general international law, certain individuals enjoy the privilege of exemption from the coer-

---

[18] The rule is usually formulated thus: A state possesses jurisdiction over all persons and things within its territory. Thus, e.g., in the case of the *Compañia Naviera Vascongado v. The Cristina* (1938 Law Reports, A.C. 485, at pp. 496 f.) Lord Macmillan in the British House of Lords (1938) said: "It is an essential attribute of sovereignty of this realm as of all sovereign independent States, that it should possess jurisdiction over all persons and things within its territorial limits and in all causes civil and criminal arising within these limits." Jurisdiction over things is, in the last instance, jurisdiction over persons.

The Essential Function of International Law 229

cive power or, as it is usual to say, from the criminal, civil, and administrative jurisdiction of the state on the territory of which they are staying. No coercive act, not even a legal procedure aiming at a coercive act, is allowed to be directed against these individuals. This privilege constitutes not only a direct restriction of the personal sphere of validity of the national legal order, but also an indirect restriction of the territorial sphere of validity of the national legal order, insofar as a state is legally prevented from exercising its coercive power against these individuals on its own territory. It is this aspect of the privilege which explains the term "exterritoriality," implying the fiction that the individuals concerned shall be treated as if they were not on the territory of the state the coercive power of which is restricted.

It is usually contended that the individuals who enjoy the privilege of exterritoriality, being exempt from the coercive power of the state on the territory of which they are staying, are nevertheless subjected to the law of this state, that is to say are obliged to comply with its provisions. This is true insofar as prosecution of these individuals for violations of the law committed during the time they enjoy the privilege is possible as soon as they lose this privileged status. In this sense the privilege of exterritoriality means that the exercise of coercive power against the privileged individuals is only suspended. But this holds true only with respect to certain and not to all norms of the legal order of the receiving state whose coercive power is restricted. Thus, for instance, no state is allowed to inflict upon a person who was a diplomatic envoy to this state a sanction for not having paid an income tax during the tenure of his office after he ceases to be a diplomatic envoy in relation to the state concerned. But the receiving state may prosecute the former diplomatic envoy for a criminal delict committed during the time of his diplomatic mission. Prosecution is possible also in case the exemption from jurisdiction is waived by the sending[19] state.

---

[19] In the case *Dickinson v. Del Solar* (Annual Digest 1929–1930, Case No. 190) the English High Court of Justice (King's Bench Division) (1929) stated: "Diplomatic agents are not, in virtue of their privileges as such, immune from legal liability for any wrongful acts. The accurate statement is that they are not liable to be sued in the English Courts unless they submit to the jurisdiction. Diplomatic privilege does not import immunity from legal

As to the delicts for which prosecution is excluded, it is important to note that the privilege of exterritoriality applies to acts the privileged individuals perform as private persons. That they cannot be prosecuted for acts they perform in their capacity as organs of their state, that is to say, for acts which are acts of their state, is not a consequence of their exterritoriality but of the rule of general international law that no state has jurisdiction over the acts of another state. (See *infra*, p. 235.)

b. *Heads of foreign states and diplomatic representatives as subjects enjoying the privilege of exterritoriality.* The privilege of exterritoriality is granted by general international law to heads of foreign states and to diplomatic representatives.

The Head of the State is an organ upon which certain specific functions are conferred by the state's constitution. These functions usually include legislation or some kind of participation in legislation, conclusion of treaties, declaration of war, reception and mission of diplomatic envoys and consuls, disposition of the armed forces as commander in chief, exercise of the right of pardon, appointment of all or of the higher officials of the state. These functions may be exercised by the Head of State alone or in cooperation with other organs, such as the parliament or the cabinet. The Head of State may be an individual or a collegiate organ. In the first case the office may be hereditary. Other methods of appointment are nomination by the predecessor, election by the people, or election by the parliament. If the office is hereditary and the title of the Head of State is Emperor or King or the like, he is called a monarch; he is called president of a republic if he is elected, especially if elected only for a definite term. If elected for life with the title of Emperor or King, he is also called a monarch.

It is usual to consider a monarch as the representative of the sovereignty of the state and consequently as a "sovereign" himself. If under international law sovereignty is possible at all, it

---

liability, but only exemption from local jurisdiction. The privilege is the privilege of the Sovereign by whom the diplomatic agent is accredited, and it may be waived with the sanction of the Sovereign or of the official superior of the agent."

The Essential Function of International Law

is a quality of the state, and cannot be a quality of one of its organs. Some writers maintain that international law grants to "sovereigns" more privileges than to presidents of republics; but this holds true only with respect to certain honors which are due to a monarch but not to the president of a republic. From a legal point of view this difference is of no importance.

Some writers maintain that international law obliges the states to have a Head of State. Such a rule can hardly be proved. The constitution of a state may confer upon different organs the functions which are combined in the competence of the organ called Head of State, so that no Head of State exists. General international law leaves the organization of the state to the national legal order. But each state must have an organ or organs competent to represent it in relation to other states. Such organs are not only the Head of State—provided that such an organ exists—but also the minister of foreign affairs and the diplomatic representatives.

Each community which is a state in the sense of international law has the active and passive right of legation, that is to say, the right to send and to receive diplomatic agents. But international communities of states, competent to engage in international transactions, especially to conclude treaties, such as the League of Nations and later the United Nations, also have the right of legation.

The privilege of exterritoriality is granted in different degrees to the above-mentioned persons. The privilege comprises in all cases exemption from civil, criminal, and administrative jurisdiction, including exemption from direct personal taxes, but not from customs duties. It extends in the case of heads of states and diplomatic envoys to their domicile (immunity of domicile), which implies that officials of the state concerned are not allowed to enter the domicile in order to perform within it official acts without the consent of the privileged persons. Immunity of domicile does not imply the right to grant asylum to persons prosecuted by the receiving state.[20] In respect to the immunity of domicile the restriction of the

---

[20] Such a right may be stipulated by a special agreement as, e.g., by the Convention signed at Havana on February 20, 1928, which provides in Article 2, paragraph 1: "Asylum granted to political offenders in legations, warships, military camps or military aircraft, shall be respected to the extent in which

territorial sphere of validity of the law of the state concerned is in the foreground. The privilege of exterritoriality of heads of foreign states and diplomatic envoys extends also to members of their suite, that is, to the individuals who accompany them in official or private service. But there is no unanimity concerning the extent to which the privilege is granted to private servants, especially when they are citizens of the receiving state. In the case of the head of a foreign state, the privilege of exterritoriality extends also to his wife; but, according to some writers, not to other members of his family; whereas according to most writers, in the case of a diplomatic envoy, the privilege of exterritoriality extends to his wife and to other members of his family living within the same household; but only the wife of the diplomatic envoy has the privilege of exterritoriality to the same extent as the envoy himself. Other members of his family living with him in the same household enjoy only exemption from criminal and civil jurisdiction.

c. *Other privileged persons.* Armed forces of a state may stay on the territory of another state either in time of war, or in time of peace on the basis of a treaty conferring upon one contracting party the right to keep troops on, or to send troops through, the territory of the other contracting party. In these cases the members of the armed forces are exempt from the jurisdiction of the state on the territory of which they stay, remaining under the jurisdiction of their own state.

It is usual to say that men-of-war in foreign (territorial and national) waters are exterritorial. By this statement a legal status is designated, characterized by the fact that the state in the waters of which the foreign man-of-war stays has no jurisdiction over the vessel and, consequently, is obliged to refrain from exercising any kind of coercive power on board the man-of-war.[21] This privi-

---

allowed as a right or through humanitarian toleration, by the usages, the conventions or the laws of the country in which granted and in accordance with the following provisions. . . ."

[21] In the case *The Schooner Exchange v. McFadden* (7 Cranch 116) the Supreme Court of the United States (1812) declared: "It seems, then, to the court, to be a principle of public law, that national ships of war, enter-

The Essential Function of International Law   233

lege constitutes a restriction of the territorial but not of the personal sphere of validity of the state concerned. For if members of the crew of the man-of-war are on shore, they are under the jurisdiction of the state. Some writers, however, maintain that if the members of the crew are on shore in an official function, they are exempt from the jurisdiction of the state on the territory of which they are staying.

State-owned ships other than men-of-war enjoy, in principle,

---

ing the port of a friendly power open for their reception, are to be considered as exempted by the consent of that power from its jurisdiction." The Court presupposed as a principle of international law: "The jurisdiction of the nation within its own territory is necessarily exclusive and absolute. It is susceptible of no limitation not imposed by itself . . . . All exceptions, therefore, to the full and complete power of a nation within its own territories, must be traced up to the consent of the nation itself." In order to apply the rule of general international law granting the privilege of exterritoriality to foreign men-of-war, the Court had to assume that if a state allows a foreign man-of-war to enter its ports, consent to the exemption from its jurisdiction is implied. "The implied license, therefore, under which such vessel enters a friendly port, may reasonably be construed, and, it seems to the court, ought to be construed, as containing an exemption from the jurisdiction of the sovereign, within whose territory she claims the rites of hospitality." This construction is a legal fiction. It is superfluous, for it is a rule of general international law by which the privilege concerned is established, without any consent of the respective States.

In the case *Chung Chi Cheung v. The King* (Annual Digest 1938–1940, Case No. 87) the Judicial Committee of the Privy Council (1938) expressed the following opinion: "On the question of jurisdiction two theories have found favor with persons professing a knowledge of the principles of international law. One is that a public ship of a nation for all purposes either is, or is to be treated by other nations as, part of the territory of the nation to which she belongs. By this conception will be guided the domestic law of any country in whose territorial waters the ship finds herself. There will therefore be no jurisdiction in fact in any Court where jurisdiction depends upon the act in question, or the party to the proceedings, being done or found or resident in the local territory. The other theory is that a public ship in foreign waters is not, and is not treated as, territory of her own nation. The domestic Courts, in accordance with principles of international law, will accord to the ship and its crew and its contents certain immunities, some of which are well settled, though others are in dispute. In this view, the immunities do not depend upon an objective exterritoriality, but on implication of the domestic law. They are conditional, and can in any case be waived by the nation to which the public ship belongs." The fact that the immunities can

the same privilege as men-of-war. With respect to state-owned commercial ships, the practice of the states is not uniform. There is a tendency to abolish the privilege of exterritoriality of state-owned ships engaged in commerce.[22] A convention signed at Brussels on April 10, 1926, and ratified only by a few States, contains the following provision: "Seagoing vessels owned or operated by States, cargoes owned by them, and cargoes and passengers carried on Government vessels, and the States owning or operating such vessels, or owning such cargoes, are subject in respect of claims relating to the operation of such vessels or the carriage of such cargoes, to the same rules of liability and to the same obligations as those applicable to private vessels, cargoes and equipments." But this provision is not applicable to men-of-war and nontrading public vessels.

By international agreements states may confer exemption of their jurisdiction to persons who do not enjoy it under general international law, such as members of an international court or consuls. Consuls are organs the main function of which is to take care of the commercial interests of their state on the territory of another state. They have not the character of diplomatic representatives and, consequently, do not enjoy the diplomatic privilege of immunity from the jurisdiction of the state on the territory of which they are active, unless such privilege is expressly conferred upon them by special treaty. In former times consuls of certain Christian states on the territory of certain non-Christian states had criminal and civil jurisdiction over the citizens of their states.

be waived by the state to which the public ship belongs is quite compatible with the view that the exterritoriality of the ship is established by an objective rule of general international law, and that this rule has the character of *jus dispositivum*.

[22] Cf. the case *The Parlement Belge* (*supra*, p. 222). In the case *Berizzi Brothers Co. v. S.S. Pesaro* (271 U.S. 562) the same question arose with respect to the ship *Pesaro*, owned, possessed, and operated for trade purposes by the Italian Government. The Supreme Court of the United States (1926) decided the case in the same way. But in *Republic of Mexico v. Hoffman* (*The Baja California*) (39 *American Journal of International Law* [1945] 585 ff.) the Supreme Court of the United States (1945) held that the courts may not allow immunity from jurisdiction *in rem* to a vessel owned by a foreign government but not in its possession and service where the political branch of the government, though consulted, has not recognized such immunity.

The Essential Function of International Law   235

But the treaties establishing this extraterritorial consular jurisdiction[23] (so-called capitulations) are now repealed.

3. No State Has Jurisdiction over Another State

A most important restriction of the personal and the territorial sphere of validity of the national legal order, or what amounts to the same, of the jurisdiction of the state, results from the principle of general international law that no state has jurisdiction over another state. This principle is usually presented as a consequence of the fundamental right of equality and formulated as *par in parem non habet imperium* ("equals do not have jurisdiction over each other"). The jurisdiction to which the principle refers is jurisdiction exercised by the courts of a state. No state is allowed to exercise through its own courts jurisdiction over another state unless the other state expressly consents. But a state may exercise jurisdiction in another way over another state. This is the case when a state ascertains under general international law that another state has violated the former's right, and resorts to reprisals or war, as the sanctions of international law. But although a state cannot be sued in the courts of another state, it may bring a lawsuit before such courts. Since a state manifests its legal existence only through acts performed by human beings in their capacity as organs of the state, that is to say, through acts of state, the principle that no state has jurisdiction over another state must be interpreted to mean that a state must not exercise jurisdiction through its own courts over acts of another state unless the other state consents. Hence the principle applies not only in case a state as such is sued in a court of another state, but also in case an individual is the defendant or the accused and the civil or criminal delict for which the individual is prosecuted has the character of an act of state. Then the delict is to be imputed to the state, not to the individual, and only the sanctions provided by international law as reactions against delinquent states, reprisals and

---

[23] "Extraterritorial" jurisdiction means the jurisdiction exercised by a state outside its territory, on the territory of another state. "Exterritoriality" means immunity from jurisdiction.

war, are applicable.[24] Hence the principle that no state has jurisdiction over another state excludes individual—civil or criminal—responsibility for acts of state. Such responsibility can be

---

[24] In the case *The Caroline*, a vessel chartered during the Canadian rebellion (1837) by insurgents and captured by a British force, two Americans were killed on the occasion of the capture. Alexander McLeod, a member of the British force, when on business in New York in 1840, was arrested and indicted for the killing of one of the Americans. In a note to the Attorney General, the Secretary of State of the United States of America stated that "since the attack on the *Caroline* is avowed as a national act, which may justify reprisals, or even general war, if the Government of the United States, in the judgment which it shall form of the transaction and of its own duty, should see fit so to decide, yet that it raises a question entirely public and political, a question between independent nations; and that individuals connected in it cannot be arrested and tried before the ordinary tribunals, as for the violation of municipal law. If the attack on the *Caroline* was unjustifiable, as this Government has asserted, the law which has been violated is the law of nations; and the redress which is to be sought is the redress authorized, in such cases, by the provisions of that code." (Moore, *Digest of International Law*, II, 26).

In the case *Underhill v. Hernandez* (168 U.S. 250), the plaintiff, an American citizen, in 1892 in charge of the waterworks of the Venezuelan city of Bolívar, brought a suit for damage against the defendant on account of the fact that the latter in his capacity as head of the army of the revolutionary government of Venezuela (later recognized by the United States) prevented the plaintiff from leaving the city and forced him to operate the waterworks for the benefit of the revolutionary forces. The Supreme Court of the United States (1897) decided in favor of the defendant because "the courts of one country will not sit in judgment on the acts of another done within its own territory," regardless of whether the acts are performed by an organ representing the *de jure* or the *de facto* government.

As early as 1797 the Attorney General of the United States declared in the case *Governor Collot*, governor of the French island of Guadeloupe, against whom a civil action was brought based on his seizure and condemnation of a vessel while acting as governor of the island: "I am inclined to think, if the seizure of the vessel is admitted to have been an official act, done by the defendant by virtue, or under color, of the powers vested in him as governor, that it will of itself be a sufficient answer to the plaintiff's action; that the defendant ought not to answer in our courts for any mere irregularity in the exercise of his powers; and that the extent of his authority can, with propriety or convenience, be determined only by the constituted authorities of his own nation." (Moore, *op. cit.*, II, 23.)

In *The Invincible* (United States Circuit Court, D. Massachusetts, 1814, 2 Gallison 29) the court declared: "The acts done under the authority of one sovereign can never be subject to the revision of the tribunals of another sovereign; and the parties to such acts are not responsible therefor in their

The Essential Function of International Law

established only with the consent of the state for the act of which an individual is to be made responsible.[25] The principle that no state has jurisdiction over another state implies also that no court

---

private capacities." And in *The Zamora* (1916 Law Reports, 2 A.C. 77) the Judicial Committee of the Privy Council, after referring to this statement, declared: "It follows that but for the existence of Courts of Prize no one aggrieved by the acts of a belligerent power [i.e., acts of state] in time of war could obtain redress otherwise than through diplomatic channels at the risk of disturbing international amity."

In the case *Bigelow v. Zizianoff* (23 *American Journal of International Law* [1929] 172 ff.) Mr. Bigelow, Director of the Passport Service of the American Consulate General in Paris, furnished representatives of the press information, later published in a newspaper, that Princess Zizianoff's application for a visa was refused because she was an international spy. Cited before a French correctional tribunal, Mr. Bigelow denied the competence of the French court on the ground that he furnished the information in the performance of his duties, which statement was confirmed by the Government of the United States. Nevertheless, the French Court of Appeal rejected the contentions of Bigelow on appeal. In conformity with the statement of the French Attorney General that "French courts cannot be bound by the opinion of the Government of the United States which thinks that Consul Bigelow has acted within the scope of his duty," the Court declared that it could not consider the information furnished by Consul Bigelow as "performance of an official act," and decided that the wrong constituted by this information was "clearly unconnected with the duty performed by Bigelow."

[25] As to the question whether commercial activities of states are exempt from the jurisdiction of another state, the case *United States v. Deutsche Kalisyndikat Gesellschaft* (31 Federal Reporter [2d] 199) is of interest. A suit was brought by the United States to enjoin violations of the antitrust laws by the Deutsche Kalisyndikat Gesellschaft, the Société Commerciale des Potasses, and others. The ambassador of the Republic of France intervened. A motion was made to set aside the service of process on the ground that the court had no jurisdiction. In a letter to the Secretary of State of the United States, the French ambassador maintained that "the Société Commerciale des Potasses d'Alsace is an organization created and controlled by the Republic of France for the purpose of administering potash mines, some of which the French Republic acquired on the cession of Alsace-Lorraine by the treaty of Versailles in 1919, and some of which belong to French nationals, and that the suit commenced against the Société Commerciale des Potasses d'Alsace and its officers and agents was in fact begun against the French government." The United States District Court, S. D. New York (1929) denied the motion. The court held *inter alia:* "Société Commerciale was organized, like any other business corporation, under the general corporation laws of France. Its stockholders include private persons, as well as officials. It sold potash for others, as well as for the Republic of France. The law under which it was incorporated, as well as its certificate of incorporation, provide that it may be sued. It thereby was stripped of any

of a state is allowed to exercise jurisdiction by directing coercive measures against the property of another state as a consequence of or in connection with a delict committed by an individual in his capacity as organ of another state.

The principle that no state has jurisdiction over acts of another state applies also to the jurisdiction of a tribunal established by an international agreement with respect to acts of a state not a contracting party to the agreement. In relation to that state such a tribunal is not an "international" tribunal, but a common tribunal of the state parties to the agreement. This was the case with the so-called International Military Tribunal established by the London Agreement of 1945 for the Prosecution of European Axis War Criminals, to which the European Axis Powers were not contracting parties. Nevertheless, the London Agreement authorized the

---

sovereign immunity it otherwise may have enjoyed. . . . France holds it amenable to the process of its courts. The French law, like the law of the United States, regards a corporation as an entity distinct from its stockholders. A suit against a corporation is not a suit against a government merely because it has been incorporated by direction of the government, and is used as a governmental agent, and its stock is owned solely by the government. . . . The defendant company being an entity distinct from its stockholders, immunity cannot be claimed by it or on its behalf on the ground that it and the government of France are identical in any respect. Private corporations in which a government has an interest, and instrumentalities in which there are private interests, are not departments of government. . . . Nor can immunity be claimed by the defendant corporation, or on its behalf, or by or on behalf of any of its officers, agents, or employees, on the ground that they are acting as agents of a foreign government. An agent does not cease to be answerable personally for his illegal acts because he is an agent, even though he may be an instrumentality of government. . . . Officers and agents of a corporation are not officers or agents of its stockholders . . . and it therefore cannot be successfully urged that an action against an officer or agent of a corporation in which a sovereign state is a stockholder is in fact an action against the sovereign state. . . . A foreign sovereign cannot authorize his agents to violate the law in a foreign jurisdiction or to perform any sovereign or governmental function within the domain of another sovereign, without his consent. He, therefore, cannot claim as a matter of comity or otherwise that the act of the alleged agent in such case is the act of the sovereign, and that a suit against the agent is in fact a suit against the sovereign." Cf. also the cases *The Parlement Belge, supra,* pp. 222, 234, *Berizzi Bros. v. Pesaro* and *The Baja California, supra,* p. 234.

As to another exception to the principle that no state has jurisdiction over acts of another state (espionage), cf. *supra,* p. 129.

The Essential Function of International Law

Tribunal to sit in judgment on acts of these states, by conferring upon it the power of punishing individuals for having performed, in their capacity as organs of these states, certain acts declared as criminal by the Agreement.[26]

The principle that no state has jurisdiction over acts of another state implies the principle that the courts of one state are not entitled to question the validity of acts of another state performed within its jurisdiction.[27] But the courts of a state usually refuse to

---

[26] Cf. *supra*, p. 133. The International Military Tribunal, established by the London Agreement for the Prosecution of European Axis War Criminals of 1945 (cf. *supra*, p. 134) rejected in its judgment the principle of general international law, that an individual can be made responsible by the tribunal of a state (or by a common tribunal of several states) for acts performed in his capacity as organ of another state only with the latter's consent. The tribunal stated: "It was submitted that international law is concerned with the actions of sovereign States, and provides no punishment for individuals; and further, that where the act in question is an act of state, those who carry it out are not personally responsible, but are protected by the doctrine of the sovereignty of the State. In the opinion of the Tribunal, both these submissions must be rejected. That international law imposes duties and liabilities upon individuals as well as upon States has long been recognized. . . . The principle of international law, which under certain circumstances, protects the representatives of a state, cannot be applied to acts which are condemned as criminal by international law. The authors of these acts cannot shelter themselves behind their official position in order to be freed from punishment in appropriate proceedings." The statement that international law is concerned not only with states but also with individuals is certainly correct. As to the question under what conditions the act of an individual is to be considered as "criminal" under international law, that is to say, under what conditions an individual is criminally responsible under international law, cf. *supra*, pp. 124ff.

In the numerous trials of war criminals conducted by military tribunals of the Allied and Associated Powers in connection with the Second World War, the plea of an accused of having acted in his capacity as organ of his State or in conformity with the law of his State, has not been regarded as constituting a defense. Cf. *Law Reports of Trials of War Criminals.* Selected and prepared by the United Nations War Crimes Commission (1949), XV, 160–161.

[27] In the case *A. M. Luther Company v. Sagor & Co.* (1921 Law Reports, 3 King's Bench Division 532 ff.) the British Court of Appeal stated: "It is well settled that the validity of the acts of an independent country in relation to property and persons within its jurisdiction cannot be questioned in the courts of this country."

In the case *Bernstein v. Van Heyghen Frères S.A.* (163 Federal Reports, 2d Series, 249) the Circuit Court of Appeals, Second Circuit, stated in 1947: "We have repeatedly declared, for over a period of at least thirty years, that a court of the forum will not undertake to pass upon the validity under the

give effect to the laws of another state if they are contrary to the public order of the former.[28] By "public order" or "public policy" the basic principles of a national legal order are understood.

C. DETERMINATION OF THE MATERIAL SPHERE OF VALIDITY OF THE NATIONAL LEGAL ORDER (COMPETENCE OF THE STATE) BY INTERNATIONAL LAW

Besides the questions as to the space and the individuals for which the national legal order is valid, the question arises as to the subject matters which this order may regulate. It is the question of the material sphere of validity of the national legal order, presented usually as the problem of the competence of the state.

1. No Natural Limits to the Competence of the State

The national legal order can regulate human behavior in very different respects and to very different degrees. It can regulate different subject matters and can, by doing so, limit more or less the personal freedom of individuals. The more that subject matters are positively regulated by the legal order, the wider its material sphere of validity; the more the competence of the state is expanded,

---

municipal law of another state of the acts of officials of that state, purporting to act as such."

[28] In *Dougherty v. Equitable Life Insurance Society* (United States, Court of Appeals of New York, 1934, 266 N.Y. 71, 193 N.E. 897) the Court stated that "recognition of a Government does not compel our courts to give effect to foreign laws if they are contrary to our public policy." In *État Russe v. Cie. Ropit* (Annual Digest 1925–1926, Case No. 17) the Cour d'Aix (First Chamber) (1925) stated that although, as the result of recognition *de jure* the judge is no longer at liberty to ignore the Soviet laws and to reject them *en bloc*, the recognition has not the effect of preventing him from examining them in each individual case and from refusing to give them legal effect if he considers that they violate the essential principles of French political and social organisation.

The Essential Function of International Law 241

the more limited is the personal freedom of its subjects. The question as to the proper extent of this limitation (and this is the question as to the subject matters which the national legal order may, or may not, regulate by establishing obligations to behave in a definite way) is answered differently by different political systems. Liberalism stands for the utmost restriction of the material sphere of the national legal order, especially in matters of economy and religion. Other political systems, such as socialism, maintain the opposite view ("Etatism," totalitarianism).

Again and again the attempt has been made to derive from the very nature of the state and the human individual a limit beyond which the competence of the state must not be expanded, the freedom of the individual must not be limited. This attempt is typical of the theory of natural law. A scientific theory of the state is not in a position to establish a natural limit to the competence of the state in relation to its subjects. Nothing in the nature of the state or the individuals prevents the national legal order from regulating any subject matter in any field of social life, from restricting the freedom of the individual to any degree. The competence of the state is not limited by its nature; and in historical reality the actual competence of the different states is very different. Between the liberal state of the nineteenth century and the totalitarian state of our days there are many intermediate stages.

The fact that the competence of the state is not limited "by nature" does not prevent the material sphere of validity of the national legal order from being limited legally. The question arises whether international law, which limits the territorial and the personal sphere of validity of the national legal order, does or does not also limit its material sphere.

The material sphere of validity of the national legal order or the competence of the state is limited by international law insofar as certain subject matters cannot be regulated by national but only by international law. This question has been considered in connection with the problem of the material sphere of validity of international law. The material sphere of validity of the national legal order or the competence of the state may be limited also insofar as certain subject matters may be regulated by national law, but must be regulated in conformity with international law, the latter prescribing a definite regulation of these matters.

The states, it is true, are competent, under general international law, to regulate in principle all matters which can be regulated by an order limited in its territorial sphere; but they retain this competence only insofar as international law does not regulate positively a particular subject matter. The fact that a subject matter is regulated by a norm of international law stipulating an obligation with respect to this matter has the effect that this matter can no longer be regulated arbitrarily by national law. There are subject matters which, according to general international law, and subject matters which, according to particular international law, especially treaties, must be regulated in a certain way by national law.

2. Protection of Organs and Citizens of Foreign States

General international law does not impose upon the state any obligation concerning the treatment of its own citizens. In this respect the state is free, that is to say, the national legal order is not limited as to the rights which it confers or does not confer and the legal protection it grants or does not grant to individuals who are citizens of the state constituted by that legal order. Only by a special treaty may a state assume obligations to treat its own citizens in a certain way, to confer upon them certain rights and grant them a certain protection. But general international law obligates the state to protect individuals who stay within its territory but belong as organs or citizens to another state.

The Head of a State, if he is staying on the territory of another state in time of peace and with the knowledge and consent of the government, and diplomatic envoys of a state received by another state must be afforded special protection by the other state. The protection consists in that the government concerned is obliged to prevent violations of their personal dignity, their personal safety, and their intercourse with their government at home; and if prevention proves to be impossible, to punish severely the delinquents. This is the so-called inviolability of heads of state and diplomatic envoys. The privilege of inviolability is related to, but different

The Essential Function of International Law 243

from, the privilege of exterritoriality or immunity from jurisdiction. The latter has a negative, the former a positive, character.

Under general international law the states are obliged to permit passage through their territory to diplomatic envoys sent by another state to a third state on their way from the sending state to the receiving state, provided that passing through the territory is necessary because the sending state and the receiving state are not neighbors.

International law obligates the states not only to protect heads of other states and diplomatic envoys but also other states as such by imposing upon each state the obligation to prevent individuals from committing on its territory acts injurious to another state such as, e.g., the organization of an expedition for the purpose of overthrowing by force the legitimate government of another state.

If aliens are admitted,[29] the legal order of the state in the territory of which they are staying has to grant these individuals a minimum of rights, and must not impose upon them certain duties; otherwise a right of the state to which they legally belong is considered to be violated. As far as the rights are concerned, every state is by general international law obliged to grant to aliens at least equality before the law with its citizens in respect to safety of persons and property. This, however, does not mean that the law of the state must confer upon aliens the same rights as upon its citizens. Aliens may be excluded from political rights, from certain professions, and even from acquiring property in land. But the legal status granted to aliens must not remain below a certain minimum standard of civilization. The fact that the legal status granted to the citizens by the national law does not correspond to this standard is no excuse.[30] Even if under the law of a state its own citizens may be deprived of their property for public pur-

[29] In the case *Nishimura Ekiu* (142 U.S. 659) the Supreme Court of the United States (1891) held: "It is an accepted maxim of international law, that every sovereign nation has the power, as inherent in sovereignty and essential to self-preservation, to forbid the entrance of foreigners within its dominions, or to admit them only in such cases and upon such conditions as it may see fit to prescribe."

[30] In the *H. Roberts Case* (United States and Mexico, General Claims Commission, 1926; Annual Digest 1925–1926, Case No. 166) the United States put forward a claim on behalf of Harry Roberts, an American citizen,

244   Principles of International Law

poses without compensation, confiscation of the property of aliens is a violation of international law. The state to which the alien belongs may claim compensation. A state may annul its debts in relation to its own citizens; but if the creditor is a citizen of another state, the latter is entitled to intervene to protect its national.[31] No state is

---

inter alia on the ground of cruel and inhuman treatment during imprisonment. The Mexican agent stated that Roberts was accorded the same treatment as that meted out to other prisoners confined in the jail. The commission held that Mexico was liable in damages. In regard to the maltreatment in prison the commission stated that the imprisonment was cruel and inhuman. Equality of treatment of aliens and nationals did not constitute in the light of international law the ultimate test of the propriety of acts of authorities in regard to aliens. The test was whether aliens are treated in accordance with the ordinary standards of civilization.

[31] Sometimes a clause is inserted into a contract concluded between a government and a foreigner, to the effect that a dispute arising out of the contract shall not be the subject of a diplomatic intervention on the part of the state to which the foreigner belongs (the so-called Calvo Clause). Most of the writers agree that such a clause has not the effect of depriving the state concerned of the right it has under international law to protect its own citizen.

In the case *Mexican Union Railway (Limited)* (Great Britain and Mexico, Claims Commission, 1930; Annual Digest 1929–1930, Case No. 129) the British Government brought a claim on behalf of the Mexican Union Railway (Limited), a British company operating in Mexico, before the British-Mexican Claims Commission for losses suffered in connection with revolutionary disturbances in Mexico between 1912 and 1920. The concession granted by the Mexican Government to the company contained the clause: "They [the company] shall only have such rights and means of asserting them as the laws of the Republic grant to Mexicans, and Foreign Diplomatic Agents may consequently not intervene in any manner whatsoever." The commission held: "In holding that under the rules of international law an alient may lawfully make a promise, as laid down in the concession, the majority of the Commission holds at the same time that no person can, by such a clause, deprive the Government of his country of its undoubted right to apply international remedies to violations of international law committed to his hurt. A Government may take a view of losses suffered by one of its subjects different to that taken by such subject himself. Where the Government is concerned, a principle higher than the mere safeguarding of the private interests of the subject who suffered the damage may be involved. For the Government the contract is *res inter alios acta*, by which its liberty of action cannot be prejudiced."

But in the *North American Dredging Company of Texas Case* (United States and Mexico, General Claims Commission, 1926; Annual Digest 1925–1926, Case No. 191) the commission held that the contention of the United States— that the so-called Calvo Clause could not in the present case be allowed to oust the jurisdiction of the commission on the ground, *inter alia*, that individuals could in no case have an influence upon the international rights and

The Essential Function of International Law

allowed to impose upon citizens of another state the obligation to do military service,[32] but it may accept voluntary military service on the part of the foreigner. So-called foreign legions are not incompatible with international law. But a state is not allowed to force foreigners who voluntarily entered its military service, to participate in war operations against their own state.

Each state has the right to protect its own citizens against violations of the rules of international law concerning the treatment of aliens. From the point of view of international law, this is a right of the state, not of its citizens;[33] and it is a right which a state

---

duties of states relating to private persons—must be rejected. In its opinion the commission stated that the problem of the lawfulness of the so-called Calvo Clause is oversimplified by the argument either that it is in no case effective, or that it is in every case effective, to oust the jurisdiction of an international tribunal. Each case must be considered on its merits.

[32] In *Polites v. The Commonwealth and Another* and *Kandiliotes v. The Commonwealth and Another* (High Court of Australia, 1945; Annual Digest 1943–1945, Case No. 61) the plaintiffs, although Greek nationals and not British subjects, had been served with notices requiring them to serve in the military forces of the Commonwealth. The notices had been issued in pursuance of the National Security (Aliens Service) Regulations. The Court held that the Regulations and the notices served under them were valid. In his opinion the Chief Justice admitted: "The Regulations provide for compulsory service of aliens in Australian armed forces and place the aliens in the same position as British subjects in Australia. They must be held to be contrary to an established rule of international law." But he referred to the principle recognized by "all the authorities in English law . . . that courts are bound by the statute law of their country, even if that law should violate a rule of international law." He further stated: "It is not for a court to express an opinion upon the political propriety of this action. It is for the Government of the Commonwealth to consider its political significance, taking into account the obvious risk of the Commonwealth having no ground of objection if Australians who happen to be in foreign countries are conscripted for military service there. Parliament has, in my opinion, placed upon the Executive the responsibility of making agreements with other countries which will remove international difficulties or of accepting the risk of such difficulties being created. In my opinion, the regulations are valid . . . ."

[33] In the case *The Mavrommatis Palestine Concessions* (Publications of the Permanent Court of International Justice, Series A, No. 2, p. 12) the Permanent Court of International Justice (1924) stated: "By taking up the case of one of its subjects and by resorting to diplomatic action or international judicial proceedings on his behalf, a State is in reality asserting its own rights—its right to ensure, in the person of its subjects, respect for the rules of international law."

has only with respect to its own citizens.[34] Whether a citizen has a right to be protected by his state depends on the national law of that state.[35] It is especially against so-called denial of justice that a state is entitled to protect its citizens. Denial of justice is denial of proper protection by the courts (due process of law).[36]

---

[34] In *United States v. Germany* (*Nationality of Claims*) (Annual Digest 1923–1924, Case No. 100) the United States and Germany Mixed Claims Commission (1924) held that, as a rule, states do not espouse a private claim against another state unless in point of origin it possesses the nationality of the claimant nation. The reason for the rule is that the nation is injured through injury to its national, and it alone may demand reparation, as no other nation is injured. "Only the injured nation will be heard to assert a claim against another nation. Any other rule would open wide the door for abuses and might result in converting a strong nation into a claim agency in behalf of those who after suffering injuries should assign their claims to its nationals or avail themselves of its naturalization laws for the purpose of procuring its espousal of their claims."

[35] In the case *Gschwind v. Swiss Confederation* (Annual Digest 1931–1932, Case No. 120) the Swiss Federal Court (1932) held: "The granting of diplomatic protection in respect of injuries inflicted upon nationals by authorities or servants of a foreign State in disregard of rules of international law is not merely a right, under international law, of the home State as against the foreign State. From the point of view of internal constitutional law, diplomatic protection is also an administrative duty generally towards the nationals who have suffered injury. . . . Such protection is part of the administration of the State. All citizens are entitled to it under equal conditions and in the same way. However, the acts of the public authority in this matter must be governed by objective rules of general application. Therefore, if a Swiss subject alleges that he has suffered damage as the result of a breach of international law, and applies to the Federal Council for intercession with the foreign State and for steps to be taken with a view to obtain compensation, such application can only have the object of drawing the attention of the federal authority to the case and of inducing it to examine the matter. The steps to be taken are not determined by the request of the applicant, but by the substantive law governing the duties of the competent authorities in such matters. The fact that he has been injured in breach of international law does not confer upon the citizen a right to assistance by the Confederation in a manner desired by him."

[36] In the broadest sense of the term, "denial of justice" means any violation of the obligations a state has under general international law with respect to the treatment of aliens; in the narrowest sense, only denial of access to the courts. Most writers limit the concept to acts of courts, including denial of access to the courts. Article 9 of the Harvard Draft Convention on Responsibility of States contains the following definition: "Denial of justice exists when there is a denial, unwarranted delay or obstruction of access to courts, gross deficiency in the administration of judicial or remedial process, failure to provide those guarantees which are generally considered indispensable to the proper

The Essential Function of International Law 247

But it is a generally recognized rule that the alien must exhaust any legal remedies available under the law of the state responsible for the violation of international law before the state to which the alien belongs can make claims for reparation.[37] An individual who has no citizenship, a stateless individual, is not protceted by international law.[38]

---

administration of justice, or a manifestly unjust judgment. An error of a national court which does not produce manifest injustice is not a denial of justice." (*Research in International Law*, Harvard Law School [1929], p. 173.)

[37] In the case *William J. Blumhardt v. Mexico* (John Bassett Moore, *History of International Arbitrations* [1895], III, 3146) the claimant demanded indemnity for ill-treatment and illegal imprisonment by a Mexican inferior judge. The umpire held "that the Mexican Government cannot be held responsible for the losses occasioned by the illegal acts of an inferior judicial authority, when the complainant has taken no steps by judicial means to have punishment inflicted upon the offender and to obtain damages from him. The umpire does not believe that the Government of the United States, or of any nation in the world, would admit such a responsibility under the circumstances which appear from the evidence produced in the part of the claimant, showing that Judge Alvarez was the person to blame in the matter, and that it was against him that proceedings should have been taken."

In *United States (The R. T. Roy) v. Great Britain* (Nielsen's Report, p. 406) an American fishing vessel called the *R. T. Roy* was seized by an inspector of fisheries for Northwest Ontario and taken into a Canadian port. The arbitral tribunal (1925) held that the claim of the United States must be disallowed because of failure on the part of the claimant to obtain satisfaction through the legal remedies which were open to him or placed at his disposal: "The Tribunal is constrained to emphasize the failure of the claimant to submit to the orderly legal procedure provided for the determination of the issue at the time. The seizure here complained of was the initial step in a procedure which, if it had been permitted to pursue its normal course, would have led to a judicial inquiry in which the very issue here presented would have been considered with full opportunity to elicit all the facts by examination of records and cross-examination of material witnesses. This procedure was interrupted, and its logical completion rendered impossible, by the affirmative act of the claimant's representative in withdrawing the vessel from the only jurisdiction where the matter could be duly and promptly dealt with. The circumstances do not justify us in finding that the Canadian authorities had abandoned the seizure when such withdrawal took place. Moreover, proceedings might have been taken in the Canadian courts at any time against the Fisheries Inspector personally or against the Canadian Government by way of Petition of Right."

[38] In *United States of America on Behalf of Dickson Car Wheel Company v. The United Mexican States* (United States and Mexico, Special Claims Commission, 1931; Annual Digest 1931–1932, Case No. 115) the commission stated: "The relation of rights and obligations created between two States upon the commission by one of them of an act in violation of International Law,

3. Citizenship (Nationality)

a. *Citizenship as a legal status.* Citizenship or nationality is the status of an individual who legally belongs to a certain state or—formulated in a figurative way—is a member of that community. The acquisition and loss of this status are regulated by the national legal order, which, normally, makes this status the condition of certain duties and rights. The most prominent among those duties that can be imposed only upon citizens is the duty to do military service. The most prominent among those rights which may be conferred only upon citizens are the political rights. Only citizens have, as a rule, a right to reside within the territory of the state, that is, the right not to be expelled therefrom. The government may expel aliens at any time and for any reason. This power may be limited by special treaties. In earlier periods some legal orders provided for expulsion of their own citizens as a punishment, which was called "banishment." Even now, international law does not forbid it as such, but its practical applicability is limited. For the banished individual is a foreigner in any other state; and every state has the right of refusing to permit a foreigner to enter its territory, and at any time to expel any foreigner. The expelled foreigner's own state would violate this right by refusing to permit him to return.

---

arises only among those States subject to the international juridical system. There does not exist, in that system, any relation of responsibility between the transgressing State and the injured individual for the reason that the latter is not subject to international law. The injury inflicted upon an individual, a national of the claimant State, which implies a violation of the obligations imposed by International Law upon each member of the Community of Nations, constitutes an act internationally unlawful, because it signifies an offense against the State to which the individual is united by the bond of nationality. The only juridical relation, therefore, which authorizes a State to exact from another the performance of conduct prescribed by International Law with respect to individuals is the bond of nationality. This is the link existing between that law and individuals and through it alone are individuals enabled to invoke the protection of a State and the latter empowered to intervene on their behalf. A State, for example, does not commit an international delinquency in inflicting an injury upon an individual lacking nationality, and consequently, no State is empowered to intervene or complain on his behalf either before or after the injury."

Under national law a difference may exist between full citizens, that is to say, subjects of the state who have, and subjects who—although legally belonging to the state—have not all the rights and duties of a full citizen. Only the former may be called "citizens," this term being used in a narrower sense. Thus, according to a German statute of September 1935, only subjects of German blood had political rights and were called *Reichsbuerger,* whereas the other subjects, especially Jewish subjects, were called *Reichsangehoerige.* Individuals may legally belong to a colony and thus to the state concerned, but may not be "citizens" of that state, not having the rights and duties of a full citizen, especially political rights. Such differences are irrelevant from the point of view of international law. Citizenship or nationality in the sense of international law is nothing but the status of legally belonging to a state, irrespectively of the rights and duties which under national law are connected with this status. Under international law a state has the right to protect its citizens (nationals) against certain violations of their interests by another state.

b. *Extradition.* Extradition is distinct from expulsion. A state may ask another state for the extradition of an individual in order to be able to prosecute him legally because of a crime he has committed on the territory of the state which asks for extradition. A state is obliged to grant the request only on the basis of a special treaty. There are, in fact, numerous treaties of extradition. Normally, the individuals who are the object of extradition have no right to be or not to be extradited. Citizenship of the individual to be extradited is relevant only if by an extradition law a state is not allowed, or by an extradition treaty not obliged, to extradite one of its own citizens. The crimes for which extradition is to be granted must be determined in the extradition treaty. It is usual to insert into the treaty a clause according to which extradition shall be granted only for an act which is a crime both under the law of the state asking for extradition and under the law of the state which is asked for extradition. As a rule, no extradition is granted for political crimes, that is to say, crimes committed for political purposes or from a political motive. This rule has an important restriction, the so-called *attentat* clause, according to which murder of the head of a foreign state or a member of his family is not to be considered a political crime.

c. *Acquisition and loss of citizenship.* Acquisition and loss of citizenship are, in principle, regulated by the national legal orders.[39] The various legal orders contain quite different stipulations concerning the acquisition and loss of citizenship. Usually the wife shares her husband's citizenship, legitimate children their father's, and illegitimate children their mother's. Citizenship is often acquired through birth within the territory of the state, or through residence of a certain length of time. Other grounds of acquisition are legitimation (of children born out of wedlock), or adoption, or a legislative or administrative act conferring citizenship upon a person.

Naturalization is an administrative act of the state, conferring citizenship upon an alien. But there is a rule of general international law prohibiting the conferring of citizenship upon an alien without his consent. Hence naturalization is admissible only in case the alien applies for it. The law of a state providing that every alien entering the territory of the state becomes *ipso facto* a citizen of this state would be in contradiction to general international law. However, when the territory of one state becomes the territory of another state by cession or annexation, the citizens of the former inhabiting the ceded or annexed territory become citizens of the state which acquires the territory. By acquiring the new citizenship they lose their old citizenship. In these cases acquisition and loss of citizenship are regulated directly by general international law.[40]

Some writers deny that the inhabitants of an annexed or ceded

[39] In *Stoeck v. Public Trustee* (England, High Court of Justice, Chancery Division, 1921; Annual Digest 1919–1922, Case No. 156) the Court held that "whether a person is a national of a country must be determined by the municipal law of that country . . . ."

[40] In *Romano v. Comma* (Annual Digest 1925–1926 Case No. 195) the Egyptian Mixed Court of Appeal (1925) held with respect to the Papal State the territory of which was annexed by Italy in 1870, that all the nationals of the annexed state became automatically subjects of the annexing state without necessity for an express declaration on their part, and that no option for nationality is possible when the former state disappears completely.

The Essential Function of International Law 251

territory automatically become citizens of the annexing or cessionary state. They admit only that in case the entire territory of a state is acquired by another state, the latter is entitled to impose its citizenship upon all citizens of the perished state; and that in case only part of the territory of one state is acquired by another state the latter is entitled to impose its citizenship on those citizens of the other state who have their residence on the territory in question or are in some other local relation to it (e.g., legally belong to—have *Heimatsrecht* in—a municipality situated on the territory). Treaties of cession often confer upon the inhabitants of the ceded territory the right to decide, by a declaration called "option," whether they will become nationals of the acquiring state or will keep their old nationality. In the latter case, they can be compelled to leave the territory.

The loss of citizenship takes place in ways corresponding to those in which it is acquired. It may be lost through emigration or long residence abroad, or by entering into foreign military or civil service without permission of one's own state, or by acquiring the citizenship of another state, or by so-called expatriation. Expatriation is release from citizenship granted on the application of the individual concerned. Recently, some governments have practiced denationalization, that is, deprivation of citizenship by an administrative or legislative act without the consent of the individual concerned.

Since the acquisition of a new citizenship is normally not dependent upon, and often does not cause, the loss of the previously existent citizenship, cases of individuals having two or more citizenships, as well as individuals having no citizenship at all, are not uncommon. If an individual is a citizen of two or more states, each of these states may consider him as its own citizen,[41]

---

[41] In *United States (Alexander Tellech) v. Austria and Hungary* (United States-Austria and Hungary, Tripartite Claims Commission, 1928; Decisions and Opinions [1929], p. 71) the question was to be decided whether the Austrian Government was entitled to subject Alexander Tellech, who was by parentage an Austrian citizen and by birth a citizen of the United States, to compulsory military service. The commission held: "The action taken by the Austrian civil authorities in the exercise of their police powers and by the

but none of them is able to give him diplomatic protection against the others. If an individual is without any citizenship, no state can protect him against any other state. The situation becomes especially difficult when—as sometimes occurs—an individual is a citizen of two states that are at war with one another. International agreements have been concluded with a view to preventing dual or

---

Austro-Hungarian military authorities, of which complaint is made, was taken in Austria, where claimant was voluntarily residing, against claimant as an Austrian citizen. Citizenship is determined by rules prescribed by municipal law. Under the law of Austria, to which claimant had voluntarily subjected himself, he was an Austrian citizen. The Austrian and the Austro-Hungarian authorities were well within their rights in dealing with him as such. Possessing as he did dual nationality, he voluntarily took the risk incident to residing in Austrian territory and subjecting himself to the duties and obligations of an Austrian citizen arising under the municipal laws of Austria."

In the *Canevaro Case* (Tribunal of the Permanent Court of Arbitration, 1912; Scott, Hague Court Reports [1916], p. 284) the tribunal held that "whereas, according to Peruvian legislation (Article 34 of the Constitution), Rafael Canevaro is a Peruvian by birth because born on Peruvian territory, and, whereas, on the other hand, according to Italian legislation (Article 4 of the Civil Code) he is of Italian nationality because born of an Italian father; whereas, as a matter of fact, Rafael Canevaro has on several occasions acted as a Peruvian citizen, both by running as a candidate for the Senate, where none are admitted except Peruvian citizens and where he succeeded in defending his election, and, particularly, by accepting the office of Consul General for the Netherlands, after having secured the authorization of both the Peruvian Government and the Peruvian Congress; whereas, under these circumstances, whatever Rafael Canevaro's status as a national may be in Italy, the Government of Peru has a right to consider him a Peruvian citizen and to deny his status as an Italian claimant . . . ."

In the case *Baron Frederic de Born v. Yugoslavian State* (Yugoslavian-Hungarian Mixed Arbitral Tribunal, 1926; Annual Digest 1925–1926, Case No. 205) the tribunal held that when a person was entitled to claim one nationality in one country and another nationality in another country, and an international tribunal was called upon to decide whether the nationality actually claimed by a person should be recognized, it was the duty of the tribunal to examine in which of the two countries existed the elements essential in law and in fact for the purpose of creating an effective link of nationality and not merely a theoretical one. But in the *Salem Case* (United States and Egypt, 1932; Annual Digest 1931–1932, Case No. 98) an arbitral tribunal stated: "The principle of the so-called 'effective nationality,' referred to by the Egyptian Government, does not seem to be sufficiently established in International Law. It was used in the famous Canevaro case; but the decision of the Arbitral Tribunal appointed at that time has remained isolated. In spite of the Canevaro case, the practice of several Governments, for instance, the German, is that if

The Essential Function of International Law

multiple citizenship and complete lack of citizenship (statelessness).

The Convention on certain questions relating to the conflict of nationality laws, signed at The Hague, April 12, 1930, establishes the following general principles: "ARTICLE 1. It is for each State to determine under its own law who are its nationals. This law shall be recognized by other States in so far as it is consistent with international conventions, international custom, and the principles of law generally recognized with regard to nationality. ARTICLE 2. Any question as to whether a person possesses the nationality of a particular State shall be determined in accordance with the law of that State. ARTICLE 3. Subject to the provisions of the present Convention, a person having two or more nationalities may be regarded as its national by each of the States whose nationality he possesses. ARTICLE 4. A State may not afford diplomatic protection to one of its nationals against a State whose nationality such person also possesses. ARTICLE 5. Within a third State, a person having more than one nationality shall be treated as if he had only one. Without prejudice to the application of its law in matters of personal status and of any conventions in force, a third State shall, of the nationalities which any such person possesses, recognize exclusively in its territory either the nationality of the country in which he is habitually and principally resident, or the nationality of the country with which in the circumstances he appears to be in fact most closely connected. [So-called 'effective' or 'active' nationality.] ARTICLE 6. Without prejudice to the liberty of a State to accord wider rights to renounce its nationality, a person possessing two nationalities acquired without any voluntary act on his part may renounce one of them with the authorization of the State whose nationality he desires to surrender.—This authorization may not be refused in the case of a person who has his habitual and principal residence abroad, if the conditions laid down in the law of the State whose nationality he desires to surrender are satisfied."

---

two Powers are both entitled by International Law to treat a person as their national, neither of these Powers can raise a claim against the other in the name of such person . . . ."

4. Conflict of Laws (Private International Law)

In close connection with the territorial, personal, and material spheres of validity of the different national legal orders is the problem of so-called conflict of laws or private international law (in contradistinction to public international law). This concept is usually defined as that body of legal rules which are to be applied to a conflict between two systems of law in the decision of cases having contact with more than one territory. The principal topic of these rules is considered to be the decision concerning which law in such cases has superiority, or the choice of the law to be applied to the cases.

a. *The problem involved: Application by organs of one state of the law of another state.* As a rule, the law-applying organs of a state, especially the courts (but not only the courts), are legally bound to apply—apart from international law—norms of the national legal order only; that is to say, the law of the state whose organs they are. This law is formed of the legal norms created according to the written or unwritten constitution of the state, by custom, by the legislative organs of the state, by its courts or by other agents competent to create law. As an exception to this rule, the law-applying organs of a state, especially its courts, may be bound to apply norms of another national legal order, that is to say, the law of another state, to certain cases determined by their own law. These cases are characterized by the fact that they stand in a certain relationship to the territorial or personal sphere of validity of a foreign national legal order. Typical cases of so-called conflicts of laws or private international law are the validity of a marriage contracted on the territory of a foreign state, rights and duties concerning real estate located on the territory of a foreign state, a crime committed on foreign territory, the acquisition or the loss of a foreign citizenship of a person who has his residence in the state claiming jurisdiction.

The norms of the foreign law which are to be applied by the organ of a state may be norms of the private or of the public law of the other state, and in the latter case, norms of criminal or administrative law. If the rules prescribing the application of a

The Essential Function of International Law

foreign law are called "private" international law, this term is not quite correct, since there exist—in this sense—also a criminal and an administrative international law. The legal problem is exactly the same in all these cases.

The essential point of the problem seems to be the application of the law of one state by the organs of another state. But, if the organ of a state, bound by the law of this state, applies the norm of a foreign law to a certain case, the norm applied by the organ becomes a norm of the legal order of the state whose organ applies it. The organ of a state, especially a court, is in a position to apply the norm of the law of another state only if bound to do so by the law of its own state, in the last resort by its written or unwritten constitution. The norm applied by the organ of the state is valid for the sphere of validity of the state's law only if its application is prescribed by that law. With reference to its reason of validity it is a norm of the legal system of that state. The rule obliging the courts of a state to apply norms of a foreign law to certain cases has the effect of incorporating the norms of the foreign law into the law of this state.

The norm of a foreign law applied by the organ of a state is "foreign" only with respect to its content. With respect to the reason for its validity it is a norm of the law of the state whose organ is bound to apply it. Strictly speaking, the organ of a state can apply—apart from international law—only norms of the legal order of its own state. Consequently, the statement that a rule of the legal order of a certain state obliges an organ of this state to apply—in certain cases—a norm of the legal order of another state is not a correct description of the legal facts involved. The true meaning of the rules of so-called private international law is this: The law of a state directs its organs to apply to certain cases norms which are norms of the state's own law, but which have the same contents as corresponding norms of another state's law. Only if we constantly keep in mind its true meaning may we say that one state applies the law of another state.

b. *So-called private international law: National, exceptionally international law.* With respect to the application of the law of one state by the organs of another state two different possibilities may be distinguished: (a) the state is legally free to apply or not to apply the law of another state to certain cases; (b) the state is legally bound by general or particular international law to apply the law of another state to certain cases. Some writers deny that there are rules of general international law obliging the state to apply the law of another state to certain cases. This seems to be true with respect to the application of norms of the private law of another state. If, however, not only the application of the private law but also of the public law of another state is taken into consideration, it cannot be denied that there are norms of general international law obligating the state to apply to certain cases the law of another state, for instance, the norm of general international law that the courts of a state are not allowed to question the legality of acts of another state performed within its jurisdiction. If, e.g., the court of a state has to decide the question whether a person has been legally deprived of his property by a confiscatory decree or a corporation has been abolished by a nationalization decree of another state or whether a person has acquired the nationality of another state by an act of naturalization, the court has to decide these questions in accordance with the law-creating act of the other state. That means that the court is bound by general international law to apply the law of another state.[42] But even the

---

[42] In the case *Lazard Bros. v. Midland Bank Ltd.* (1933 Law Reports, A.C. 289) the House of Lords upheld the decision of the Court of Appeal that a Russian bank, nationalized by the Soviet Government, no longer existed. Lord Wright stated: "The Bank was a corporation established by an Act of the Tsar; but the governing authority in Russia, as recognised in the English Courts, is now and has been since October, 1917, the Soviet State. Soviet law is accordingly the governing law from the same date in virtue of the recognition *de facto* in 1921 and *de jure* in 1924 by this country of the Soviet State as the sovereign power in Russia. . . . The question, therefore, is whether by Soviet law the Bank was at that date . . . an existing juristic person . . . I think (the evidence given by Russian lawyers as expert witnesses on both sides) compels the conclusion of fact that the Bank was by Soviet law, which is the material law, non-existent in Russia in 1930 . . ."—In the *United States v. Bank of New York & Trust Co.* (77 Federal Reporter [2d] 866) the United States Circuit Court of Appeals (2d) held (1935) that the plaintiff's motion for an injunction must be denied on the basis of the assumption that the Moscow Fire Insurance Company was dissolved by decrees of the Russian state and all of its right, title and interest and all the right, title and interest

The Essential Function of International Law

application of norms of the private law of another state may be obligatory, e.g., as the consequence of the norms of general international law concerning treatment of aliens. Some writers maintain that a state is obliged by general international law to judge the validity of rights acquired by an alien under the law of his own state in accordance with that law.[43] It is true, however, that general international law imposes the obligation of applying foreign law only to a limited extent. If there is no treaty obliging a state to apply foreign law to certain cases, the state is, as a rule, legally free in this respect. It may regulate by its own law the application of foreign law to certain cases according to principles which it considers to be adequate, just, and the like. Consequently, private (criminal, administrative) international law is, insofar as there is no rule of general or particular international law obliging the state to apply foreign law to certain cases, not international but national law. As a rule, only so-called "public" international law is international law.

D. DETERMINATION OF THE TEMPORAL SPHERE OF VALIDITY OF THE NATIONAL LEGAL ORDER (EXISTENCE OF THE STATE IN TIME) BY INTERNATIONAL LAW

1. Time as Element of the State

It is characteristic of traditional theory that it considers space—the territory—but not time as an "element" of the state. A state

---

of all of its stockholders in its property, including the deposits with the Superintendent of Insurance of the State of New York, were confiscated and appropriated by the Russian state. The court stated: "When the executive branch recognized the Soviet Government, the judicial branch became bound to recognize the validity of Soviet decrees in Soviet territory from the beginning of the Soviet regime." Cf. also the cases *Luther v. Sagor* and *Bernstein v. Van Heyghen Frères, supra,* pp. 239f.

[43] Cf. Alfred Verdross, *Voelkerrecht* (1937), p. 143.

exists, however, not only in space but also in time; and if we regard territory as an element of the state, then we have to regard the period of its existence as an element of the state, too. When it is said that not more than one state can exist within a given space, it is obviously meant that not more than one state can exist within the same space at the same time. It is taken as self-evident that, as history shows, two different states can exist one after the other, at least partly, within the same space.

Just as territory is an element of the state not in the sense of a natural space which the state fills up like a physical body, but only in the sense that it is the territorial sphere of validity of the national legal order, so time, the period of existence, is an element only in the sense that it is the corresponding temporal sphere of validity. Both spheres are limited. Just as the state is spatially not infinite, it is temporally not eternal. It is the same order which regulates the spatial coexistence of the many states and their temporal sequence. It is international law which delimits the territorial as well as the temporal sphere of validity of the national legal order. The time when a state begins to exist, that is, the moment when a national legal order begins to be valid, as well as the moment when a state ceases to exist, that is to say, when a national legal order ceases to be valid, is determined by positive international law according to the principle of effectiveness. It is the same principle according to which the territorial and personal spheres of validity of the national legal order are determined.

2. Birth and Death of the State

The problem of the temporal sphere of validity of the national legal order is usually presented as the problem of the birth and death of the state. It is generally recognized that the question whether a new state has come into existence or an old state has ceased to exist is to be answered on the basis of international law. The relevant principles of international law are commonly stated as follows: A state comes into existence when a group of individuals living on a definite territory are organized under an effective and independent government; and a state ceases to exist when it loses

The Essential Function of International Law

one of its essential elements—its population, its territory, or its independent effective government. A government is independent if it is not legally under the influence of the government of another state; and it is effective if it is able to obtain permanent obedience to the coercive order issued by it. It is evident that since the state is the national legal order, the problem of the birth and death of the state amounts to this question: Under what circumstances does a national legal order begin and cease to be valid? And the meaning of the usual answer to the question as to when a state comes into existence and ceases to exist is that a national legal order begins to be valid as soon as it has become—on the whole—effective, and that it ceases to be valid as soon as it loses this efficacy.

If it is assumed that a state comes into existence when a coercive order established by an independent government becomes effective for a group of individuals living on a definite territory, it is presupposed that the territory for which the coercive order has been put into force has not before formed, together with the individuals living thereon, the territory and the population of one state. It must be a territory which, together with the individuals living thereon, has until now belonged to no state at all, has belonged to two or more states, or has formed only part of the territory and population of one state. If a government has established itself which is able to obtain permanent obedience to its order for a territory and over a population which were already the territory and the population of one state, i.e., if the territory and the population over which a new government is established are identical with the territory and the population over which another government has previously been established, then no new state in the sense of international law has come into existence; only a new government has been established. However, the existence of a new government in this sense is assumed only if it is established in the way of revolution or *coup d'état*.

3. The Identity of the State

The question as to the identity of the state, that is, the question whether a state remains the same in spite of certain changes of the content and sphere of validity of the national legal order, is of importance in international law in the first place with respect to the question as to whether the international obligations, responsibilities, and rights of a state remain the same, in spite of these changes. If the state remains the same, no change in its obligations, responsibilities, and rights takes place. As to the question of the identity of the state, no clear and generally accepted answer has been reached in the traditional doctrine; partly because the general concept of identity is highly problematical,[44] partly because the particular question of the identity of the state may be answered in a different way from two different points of view. From the point of view of its own national legal order, a state remains the same as long as the changes of this order, even fundamental changes in the contents of the legal norms or in the territorial sphere of validity, are the result of acts performed in conformity with the constitution, provided that the change does not imply the termination of the validity of the national legal order as a whole. The latter is the case, e.g., when a state, by an act of its own legislation merges into another state. Thus the Austrian Republic, by a law voted by its National Assembly on November 12, 1918 (but not executed), was declared a part of the German Reich. By an analogous Austrian law issued on March 13, 1938, Austria was incorporated into the German Reich.

From the point of view of the national legal order itself, its continuity always coincides with the identity of the state constituted by this legal order. If, however, the change is the result of a revolution or *coup d'état*, the question of the identity of the state can be answered in the affirmative only from the point of view of the international legal order. According to international law, in case of revolution or *coup d'état*, the state remains the same if the territory remains essentially the same. The identity of the state in time is then based directly upon the identity of the territory and only indirectly upon the identity of the population living on the territory.

If the territorial changes take place without interruption of the

---

[44] Some philosophers deny that there exists such a thing as identity at all. Well known is the saying of Heraklitus "You cannot step twice in the same river."

The Essential Function of International Law 261

continuity of the national legal order, that is to say, in a way which is legitimate from the point of view of the national law of the state, the identity of the state is also considered to be unaffected from the point of view of international law. Thus Yugoslavia is considered from the point of view of international law to be the same state as Serbia, although the territory of this state was very much enlarged by the peace treaties of 1918–1919;[45] and the Turkish Republic is regarded as identical with the Turkish Empire, in spite of the fact that the territory of this state has been remarkably reduced as an effect of the First World War.[46] Identity of the name of a state is not essential to the identity of its personality. A state may change its name without losing its identity. On the other hand, the Austrian Republic is not identical with the Austrian Monarchy, although it has the same name as the state which disappeared as an effect of the First World War.[47]

---

[45] In *Katz and Klump v. Yugoslavia* (Annual Digest 1925–1926, Case No. 24) the German-Yugoslav Mixed Arbitral Tribunal (1925) decided that the Kingdom of the Serbs, Croats, and Slovenes was not a "new state" within the meaning of Article 297 (h) of the Treaty of Versailles.

[46] In the *Ottoman Debt Arbitration* (Annual Digest 1925–1926, Case No. 57) the arbitrator decided (1925) that in international law the Turkish Republic was deemed to continue the international personality of the former Turkish Empire.

[47] In the Peace Treaty of St. Germain, the Austrian Republic was treated as identical with the Austrian Monarchy. The Republic was forced to conclude a peace treaty with the Allied and Associated Powers, which implied that the Republic had been at war with these powers; and in Article 177 of the peace treaty the Republic "accepts the responsibility of Austria . . . for causing the loss and damage to which the Allied and Associated Governments and their nationals have been subjected as a consequence of the war imposed upon them by the aggression of Austria-Hungary and her allies," which means that the Austrian Republic was made responsible for damages caused by the Austrian Monarchy as part of the Austro-Hungarian Empire. All this in spite of the fact that the Austrian Republic did not come into existence in conformity with the constitution of the Austrian Monarchy, and that the territory of the Republic was only a small part of the territory of the former Monarchy. But, in *Austrian Pensions Case* (Annual Digest 1925–1926, Case No. 25) the Austrian Supreme Court (1925) decided that the Austrian Republic was not the same state as the Austrian Empire. The Court interpreted the Peace Treaty of St. Germain as not opposed to that view. This interpretation is hardly correct. In the *Military Decoration Pension Case* (Annual Digest 1925–1926, Case No. 58) the Austrian Constitutional Court (*Verfassungsgerichtshof*) (1926) decided that the Austrian Republic was not bound by the liabilities

The principle that, from the point of view of international law, a state remains, in spite of a revolutionary change of government, the same if the territory—and the population living on it— remains by and large the same applies only if the continuity of its existence under international law is not interrupted. It is interrupted if a state according to international law ceases to exist, e.g., because its territory has been annexed by another state, and, later, on the same territory inhabited by the same population an independent state has been established. Although it is usual to speak of a re-establishment of the old state, it is, from the point of view of international law, a new state, which has come into existence. Thus, in 1938, the territory of the Austrian Republic was incorporated into the German Reich, and consequently the Austrian Republic ceased to exist. In 1945, the Austrian Republic was "re-established," that is to say, on the territory annexed in 1938 by the German Reich, still inhabited by the former Austrian people, a state was established under the name of Austria, under a constitution that was not identical with the constitution in force at the time of the annexation, but under a constitution that has the same content as the constitution in force in 1929. The second Austrian Republic is a new state, since there is no legal continuity in the relationship between the first and the second Republic either from the point of view of national law or from the point of view of international law.

According to traditional view, a state ceases to exist when it loses one of the essential elements of statehood. A state may lose its population by emigration, or its territory in case the territory is an island and this island is swallowed by the sea as the effect of an earthquake. A state also ceases to exist when the government ceases to be effective, that is to say, when the government is no longer able to obtain obedience to the coercive order which has been until then effective for this territory; or when the government ceases to exist, that is, when the community which was until that moment a state

---

of the former Austrian Monarchy except when otherwise provided by a treaty entered into by the Republic or by the municipal law of the Austrian Republic. This implied that the Austrian Republic was not identical with the Austrian Monarchy.

The Essential Function of International Law 263

loses it own independent government. A state ceases to exist by loss of its own government if there is no longer a government independent of governments of other states and able to obtain permanent obedience to the coercive order valid for the territory under discussion. Then the latter may become no-state's land, or part of the territory of another state by annexation, that is to say, by being definitively incorporated in the territory of the other state, or by being placed in some other way under the sovereignty, i.e., the government, of another state. If different territories are legally under one and the same government, they belong to one and the same state, since one state can have only one government in the sense of international law, as one state can have only one territory; and if there is only one government, there can be only one state. A state may cease to exist when its territory becomes the territories of two or more other states (dismemberment), or the common territory of two or more states (condominium). The latter is established if the territory of a state, after its own government has ceased to exist, is placed under the governments of two or more other states. The Austrian Monarchy ceased to exist, as an effect of the First World War, by dismemberment; on its territory new states—the Czechoslovakian and the Austrian Republics, and part of the Polish Republic—were established. The German Reich ceased to exist as an effect of the Second World War by the loss of its own government, the last national government of Germany being abolished and its members prosecuted as criminals. Its territory was placed under the governments and hence under the condominium of the four powers which occupied this territory—the United States, Great Britain, France, and the Soviet Union—and which governed this common part of their territories by the Control Council in which each of the four powers was represented by one delegate. The Western and the Eastern German Republic are two new states, provided they are true states in the sense of international law. This is doubtful, since the governments they have under their constitutions are legally not independent of the governments of the occupant powers.

If the territory in question remains, in its entirety, territory of one state, and if the continuity of the existence of the state under international law is not interrupted, it is not possible to assume that one state has ceased to exist and another state has come into existence on the same territory. It is the same state which continues to exist, but under a new government which came into power by revolution or *coup d'état*.

The result of the foregoing considerations is that a state, in spite of changes of the content and sphere of validity of its legal order, remains the same (in other terms, the identity of a state, in spite of these changes, is not affected) in case the changes are brought about in a constitutional way; but in case the changes are brought about by revolution or *coup d'état*, the state remains the same only if the territory (and the population living on it) remains, by and large, the same, provided that the continuity of its existence under international law is not interrupted. A victorious revolution or a successful *coup d'état* does not destroy the identity of the legal order which it changes, provided that its territorial sphere of validity remains identical. The order established by revolution or *coup d'état* has to be considered as a modification of the old order, not as a new order, if this order is valid for the same territory. The government brought into permanent power in an unconstitutional way is, according to international law, the legitimate government of the state whose identity is not affected by these events. Hence, according to international law, victorious revolutions or successful *coups d'état* are to be interpreted as procedures by which a national legal order can be changed. Both events are, viewed in the light of international law, law-creating facts. By mere revolution or *coup d'état*, the legal continuity, though interrupted under national law, is not interrupted under international law. Again *ex injuria jus oritur* ("a right may originate in an illegal act") and it is again the principle of effectiveness that is applied.

4. Recognition of a Community as a State

a. *Recognition as ascertainment of a fact determined by the law*. General international law determines the conditions under which a community is a state and, as such, a subject of international law. If states are subjects of international law, the latter must determine

The Essential Function of International Law 265

what a state is, just as national law has to determine who are the subjects of duties and rights stipulated by it—for instance, only human beings and not animals, or only free men and not slaves. If international law did not determine what a state is, then its norms would not be applicable.

According to international law, a social order is a national legal order, i.e., the law of a state, if it is a relatively centralized coercive order regulating human behavior, if this order is inferior only to the international legal order, and if it is effective for a certain territory. The same rule, if expressed in the usual language of personification, runs as follows: A community is a state if the individuals belonging to this community are living on a certain territory, organized under an independent and effective government. This is the fact "state in the sense of international law." It is a fact to which international law attaches various important consequences.

If a legal order in an abstract rule attaches certain consequences to a certain fact, it must determine a procedure through which the existence of the fact, in a concrete case, is ascertained by a competent authority. In the realm of law, there is no fact "in itself," no immediately evident fact; there are only facts ascertained by the competent authorities in a procedure determined by law.

Under modern national law the procedure for the ascertainment of legally relevant facts is, as a rule, centralized, that is to say, national law establishes special organs to fulfill this function, especially to ascertain the existence of criminal delicts. The ascertainment of other facts, too, is conferred upon special organs, at least in case the existence of the fact is disputed by the parties concerned. Thus, for instance, the decision of the question as to whether a contract has been concluded is left to the contracting parties; but if they do not agree upon it, if there is in respect of this question a dispute between them, one party maintaining, the other party denying, that a contract has been concluded, then a civil court is competent to decide this question, that is to say, to ascertain in an authentic way the fact concerned.

Since general international law does not establish—as national law does—special organs competent to ascertain the facts to which the law attaches legal consequences, it is always left to the states concerned, that is, the states interested in the fact, to fulfill this function by an agreement (if two or more states are involved). But, if no such agreement can be brought about, each state is authorized to ascertain the existence of the fact concerned for itself. As pointed out in a previous connection,[48] this is the procedure for the ascertainment of an international delict under general international law. It is the procedure for the ascertainment of any fact whatever relevant according to general international law.[49]

Since general international law consists of general norms, it can determine the legal fact "state" in abstract terms only. But how,

[48] Cf. *supra*, pp. 20f.

[49] If the states concerned cannot agree as to the existence of a fact or its legal qualification, a conflict may arise which is to be settled according to the norms of general or particular international law (cf. *infra*, pp. 367ff.) In the *Colombian-Peruvian Asylum case* (International Court of Justice, Reports, 1950, p. 266) the International Court of Justice (1950) had to decide the question as to whether the Colombian Government, which, on the basis of the convention signed at Havana on February 20, 1928 (cf. *supra*, p. 231), had granted asylum in its legation in Lima (Peru) to Mr. Haya de la Torre, prosecuted by the Peruvian Government, was competent to qualify the nature of the offense for the purpose of the said asylum by a unilateral and definitive decision, binding upon Peru. In its judgment the Court stated in respect to general international law that "the diplomatic representative who has to determine whether a refugee is to be granted asylum or not must have the competence to make such a provisional qualification of any offence alleged to have been committed by the refugee. He must in fact examine the question whether the conditions required for granting asylum are fulfilled. The territorial State would not thereby be deprived of its right to contest the qualification. In case of disagreement between the two States, a dispute would arise which might be settled by the methods provided by the Parties for the settlement of their disputes." The Court stated further that "the principles of international law do not recognize any rule of unilateral and definitive qualification by the State granting diplomatic asylum." The Court referred to "the equal rights of qualification which, in the absence of any contrary rule, must be attributed to each of the States concerned." As to the Havana Convention of 1928, the Court stated: "This Convention lays down certain rules relating to diplomatic asylum, but does not contain any provision conferring on the State granting asylum a unilateral competence to qualify the offence with definitive and binding force for the territorial State." The Court rejected the submission of the Government of Colombia "in so far as it involves a right for Colombia, as the country granting asylum, to qualify the nature of the offence by a unilateral and definitive decision, binding on Peru . . ."

The Essential Function of International Law 267

according to general international law, is the question to be decided: Does the legal fact "state in the sense of international law" exist in a concrete case? Does a given community of men actually possess the qualities required of a subject of international law? In other words, is international law applicable to this community in its relations to other states? What is the procedure by which the fact "state in the sense of international law" is to be ascertained; who is competent to ascertain the fact in question? The procedure provided by general international law to ascertain the fact "state in the sense of international law," in a concrete case, is called recognition; competent to ascertain the existence of this fact are the governments of the other states interested in the existence of the state in question. Recognition of a community as a state is, insofar as it implies the ascertainment of the fact that a community is a state in the sense of international law, the application of the procedure provided for by general international law for the ascertainment of legally relevant facts.

b. *Legal and political recognition.* The nature of the act called recognition of a community as a state is very much discussed in the theory of international law. According to one doctrine, the act of recognition has a constitutive character, that is to say, it is essential to the coming into legal existence of the state, which, without such recognition on the part of other states, legally does not exist in relation to them. According to another doctrine, the act of recognition has no such constitutive character; it is only declaratory. A state can come into legal existence even without and independently of any recognition on the part of other states. To recognize a community as a state means only to declare that this community exists as a state, that the recognizing state takes cognizance of the existence of the recognized state; but such declaration has no legal effect.[50] Even without it the state concerned legally exists, especially in relation to states which have not recognized it.[51] Some

---

[50] The author, in his *Théorie générale du droit international public*. Recueil des Cours. Académie de droit international, Vol. XLII (1932), adhered to the doctrine of the declaratory character of recognition. But the considerations presented in the text forced him to abandon this doctrine.

[51] In the case of *Deutsche Kontinental-Gasgesellschaft* (published in *Zeitschrift fuer auslaendisches oeffentliches Recht und Voelkerrecht* [1931] Vol. II,

writers consider recognition as a unilateral act; others, as a treaty entered into by the recognizing and the recognized state.

This strange disagreement with respect to one of the most important acts frequently performed in international relations is probably due to some confusion which prevails as to the problem of recognition. The reason for this confusion is that one does not distinguish clearly between two totally different acts or two different functions of one and the same act, both called "recognition." The meaning of one of these two acts or functions is that the recognizing state ascertains that the recognized community is a state in the sense of international law. This is recognition in a legal sense of the term. The meaning of the other act or function is that the recognizing state is willing to enter into political and other relations with the recognized state, relations of the kind which normally exist between members of the family of nations. This act or function, if called recognition, should be designated as political recognition, in contradistinction to legal recognition, the ascertainment of the fact "state in the sense of international law." Since a state, according to general international law, is not obliged to entertain such relations with other states, namely, to send or receive diplomatic envoys, to conclude treaties, and the like, political recognition of a state is an act which lies within the arbitrary decision of the recognizing state.

The declaration of political recognition in itself has not necessarily a legal consequence, although it may be of great political importance, especially for the prestige of the state to be recognized. The declaration by a state that it is willing to enter into the normal political, economic, and diplomatic relations with a new state may be made without the intent to assume a legal obligation to this effect. Political recognition establishes the obligation of the recognizing state to enter into the normal relations with the recognized

---

p. 14) the German-Polish Arbitral Tribunal (1929) declared (translation from the French original): ". . . recognition of a state is not a constitutive but merely a declaratory act. The state exists by itself, and recognition is nothing but the ascertainment (*constatation*) of that existence . . ." But a dissenting member of the tribunal expressed this opinion: "Recognition of a new state means that the recognizing states confer upon the recognized state the quality of a juristic person; they admit the new state as a member of the international community."

The Essential Function of International Law

state only if it is accepted by the latter, that is to say, if there is a treaty concluded by the recognizing and the recognized state concerning the establishment of certain relations. Such a treaty presupposes the existence of the new state. Hence the treaty cannot have a constitutive character with respect to this existence.

Entirely different from the political is the legal recognition of a community as a state, that is, the act by which a state ascertains that a community is a state in the sense of international law. This act may be performed in any form whatever, its meaning may be expressed directly or indirectly, expressly or tacitly. As a matter of fact, legal recognition is usually combined with political recognition in one and the same act. This is the reason why the two fundamentally different functions which this act called "recognition" has are not clearly distinguished in the traditional theory of international law and why this theory is entangled in most undesirable contradictions with respect to the nature of recognition.

According to international law, legal recognition is indeed necessary. General international law determines under what conditions a community has to be considered a state; consequently, it provides a procedure to decide whether or not in a concrete case a community fulfills these conditions and therefore is, or is not, a state in the sense of international law. To decide this question international law authorizes the governments of the states which—according to general international law—have duties and rights in relation to the community under discussion, provided that this community is a state. The government of a state interested in the existence or nonexistence of another state is, it is true, not an objective and impartial authority to decide that question. But since general international law does not institute special organs to create and apply the law, the existence of legal facts can be ascertained only by the interested governments. This ascertainment is called "recognition." Legal recognition of a community as a state is, as pointed out, only a particular case of the general principle according to which the existence of facts to which international law attaches legal consequence has to be ascertained by the governments which are interested in these facts in a concrete case.

This is a consequence of the far-reaching decentralization of international law.

c. *Constitutive character of the act of legal recognition.* In deciding the question whether a community which claims to be a state is actually a state in the sense of international law, the governments of the other states are by no means free. It may be doubted whether the existing states are legally obliged to recognize a community as a state if this community fulfills—according to the opinion of the former—the requirements of international law. But there can be no doubt that, if a state does recognize another community as a state, it is bound by international law, which determines, in a general way, the essential elements of a state. A state violates international law and thus infringes upon the rights of other states if it recognizes as a state a community which does not fulfill the requirements of international law. As soon as a state, through its government, has certified that a community is a state in the sense of international law, that is to say, as soon as a state has recognized the community as a state, the recognizing state has toward the recognized community all the obligations and all the rights that are stipulated by general international law, and vice versa. International law becomes applicable to the relationship of the recognizing to the recognized state.

International law requires that a new state be recognized as such by an old state in order that international law be applicable to the relations between the old and the new state. But international law does not require that international law be recognized by the new state in order to be applicable to this state. International law cannot contain a binding norm, according to which international law shall be binding upon a new state only if recognized by this state. The requirement of a recognition of international law as a condition of its validity cannot be based on international law because this would imply a logical fallacy, a so-called *petitio principii* ("begging the question"). International law cannot provide that international law is valid in relation to a state only if this state recognizes international law. That international law "provides" something with respect to a state implies that international law is already valid in relation to that state. The recog-

The Essential Function of International Law 271

nition of international law cannot be required by a norm of positive international law. But the recognition of a community as a state by a community already subjected to international law can be required by a norm of positive international law. As a matter of fact, international law does provide that a community, in order to be a state in the sense of international law, must be recognized as such by a state already existing under international law. Consequently by its recognition as a state the recognized community comes legally into existence in relation to the recognizing state. That means that the legal existence of a state under international law is a relative existence, that is to say, that a state legally exists only in relation to other subjects of international law. Consequently, it is possible—and frequently the case—that a newly established community is recognized by one state and hence a state in relation to this state, but not recognized by another state and hence no state in relation to that state; so that international law applies to the one, but not to the other, relationship.

This is one of the many unsatisfactory consequences of the complete decentralization of general international law. It would be more satisfactory, of course, if the question as to whether a community fulfills the requirements of international law were to be decided by a central organ of the international community, or if there were a rule of general international law that if a community is recognized as a state by a certain number of states, it has to be considered as a state by all the others. But as long as no such central organ or no such rule exists, the recognition procedure remains completely decentralized.

In view of the essential legal effect which the act of recognition has on the relation between the recognizing and the recognized state, recognition of a community as a state must be considered as a constitutive act,[52] just as the act by which a court ascertains

---

[52] In *Kennett v. Chambers* (United States, Supreme Court, 1852, 14 Howard 38) the validity of a contract entered into between a general of a revolutionary army fighting for the independence of Texas against the Government of Mexico, and some citizens of the United States, depended upon the answer to the question whether Texas, at the time the contract was concluded, was an independent state. The Court decided this question in the negative because Texas was at that time not recognized as a state by the Government of the United

that a contract has been concluded or a crime committed. No fact has, by itself, legal effects; it has legal effects only together with the act by which the existence of the fact is ascertained. An act which has this legal effect is "constitutive."

If recognition of a community as a state is a constitutive act, it

---

States. In its opinion the Court stated: "But it has been urged in the argument that Texas was in fact independent, and a sovereign state at the time of this agreement; and that the citizen of a neutral nation may lawfully lend money to one that is engaged in war, to enable it to carry on hostilities against its enemy. It is not necessary, in the case before us, to decide how far the judicial tribunals of the United States would enforce a contract like this, when two states, acknowledged to be independent, were at war, and this country neutral. It is a sufficient answer to the argument to say that the question whether Texas had or had not at that time become an independent state, was a question for that department of our government exclusively which is charged with our foreign relations. And until the period when that department recognized it as an independent state, the judicial tribunals of the country were bound to consider the old order of things as having continued, and to regard Texas as a part of the Mexican territory. And if we undertook to inquire whether she had not in fact become an independent sovereign state before she was recognized as such by the treaty-making power, we should take upon ourselves the exercise of political authority, for which a judicial tribunal is wholly unfit, and which the Constitution has conferred exclusively upon another department . . . ."

In *The Gagara* (Annual Digest 1919–1922, Case No. 25) the plaintiffs, the West Russia Steamship Company, stated in an affidavit to be a corporate body having their registered office at Petrograd, issued a writ *in rem* in the Admiralty Division of the High Court (England, 1919), claiming possession of "the steamship *Gagara,* now sailing under the name of the *Kajak.*" Thereupon the Estonian Government entered an appearance under protest and moved to set aside the writ of summons, service, and all subsequent proceedings on the ground that they were the owners of the *Gagara,* and that, as they were an independent sovereign government, the Court had no jurisdiction. When the motion came before the Admiralty Court, the judge invited the assistance of the Foreign Office as to the status of the Estonian Government. Thereupon the law officers appeared and stated on behalf of the Foreign Office: "Our own Government [and likewise the Governments of France and Italy] has for the time being provisionally, and with all necessary reservations as to the future, recognized the Estonian National Council as a *de facto* independent body, and accordingly has received a certain gentleman as the informal diplomatic representative of the Provisional Government. The state of affairs is of necessity provisional and transitory . . . ." The meaning of this statement was that the British Government has recognized the Estonian Republic as a state in the sense of international law. Cf. *infra,* p. 276. In view of this recognition the Court refused to exercise jurisdiction in conformity with the principle of international law that no court of a state has jurisdiction over the acts of another state.

must be a unilateral transaction; it cannot be a treaty between the recognizing state and the recognized community, because the latter becomes a state in relation to the former only by the recognition, and a treaty can be concluded only by states. But after being recognized as a state, the recognized community must, on its part, recognize the recognizing state. Recognition must be reciprocal. The recognition of the recognizing by the recognized state is no practical problem; it is implied in the act by which the new community accepts the recognition granted to it.

The constitutive character of the recognition (in the legal sense of the term) of a community as a state seems to be not consistent with the practice of states in making a community not yet recognized as a state responsible for violations of international law. Thus, e.g., the British Government declared in 1949 that it would demand compensation from the Government of Israel for the shooting down of British airplanes, although Great Britain had not yet recognized Israel as a state.[53] But if a state maintains that the community in question has violated international law in relation to the former and hence is obligated to repair the wrong, the state

[53] On January 8, 1949, the British delegate to the United Nations handed the following memorandum to the Israeli Consul General in New York, acting representative of the Provisional Government of Israel at the Security Council of the United Nations: "His Britannic Majesty's Government takes a grave view of the events recorded in the attached statement which have resulted in the loss of five British aircraft as a result of unprovoked attacks by Jewish aircraft over Egyptian territory. They have informed the United Nations Acting Mediator of these events and wish also to make strong protest to the Jewish Authorities at Tel Aviv and to reserve all their rights both with regard to claims for compensation and to all possible subsequent actions.—The United Kingdom Delegation at the United Nations have been instructed to request the Jewish Delegation to transmit this protest to Tel Aviv as soon as possible and to call the particular attention of the authorities there to the last paragraph of the attached statement.—A copy of this memorandum and of the statement is also being communicated via His Britannic Majesty's Consul General at Haifa."

On the same day the British Consul General in Haifa handed an identical memorandum to an official of the Israeli Foreign Ministry permanently stationed in Haifa (according to an information received by the author from Mr. S. Rosenne, legal adviser to the Israeli Minister of Foreign Affairs). It should be noted that the above-quoted memorandum was addressed to the "Jewish authorities at Tel Aviv," not to the Provisional Government of Israel, in order to indicate that Great Britain had not "recognized" this state.

demanding reparation recognizes the community as a state. Legal recognition is implied in the act of demanding reparation, although political recognition may be withheld.

d. *Withdrawal of recognition.* Not only may the government of a state recognize a community as a state; it may also directly or indirectly, expressly or tacitly, ascertain that a community which claims to be a state is no state in the sense of international law, or that a community which it has recognized as a state has ceased to be a state in the sense of international law. In the latter case one speaks of "withdrawal" of recognition. Such withdrawal of recognition is usually not expressly declared. But when a state loses its own government as a result of an annexation of its territory by another state, and if a third state recognizes this fact, the recognition of the annexation implies the withdrawal of the recognition previously granted to the perished state. The recognition of the annexation, and that means the recognition that the annexed state has ceased to exist, may be implied in the establishment of consuls on the annexed territory, for the establishment of consuls on a definite territory is possible only with the consent of the authority which is the legitimate government over that territory. This consent is called *exequatur*. If a government asks another government for the exequatur to be granted to a consul to be established on a certain territory, the first-mentioned government recognizes that the other government is the legitimate government over the territory concerned, and, hence, that this territory is part of the territory of the state whose government is asked to grant the exequatur. Some writers maintain that the government of a state may ask the government of another state to grant the exequatur for a consul to be established on a certain territory, without recognizing that this territory belongs to the state the government of which is asked to grant the exequatur. Such nonrecognition can have only a political and not a legal character; it cannot mean that the nonrecognizing state still considers the annexed community as a state in the sense of international law.

When a state, through its government, certifies that a community hitherto recognized as a state no longer corresponds to the requirements of international law, that is to say, when a state "withdraws" recognition from a community, the latter ceases to exist legally as a state in relation to the former. The legal existence of states has, as pointed out, a thoroughly relative character.

Just as international law can be violated by an act of recognition, it can also be violated by the act of withdrawing recognition. Recognition as well as the *actus contrarius* may be performed in contradiction to international law. A state may declare that a community which has been a state ceases to be a state, although the community in fact still fulfills all conditions laid down by international law. Thus the right of the community in question is violated. The question of its legal existence is disputed between the community and the state which denies its existence. The same rules then become applicable which, according to general international law, are to be applied in case the question is disputed whether a state has violated the right of another state.

e. *Conditional recognition.* Since the recognition of a state is, as a legal act, the ascertainment of a fact determined by international law, it cannot be conditional. The question whether a given community is a state in the sense of international law can only be answered "Yes" or "No." The content of the declaration of recognition excludes any possibility of a condition. Legal recognition of a state can only be unconditional. In the case of a conditional recognition, e.g., the declaration of State A to recognize the new State B on condition that the new state grant specific rights to a certain minority of its population, the condition cannot refer to legal recognition, i.e., to the ascertainment of the fact that Community B is a state in the sense of international law. The condition can only refer to the political recognition, which is in this case connected with the legal recognition in one and the same act. If Community B, recognized as a state, has accepted the declaration of State A, i.e., if B is under obligation to A to grant to a certain minority of its population specific rights and does not fulfill this obligation, then B violates a right of A with all the consequences of a violation of law according to general international law. For the legal existence of State B in relation to State A, based on the legal recognition, this violation of law has no importance.

f. De jure *and* de facto *recognition.* It is usual in theory and in practice to distinguish between *de jure* and *de facto* recognition. The significance of this distinction is not quite clear. In general it is assumed that *de jure* recognition is final, whereas *de facto* recognition is only provisional and thus may be withdrawn. If such a distinction is made with reference to political recognition, it must be observed that the declaration of willingness to enter into normal political and economic relations with the new state does not necessarily constitute any legal obligation. Even if this political recognition has no provisional character, it is not a legal act, and thus, in this sense, is not *de jure*. In order that political recognition may not be withdrawn unilaterally, it has to have the form of a treaty between the recognizing and the recognized state, a treaty constituting legal obligations. Then it is *de jure*, even if it is declared to be *de facto*, meaning provisional.

The distinction in question can be applied to legal recognition only with the restriction that the so-called *de facto* recognition is also a *de jure* recognition because it has a legal effect. But perhaps this legal effect of a so-called *de facto* recognition differs somehow from the effect of a *de jure* recognition, using the term in a narrower sense? This is not the case. It is true that it is sometimes difficult to answer the question whether a given community fulfills all the conditions prescribed by international law in order to be a state. Immediately after a new community which claims to be a state has come into existence, it is in some cases doubtful whether the given facts correspond completely to the requirements of international law, especially whether the new order is permanently effective and independent. If the legal act of recognition is made in this stage, the recognizing state may wish to refer to the situation in its act by declaring its recognition to be merely *de facto*. The expression is, as indicated, not quite exact, for even such a recognition is a legal act and has in the relations between the recognizing and the recognized state the same effects as a *de jure* recognition. If it turns out later that the recognized community does not in fact fulfill all the conditions prescribed by international law, the recognizing state may at any time establish this; but this is also possible if the recognition was announced not as a *de facto* but as a *de jure* recognition. Any state is entitled, according to general international law, at any time to ascertain the fact that a community which has been a state in the sense of international law has ceased to be such, because it no longer fulfills the conditions prescribed by general international law. If the ascertainment of such a fact is called "withdrawal" of recognition, so-called withdrawal of recognition is an *actus contrarius* as compared with the act of recognition.

From the juristic point of view, the distinction between *de jure* and *de facto* recognition has no importance.

g. *Recognition with retroactive force*. Since states, according to general international law, are not obliged, but only authorized, to determine whether a community is a state, or has ceased to be a state, this can be established at any time regardless of the date when, in the opinion of the state so determining, the community in question began to fulfill the prescribed conditions. The state competent to establish this fact can fix the date in its declaration. The recognizing state may perform its recognition or the *actus contrarius* with retroactive force by declaring that the community in question began to or ceased to fulfill the conditions prescribed by international law before the date of the recognition or the *actus contrarius*. Legal acts with retroactive force are possible according to general international law. There is no reason to suppose that the act of recognition or its *actus contrarius* forms an exception to this rule. Whether these acts have retroactive force or not is to be decided according to the intention of the acting state. This intention must be expressed in some way. No special form is prescribed by general international law; in fact, neither is there one for the act of recognition nor for its *actus contrarius*.

h. *Recognition by admission into the United Nations*. A state can transfer its competence to recognize the existence of another state by means of a treaty to another state or to a union of states or its organs. It is in this sense that we must interpret Article 4 of the Charter of the United Nations: "1. Membership in the United Nations is open to all other peace-loving states which accept the obligations contained in the present Charter and, in the judgment of the Organization, are able and willing to carry out these obligations. 2. The admission of any such state to membership in the

United Nations will be effected by a decision of the General Assembly upon the recommendation of the Security Council."

This provision does not mean that only communities recognized as states by all members of the United Nations can be admitted to the United Nations. Thus it is possible that a community may become a member of the United Nations even if this community has not yet been recognized as a state by one or another member voting for or against its admission. By admission into the United Nations the community in question becomes a subject of the duties and rights stipulated by the Charter in relation to all the other members, even to those who have voted against the admission of the new member; and the other members of the United Nations, even those who voted against its admission, obtain, according to the rules laid down in the Charter, certain rights and incur certain obligations in relation to the newly admitted member. This is only possible under the supposition that the new member, by admission into the United Nations, is recognized as a state also in relation to those members which have not yet recognized it. The resolution of the General Assembly by which the new member is admitted implies the act of recognition for those members which have themselves not yet recognized the new member as a state. A state, by subjecting itself to the Charter of the United Nations, transfers to the General Assembly and the Security Council the competence to recognize as a state a community which it has not yet recognized, that is to say, the power of ascertaining the fact that this community is a state in the sense of international law. This transfer of competence, however, is limited to the case that the community in question is admitted to the United Nations. Article 1, section 2, of the Covenant of the League of Nations concerning admission of new members has been interpreted in this way.

If it is maintained that admission of a community into the United Nations does not imply recognition on the part of the members, this can mean only that admission of a community into the United Nations does not imply political recognition of the community on the part of the members, that is to say, that the members are not obliged to enter into the normal diplomatic, political, and economic relations with the community admitted into the United Nations.

The Essential Function of International Law

According to the wording of the Charter, the members are indeed not obliged to do so. But it is doubtful whether such an interpretation is consistent with the spirit of the Charter, which in its Preamble declares that the peoples of the United Nations are determined to live together "as good neighbors."[54]

5. Recognition of a Government

Recognition of a government, as distinct from the recognition of a community as a state, comes into consideration only in case of a new government, that is to say, a government established by revolution or *coup d'état*. In case of changes in the government established in conformity with the constitution, as a rule, no recognition is required or granted.

a. *Legal and political recognition of a government.* The recognition of an individual or a body of individuals as the government of a state offers problems similar to those involved in the recognition of a community as a state. The legal recognition of a government must in principle be distinguished from the political recognition. The first is the ascertainment of the fact that an individual or a body of individuals is actually the government of a state. And an individual or a body of individuals is the government of a state in the sense of international law if the individual or the body of individuals is independent and in effective control of a population living on a definite territory. Political recognition of a government is the expression of willingness to enter into mutual relations with this government. Since a state in the sense of international law must have a government, and a community which has no government is no state, the recognition of a community as a state implies that the community has a government. So long as a state admits that another community is a state in the sense of international law, and so long as it does not declare that this community has ceased to be a state, it cannot declare that this state has no

---

[54] In a memorandum of the Secretary-General of the United Nations on the legal aspects of the problem of representation (UN Doc. S/1466), the view that admission to the United Nations constitutes an implied recognition by all members is rejected. This interpretation can be maintained only if by "recognition" not legal but only political recognition is meant.

government. Recognition or nonrecognition of a government must not be mixed up with recognition or nonrecognition of a state.[55] Only if recognition of a community as a state and recognition of an individual or a body of individuals as the government of a state are not clearly distinguished, nonrecognition of a government—not implying nonrecognition of the state—can be misinterpreted to mean that legally no government exists.[56]

---

[55] In *Lehigh Valley Railroad Co. v. State of Russia* (United States, Circuit Court of Appeals, Second Circuit, 1927, 21 Federal Reporter [2d] 396) the Court stated: "The granting or refusal of recognition of a government has nothing to do with the recognition of the state itself. If a foreign state refuses the recognition of a change in the form of government of an old state, this latter does not thereby lose its recognition as an international person."

[56] This misinterpretation is partly due to the fact that in the English language the term "government" is frequently used as equivalent to the term "state." Thus, e.g., in *Wulfsohn v. Russian Socialist Federated Soviet Republic* (United States, Court of Appeals of New York, 1923, 234 N.Y. 372, 138 N.E. 24) the question as to whether the Soviet Russian State under the unrecognized Soviet Government was immune from jurisdiction by American courts was certified as follows: "Can the defendant, which has not been recognized as a sovereign state by the United States government, be sued in the courts of this state as a foreign corporation?" The Court stated: "The Russian Federated Soviet Republic is the existing *de facto* government of Russia. . . . Whether or not a government exists, clothed with the power to enforce its authority within its own territory, obeyed by the people over whom it rules, capable of performing the duties and fulfilling the obligations of an independent power, able to enforce its claims by military force is a fact, not a theory. For its recognition does not create the state, although it may be desirable."

In *Russian Socialist Federated Soviet Republic v. Cibrario* (United States, Court of Appeals of New York, 1923, 235 N.Y. 255, 139 N.E. 259) the Court declared regarding certain confiscation decrees of the Soviet Government: "Should there be any government which appropriates other people's property without compensation, the remedy appears to be to refuse to recognize it as a sovereign state." By "to refuse to recognize it as a sovereign state" was evidently meant to refuse to recognize the government; not to refuse to recognize the state.

In *Sokoloff v. National City Bank* (United States, Court of Appeals of New York, 1924, 239 N.Y. 158, 145 N.E. 917) the Court stated: "The government of the United States refuses recognition of the Soviet Republic as the government of Russia," which means only that the Government of the United States refuses recognition of the government of the Soviet Republic, and not that the Government of the United States refuses recognition of the Soviet Republic.

In *Dougherty v. Equitable Life Assurance Society* (cf. *supra*, p. 240) the Court stated: "On November 16, 1933, the United States extended formal recognition to the Soviet Republic," meaning that the United States extended

The Essential Function of International Law

During a civil war it may be doubtful which individual or which body of individuals claiming to be the government is the government; then legal recognition of the new government is necessary.

recognition to the Government of the Soviet Republic, not to the Soviet Republic as a state.

As the recognition of a government is represented as recognition of a state, the recognition of a state is represented as recognition of a government. Thus, e.g., in *Jones v. Garcia del Rio* (Great Britain, High Court of Chancery, 1823, 1 Turner & Russell 297) the validity of a contract entered into with persons who maintained that they were representatives of the Government of Peru, which had established itself as a state by revolutionary separation from Spain, depended on the answer to the question whether Peru was a new state in the sense of international law. The Court stated: "We all know that Peru was part of the dominions of Spain, and that Spain and this country are at peace, and that this country has not acknowledged the government of Peru; I want to know, whether, supposing Peru to be so far absolved from the government of Spain that it never can be attached to it again, the King's Courts will interfere at all while the Peruvian government is not acknowledged by the government of this country. What right have I, as the King's Judge, to interfere upon the subject of a contract with a country which he does not recognize?"

A clear distinction between "government" and "state" was made in the two cases *The Government of Spain v. The Chancery Lane Safe Deposit, Ltd.* and *The State of Spain v. The Same Parties* (England, High Court, 1939; Annual Digest 1941–1942, Case No. 7). In the first case the Government of General Franco, recognized in February, 1939, by the British Government as the *de jure* government of Spain, brought an action in an English court, in which it made—in the name of the Spanish Government—a claim based on the repudiation of an act of the Republican government of Spain, done when the latter was still the *de jure* government of Spain. The Court held that before the English courts General Franco's Government after February, 1939, and the Republican Government before that date, were the same legal entity, though composed of different persons, and the Government of Spain could not base a claim on the illegality of its own acts.

In the second case, the same claim was brought forth in the name of the Spanish State; this claim was successful. The Court held that the government is an organ of the state, and, though a most important organ of the state and that which ordinarily represents the state in relation to the outside world, the government is not legally the same thing as the state. Governments may act illegally and *ultra vires* their powers under the law of the state, and the state can claim that the acts of its government at a given time were *ultra vires* and illegal. Consequently it was possible for an action to be brought in the English courts in the name of the Spanish state, based on the contention that certain acts of the Spanish Government at a certain time were illegal. The Court stated that the claim of the Government of Spain was one thing and the claim of the State of Spain another, although the same persons were interested.

Such a recognition is constitutive with respect to the legal existence of the recognized government in relation to the recognizing government. If a state recognizes an individual or a body of individuals as a government although it does not fulfill the requirements of international law, that state violates international law and the right of the state concerned. If, however, the government of a state has no doubt that the individual or the body of individuals who presents itself as the new government of another state is independent and in effective control of the territory and the population, nonrecognition of this government by the first-mentioned government cannot mean that the nonrecognized government does legally not exist in relation to the nonrecognizing government. By withholding recognition, the nonrecognizing state refuses to enter into normal relations with the state whose government it does not recognize. In other words, if nonrecognition of a government is not intended to mean that the community whose government is not recognized has no government at all and hence is no state—has ceased to be a state—nonrecognition of a government has no legal effect as to the existence of the government, and insofar has only a political character.[57] But this does not exclude the fact that

---

[57] In the case *The Tinoco Arbitration* (Great Britain-Costa Rica, 1923, 18 *American Journal of International Law* [1924] 147) the arbitrator held that the government of Federico Tinoco, which came into power by revolution and exercised effective control over the territory of Costa Rica from June, 1917, to August, 1919, was the (*de facto*) government of Costa Rica in spite of the fact that Great Britain did not recognize this government. In his opinion the arbitrator stated: "For a full two years Tinoco and the legislative assembly under him peaceably administered the affairs of the Government of Costa Rica, and there was no disorder of a revolutionary character during that interval. No other government of any kind asserted power in the country. The courts sat, Congress legislated, and the government was duly administered. Its power was fully established and peaceably exercised. . . . The non-recognition by other nations of a government claiming to be a national personality, is usually appropriate evidence that it has not attained the independence and control entitling it by international law to be classed as such. But when recognition *vel non* of a government is by such nations determined by inquiry, not into its *de facto* sovereignty and complete governmental control, but into its illegitimacy or irregularity of origin, their non-recognition loses something of evidential weight on the issue with which those applying the rules of international law are alone concerned. . . . Such non-recognition for any reason, however, cannot outweigh the evidence disclosed by this record before me

The Essential Function of International Law

nonrecognition of a government (not implying nonrecognition of the community concerned as a state) may have other legal effects. These effects will be discussed later.

Each state is free to enter or to refuse to enter into political and other relations with a new government for any reason whatever, for no state is obliged by general international law to enter into or to maintain such relations with other states. A state may, e.g., make its political recognition of the new government of another state dependent on the fact that the government is supported, or that the revolutionary change is approved, by the majority of the people. It may refuse its recognition because it does not want to be in the normal relations with a state in which by revolution or *coup d'état* a communistic or fascistic regime has been established, or for other reasons.

b. *Effects of nonrecognition.* Political nonrecognition has the effect that the state withholding recognition will neither send nor receive diplomatic representatives or consuls to and from the state whose government it refuses to recognize, and will not conclude treaties with the state. But what about the mutual obligations

---

as to the *de facto* character of Tinoco's government, according to the standard set by international law. . . . Here the executive of Great Britain takes the position that the Tinoco Government which it did not recognize, was nevertheless a *de facto* government that could create rights in British subjects which it now seeks to protect." In this case nonrecognition of the Tinoco Government by the British Government did not imply the opinion of the British Government that the Tinoco Government was not the government of Costa Rica.

But in *Sokoloff v. National City Bank* (cf. *supra*, p. 280) the Court held with respect to the Soviet Government, which neither the United States Government nor the Court denied was in effective control of the Soviet Union: "Juridically, a government that is unrecognized may be viewed as no government at all, if the power withholding recognition chooses thus to view it." But the Court added: "In practice, however, since juridical conceptions are seldom, if ever, carried to the limit of their logic, the equivalence is not absolute, but is subject to self-imposed limitations of common sense and fairness. . . ." If nonrecognition of the Soviet Government did not imply nonrecognition of the Soviet Russian State, then the legal nonexistence of the Soviet Government was not at all a logical consequence of the concept of nonrecognition. On the contrary, the legal existence of the Soviet Government was the logical consequence of the continued recognition of the Soviet Russian State. Considerations of "common sense and fairness" were not at all necessary to accept this consequence.

and rights of the two states, established by general international law and by treaties concluded with the recognized predecessor of the nonrecognized government? It is hardly possible to maintain that the state which as such is recognized by another state but whose government is not recognized by that state is not obliged to comply with the rules of general international law in its relations with the state which withholds the recognition, and vice versa. For the state whose government is not recognized by another state remains a state in its relation with the other state; hence general international law remains applicable. As to treaty obligations and rights established prior to the coming into power of the nonrecognized government, it should not be overlooked that the binding force of treaties rests on a rule of general international law: *pacta sunt servanda*. There is no reason to assume that just this rule ceases to be valid in the relation between two states of which one refuses to recognize, not the existence as a state, but only the government of the other.

In this respect, especially, multilateral treaties are of importance. Revolutionary change of government of a state which is a member of the United Nations does not change the obligations and rights which this state has under the Charter in relation to any other member of the United Nations, whether this member recognizes or refuses to recognize the new government. As pointed out,[58] even nonrecognition of a community as a state by a member of the United Nations cannot prevent admission of this community to the United Nations and that means the application of the Charter to the relation between the two states. When a revolutionary change of government takes place within a state which is a member of the United Nations, the new government is certainly entitled to send its representatives to the General Assembly and to the Councils in which the state is a member. And each of these bodies must approve the credentials of the representatives of the new government. If the old government still maintains the claim to send representatives to the General Assembly or the Councils of the United Nations, each of these bodies must approve the credentials of the representatives of the new government and

---

[58] Cf. *supra*, p. 278.

rescind the credentials of the representatives of the old government, provided the body is of the opinion that the individual or group of individuals which presents itself as the new government fulfills the requirements of international law, that is to say, is independent and in effective control of the territory and the population of the member state. In such a case the approval of the credentials implies the legal and political recognition of the new government. The recognition, implied in the approval of the credentials, cannot be refused under the Charter, which confers upon the state as such, not upon its government, the right to be represented in the General Assembly and the Councils of the United Nations; whereas the political recognition of a new government can be refused by any state under general international law.[59]

As to the effect of the political nonrecognition of the government of a recognized state, the only interpretation consistent with the

---

[59] On December 14, 1950, the General Assembly of the United Nations adopted the following resolution: "The General Assembly, considering that difficulties may arise regarding the representation of a Member State in the United Nations and that there is a risk that conflicting decisions may be reached by its various organs, considering that it is in the interest of the proper functioning of the Organization that there should be uniformity in the procedure applicable whenever more than one authority claims to be the government entitled to represent a Member State in the United Nations, and this question becomes the subject of controversy in the United Nations, considering that, in virtue of its composition, the General Assembly is the organ of the United Nations in which consideration can best be given to the views of all Member States in matters affecting the functioning of the Organization as a whole, 1. recommends that, whenever more than one authority claims to be the government entitled to represent a Member State in the United Nations and this question becomes the subject of controversy in the United Nations, the question should be considered in the light of the Purposes and Principles of the Charter and the circumstances of each case; 2. recommends that, when any such question arises, it should be considered by the General Assembly, or by the Interim Committee if the General Assembly is not in session; 3. recommends that the attitude adopted by the General Assembly or its Interim Committee concerning any such question should be taken into account in other organs of the United Nations and in the specialized agencies; 4. declares that the attitude adopted by the General Assembly or its Interim Committee concerning any such question shall not of itself affect the direct relations of individual Member States with the State concerned; 5. requests the Secretary-General to transmit the present resolution to the other organs of the United Nations and to the specialized agencies for such action as may be appropriate."

fact that the state whose government is not recognized by another state remains—in the relation to this state—a state in the sense of international law, is this: As long as the government is not recognized, no diplomatic and consular relations will be established and no treaties will be concluded between the two states. But the practice of states and a doctrine advocated by some writers are not in agreement with this view. It is maintained that treaties entered into by the two states prior to the coming into power of the new government are not in force; that they come into force only after recognition of the government; that a state whose government is not recognized by another state does not enjoy immunity from jurisdiction of the courts of the nonrecognizing state; that a state under a nonrecognized government cannot claim that the validity of the acts of its government is not to be questioned by the courts of states which have refused to recognize that government; that a state under a nonrecognized government is not entitled to demand and to receive possession of property within the nonrecognizing state—all this as if the privileges and rights concerned were privileges and rights of a government, and not privileges and rights of the state.[60]

Even if this doctrine is accepted, it is not possible to maintain, with respect to the relation between the state which withholds

[60] In *Wulfsohn v. Russian Socialist Federated Soviet Republic* (cf. *supra*, p. 280) the court answered in the affirmative the question as to whether the Soviet Union, although its government was not recognized by the United States, enjoyed the privilege of immunity from jurisdiction by American courts. In *Russian Socialist Federated Soviet Republic v. Cibrario* (cf. *supra*, p. 280) the court decided that a state is not obliged to permit another state, the government of which is not recognized, to bring an action in the courts of the non-recognizing state. The court did not refer to international law, but to "comity": "Does any rule of comity, then, require us to permit a suit by an unrecognized power? In view of the attitude of our government, should we permit an action to be brought by the Soviet government? To both queries we must give a negative answer." It is not very clear what the court meant by "comity." Probably the same as international law, because the court stated: "Rules of comity are a portion of the law that they enforce."

In *The Soviet Government v. Ericsson* (Annual Digest 1919–1922, Case No. 30) the Swedish Supreme Court (1921) upheld the decision of the court of Stockholm that the action was brought by the Soviet Government, that this government was not recognized by the Swedish Government, that, moreover, there was no information as to the composition of the Soviet Government,

The Essential Function of International Law

recognition of the new government of another state and that state, that their mutual obligations and rights established by general international law and by treaties entered into prior to the coming into power of the new government cease to be valid; but only that the fulfillment of these obligations and the exercise of these rights are suspended. It seems that those who advocate the doctrine

and that in these circumstances the Soviet Government could not be allowed to appear as a party before the court.

In *A. M. Luther v. James Sagor & Co.* (cf. *supra*, pp. 239, 257) the lower court refused to consider a nationalization decree of the (at the time of the decision) not yet recognized Government of Soviet Russia, and consequently gave judgment for the plaintiff. But the Court of Appeal reversed the decision, since in the meantime the British Government had recognized the Soviet Government. In *Sokoloff v. National City Bank* (cf. *supra*, pp. 280, 283) the court, refusing to apply to the acts of the unrecognized Government of Soviet Russia the principle of international law that no court of a state is entitled to question the validity of the acts of another state, declared that the acts of an unrecognized government may be given "a validity quasi-governmental, if violence to fundamental principles of justice or to our own public policy might otherwise be done." In *Petrogradsky M. K. Bank v. National City Bank* (253 N.Y. [1930] 23) the court refused to recognize the decrees of the unrecognized Soviet Government as legally valid, and went even as far as to state that they were not even law in Soviet Russia. But in *Salimoff & Co. v. Standard Oil Co. of New York* (United States, Court of Appeals of New York, 1933, 262 N.Y. 220) the court held that "the existing government cannot be ignored by the courts of this state, so far as the validity of its acts in Russia is concerned, although the attempt is here made to nullify such acts and create a cause of action in tort in favor of Russian nationals against American corporations, purchasers for value from the Soviet government of property in Russia in accordance with Soviet law . . . . Nonrecognition is no answer to defendant's contention, no reason for regarding as of no legal effect the laws of an unrecognized government ruling by force, as the Soviet government in Russia concededly was. 'Within its own territory the Soviet was a sovereign power' . . . ." In this case the court referred to the following statement made by the Secretary of State of the United States:

"1. The Government of the United States accorded recognition to the Provisional Government of Russia as the successor of the Russian Imperial Government, and has not accorded recognition to any government in Russia since the overthrow of the Provisional Government of Russia.

"2. The Department of State is cognizant of the fact that the Soviet regime is exercising control and power in territory of the former Russian Empire and the Department of State has no disposition to ignore that fact.

"3. The refusal of the Government of the United States to accord recognition to the Soviet regime is not based on the ground that that regime does not exercise control and authority in territory of the former Russian Empire, but on other facts."

that nonrecognition of the government of a recognized state has such legal effect do not assume that the entire general customary and particular (conventional) international law is suspended in the relation between the two states. But to what extent this effect takes place is not clear. Whatever legal effects nonrecognition of a government (not implying nonrecognition of the community concerned as a state) may have, subsequent recognition of the government is—with the exception of the above-mentioned case of two authorities claiming to be the government—not constitutive with respect to the legal existence of the government and insofar has only a political character.

6. So-Called Governments in Exile

As pointed out, an individual or a body of individuals is, according to general international law, the government of a state if it is independent, that is to say, legally not subjected to the government of another state, and if it is in effective control of the territory and the population living thereon. The control is effective if it is firmly established. This rule, however, does not apply to so-called governments in exile; and, hence, it seems as if the principle of effectiveness could not be considered as the decisive criterion in this case.

When in the course of war the territory of a belligerent is occupied by armed forces of the enemy, the government of the state under belligerent occupation may establish its seat temporarily on the territory of an allied state, which, of course, is legally possible only with the consent of the government of that state.[61] During the period of belligerent occupation the territory is actually under the control of the occupying power. But as long as the status of the territory is that of belligerent occupation, and that means as long as there is a state of war between the occupied state and the occupying state, the control exercised by the latter cannot be considered as "effective." Apart from the fact that it is restricted by international law, it is not firmly established; for there is a war going on the

---

[61] During the Second World War the governments of several states occupied by Germany's armed forces, e.g. the governments of Poland, Belgium, the Netherlands, Greece, Yugoslavia, established their seat in England.

The Essential Function of International Law

purpose of which is to reestablish the effective control of the government now in exile. On the other hand, the exiled government, too, is not in effective control of the territory concerned. Nevertheless it is this government—and not the government of the occupying state—which is competent under general international law to exercise, as organ of the occupied state, all the functions of a state in relation to other states, such as sending and receiving diplomatic envoys, concluding treaties, especially a peace treaty with the occupying state, directing the armed forces at its disposal in the war against the occupying state. It may even exercise legislative, administrative, and judicial functions. Finally, certain privileges, such as immunity from jurisdiction, may be granted to the members of the government in exile by the government of the state on the territory of which it is established.[62] All this in spite of the fact that the government in exile has lost the control of the territory of its state. To consider a government in exile as the government of the state under belligerent occupation is, however, possible only as long as the loss of control is to be considered as temporary only, and that means as long as the government in exile is making efforts to regain the effective control of the territory of its state by means of war waged through its own armed forces or by participating in a war waged by other states against the occupying state. The requirement of exercising effective control of the territory is replaced by the requirement of making efforts to regain effective control. This requirement, too, is an application of the principle of effectiveness. The efforts of the government in exile to regain control of the territory under belligerent occupation must be "effective" in a sense similar to that in which a blockade must be effective. Blockade is effective—and not fictitious—if it is maintained by armed forces sufficient to prevent (as a rule, exceptional breach of blockade not excluded) access to the enemy coast. The efforts of a government in exile to regain control are effective if they are made by means of war, that is to say, by armed forces sufficient

---

[62] A statute adopted by the British Parliament in 1941, the Diplomatic Privileges (Extension) Act, conferred diplomatic privileges upon the members of the exile governments established in the United Kingdom and their official staff, as well as on the envoys accredited to them.

to prevent the control of the occupying power from becoming firmly established. That a government in exile is considered to be the government of the occupied state in spite of the fact that it has temporarily lost effective control of the territory does not mean that the principle of effectiveness does not apply at all in this case; it means only that the principle of effectiveness does not refer to the control of the territory but to the efforts to regain such control.

Since the decisive reason for considering a so-called government in exile as the government of an occupied state is its effective effort to obtain control over the territory of that state, it is irrelevant whether or not this government is established in conformity with the constitution. The fact that the territory of a state is under belligerent occupation may render compliance with the provisions of the constitution concerning the establishment of the government impossible, for instance, when the head of the state dies or resigns and the popular election prescribed by the constitution cannot take place. Just as international law does not require constitutionality of a government established on the territory of its own state, it does not require constitutionality of a government in exile. The difference which exists between these two cases is that in the first one effective control of the territory, in the second one effective efforts to obtain such control is required.

As to the recognition of governments in exile the same principles apply as to recognition of governments in general. If the government in exile is unconstitutionally established, recognition may or may not be granted. Recognition may be implied in the act by which a state gives its consent to the establishment of the seat of the exile government on its territory.

From the preceding analysis it follows that the so-called government in exile can be considered as the government of the occupied state only as long as it continues its efforts to obtain by means of war control of the territory of the state concerned. When the war is terminated without the government in exile having obtained control of the territory, if, for instance, this territory has been annexed by the occupying power in the way of subjugation or if it has been placed under a new national government different from the government in exile, then the latter can no longer be considered as the government of a state. Those who call it still a government and treat it as if it were a government are using a fiction. The same holds in case a so-called government in exile is established only after the war is terminated or after a successful revolution.

7. Recognition of Insurgents As a Belligerent Power

Besides the recognition of states and governments, the recognition of insurgents as a belligerent power is also of importance in international law. It presupposes a civil war. Under certain conditions determined by international law, this civil war may assume the character of an international war.

These are the conditions: (1) The insurgents must have a government and a military organization of their own. (2) The insurrection must be conducted in the technical forms of war, i.e., it must be more than a petty revolt and must assume the true characteristics of a war, especially regarding the means of destruction used by the parties. (3) The government of the insurgents must in fact control a certain part of the territory of the state in which the civil war takes place, i.e., the order established by the insurgents must be effective for a certain part of the territory of this state.

The legal recognition of insurgents as a belligerent power implies that the above-mentioned facts, determined generally by international law, exist in a given case. This recognition may be made by the legitimate government against which the insurrection is directed as well as by the governments of other states.

The two most important effects of this act of recognition are as follows: (1) Application of the norms of international law concerning conduct of war and neutrality to the relations between the recognizing state and the community recognized as belligerent power. That implies the transformation of civil war into international war with all its legal consequences, among which are: that a state, after having recognized the insurgents as a belligerent power, is under the obligations of a neutral state in relation to the government of the insurgents as well as to the legitimate government against which the insurrection is directed; and that after the legitimate government has recognized the insurgents as a belligerent power, the individuals involved in the civil war, when they fall into the hands of the other side, must not be prosecuted by the latter, especially by the legitimate government against which the civil war is waged, as criminals for high treason, murder, and the like, but must be treated as prisoners of war according to the rules of international law. And (2) the regulation of international responsibility corresponding to the change of political power within the state involved in civil war, not only with respect to the legitimate government, which is released from all responsibility for events which may happen in the territory under the control of the insurgents, but also with respect to the insurgent government, which is now responsible for these events.

The recognition of insurgents as a belligerent power resembles more the recognition of a community as a state than the recognition of an individual or a group of individuals as a government. By the effective control of the insurgent government over part of the territory and people of the state involved in civil war an entity is formed which indeed resembles a state in the sense of international law.

Recognition of insurgents as a belligerent power, as recognition of belligerency, is different from the so-called recognition of insurgency. Sometimes a state recognizes the existence of an insurrection within another state, without recognizing the insurgents as a belligerent power because they do not fulfill the conditions under which such a recognition is admissible. A state may recognize insurgents as such in order to avoid treating them as criminals. But so-called recognition of insurgency does not confer upon the insurgents a legal status under international law.[63]

---

[63] During an insurrection in Cuba the Government of the United States, in a proclamation of the President on June 12, 1895, recognized the existence of this insurrection, and admonished all persons concerned to abstain from any violation of the neutrality law of the United States. In *The Three Friends* (166 U.S. 63) the Supreme Court of the United States (1897) decided that the neutrality law of the United States was applicable in spite of the fact that the United States Government had not recognized the insurgents as a belligerent power. The Court stated: "The distinction between recognition of belligerence and recognition of a condition of political revolt, between

8. Recognition and Nonrecognition of Illegally Established Situations (Stimson Doctrine)

Starting from the problematical presumption that by an illegal act no legal result can be produced, especially no right acquired (*ex injuria jus non oritur*),[64] some writers maintain that the legal defect may be cured, and the right, in spite of the illegality of its origin, acquired, by recognition on the part of other states. If, for instance, a state in violation of international law incorporates in its own territory, territory of another state, the illegality of the acquisition may be validated by recognition on the part of third states. Such recognition is an act quite different from the legal recognition of a community as a state or an individual or a body of individuals as the government of a state. It is not the ascertainment of a legally relevant fact. It is an act by which—according to this doctrine—one state creates law applicable in the relationship between two other states. It is, however, more than doubtful that the unilateral act of one state can have legal effect on a relation-

---

recognition of the existence of war in a material sense and of war in a legal sense, is sharply illustrated by the case before us. For here the political department has not recognized the existence of a *de facto* belligerent power engaged in hostility with Spain, but has recognized the existence of insurrectionary warfare prevailing before, at the time, and since this forfeiture is alleged to have been incurred. . . . We are thus judicially informed of the existence of an actual conflict of arms in resistance of the authority of a government with which the United States are on terms of peace and amity, although acknowledgement of the insurgents as belligerents by the political department has not taken place; and it cannot be doubted that, this being so, the act in question is applicable." The decision of the Court was based on an interpretation of a national law of the United States which provided: "Every person who, within the limits of the United States, fits out . . . any vessel with intent that such vessel shall be employed in the service of any foreign prince or state, or of any colony, district or people, to cruise or commit hostilities against the subjects, citizens or property of any foreign prince or state, or of any colony, district or people, with whom the United States are at peace . . . shall be deemed guilty of a high misdemeanor, and shall be fined . . ." The decision was essentially based on the words "colony, district or people." The Court stated: ". . . why should the meaning of the words 'colony, district or people' be confined only to parties recognized as belligerent?" The Court applied national, not international, law.

[64] Cf. *supra*, p. 216.

ship between other states. There can be no doubt that a change of the legal relations between two states, especially a territorial change, if brought about legally, does not need the recognition of third states in order to be valid; and if the change has been brought about illegally, it is difficult to see how it can be validated by the interference on the part of other states. Besides, no' third state is competent under general international law to decide whether the act of one state is legal or illegal in relation to another state, that is to say, whether one state has, or has not, violated the right of another state. If, however, the effect of the recognition in question, as some writers maintain, consists only in the waiver of claims of the recognizing state conflicting with the right thus recognized, it is the violation of its own right which the recognizing state validates by its consent called "recognition." Recognition of a change in the legal relations of other states may have a political effect; it can hardly have a legal effect under general international law. The same is true with respect to nonrecognition.

After Japan invaded the Chinese province of Manchuria, the Secretary of State of the United States of America (Henry L. Stimson), on January 7, 1932, sent two identical notes to the Japanese and Chinese governments in which he stated that the United States "does not intend to recognize any situation, treaty or agreement which may be brought about by means contrary to the covenants and obligations of the Pact of Paris of August 27th, 1928, to which treaty both China and Japan as well as the United States are parties" (Stimson Doctrine). On March 11, 1932, the Assembly of the League of Nations adopted a resolution which declared that "it is incumbent upon the Members of the League of Nations not to recognize any situation, treaty or agreement which may be brought about by means contrary to the Covenant of the League of Nations, or to the Pact of Paris." Neither the Covenant of the League of Nations nor the Kellogg-Briand Pact provides that a change in the legal relations between two parties brought about illegally, can be validated by recognition or that such a change can be prevented by nonrecognition on the part of a third party. Hence mere nonrecognition in conformity with the Stimson Declaration or with the resolution of the Assembly can

The Essential Function of International Law

have only political, no legal effects. If, for instance, a war resorted to by one state against another in violation of the Kellogg-Briand Pact leads to a peace treaty in which the state against which the illegal war was directed cedes part of its territory to the victor, and if the vanquished state does not refuse to carry out the treaty, nonrecognition of the treaty on the part of third states can hardly have any legal effect on the situation.

9. Succession of States

The territory of one state may become part of the territory of another state or of several other states when a state merges voluntarily into another or into several other states by treaty; or when the whole territory of one state is forcibly annexed by another or by several other states; or when several states establish a federal state by a treaty, provided that the so-called component states retain no international personality at all. The territory of one state may become, by dismemberment, the territories of several new states, as did the territory of the Austro-Hungarian Monarchy, as a result of the First World War, or the territory of the German Reich as a result of the Second World War. Part of the territory of one state may become the territory of a new state by treaty, as, for instance, Danzig, or the State of the Vatican City; or by revolution when a part of the population of a state breaks away and establishes, on the territory where it lives, a new state. Part of the territory of one state may become part of the territory of another state by a treaty of cession or, without the consent of the government concerned, by annexation on the part of another state.

When the territory of one state bcomes, totally or partially, part of the territory of another state or of several other states, or when the territory of one state becomes the territories of several new states (dismemberment), or when part of the territory of one state becomes the territory of a new state (revolutionary separation), the question arises whether and to what extent, according to general international law, the obligations and rights of the predecessor devolve on the successor. This is the problem of so-called succession of states. The whole territory of one state can become the territory of one other state, that is to say, the territories of two states can be considered as identical only when one state ceases to exist—as, for instance, by incorporation into another state—and, later, on the same territory, a new state comes into existence.[65] Otherwise, only a change of government takes place, which does not affect the identity of the state. In this latter case, no succession of states comes into consideration. In the first case, succession of states is not excluded. But no rule of positive general international law stipulating succession of the new state in the obligations and rights of the old state can be maintained.

The fact that the predecessor state ceases to exist—as in the case of the whole territory of one state becoming part of the territory of one or several other states, or in the case of the whole territory of one state becoming the territories of several new states—does not prevent succession. The argument, brought forth by some writers, that if a state ceases to exist, its obligations and rights cease to exist and, consequently, cannot devolve on another state, does not hold. For devolution of obligations and rights of one state on another does not imply identity of these obligations and rights; it means only that general international law imposes upon the successor state certain obligations and confers upon it certain rights which have the same content as certain obligations and rights of the predecessor. This is possible even if it is assumed that the obligations and rights have ceased to exist as soon as the state which is the subject of these obligations and rights has ceased to exist.

Succession does not concern the obligations imposed and the rights conferred upon a state by general international law. These obligations and rights of the successor with respect to the territory in question exist by virtue of general international law directly, not by virtue of succession. Succession refers only to obligations and rights established (1) by particular international law, especially by treaties, and (2) by national law, as, for instance, the public debts of states. It is assumed that, according to general

---

[65] Cf. the above-mentioned case of the first and the second Austrian Republic, *supra*, p. 262.

The Essential Function of International Law   297

international law, succession takes place with regard to such international obligations and rights of the predecessor as are connected with the territory which became territory of the successor. The latter is considered to be bound by treaties concluded by its predecessor with other states if these treaties established obligations of the predecessor inherent to the territory which became territory of the successor, for instance, obligations concerning boundary lines, navigation on rivers, and the like. But the rights arising from such treaties also devolve on the successor of the state which concluded the treaty.

It is assumed that in case the entire territory of one state becomes part of the territory of another state, succession also takes place with regard to the fiscal property of the predecessor; and that in case only part of the territory of one state becomes part of the territory of another state or the territory of a new state, succession takes place with regard to the fiscal property found on the territory which becomes territory of the successor. Some writers deny that automatic succession takes place, but they admit that the successor may under its own law appropriate the property of the predecessor, for each state has, under international law, the lawmaking power regarding property. If a state acquires the territory of another state, the former may adopt the property law prevailing in the territory at the time of the acquisition, that is to say, it may adopt this law as its own law; or it may replace this law by a new law. For practical reasons, the successor usually allows the old law to prevail until new law is enacted;[66] and if under the old law the state had property, the successor becomes the owner under this law. But in this case, too, it is

---

[66] In the *Philippine Sugar Estates Development Company (Limited) v. United States* (United States, Court of Claims, 1904, 39 Ct. Cl. 225) the court stated: "The general rule of international law in regard to all conquered or ceded territory is that the old laws continue until repealed by the proper authorities." There is no such rule of international law. If the old law continues it is only because the successor state by virtue of its legislative power—tacity or expressly—allows the old law to continue as its own law, i.e., the law of the succeeding state. Although the content of the law may remain the same, its reason of validity has changed. It is now valid on the basis of the constitution of the successor state, whereas it was valid previously on the basis of the constitution of the predecessor state.

under its own law that the successor becomes the owner of the property of its predecessor. This view seems to be more correct than the one according to which succession to the property of the predecessor takes place automatically, under international law.[67] As far as the debts of the predecessor are concerned, succession takes place only when the whole territory of a state becomes part of the territory of another state or of several other states, or if the territory of one state becomes the territory of several new states, and with regard to those debts only the creditors of which are nationals of another than the succeeding state. Then their home state is entitled to claim that the successor takes over these debts.[68] When the territory becomes territory of more than one state and hence there are several successors to the fiscal property of the predecessor, the rule is that proportionate parts of the

---

[67] In *German Settlers in Poland* (Publications of the Permanent Court of International Justice, 1923, Series B, No. 6) the Court was asked to give an advisory opinion concerning the question as to whether Poland as the successor to territory ceded by Germany was obliged to respect certain rights acquired under German law by colonists who, formerly German citizens, were domiciled in the ceded territory and had acquired Polish nationality. The Court stated: "Private rights acquired under existing law do not cease on a change of sovereignty." This holds true only if the law does not change. The statement continues: "No one denies that the German Civil Law, both substantive and adjective, has continued without interruption to operate in the territory in question. It can hardly be maintained that, although the law survives, private rights acquired under it have perished. Such a contention is based on no principle and would be contrary to an almost universal opinion and practice." The Court did not consider the question "whether and under what circumstances a State may modify or cancel private rights by its sovereign legislative power," because the Court was dealing with the obligations Poland had under a special treaty, signed at Versailles on June 28, 1919; and it was with reference to this treaty that the Court held that Poland was obliged to respect the rights in question.

[68] In the *Robert E. Brown Claim* (Nielsen's Report, pp. 162–202) the Anglo-American Claims Arbitrary Tribunal, 1923, held that a state (Great Britain) which by conquest annexed the entire territory of another state (the South African Republic) is not obliged to repair a damage caused by an act of the extinct state. The same principle was applied by the tribunal in the *Hawaiian Claims,* 1925 (Nielsen's Report, p. 160) with respect to a case of contractual incorporation of the entire territory of a state (Hawaiian Republic) into the territory of another state (United States).

The Essential Function of International Law

debts must be taken over by the different successors.[69] This, however, is not possible without an agreement entered into for this purpose by the successor states.

---

[69] In the *Austrian Empire (Succession) Case* (Annual Digest 1919–1922, Case No. 39) the Austrian Constitutional Court (*Verfassungsgerichtshof*), 1919, dismissed the action of a teacher against the Ministry of Education for payment of certain bonuses due to him for his work as teacher of gymnastics from October 1, 1917, to the end of September, 1918. The court held that the claim was one against the Austrian Empire, which state was now defunct. "In the territory of the Austrian State there have arisen national States—new States which are not successors of the old State and liable for its obligations. It is true that according to the principles of international law in cases in which a territory is ceded by one State to another or when several States arise out of one State, the State acquiring the territory or the new States are bound to take over an appropriate part of the obligations of the former State in proportion to the assets which it or they have taken over and which have been created as the result of the activity or under the protection of the former State. However, in individual cases both the taking over of the liability and the extent to which it has been taken over must be determined by international agreement—in this case between the national States in the former Austrian territory. For this purpose there had been set up a Liquidation Commission composed of representatives of those States and entrusted with the function of determining the state of the assets and liabilities. Only after the share of liability of the German Austrian Republic has been determined will the plaintiff be entitled to bring an action."

IV.

CREATION AND APPLICATION OF INTERNATIONAL LAW

A. THE CREATION (SOURCES) OF INTERNATIONAL LAW

1. The Concept of "Source" of Law

"Sources" of law is a figurative and highly ambiguous expression. It is used not only to designate the different methods of creating law but also to characterize the reason for the validity of law, and especially the ultimate reason. But, in a wider sense, every legal norm is a source of that other norm the creation of which it regulates. It is a characteristic element of the law in general, and hence also of international law, that it regulates its own creation. It is especially the function of a constitution to regulate the creation of general norms. The creation of general norms by special organs within national law is called legislation. The constitution of a state determines the organs and the procedure of legislation. General international law or the community constituted by general international law also has its "constitution." The constitution of the international community is the set of rules of international law which regulate the creation of international law, or, in other terms, which determine the "sources" of international law.

The norm which regulates the creation of other norms is "superior" to the norms which are created according to the former. The norms created according to the provisions of another norm are "inferior" to the latter. In this sense, any superior legal norm is the source of the inferior legal norm. Thus the constitution of a state is the source of the statutes created on the basis of the constitution, a statute is the source of the judicial decisions based thereon, a judicial decision is the source of the duty it imposes upon the party, and so on.

Traditional jurisprudence opposes the function of creating law to the function of applying law. It considers the function of judicial organs only as application of law, and the function of legislative organs only as creation of law. But the creation of an inferior norm is at the same time the application of the superior norm determining the creation of the inferior norm. In applying the constitution, the legislative organ creates the general norms contained in a statute; in applying the statute, the judicial organ creates an individual norm implied in its decision. Creation and application of law are only relatively, not absolutely, opposed to each other. In regulating its own creation, law regulates also its own application. By "source" of law not only the methods of creating law but also the methods of applying law may be understood.

Finally, the expression "source" of law is used also in an entirely nonjuristic sense. One thereby denotes all those ideas which actually influence the law-creating organs, for instance, moral norms, political principles, legal doctrines, the opinions of juristic experts, and so on. In contradistinction to the previously mentioned sources of law, these sources do not as such have the character of law; they do not have any binding force.

The ambiguity of the term "source" of law seems to render the term rather useless. Instead of a misleading figurative expression, one ought to introduce an expression that clearly and directly describes the phenomenon one has in mind.

2. The So-Called "Gaps" in the Law

In this treatise, by "sources" of international law the methods of creating international law are meant. Whereas the two principal methods of creating national (municipal) law are custom and legislation, the two principal methods of creating international law are custom and treaties. Custom is the older and the original source of international law, of particular as well as of general international law. At present, treaties play an important part in the development of international law. Hence the international legal order is composed of norms created by custom—customary international law—and norms created by treaties—conventional international law. General international law is customary law. There

Creation and Application of International Law 305

is no treaty to which all the states of the world are contracting parties.[1]

In the application to concrete cases, particular conventional (or particular customary) law precedes general customary law. If there is no treaty (or particular customary law) referring to the case, rules of general customary law apply. That neither conventional nor customary international law is applicable to a concrete case is logically not possible. Existing international law can always be applied to a concrete case, that is to say, to the question as to whether a state (or another subject of international law), is or is not obliged to behave in a certain way. If there is no norm of conventional or customary international law imposing upon the state (or another subject of international law) the obligation to behave in a certain way, the subject is under international law legally free to behave as it pleases; and by a decision to this effect existing international law is applied to the case. But this decision, though logically possible, may be morally or politically not satisfactory. Only in this sense are there "gaps" in the international as in any legal order.

The assumption that the law-applying organs are authorized to fill such gaps, by applying to the particular case norms other than those of existing conventional or customary international law, implies that the law-applying organs have the power to create new law for a concrete case if they consider the application of existing law as unsatisfactory. From the point of view of legal positivism, such a law-creating power must be based on a rule of positive international law. Whether there exists such a rule of general international law is doubtful, although many writers take it for granted that there are gaps in existing international law, and that the states or international agencies competent to apply international law are authorized to fill these gaps.[2] But they

[1] As to the question as to whether the Charter of the United Nations, a treaty to which not all the states of the world are contracting parties, has the character of general international law, cf. *supra*, pp. 247f.

[2] The Tribunal of Arbitration in the dispute between the United States and Norway (1922) (17 *American Journal of International Law* [1923] 384), referring to H. Lammasch, *Die Rechtskraft internationaler Schiedssprueche*

suppose that these gaps consist in the cases to which the existing law logically cannot be applied because there is no rule in existing international law which refers to them. That there is no rule referring to a case can only mean that there is no rule imposing upon a state (or another subject of international law) the obligation to behave in this case in a certain way. He who assumes that in such a case the existing law cannot be applied ignores the fundamental principle that what is not legally forbidden to the subjects of the law is legally permitted to them. The rule authorizing the law-applying organs not to apply existing law but to create new law in case the application of existing law is, though logically possible, morally or politically unsatisfactory, confers an extraordinary lawmaking power upon the law-applying organs. It is doubtful whether the writers who adhere to the traditional doctrine of "gaps in international law" are aware of the consequence of this doctrine when they maintain the existence of rules of general international law conferring upon the states and agen-

---

(1913), p. 37, stated that "the arbiter shall decide in accordance with equity, *ex aequo et bono*, when positive rules of law are lacking . . . ." In *Great Britain (Eastern Extension etc. Telegraph Co. Claim) v. United States* (United States-Great Britain, Claims Arbitration, 1923; Nielsen's Report, p. 73) the tribunal stated: "Even assuming that there was . . . no treaty and no specific rule of international law formulated as the expression of a universally recognized rule governing the case . . . . it cannot be said that there is no principle of international law applicable. International law, as well as domestic law, may not contain, and generally does not contain, express rules decisive of particular cases; but the function of jurisprudence is to resolve the conflict of opposing rights and interests by applying, in default of any specific provision of law, the corollaries of general principles, and so to find—exactly as in the mathematical sciences—the solution of the problem. This is the method of jurisprudence; it is the method by which the law has been gradually evolved in every country resulting in the definition and settlement of legal relations as well between States as between private individuals." If the court does not apply the rules of positive international law, but "the corollaries of general principles," the court creates new law for the case at hand, whether the "principles" are presented as generalizations of existing rules of international law or as general principles of law in the sense of Article 38 (c) of the Statute of the International Court of Justice. But the tribunal declared also that "the duty of this Tribunal . . . is not to lay down new rules. Such rules could not have retroactive effect, nor could they be considered as being anything more than a personal expression of opinion by members of a particular tribunal, deriving its authority from only two Governments."

Creation and Application of International Law

cies competent to apply international law the power to fill the gaps. There can be no doubt that such a power may be conferred upon a law-applying organ by a treaty. It is from this point of view that the provision of Article 38 of the Statute of the International Court of Justice is to be understood: that the Court "whose function is to decide in accordance with international law such disputes as are submitted to it, shall apply" not only conventional and customary international law but also "the general principles of law recognized by civilized nations." These "general principles of law" are probably supposed to be a supplementary source of international law, to be applied if the two others—treaty and custom—cannot be applied.[3]

3. Custom

a. *Customary and statutory law.* Customary law is law created by custom. Custom is a usual or habitual course of action, a long-established practice; in international relations, a long-established practice of states. But the frequency of conduct, the fact that certain actions or abstentions have repeatedly been performed during a certain period of time, is only one element of the law-creating fact called custom. The second element is the fact that the individuals whose conduct constitutes the custom must be convinced that they fulfill, by their actions or abstentions, a duty, or that they exercise a right. They must believe that they apply a norm, but they need not believe that it is a legal norm which they apply. They have to regard their conduct as obligatory or right. If the conduct of the states is not accompanied by the opinion that this conduct is obligatory or right, a so-called "usage," but not a law-creating custom, is established.

The basis of customary law is the general principle that we ought to behave in the way our fellow men usually behave and during a certain period of time used to behave. If this principle assumes the character of a norm, custom becomes a law-creating fact. This is the case in the relations between states. Here custom, i.e., a long-established practice of states, creates law. Custom

---
[3] Cf. *infra*, pp. 393f.

creates law just as legislation does. There are two differences between legislation and custom: (1) Legislation is conscious and deliberate lawmaking—men who legislate know that they are making law and intend by their activity to make law; custom is unconscious and unintentional lawmaking. In establishing a custom, men do not necessarily know that they create by their conduct a rule of law, nor do they necessarily intend to create law. The rule of law is the effect and not the purpose of their activity. (2) Legislation is lawmaking by a special organ instituted to this end, according to the principle of division of labor, this organ being different from and more or less independent of the individuals subject to the law created by the organ. Custom is lawmaking by the individuals themselves who are subject to the law created by their conduct. The individuals creating the law and the individuals subject to the law are at least partly identical. Custom is a decentralized—legislation a centralized—creation of law. The law created by legislation is usually called statutory law.

Legislation is not the only sort of conscious and deliberate lawmaking by special organs. Another kind of conscious and deliberate lawmaking by special organs is the creation of law by decisions of courts. A treaty (contract in national law) is also conscious and deliberate lawmaking; but it is lawmaking not by special organs. The individuals who make the treaty (or the contract) that is, the contracting parties, are in principle identical with the individuals who are subject to the norm created by the treaty (or contract). In this point there exists a certain similarity between custom and treaty; the difference is that the latter is conscious and deliberate—the former, unconscious and unintentional—lawmaking.

b. *Custom as a law-creating fact.* The opinion that custom is a law-creating fact, however, is not generally accepted. Some writers maintain that custom is not able to create a legal norm; it is only an evidence of the existence of a legal norm. According to this theory, custom has only a declaratory, not a constitutive character. This theory has obviously influenced the Statute of the Permanent Court of International Justice. Article 38 of this statute, which is identical with Article 38 of the Statute of the International Court of Justice, determines the sources of international law to be applied by the Court. It runs as follows: "The Court . . . shall apply: a. International conventions, whether general or particular, establishing rules expressly recognized by the contesting States; b. International custom, as evidence of a general practice accepted as law . . . ."

The doctrine that custom does not create law but is only an evidence of the existence of a legal norm presupposes that this norm is created by another fact than custom, that the true creator of law stands—so to speak—behind custom. But who is this true creator of law? To this question different answers are given. According to the doctrine of the historical school, which was very influential in Germany during the nineteenth century, national law is created by the national spirit (*Volksgeist*); a custom, the fact that men usually behave in conformity with a certain rule, only indicates that there already exists a general legal norm as the product of the national spirit's invisible and mysterious activity. The most outstanding representative of this school, F. K. von Savigny, consistently denied any competence of the state to legislate.[4] According to a school of sociological jurisprudence which is prevailing in France, "the true law," the "objective" law (*droit objectif*), is created by a fact which this school calls "social solidarity" (*solidarité sociale*). Consequently, as e.g., Léon Duguit, a typical representative of this school maintains,[5] any act or fact which seems to create positive law, be it legislation or custom, is not true creation of law but a declaratory statement (*constatation*) of a legal norm previously created by social solidarity. Positive law that is not in conformity with the "objective" law, the product of social solidarity, has no chance of becoming effective.

Neither the existence of the *Volksgeist* nor that of the *solidarité sociale* can be proved in a scientific way. Both are assumptions of social metaphysics, the purpose of which is to present moral-political postulates, based on subjective value judgments, as ob-

---

[4] Friedrich Karl von Savigny, *Vom Beruf unserer Zeit fuer Gesetzgebung und Rechtswissenschaft* (1815).

[5] Léon Duguit, *L'État, le droit objectif, et la loi positive* (1901).

jectively valid principles. In this respect the German doctrine of the *Volksgeist* and the French doctrine of the *solidarité sociale* as the true creators of the law are very similar to the natural-law doctrine, which was the dominant philosophy of law during the seventeenth and eighteenth centuries and which has still some influence on the juristic thinking of our time. According to this doctrine[6] there exists, behind and above the positive law, customary or statutory, an absolutely just law which can be deduced from nature—the nature of man, the nature of society, or even the nature of things. It is nature which as the supreme legislator creates the true, the "natural" law, and it is from this natural law that all positive law derives its validity. Hence custom, legislation, treaties, i.e., the sources of positive law, cannot produce true law, they only reproduce law when their product has binding force. It is with respect to the nature of these sources of law that the natural-law doctrine is opposed to legal positivism, which considers custom, legislation, and treaties as law-creating facts.[7]

The natural-law doctrine is based on the illusion that it is possible to obtain from our insight in nature, that is, from our knowledge of facts, a knowledge of what is right and wrong. To infer from that which is that which ought to be is a logical fallacy. Hence the most contradictory principles have been de-

---

[6] Cf. *supra*, pp. 149f., 241.

[7] The antagonism of the natural-law doctrine and legal positivism in the field of international law appears in decisions of two American courts, rendered with respect to the question as to whether slave trade on the sea is forbidden by general international law. The one is a decision of the United States Circuit Court in the case *United States v. The Schooner La Jeune Eugénie* (1822, 2 Mason's Reports 409), the other the decision of the United States Supreme Court in the case *The Antelope* (1825, 10 Wheaton 66). In the first case the court stated that a traffic such as slave trade, which "is unnecessary, unjust, and inhuman," cannot be "countenanced by the eternal law of nature, on which rests the law of nations"; that "no practice whatsoever can obliterate the fundamental distinction between right and wrong, and that every nation is at liberty to apply to another the correct principle, whenever both nations by their public acts recede from such practice, and admit the injustice or cruelty of it." The court declared to be bound "to consider the trade an offense against the universal law of society," which, probably, means the law of nature. In *The Antelope Case* the Court declared that the slave trade, although "contrary to the law of nature," is not illegal under international law.

Creation and Application of International Law 311

duced from nature as rules of "natural law," which, in truth, are nothing but maxims, differing according to the moral-political creed of their author. It stands to reason that any lawmaker is determined in his activity by such maxims. Hence it is quite understandable that principles presented by writers such as Grotius,[8] Pufendorf,[9] Vattel,[10] and others, as natural law allegedly deduced from the nature of the state or the international community,[11] were of decisive influence on the practice of states by which customary international law has been developed.

c. *Common consent as basis of international law.* In answering the question as to the fact by which the customary rules of international law are created or—what amounts to the same—in designating the fact on which general international law, which is customary law, is based, modern writers advocate a view which is hardly different from a natural-law doctrine. They maintain that customary international law is created by the common consent of the states; and since there is no express manifestation of this consent, a tacit consent is assumed.

(1) CUSTOMARY LAW BINDING ON STATES WHICH HAVE NOT PARTICIPATED IN THE ESTABLISHMENT OF THE LAW-CREATING CUSTOM. The assumption that such a consent has actually been given by all the states is a political fiction of exactly the same nature as the assumption of the German historical school that the "national spirit" actually creates the law, or the assumption of the French sociological school that the "social solidarity" creates it. International customary law could be interpreted as created by a consent of the states only if it were possible to prove that the custom which evidences the existence of a norm of international law is constituted by the acts of all the states which are bound by the norm of customary law, or that a norm of customary law is binding

---

[8] Cf. *supra*, pp. 26, 219, 224.
[9] Samuel Pufendorf, *De jure naturae et gentium*, libri octo (1688).
[10] Cf. *supra*, p. 35.
[11] Henry Wheaton, *Elements of International Law* (1866) (Classics of International Law No. 19 [1936]), p. 20, defines international law as "those rules of conduct which reason deduces, as consonant to justice, from the nature of the society existing among independent nations; with such definitions and modifications as may be established by general consent."

upon a state only if this state by its own acts participated in establishing the custom in question. Since general international law is customary law and since it is binding upon all states of the international community, it would—according to the theory that custom is a tacit consent—be necessary to prove that all the states of the international community have consented to all the norms of general international law by their actual conduct, by participation in the establishment of the custom which evidences the law. Such a proof is not required by international law and is in all instances excluded where general international law is applied to states which never had the opportunity to participate in the establishment of the law-creating custom.

Let us suppose that a state which has no access to the sea, and never had such an access, by a treaty acquires a territory situated between its old territory and the sea. Now the state has become a maritime (littoral) state; it has ports and ships—commercial as well as warships—and a maritime flag under which these ships sail. Previous to the acquisition of the new territory it had no opportunity to apply the norms of maritime law, that is, the norms of customary international law regulating the conduct of states on the sea. It had no opportunity to contribute, by its actions, to the custom by which these norms of international law have been created or—according to the theory in question—by which the existence of the norms is evidenced. If these norms of international law are considered to be applicable to the state concerned from the very beginning of its becoming a maritime state, these norms of customary international law cannot have been created by all the states upon which they are binding.

Another striking instance is the birth of a new state. The new state obviously had no opportunity to participate in the establishment of the custom by which all the norms of general international law have been created, norms that existed long before the new state came into existence. If the new state is considered to be subjected, from the very beginning of its existence, to the norms of general customary international law, then these norms cannot have been created by a common consent of all the states.

Finally, the custom by which a norm of general international law

Creation and Application of International Law   313

is created, a norm which is binding upon all the states of the international community, is not necessarily a long-established practice of all the states. A long-established practice of a great number of states, including the states which, with respect to their power, their culture, and so on, are of certain importance, is sufficient. Hence customary law cannot be interpreted as created by the common consent of the members of the international community.

However, it may be assumed that international law is binding upon a new state, which has not participated in its creation, only if this state has recognized the pre-existing customary international law as binding upon itself. International law requires, it is true, that the new state be recognized by the old states in order to be a state in the sense of international law.[12] But, as pointed out, international law does not require that international law be recognized by the new state in order to be binding upon it. Hence international law may be applied to the new state even if the latter has not recognized this law as binding upon it. The statement that international law is applicable to a state only if it is recognized by this state is not based on a norm of international law; it is an assumption made on the basis of a definite view of the relationship between international law and national law, the view according to which international law is binding only as part of national law. This view is, as we shall see later,[13] not impossible. But to assume that international law is actually recognized by all states is a fiction. If it is assumed that international law is binding upon a state only if it is recognized by this state, it is inconsistent to apply international law to a state without a proof of such recognition, and to admit that a state cannot, by nonrecognition of international law or by withdrawing its recognition, prevent the application of this law.

(2) CUSTOMARY INTERNATIONAL LAW AS BASIS OF CONVENTIONAL INTERNATIONAL LAW. Treaties are a second source of international law. This method of creating international law will be considered in the following section.[14] Here it should be pointed out only that

---
[12] Cf. *supra*, pp. 264ff.
[13] Cf. *infra*, pp. 435ff.
[14] Cf. *infra*, pp. 317ff.

a treaty is an agreement between two or more states by which the expression of their common consent concerning a mutual behavior is established. By this agreement a norm is created imposing obligations and conferring rights upon the contracting parties relating to the mutual behavior about which they agree. Hence, in principle, a treaty creates law only for the contracting parties. That a treaty is a law-creating fact, that by a treaty obligations and rights are established, or, in other terms, that a treaty has binding force, is due to a rule of customary international law which is usually expressed in the formula *pacta sunt servanda*. This rule is the reason for the validity of treaties, and hence the "source" of all the law created by treaties, the so-called conventional international law in contradistinction to customary international law. With respect to its reason of validity, the conventional international law is inferior to the customary international law. The latter represents a higher level in the hierarchical structure of the international legal order than the former.

What, however, is the reason for the validity of customary international law? Why has a rule of customary international law binding force? The binding force of customary international law rests in the last resort on a fundamental assumption: on the hypothesis that international custom is a law-creating fact. This hypothesis may be called the basic norm. It is not a norm of positive law; it is not created by acts of will of human beings; it is presupposed by the jurists interpreting legally the conduct of states.[15]

(3) THE DOCTRINE OF SOCIAL CONTRACT IN INTERNATIONAL LAW. There is, however, another theory, mentioned before, according to which customary international law is valid because it is based on the recognition and thus on the consent of the states which are bound by its norms. Hence, there is according to this doctrine no essential difference between customary international law and conventional international law, i.e., law established by treaties, as far as their basis, the reason of validity, is concerned. A treaty is binding upon the contracting parties because both of them have consented to the norm created by their agreement. The basis of the treaty, that is, the reason of validity of the conventional

---
[15] Cf. *infra*, pp. 408ff., 417f.

Creation and Application of International Law 315

norm, is the common consent of the contracting parties. But why is the common consent, and only the consent, binding upon the contracting states? The fundamental principle which is at the basis of this theory is the principle of individual liberty, which in the relation between states is called sovereignty. It is the principle usually presented as a rule of natural law, according to which an individual can be bound only by his own will, for the individual is by his very nature free. Hence it is impossible to obligate an individual against his own will. When the individual lives together with other individuals, and when it is necessary to regulate the mutual behavior of the individuals, the only way in which a social order can be established is a contract concluded between the free individuals. They are bound by this contract, for this contract is based on their common consent. This is the doctrine of social contract derived from the idea of individual liberty. It is an essential element of the natural-law doctrine and presented in a classical form by the French philosopher Jean Jacques Rousseau.[16]

This doctrine, when applied to the states and their mutual relations, presents itself as the dogma that the state, by its very nature, is sovereign, and consequently can be bound by a norm regulating its behavior only if it consents to this norm; that means, if mutual behavior of the states is in question, only by a treaty.

In order to harmonize the existence of customary international law with this doctrine, and to maintain the idea of the sovereignty of the state, it is necessary to assume international customary law as binding upon the states only if directly or indirectly recognized by them, or, which amounts to the same, to maintain that the binding force of general customary international law is based on the common consent[17] of, or on a treaty tacitly entered into by, the

---

[16] Jean Jacques Rousseau, *Contrat social* (1762).

[17] In *West Rand Central Gold Mining Co., Ltd. v. The King* (1905 Law Reports 2 King's Bench Division 391) the Court stated: "There is an essential difference, as to certainty and definiteness, between municipal law and a system or body of rules in regard to international conduct, which, so far as it exists at all (and its existence is assumed by the phrase 'international law'), rests upon a consensus of civilized States, not expressed in any code or pact, nor possessing, in case of dispute, any authorized or authoritative interpreter; and capable, indeed, of proof, in the absence of some express international agreement, only by evidence of usage to be obtained from the

members of the international community. Just as the natural-law doctrine maintains that the state, the national community, is based on a social contract entered into voluntarily by the individuals belonging to it, so most of the writers on international law maintain that the international community is based on a contract, i.e., the common consent of the states belonging to this community. According to this doctrine the basic norm of customary international law is identical with the basic norm of conventional international law; that is to say, the principle *pacta sunt servanda*, as a rule of natural law, serves as the basic norm of the whole legal system we call international law. The essential function of this theory is to maintain the principle that a state can be legally bound only by its own will, and hence by its consent to the norms regulating its behavior. In this way the theory maintains the dogma of the sovereignty of the state.

Although this theory is nothing but a variety of the old natural-law doctrine of the social contract, long ago abandoned in the field of national law, it is still applied in the field of international law and is advocated by many outstanding internationalists. Its fundamental assumption, "the common consent of the states, the members of the international community" is exactly the same fiction as the social contract of the natural-law doctrine; and the states, subjected to international law, are, by their very nature, no more "sovereign" than the individuals, subjected to the national legal order, are, by their very nature, "free."

Some writers advocating the doctrine of the common consent of the states as the basis of international law became aware of the fact that general international law is binding upon many states which never, expressly or tacitly, consented to it. Consequently, they modified the doctrine by maintaining that by "common consent" they mean only the tacit consent of such an overwhelming majority of the members of the international community that "those who dissent are of no importance whatever and disappear from the view of one who looks for the will of the community as an entity

---

action of nations in similar cases in the course of their history. It is obvious that, in respect of many questions that may arise, there will be room for difference in opinion as to whether such a consensus could be shown to exist."

Creation and Application of International Law 317

in contradistinction to the wills of its single members."[18] It is quite interesting to note that this is the old fictitious distinction of Jean Jacques Rousseau between *volonté générale* ("general will") and *volonté de tous* ("will of all"), a distinction made to the effect to interpret a majority-vote decision as the will of the whole community. By so doing Rousseau tries to maintain the illusion that the individual, although subject to the "general will," remains "free" even if he has voted against the majority. But if just one single member of the community does not consent, there is no common consent; and then it is a fiction to maintain that all individuals are free. In reality, the dissenting member does not "disappear." If only the overwhelming majority of states consent, the statement that there is a common consent and the presupposition that all states are sovereign are fictitious.

It is certainly possible to assume that a state is bound by international law only if it recognizes this law as binding upon it, just as it is possible to assume that an individual is bound by national law only if he recognizes this law as binding upon him. In other words, it is possible to proceed from the assumption that the state is sovereign, i.e., the highest legal authority, just as it is possible to start from the assumption that the individual is free and hence can be bound only by his own will. But there is hardly a writer ready to accept all the consequences of such an assumption.

4. Treaties

a. *General remarks.* (1) CONCEPT OF TREATY. A treaty is an agreement normally entered into by two or more states under general international law. If only two states are the contracting parties, it is called a bilateral treaty, if more than two states are the contracting parties, a multilateral treaty. An agreement is an act of coming into accord, or the state of being in accord—accord of opinion or will. A treaty is an accord of will. The accord must be manifested by signs, spoken or written words. A treaty is a manifested accord of the will of two or more states. The "will" of the state is expressed by an individual acting in his capacity as organ

---

[18] Oppenheim, *op. cit.* I, § 11.

of the state. The national as well as the international legal order annexes legal effects to the manifested accord of will of two or more persons. When it is the national legal order that makes this accord effective, we speak of a contract; when it is the international legal order, we speak of a treaty.[19] Sometimes a treaty is called an international agreement, a convention, a protocol, an act, a declaration, and the like. However, the name is of no importance.[20]

A treaty, like a contract, is a legal transaction by which the contracting parties intend to establish mutual obligations and rights. The legal effect which the law annexes to this legal transaction is that the contracting parties are legally obliged and correspondingly entitled to behave as they have declared that they will behave, that is to say, that the contract or treaty creates the intended obligations and rights of the contracting parties. This is the difference between a legal transaction and a delict which also has legal effects, but not those intended by the delinquent. That the contracting parties are legally obliged to behave in conformity with the contract or treaty means that if they do not behave in this way they are exposed to sanctions. By concluding contracts or treaties, the

---

[19] In the case of *Serbian Loans* the Permanent Court of International Justice, 1929 (Publications of the Permanent Court of International Justice, Series A, Nos. 20–21, p. 41) stated: "Any contract which is not a contract between States in their capacity as subjects of international law is based on the municipal law of some country."

[20] In American jurisprudence it is usual to distinguish between "treaties" as international agreements which according to the Constitution are to be concluded by the President with the advice and consent of the Senate, and so-called "executive agreements," which are treaties concluded by the President or with the authorization of the President without the advice and consent of the Senate (Cf. *infra*, p. 323.) In the case of *Four Packages of Cut Diamonds v. United States* (256 Federal Reporter [1919] 305) it was held that postal conventions with foreign countries, concluded by the Postmaster General by and with the advice and consent of the President "are not treaties, because not made by and with the advice of the Senate, and they are not laws, because not enacted by Congress." But, previously, in *B. Altman & Co. v. United States* (224 U.S. 583) the Supreme Court (1912) held that "an international compact, negotiated between the representatives of two sovereign nations and made in the name and on behalf of the contracting countries, and dealing with important commercial relations between the two countries, and . . . proclaimed by the President" is a treaty both internationally and constitutionally, even though being an "executive agreement."

Creation and Application of International Law

contracting parties regulate legally their mutual relations. The states have the power to conclude treaties, since general international law authorizes the states to conclude treaties for the purpose of regulating their mutual relations. States have the power to create, by treaties, mutual obligations and rights because and insofar as general international law obligates the states to respect the treaties which they have concluded and to fulfill the obligations established by their treaties.

(2) THE RULE PACTA SUNT SERVANDA. By concluding a treaty the contracting states apply a norm of customary international law—the rule *pacta sunt servanda*—and at the same time create a norm of international law, the norm which presents itself as the treaty obligation of one or of all of the contracting parties, and as the treaty right of the other or the others. Legal obligations and legal rights are always the function of a legal norm determining the behavior of an individual. The term "norm" designates the objective phenomenon whose subjective reflections are obligation and right. The statement that the treaty has "binding force" means nothing but that the treaty is or creates a norm establishing obligations and rights of the contracting parties. Thus the treaty has a law-applying and at the same time a law-creating character. It has a law-applying character because every conclusion of a treaty is the application of the rule of general international law *pacta sunt servanda*; it has a law-creating function because every treaty constitutes obligations and rights that, prior to the conclusion of the treaty, had not yet existed, obligations and rights which come into existence by the treaty.

(3) THE SO-CALLED "LAW-MAKING" TREATIES. It is usual to distinguish law-making treaties from other treaties which do not make law. This distinction is based on the view that some treaties are concluded for the purpose of laying down rules of conduct among states, that is to say, for the purpose of making law, whereas other treaties are concluded for other purposes. However, this distinction is incorrect. For law in general and conventional law in particular is a means to an end, not an end in itself. It is the essential function of any treaty to make law, that is to say, to create a legal norm, whether a general or an individual norm. Any purpose—

political or economic—of states, when pursued by means of a treaty, is realized in the form of law; and any so-called law-making treaty has a political or economic purpose. Hence a logically correct classification of treaties, i.e., a classification from the point of view of international law, must differentiate between different law-making treaties, and must not differentiate between treaties for law-making and treaties for other purposes. There is indeed a remarkable difference between treaties concluded by many states —multilateral treaties—by which general norms are created, regulating the mutual behavior of the contracting states, as the Covenant of the League of Nations or the Charter of the United Nations, and treaties concluded by only two states—bilateral treaties—by which an individual norm is created, establishing only one obligation of one state and one right of the other state, as for instance, a treaty of cession. The so-called law-making treaties are treaties creating general norms, whereas the others are law-making treaties creating individual norms. There are, however, many intermediate stages between the two types of law-making treaties, the term "law-making treaty" being a pleonasm.

(4) LEGAL AND POLITICAL TREATIES. In close connection with the logically erroneous classification of treaties in law-making and other treaties is the distinction between legal and political treaties, based on the view that there are treaties which are legal instruments and treaties which are political instruments, and that political instruments, in contradistinction to legal instruments, are to be interpreted not according to legal but according to political principles. A treaty, even if concluded for political purposes, is always a legal instrument, and can be interpreted only according to legal principles. To interpret a treaty according to political principles means to interpret it according to its political purpose, that is to say, according to the intentions of the contracting parties. But this is a legal interpretation—one of the legal methods of interpreting legal instruments.

(5) INTERPRETATION OF TREATIES. In order to ascertain the intentions of the authors of a legal instrument, the historical, i.e., political and economic, circumstances may be taken into consideration

under which the instrument was established. In the case of a statute, the preceding parliamentary debates may be resorted to; in the case of a treaty, the negotiations which led to its conclusion. Another method of interpreting a legal instrument in general, and a treaty in particular, is the interpretation according to its wording—the so-called logico-grammatical interpretation. The wording of a legal instrument may not be in conformity with the ascertainable intentions of its authors. The wording may go beyond, or remain behind their intentions. Then an interpretation according to the intentions of the authors is, with respect to the wording, in the first case restrictive, in the second case extensive. None of these methods of interpretation excludes the other. The subject or organ competent to apply the law laid down in the legal instrument has the choice among them—whether the instrument is a statute or a treaty, and whether the treaty is concluded for political or for other purposes—unless a norm of the legal instrument itself or another norm of the legal order to which the legal instrument belongs prescribes a definite method of interpretation. General international law does not contain such a norm; but a treaty may stipulate rules concerning its interpretation. It may, in particular, confer upon an international agency, e.g., an international tribunal, the power to interpret the treaty with binding force for the contracting parties. Sometimes a statute or a treaty has no other purpose than that of interpreting a previous statute or treaty. If the interpretation has binding force, we speak of an authentic interpretation.

The principles concerning legal interpretation in general apply also to the interpretation of treaties. There are no principles concerning the interpretation of treaties different from those concerning the interpretation of other legal instruments.

(6) INTERNATIONAL LEGISLATION. Some writers speak of "international legislation," meaning by this term the establishment of multilateral treaties by which general norms are created regulating the behavior of the contracting states. This terminology is not quite adequate, since it ignores the essential difference which exists between legislation and conclusion of contracts or treaties.

The term "treaty" is ambiguous insofar as it designates not only the law-creating act, the act by which the accord is brought about, but also the result of this act, the legal norm created by this act, the conventional norm constituting the obligations and the rights of the contracting parties. When we speak of the treaty as a source of law, we have in mind the law-creating act, the procedure by which the conventional norm is created. When we say that a treaty has been concluded or that, according to a treaty, the state is obliged to do thus and so or entitled to do thus and so, the term "treaty" designates the norm created by a procedure the essential element of which is to bring about an accord of will, a law-creating procedure, which is likewise named "treaty" (contract). It is of importance to distinguish clearly between treaty as norm-creating act and treaty as norm, created by a specific act. The confusion of these two different meanings of the term "treaty" is the source of many misunderstandings and mistakes of the traditional theory of the treaty.

b. *The treaty as a law-creating procedure.* (1) THE CONTRACTING PARTIES. As a rule, contracting parties to an international agreement are states. But exceptionally also communities which have not the character of a state in the sense of international law may be contracting parties to a treaty. We have already mentioned the Roman Catholic Church as contracting party to the so-called concordats,[21] international organizations endowed with international personality[22] and some statelike communities, as component states[23] of federal states, and states under protectorate,[24] as possible parties to international agreements. Private individuals cannot conclude treaties under existing international law.

The power of the state to conclude treaties under general international law is in principle unlimited. States are competent to make treaties on whatever matter they please. But the content of the treaty must not conflict with a norm of general international law

---

[21] Cf. *supra*, p. 159.
[22] Cf. *supra*, pp. 168ff.
[23] Cf. *supra*, pp. 161ff.
[24] Cf. *supra*, pp. 161f.

Creation and Application of International Law 323

which has the character of *jus cogens,* and not that of *jus dispositivum.*[25] The competence of the state to conclude treaties may be limited also by particular international law. Thus, for instance, the members of the League of Nations were obliged not to conclude treaties inconsistent with the Covenant of the League of Nations (Article 20, paragraph 1, of the Covenant).

(2) THE STATE ORGANS COMPETENT TO CONCLUDE TREATIES. As a rule, general international law does not directly determine the state organ which is competent to conclude a treaty on behalf of its state. International law leaves the determination of this organ to the national legal order. Normally the Head of State is authorized by the constitution to conclude treaties, either alone, or in cooperation with other organs, such as the parliament, or a cabinet minister, or the whole cabinet. Sometimes the constitution distinguishes between different categories of treaties, especially between peace treaties and politically or economically important treaties on the one hand, and other treaties on the other hand, and submits the former to the approbation of parliament, whereas the latter may be concluded by the Head of State or by the cabinet or a member of the cabinet (the Minister of Foreign Affairs) without the cooperation of the parliament. Such restrictions play a prominent part in the constitutions of most states.

The rule that international law leaves to the constitution of the state the determination of the organ or the organs competent to conclude treaties must be interpreted to mean that international law leaves to the effective constitution of the state the determination of the organs competent to conclude treaties. The effective constitution of the state may be not quite identical with its written constitution, and it is quite possible—and frequently occurs—that the practice of a state with regard to its treaty-making power differs from the norms of its written constitution. Characteristic examples are the so-called executive agreements concluded by the President of the United States of America. Although Article II, section 2, paragraph 2, of the Constitution expressly confers upon the President the power to make treaties only "by and with the

---

[25] Cf. *supra,* p. 89.

advice and consent of the Senate," numerous politically highly important treaties are concluded by the President without the advice and consent of the Senate under the name of "executive agreements."

(3) CONSTITUTIONALITY OF TREATIES. The answer to the question whether a treaty has been concluded in conformity with the constitution of the contracting state depends on the interpretation of the constitution; and it is within the competence of the government to interpret, in its relation to other states, its own constitution.[26] Hence, when a state through its government concludes a treaty with another state, the government of the latter has no reason and is not entitled to question the constitutionality of the act of the former. But this does not prevent the government of a state after having concluded a treaty with another state, from declaring the treaty null and void because concluded in violation of its own constitution.[27] However, some writers maintain that if a treaty is concluded in violation of the constitution of the contracting state by that organ which is usually competent to conclude treaties, namely, the Head of State, the treaty is under international law valid, al-

---

[26] When in international relations the interpretation of the national law of a state is in question, it is the actual interpretation of this law by the competent organs of the state concerned which is to be accepted. In the case of *Serbian Loans* (cf. *supra*, p. 318) the Permanent Court of International Justice, after having decided that French law was to be applied in the case, stated: "The Court, having in these circumstances to decide as to the meaning and scope of a municipal law, makes the following observations: For the Court itself to undertake its own construction of municipal law, leaving on one side existing judicial decisions, with the ensuing danger of contradicting the construction which has been placed on such law by the highest national tribunal and which, in its results, seems to the Court reasonable, would not be in conformity with the task for which the Court has been established and would not be compatible with the principles governing the selection of its members. It would be a most delicate matter to do so, especially in cases concerning public policy—a conception the definition of which in any particular country is largely dependent on the opinion prevailing at any given time in such country itself—and in cases where no relevant provisions directly relate to the question at issue. It is French legislation, as applied in France, which really constitutes French Law" (p. 46).

[27] A treaty of commerce concluded on August 14, 1920, between Rumania and Austria was declared null and void by Rumania because not approved by the parliament in conformity with the constitution.

Creation and Application of International Law 325

though, under the national law concerned, the individual responsible for the violation of the constitution may be exposed to a sanction. If this is a rule of positive international law—which is doubtful—the principle that international law leaves it to the national legal order to determine the organs competent to represent the state in its international relations must be considered to be restricted by the rule concerning the conclusion of treaties.[28]

Another fact, which seems to constitute such a restriction, is that certain functionaries, without being expressly authorized by the constitution, actually conclude treaties on behalf of their states with regard to matters of merely administrative or technical character falling within their competence. Thus, e.g., a cabinet minister charged with the administration of postal affairs usually concludes treaties concerning such affairs; military commanders, in time of war, conclude treaties concerning temporary suspension of arms, surrender of a fortified place, and the like. If the validity of these treaties cannot be based on a norm of the unwritten constitution of the state concerned, it can be based only on the above-mentioned rule of international law.[29]

---

[28] Cf. *supra*, p. 324. In the dispute between *Switzerland* and *France* concerning *the interpretation of a regulation of the commercial convention and report signed at Berne, October 20, 1906*, the arbitral tribunal (1912) stated: "Considering that the treaty of commerce and the regulations are international conventions governed by the sanction which the contracting parties, represented by their plenipotentiaries, have given thereto; the tribunal is not called upon to consider whether or not the regulations must be submitted to the sanction of the legislature; that is a matter pertaining to internal law." (6 *American Journal of International Law* [1912] 1000.)

In the *Case of the Free Zones of Upper Savoy and District of Gex* the Permanent Court of International Justice (Publications of the Permanent Court of International Justice, Series A/B, No. 46, p. 170) (1932) stated with respect to a declaration made by the Swiss agent in the course of the hearings: "It is true that, in the course of the recent hearings, the French Agent declared the Swiss proposal to be inacceptable; but it is also true that he regarded it as an offer to conclude a Special Agreement, an offer which, in this form, he had no power to entertain. It is also true that the French Agent expressed certain doubts as to the binding character, from a constitutional point of view, of the Swiss declaration; having regard to the circumstances in which the declaration was made, the Court must however regard it as binding on Switzerland."

[29] In the *Case of the Legal Status of Eastern Greenland* (Publications of the Permanent Court of International Justice, Series A/B, No. 53, p. 71) the

(4) EFFECT OF THREAT OR USE OF FORCE ON TREATIES. The treaty, as pointed out, is an accord of will. It is to this accord of will that international law annexes the specific legal effects of a treaty. This accord of will or mutual consent is brought about by acts of the contracting parties, the one being a proposal or offer, the other the acceptance of this proposal or offer. As long as the proposal or offer of one party is not accepted by the other party and the acceptance made known to the former, no treaty exists.

One of the most important principles of the national law of civilized peoples is that the conclusion of a contract must be voluntary on both sides. A contract imposed by illegal threat or use of force is null or annullable. This principle, however, is not generally recognized as a rule of positive international law applicable to treaties. Among the most important treaties are peace treaties, and peace treaties are, as a rule, imposed by threat or use of force exercised by a victorious state against a vanquished state. But peace treaties are not considered to be null or annullable for this reason. In this respect general international law seems to have the character of primitive law, which does not recognize the principle that a manifestation of will, if enforced, can have no legal effect, that a treaty brought about as an effect of coercion exercised upon one contracting party is null and void. Even in the Roman law legal transactions brought about by extortion were not null and void, but only annullable. That the threat or use of force is not recognized as a reason for the nullity or annullability of international agreements may be considered as a consequence of the doctrine that under general international law the threat or use of armed force (war) in the relations among states is not illegal. Since, however, under the Charter of the United Nations the threat or use of force in international relations is illegal, the organs of the United Nations may consider a treaty imposed by force as null or annullable.

Permanent Court of International Justice (1933) stated with respect to a declaration made by the Norwegian Minister of Foreign Affairs to a diplomatic representative of Denmark: "The Court considers it beyond all dispute that a reply of this nature given by the Minister for Foreign Affairs on behalf of his Government in response to a request by the diplomatic representative of a foreign Power, in regard to a question falling within his province, is binding upon the country to which the Minister belongs."

Some writers interpret the rule that the threat or use of force is no reason for the nullity or annullability of a treaty in a restrictive way. According to this doctrine a treaty is null or annullable if the threat or use of force is directed personally against the individual who as representative of a state concluded the treaty (e.g., threat to kill him or make him a prisoner); but the threat or use of force directed against the state as such (e.g., threat to occupy the territory of the state by armed force) is no reason for the nullity or annullability of the treaty enforced in this way.

(5) FORM OF TREATIES (SIGNATURE AND RATIFICATION). General international law does not prescribe a definite form for the conclusion of treaties. Hence the contracting parties may express their consent by written or spoken words, by symbols, such as a white flag for instance, or even by gestures.

As a matter of fact, many treaties are concluded in a procedure which is characterized by two stages. The first is the signing of a document containing the text of the treaty as the result of the preceding negotiations; the second is the ratification of the signed text by the competent organs of the contracting states. This procedure takes place especially when the organs of the state competent under its constitution to conclude the treaty, such as the Head of State or a parliamentary body, cannot participate in the negotiation of the text of the treaty, and especially if they cannot delegate their treaty-making power to other organs. Then special organs, the so-called plenipotentiaries, are charged with the function of negotiating and signing a treaty text, to be submitted to ratification. But the treaty does not become valid before ratification by the contracting states acting through the constitutionally competent organs; and no state is obliged to ratify a treaty signed by its plenipotentiaries.

According to the traditional theory, a treaty is concluded as soon as its text is signed by the plenipotentiaries; its binding force, however, is suspended until ratification is given. The function of ratification is, according to this doctrine, to make the treaty binding. As long as ratification is not given, the treaty is, although concluded, not yet binding. This interpretation of the act of ratification is not correct. If a treaty is not binding without ratification, and a legal act is a treaty only if it is binding, it is the act of ratification by which the treaty is concluded. Against this view the following arguments are brought forth: The contracting states have always assumed that a treaty is concluded when signed by the plenipotentiaries, that their consent has been given by the signature of their plenipotentiaries. Because the treaty is concluded by the signatures of the plenipotentiaries it cannot be ratified in part; no alterations of the treaty are possible through the act of ratification; a treaty may be tacitly ratified by its execution; and, last but not least, a treaty is always dated from the day it was signed by the plenipotentiaries and not from the day of its ratification.

These arguments, however, are not convincing. They prove only that the governments share the incorrect opinion that a treaty is concluded by the signatures of the plenipotentiaries, although it comes into force only by its ratification, and that this erroneous doctrine is responsible for the practice of dating a treaty from the day it was signed by the plenipotentiaries. This date is, in itself, without any legal importance. The fact that a treaty cannot be ratified in part, that no alterations of the treaty are possible through the act of ratification, must be explained by the fact that if one party ratifies only part of the treaty, or alters its text, no consent exists; not by the fact that the treaty has already been concluded by the signatures of the plenipotentiaries. That a treaty may be tacitly ratified by its execution is possible because international law does not prescribe any formal ratification, which is necessary only if required by the contracting parties.

Some writers maintain that the government of a state signatory to a treaty, although not obliged to ratify it, is, pending ratification, not allowed to oppose its consummation and obliged to do nothing in contravention of its terms.[30] These obligations are hardly more

---

[30] On January 22, 1903, the text of a treaty concerning the Panama Canal was signed by the United States and Colombia. The treaty was ratified by the United States, but the Senate of Colombia rejected the ratification. In a communication to the United States Government, the Government of Colombia, on December 23, 1903, declared that "the Congress of Colombia, which is vested, according to our laws with the faculty or power to approve or disapprove the treaties concluded by the government, exercised a perfect right when it disapproved the . . . convention." In reply, on January 5, 1904, the

than moral in character. And even if it were admitted that there exists a legal obligation of the governments to do nothing, pending ratification, in contravention of the terms of the treaty signed by their representatives, such obligation would be quite compatible with the doctrine that the treaty is concluded by the acts of ratification, not by the acts of signature. For it is not the treaty which imposes this obligation upon the governments; it is a norm of general international law different from the rule *pacta sunt servanda* which attaches this consequence to the act of signature. The obligation to do nothing in contravention of the terms of the treaty is differ-

United States Secretary of State said: "The Department is not disposed to controvert the principle that treaties are not definitely binding till they are ratified; but it is also a familiar rule that treaties, except where they operate on private rights, are, unless it is otherwise provided, binding on the contracting parties fom the date of their signature, and that in such case the exchanging of ratifications confirms the treaty from that day. This rule necessarily implies that the two Governments, in agreeing to the treaty through their duly authorized representatives, bind themselves, pending its ratification, not only not to oppose its consummation but also to do nothing in contravention of its terms." (Papers relating to the Foreign Relations of the United States, 58th Cong., 2d Sess., House of Representatives, Document No. 1, pp. 285, 299.)

Article 256 of the Peace Treaty of Versailles stipulated: "Powers to which German territory is ceded shall acquire all property and possessions situated therein belonging to the German Empire or to the German States . . . ." In the *Case concerning Certain German Interests in Polish Upper Silesia* (Publications of the Permanent Court of International Justice, Series A, No. 7) the Polish Government contended that the treaty, signed on June 28, 1919, even before being ratified, imposed upon Germany the obligation to refrain from alienation of property and possessions of the German Reich or the German States situated in the territory to be ceded by the German Reich to Poland. The Permanent Court of International Justice (1926) decided that the treaty did not give the state to which the territory was ceded the right to consider null and void alienations effected by the ceding state before the transfer of sovereignty; that Germany retained the right to dispose of her property in the course of the normal administration of public property. But the Court admitted the possibility of a misuse of this right: "Such misuse cannot be presumed, and it rests with the party who states that there has been such misuse to prove his statement" (p. 30).

In the case *Megalidis v. Turkey* (Annual Digest 1927–1928, Case No. 272) the Turkish-Greek Mixed Arbitral Tribunal (1928) held with respect to the Treaty of Lausanne, signed by Turkey on July 24, 1923, that from the time of the signature of the treaty and before its entry into force the contracting parties were under the duty to do nothing which might impair the operation of its clauses.

ent from the obligation to fulfill the treaty, which is the effect of the ratification.

The text of a treaty signed by the plenipotentiaries may contain a clause to the effect that the treaty, in order to come into force, does, or does not, require ratification. This is no binding treaty provision, but a declaration on the part of the signatories concerning the meaning of their respective signatures. If a treaty contains a clause requiring ratification, it may also contain a provision concerning the period of time within which ratification must be given or expressly refused. If no such provision is stipulated, legally ratification can be given at any time, but actually if ratification is not given within a certain time, ratification is assumed to be refused.

Sometimes the text signed by the representatives contains provisions which become part of the valid treaty only if ratified by a special signatory. But if this signatory refuses ratification, the treaty comes into force for the other parties after their ratification, with a text that does not correspond to the legal reality. Thus, for instance, Article 1 of the Covenant of the League of Nations stipulated: "The original Members of the League of Nations shall be those of the Signatories which are named in the Annex to this Covenant . . ."; and Article 4: "The Council shall consist of Representatives of the Principal Allied and Associated Powers, together with Representatives of four other Members of the League. . . ." The United States of America was a signatory named in the Annex and, according to the preamble of the treaty, one of the Principal Allied and Associated Powers. Hence she was—according to the wording of Article 1—an original member of the League, and—according to the wording of Article 4—a permanent member of the Council. However, since she did not ratify the treaty and consequently was, although a signatory, not a contracting party, she was neither a member of the League nor a member of the Council. The inadequacy of the text consists in that no distinction is made between a signatory and a contracting party, which is the consequence of the erroneous idea that a treaty requiring ratification is concluded by the signatures of the plenipotentiaries.

In the case of a multilateral treaty, the treaty may come into force before all the signatories have ratified it, provided that the treaty

Creation and Application of International Law 331

contains such a provision. This provision, too, comes into force only by ratification. Thus, for instance, Article 110 of the Charter of the United Nations provides: "1. The present Charter shall be ratified by the signatory states in accordance with their respective constitutional processes. 2. The ratifications shall be deposited with the Government of the United States of America, which shall notify all the signatory states of each deposit as well as the Secretary-General of the Organization when he has been appointed. 3. The present Charter shall come into force upon the deposit of ratifications by the Republic of China, France, the Union of Soviet Socialist Republics, the United Kingdom of Great Britain and Northern Ireland, and the United States of America, and by a majority of the other signatory states. A protocol of the ratifications deposited shall thereupon be drawn up by the Government of the United States of America which shall communicate copies thereof to all the signatory states. 4. The states signatory to the present Charter which ratify it after it has come into force will become original Members of the United Nations on the date of the deposit of their respective ratifications."

If there is no rule of general international law prescribing a definite form for the conclusion of treaties, the question as to whether ratification is necessary is to be answered in accordance with the intention of the contracting parties. This intention may be expressed in the text of the treaty by the provision that the treaty will enter into force only after ratification. Even if the text signed by the plenipotentiaries does not contain such a clause, the meaning of the signature might not be that of a legally binding declaration of the will of the signatory, the plenipotentiary not being authorized to perform such an act. Then, in this case, too, the treaty is concluded by the ratifications. In view of the fact that in the practice of the states during the nineteenth and twentieth centuries most of the treaties, especially multilateral treaties, expressly stipulated that ratification was required, many writers and courts assume—as a presumption of law—that if a treaty does not contain a provision to the contrary, ratification is necessary.[31] But

---

[31] In *The Eliza Ann* (cf. *supra*, p. 28) the court declared: ". . . the later usage of States has been to require a ratification, although the treaty may

this practice—it may be argued—only shows that the states considered an express clause requiring ratification as necessary. Then the opposite presumption is not excluded. Sometimes it is even maintained that there exists a rule of general customary international law according to which ratification is required unless the treaty is signed or otherwise consented to by an organ of the state competent, according to its constitution, to conclude such a treaty, as, e.g., by the Head of State in case of a treaty the conclusion of which does not require the cooperation of other organs, or by another organ of the state in case of treaties which this organ is competent to conclude with regard to matters of a merely administrative or technical character.[32] If there exists such a rule of general international law, it is hardly possible to maintain that international law does not prescribe a definite form for the conclusion of treaties; and then it would be superfluous to insert into a treaty a clause requiring ratification. However, the prevailing practice does not confirm this view.

Although general international law does not prescribe a definite form of the act of ratification, it is usual to execute as many formal documents as there are parties to the treaty, signed by the respective Heads of State and the Ministers of Foreign Affairs, and to exchange these documents among the states concerned. Sometimes the documents of ratification are not exchanged but deposited with one of the governments of the states ratifying the treaty, as according to Article 110 of the Charter, quoted above.

Neither conditional nor partial ratification, nor ratification with

---

have been signed by plenipotentiaries. According to the practice now prevailing, a subsequent ratification is essentially necessary; and a strong confirmation of the truth of this position is, that there is hardly a modern treaty in which it is not expressly so stipulated; and therefore it is now to be presumed, that the powers of plenipotentiaries are limited by the condition of a subsequent ratification. The ratification may be form, but it is an essential form; for the instrument, in point of legal efficacy, is imperfect without it."

[32] In the *Case relating to the Territorial Jurisdiction of the International Commission of the River Oder* (Publications of the Permanent Court of International Justice, Series A, No. 23, p. 20) the Permanent Court of International Justice (1929) referred to "the ordinary rules of international law amongst which is the rule that conventions, save in certain exceptional cases, are binding only by virtue of their ratification."

Creation and Application of International Law 333

a reservation is admissible. But in the case of a multilateral treaty a state may sign, through its plenipotentiaries, with the consent of the other signatories, the text of a treaty with certain reservations, or the treaty text may provide for reservations that the governments may make when ratifying the treaty. Then a ratification made with such a reservation refers to the text of the treaty modified by the reservation; and then the contracting parties may have different obligations and different rights under one and the same treaty. This is possible for it is not necesssary that a treaty impose upon all the contracting parties the same obligations and the same rights. What is necessary is only that all the contracting parties agree to the content of the treaty. Reservations permitted in the text of the treaty or made by a plenipotentiary on signature with the consent of the other signatories are to be considered as part of the text of the treaties. The same principle applies to a reservation made only on ratification and afterward consented to by the other contracting parties.[33] According to a view advocated by some writers, consent of all the contracting parties to such a reservation is not necessary; but the treaty enters into force only between the state making the reservation and the states consenting to it.[34]

---

[33] The Committee of Experts for the Progressive Codification of International Law of the League of Nations stated in a Report to the Council of the League: "In order that any reservation whatever may be validly made in regard to a clause of the treaty, it is essential that this reservation should be accepted by all the contracting parties, as would have been the case if it had been put forward in the course of negotiations. If not, the reservation, like the signature to which it is attached, is null and void" (League of Nations *Official Journal* [1927], p. 881). The Report of the Secretary-General of the United Nations concerning Reservations to Multilateral Treaties (UN Doc. A/1372, September 20, 1950, p. 19) contains the following statement: "The rule adhered to by the Secretary-General . . . may be stated in the following manner: A State may make a reservation when signing, ratifying or acceding to a convention, prior to its entry into force, only with the consent of all States which have ratified or acceded thereto up to the date of entry into force; and may do so after the date of entry into force only with the consent of all States which have theretofore ratified or acceded."

[34] This is the practice adhered to by the Pan American Union. In a resolution of the Governing Board adopted on May 4, 1932, the following statement was made with respect to treaties ratified with reservations: "1. The treaty shall be in force, in the form in which it was signed, as between those countries which ratify it without reservations, in the terms in which it was

(6) SIMPLIFIED PROCEDURES. Since the usual procedure for the conclusion of multilateral treaties (conference of the states intending to conclude a treaty, signing of the text agreed upon by the plenipotentiaries, ratification of the signed texts by the governments, exchange of the ratification instruments) is complicated and slow, attempts to simplify and shorten it have been made. The main types of such simplified procedures are as follows:

1. As pointed out, instead of exchange of ratification instruments, deposit of the instruments with the government of one of the contracting parties or with the organ of an international organization constituted by the treaty may be provided for, the government or the organ being obliged to notify the other contracting parties. For instance, Article X of the treaty signed at Brussels, March 7,

---

originally drafted and signed. 2. It shall be in force as between the Governments which ratify it with reservations and the signatory States which accept the reservations in the form in which the treaty may be modified by said reservations. 3. It shall not be in force between a Government which may have ratified with reservations and another which may have already ratified, and which does not accept such reservations." (Quoted in William Sanders, "Reservations to Multilateral Treaties made in the Act of Ratification or Adherence," 33 *American Journal of International Law* [1936] 490). Cf. UN Doc. A/1372, September 20, 1950, p. 11.—The International Court of Justice in its advisory opinion concerning *Reservations to the Convention on Genocide*, given on May 28, 1951, at the request of the General Assembly of the United Nations, stated 1. "that a State which has made and maintained a reservation which has been objected to by one or more of the parties to the Convention but not by others, can be regarded as being a party to the Convention if the reservation is compatible with the object and purpose of the Convention; otherwise, that State cannot be regarded as being a party to the Convention"; 2. "(a) that if a party to the Convention objects to a reservation which it considers to be incompatible with the object and purpose of the Convention, it can in fact consider that the reserving State is not a party to the Convention; (b) that if, on the other hand, a party accepts the reservation as being compatible with the object and purpose of the Convention, it can in fact consider that the reserving State is a party to the Convention"; 3. "(a) that an objection to a reservation made by a signatory State which has not yet ratified the Convention can have the legal effect indicated in the reply to Question I only upon ratification. Until that moment it merely serves as a notice to the other State of the eventual attitude of the signatory State; (b) that an objection to a reservation made by a State which is entitled to sign or accede but which has not yet done so, is without legal effect." (International Court of Justice, Reports, 1951, p. 15.) The opinion of the Court differs from the rule adhered to by the Secretary-General, cited in Note 33.

Creation and Application of International Law 335

1948, provides: "The present Treaty shall be ratified and the instruments of ratification shall be deposited as soon as possible with the Belgian government . . . . The Belgian government shall inform the governments of the other High Contracting Parties of the deposit of each instrument of ratification and each notice of denunciation . . . ."

2. The text agreed upon and signed by all plenipotentiaries comes into force after ratification by some, not necessarily by all signatories, but only for those which have ratified the treaty. For instance, Articles 22 and 23 of the Inter-American Treaty for Reciprocal Assistance, signed at Rio de Janeiro, September 2, 1947, provides: "This Treaty shall come into force between the States which ratify it as soon as the ratification of two-thirds of the Signatory States have been deposited. . . . The ratifications shall be deposited with the Pan American Union, which shall notify the Signatory States of each deposit. Such notification shall be considered as an exchange of ratifications."

3. Instead of convoking a conference and signing the text agreed upon by the plenipotentiaries, the text of the treaty is adopted by unanimous decision of an organ of an international organization in which all the contracting parties are represented. The adopted text is submitted, in the form of a protocol, for ratification by the governments. This was the way in which the Statute of the Permanent Court of International Justice came into force. The Assembly of the League of Nations unanimously declared its approval of the draft statute of the Permanent Court, prepared by the Council under Article 14 of the Covenant. Then the draft statute, thus adopted by the Assembly, was submitted for adoption in the form of a protocol to the governments of the states that were members of the League, and to the governments of other states. The text of the Protocol ran as follows: "The Members of the League of Nations, through the undersigned, duly authorized, declare their acceptance of the adjoint Statute of the Permanent Court of International Justice, which was approved by a unanimous vote of the Assembly, on the thirteenth of December 1920 at Geneva. Consequently, they hereby declare that they accept the jurisdiction of the Court in accordance with the terms and subject to the conditions of the

above-mentioned Statute. The present Protocol, which has been drawn up in accordance with the decision taken by the Assembly of the League of Nations on the thirteenth of December 1920, is subject to ratification. Each Power shall send its ratification to the Secretary-General of the League of Nations; the latter shall take the necessary steps to notify such ratification to the other signatory Powers. The ratification shall be deposited in the archives of the Secretariat of the League of Nations. The said Protocol shall remain open for signature by the Members of the League of Nations and by the States mentioned in the Annex to the Covenant of the League. The Statute of the Court shall come into force as provided in the above-mentioned decision."

4. The text of the treaty adopted by a majority-vote decision of the organ of an international organization, and submitted to ratification by the members, becomes binding only upon those states which have ratified the treaty. Thus, for instance, according to Article 19 of the Constitution of the International Labor Organization, the General Conference of the Organization is authorized to adopt draft conventions that must be ratified by the members in order to become binding treaties. A draft international convention for ratification by the members of the International Labor Organization requires a majority of two thirds of the votes cast by the delegates present at the meeting of the General Conference (Article 19, section 2). A copy of the draft convention shall be authenticated by the signature of the President of the Conference and by the Director-General of the International Labor Office, and deposited with the Secretary-General of the United Nations. The Director-General shall communicate a certified copy of the draft convention to each of the members. Any convention duly ratified shall be registered by the Secretary-General of the United Nations, but shall be binding only upon the members which ratify it.

5. The text adopted by a majority-vote decision by the organ of an international organization becomes binding for all members of the organization when ratified by a majority of the members. This procedure has been instituted for amendments to the constitutions of international organizations. Thus, for instance, Article 26 of the Covenant of the League of Nations stipulates: "1. Amend-

Creation and Application of International Law

ments to this Covenant will take effect when ratified by the Members of the League whose Representatives compose the Council and by a majority of the Members of the League whose Representatives compose the Assembly. 2. No such amendments shall bind any Member of the League which signifies its dissent therefrom, but in that case it shall cease to be a Member of the League." Article 36 of the Constitution of the International Labor Organization provides: "Amendments to this constitution which are adopted by the Conference by a majority of two thirds of the votes cast by the delegates present shall take effect when ratified or accepted by two thirds of the Members of the Organization including five of the eight Members which are represented on the Governing Body as Members of chief industrial importance." Article 108 of the Charter of the United Nations provides: "Amendments to the present Charter shall come into force for all Members of the United Nations when they have been adopted by a vote of two thirds of the members of the General Assembly and ratified in accordance with their respective constitutional processes by two thirds of the Members of the United Nations, including all the permanent members of the Security Council." The amendment comes into force for all members of the United Nations even if "adopted" only by a majority of the General Assembly and ratified only by a majority of the members. Article 109 of the Charter provides: "1. A General Conference of the Members of the United Nations for the purpose of reviewing the present Charter may be held at a date and place to be fixed by a two-thirds vote of the members of the General Assembly and by a vote of any seven members of the Security Council. Each Member of the United Nations shall have one vote in the conference. 2. Any alteration of the present Charter recommended by a two-thirds vote of the conference shall take effect when ratified in accordance with their respective constitutional processes by two thirds of the Members of the United Nations including all the permanent members of the Security Council. 3. If such a conference has not been held before the tenth annual session of the General Assembly following the coming into force of the present Charter, the proposal to call such a conference shall be placed on the agenda of that session of the General Assembly, and the conference shall be held if so decided by a majority vote of the members of the General Assembly and by a vote of any seven members of the Security Council." The amendment comes into force for all members even if "recommended" only by a majority of the General Conference and ratified only by a majority of the members.

In contradistinction to the Covenant of the League of Nations, the Charter of the United Nations does not contain a provision to the effect that an amendment shall not bind a member which signifies its dissent therefrom and hence is authorized to withdraw from the Organization. But according to an interpretation adopted by Commission I of the San Francisco Conference, a member may withdraw from the Organization in case an amendment comes into force against its vote in the General Assembly or the General Conference, and also in case an amendment for which a member voted and which it ratified, does not come into force.[35]

6. If the constitution of an international organization confers upon an organ in which all or only some of the members are represented, the power to adopt by a majority-vote decision norms which are binding upon the members without being submitted to ratification at all, the procedure assumes the character of legislation. In this way the General Assembly, in accordance with Article 22, and the Security Council, in accordance with Article 30 of the Charter of the United Nations, adopt their respective rules of procedure. In the same way, the General Assembly adopted at its sixty-fifth meeting on December 14, 1946, regulations concerning the registration and publication of treaties, implementing Article 102 of the Charter.

(7) REGISTRATION OF TREATIES. Article 18 of the Covenant of the League of Nations provided that "every treaty or international engagement entered into hereafter by any Member of the League shall be forthwith registered with the Secretariat and shall as soon as possible be published by it. No such treaty or international engagement shall be binding until so registered." Article 102 of the Charter stipulates: "1. Every treaty and every international agreement entered into by any Member of the United Nations after

---

[35] Cf. *infra*, p. 357.

Creation and Application of International Law

the present Charter comes into force shall as soon as possible be registered with the Secretariat and published by it. 2. No party to any such treaty or international agreement which has not been registered in accordance with the provisions of paragraph 1 of this Article may invoke that treaty or agreement before any organ of the United Nations."

What was the legal consequence of a member's nonfulfillment of his duty stipulated by Article 18 of the Covenant? First, possibly but not necessarily, the general sanction provided by Article 16, paragraph 4, of the Covenant—expulsion from the League by a decision of the Council; second, a sanction provided by Article 18 itself—a treaty not registered could not become binding. Although Article 18 did not distinguish between treaties concluded by members with members of the League, and treaties concluded by members with nonmembers, registration could be a condition of the validity of the treaty only if it was a treaty concluded between members of the League. A nonmember was not subjected to the Covenant and consequently was not bound by Article 18. When a nonmember had concluded a treaty with a member of the League, the former was entitled to consider the treaty as binding upon the member, even if the treaty was not registered with the Secretariat. The wording of Article 18 obviously exceeded the legal possibilities determined by general international law.[36]

Like Article 18 of the Covenant, Article 102 of the Charter refers to treaties concluded by the members with members or with nonmembers. But the Charter does not declare an unregistered treaty to be invalid; it provides only that an unregistered treaty shall not be considered as valid by the organs of the United Nations, such

---

[36] In the *Pablo Najera (of the Lebanon) Case* (France and Mexico, Mixed Claims Commission, 1928; Annual Digest 1927–1928, Case No. 271) the commission held: With respect to the general meaning of Article 18, that its provisions do not impair the binding force as between the parties, members of the League of Nations, of a duly ratified treaty, so that, in spite of the neglect of registration, the parties cannot withdraw from it or conclude with third powers treaties contrary to it; that, however, the article precludes the parties from invoking the treaty as obligatory, not only before the Assembly and the Council of the League of Nations but also before the Permanent Court of International Justice and any other international tribunal. This interpretation is hardly compatible with the wording of Article 18.

as the General Assembly, the Security Council, and especially the International Court of Justice. If a member persistently violates his obligation under Article 102, the sanction established by Article 6 (expulsion) is applicable.

Article 102 applies only to treaties concluded by members of the United Nations with members or with nonmembers or with the United Nations or with another international organization. It does not apply to treaties concluded by nonmembers with nonmembers or with the United Nations or any other international organization. But the regulations adopted by the General Assembly on December 14, 1946, also contain provisions for the registration and publication of treaties, not provided by Article 102 of the Charter.

(8) ACCESSION TO TREATIES. Different from the conclusion of a treaty is the so-called accession by a state to a treaty already concluded by other states. By its accession, a state becomes a party to the treaty, either to the whole treaty or only to some of its provisions. In the latter case some writers speak of adhesion in contradistinction to accession, which takes place in case a state becomes party to the whole treaty. Accession and adhesion are possible only if the treaty contains a provision to this effect. Treaties, especially multilateral treaties, frequently contain the provision that the treaty shall be open either to the accession of all other states or only to the accession of a definite state or some definite states. Such accession may or may not be dependent on the consent of the states contracting parties to the treaty. Thus, e.g., Article 10 of the North Atlantic Treaty of April 4, 1949, stipulates: "The Parties may, by unanimous agreement, invite any other European state in a position to further the principles of this Treaty and to contribute to the security of the North Atlantic area to accede to this Treaty."

According to the traditional doctrine, accession to a treaty always means conclusion of a treaty. This view is not correct. There are essential differences between accession to a treaty and the conclusion of a treaty: (1) The acceding state has no opportunity to influence by negotiation the content of the treaty. The acceding state has only the choice between accepting and not accepting the unchanged treaty. And (2) at the moment of the conclusion of a treaty there must exist concordance of will of the contracting parties, especially with respect to the person of the parties. Each party must agree to conclude the treaty with another definite party; and this concordance of will must exist at the moment of the conclusion of the treaty. When a state accedes to an existing treaty by virtue of a clause of accession, such concordance of will is not necessary. Even if one of the contracting states, parties to the existing treaty, has changed its mind with respect to the possibility of accession on the part of a third state, its dissent or protest against the accession is irrelevant as long as the clause of accession is valid; and this clause, like any other stipulation of the treaty, cannot be invalidated by a unilateral declaration of will on the part of one of the contracting states. Accession to an existing treaty by virtue of a clause of accession is not the conclusion of a treaty with the contracting parties of the existing treaty; it is rather a submission by a state to a pre-existing norm or a pre-existing set of norms, created by a treaty concluded by other states. That accession to a treaty is not identical with the conclusion of this treaty or of a new treaty with the same content is particularly clear in the case of a multilateral treaty constituting an international community and containing the provision that new members may be admitted by a majority-vote decision of an organ of the community, as, for instance, Article 1, paragraph 2, of the Covenant of the League of Nations or Article 4, paragraph 2, of the Charter of the United Nations. To become a member of an established international community by entering the community or being admitted to it is equivalent to acceding to its constituent treaty. If a state is admitted as a new member by a majority-vote decision on the part of the representatives of the existing members, it is hardly possible to maintain the fiction that the new member has concluded a treaty with all the other members, even with those which voted against its admission. The treaty provision concerning admission of new members determines the conditions under which the binding force of the treaty may be extended to states not being contracting parties to the treaty. By accession (admission) the acceding state becomes a subject of the obligations, responsibilities, and rights stipulated in the treaty.

c. *The treaty as law created by a specific procedure.* Like any legal norm, the norm created by a treaty has a certain sphere of validity. As pointed out,[37] we distinguish material, personal, territorial, and temporal spheres of validity.

(1) THE OBJECTS OF TREATIES. Traditional theory presents the problem of the material sphere of validity of a norm created by a treaty as the problem of the objects of treaties. It is generally admitted that any subject matter whatever can be regulated by a treaty. In principle, general international law does not limit the material sphere of validity of the norms created by treaties. This principle, however, seems to have some exceptions. It is usually maintained that treaties imposing an obligation to perform a physical impossibility or to behave immorally are null and void. That means that such a treaty can be annulled by each of the parties for that reason. But the question as to what is physically impossible or immoral may be disputed. Under general international law there is no objective authority competent to decide this question. Besides, to conclude a treaty and later on to declare the treaty null and void because of its immoral content is certainly not less immoral than the treaty itself.

In this connection the question arises as to whether a treaty can impose upon a contracting party the obligation to conclude in the future another treaty on a certain subject matter, either with the other contracting party or with a third party. Such a treaty is called a *pactum de contrahendo.* As to a treaty to be concluded with a third party, it is obvious that a person cannot be obliged by a treaty to conclude such a treaty, because the conclusion of a treaty is not the action of one person, but depends on the cooperation of another person. The person concerned could be obliged only to try to conclude a treaty with a third person, and such an obligation is highly problematical.[38]

---

[37] Cf. *supra*, pp. 7f.

[38] In the case of *Railway Traffic between Lithuania and Poland* (Publications of the Permanent Court of International Justice, Series A/B, No. 42) the Council of the League of Nations recommended to the governments of Poland and Lithuania, on December 10, 1927, "to enter into direct negotiations as soon as possible in order to establish such relations between the two neighboring States as will ensure 'the good understanding between nations upon which

If a treaty imposes upon the contracting parties the obligation to conclude with one another in the future a treaty on certain subject matters, two cases must be distinguished: the first treaty does, or does not, constitute an agreement on certain points. If the first treaty already constitutes an agreement on certain points, it is not a *pactum de contrahendo,* but a treaty imposing substantive obligations upon the contracting parties, the obligation to do something or to forbear from doing something, not the obligation to conclude a treaty. It may be a so-called preliminary treaty, determining only certain important points, and requiring to be completed by a subsequent so-called definitive treaty, determining other, less important points. If the first treaty does not constitute an agreement on certain points, it establishes only the obligation to enter into negotiations for the conclusion of a treaty, not the obligation to conclude a treaty. A typical example of the problematical value of such a treaty is Article 43 of the Charter of the United Nations, which, according to its wording, imposes upon the members the obligation to conclude special agreements with the United Nations, represented by the Security Council, concerning the numbers and types of forces to be placed at the disposal of the Security Council, their degree of readiness and general location, and the nature of the facilities and assistance to be provided. Although the Charter is now five years in force, these special agreements are not yet concluded and probably never will be concluded. Never-

---

peace depends.'" The Permanent Court of International Justice in its advisory opinion of October 15, 1931, held: As the representatives of Lithuania and Poland participated in the adoption of the resolution of the Council of December 10, 1927, the two governments were bound by their acceptance of the Council's resolution, which constituted an engagement between them. The Court could not accept the contention of Poland that the obligation to negotiate as laid down in the resolution constituted an engagement to come to an agreement: "The Court is indeed justified in considering that the engagement incumbent on the two Governments in conformity with the Council's Resolution is not only to enter into negotiations, but also to pursue them as far as possible, with a view to concluding agreements . . . . But an obligation to negotiate does not imply an obligation to reach an agreement, nor in particular does it imply that Lithuania, by undertaking to negotiate, has assumed an engagement, and is in consequence obliged to conclude the administrative and technical agreements indispensable for the re-establishment of traffic on the Landwarow-Kaisiadorys railway sector."

theless it cannot be maintained that the members have violated their obligations under Article 43.

Another question as to the material sphere of validity of treaties is whether by a treaty the application of norms of general international law can be excluded; or, as the question is usually formulated, whether a treaty at variance with norms of general international law is to be considered as valid. It is the question as to whether the norms of customary general international law have the character of *jus cogens* or of *jus dispositivum*. No clear answer to this question can be found in the traditional theory of international law. Some writers maintain that there exists complete, or almost complete, freedom of contract in this respect; others maintain that treaties which are at variance with universally recognized principles of international law are null and void. But they do not and cannot precisely designate the norms of general international law which have the character of *jus cogens*, that is to say, the application of which cannot be excluded by a treaty. It is probable that a treaty by which two or more states release one another from the obligations imposed upon them by the norm of general international law prohibiting occupation of parts of the open sea, will be declared null and void by an international tribunal competent to deal with this case. But it can hardly be denied that states may by a valid treaty renounce in their mutual relations the right of exercising protection over their own citizens, a right conferred upon them by general international law.[39]

(2) THE SUBJECTS UPON WHOM TREATIES ARE BINDING. As far as the personal sphere of validity of the norms is concerned which

---

[39] Vattel, *op. cit.*, Introduction, pars. 7–9, says: "We use the term *necessary Law of Nations* for that law which results from applying the natural law to Nations. It is *necessary*, because Nations are absolutely bound to observe it. It contains those precepts which the natural law dictates to States, and it is no less binding upon them than it is upon individuals. . . . Since, therefore, the necessary Law of Nations consists in applying the natural law to States, and since the natural law is not subject to change, being founded on the nature of things and particularly upon the nature of man, it follows that the necessary Law of Nations is not subject to change. Since this law is not subject to change and the obligations which it imposes are necessary and indispensable, Nations can not alter it by agreement, nor individually or mutually release themselves from it."

Creation and Application of International Law 345

are established by treaties, it is usually assumed that a treaty imposes duties and confers rights only and exclusively upon the contracting states—*Pacta tertiis nec nocent nec prosunt* ("Treaties are neither of benefit nor of detriment to third parties"). Another principle advocated by international jurists is that treaties can have effect upon states only and not upon their subjects, private individuals. Both principles, however, have important exceptions in positive international law.

(a) Treaties Imposing Duties upon Third States.

1. Treaties by which so-called state servitudes are established. The term "servitude" is taken from private law. According to the usual definition, a servitude is a charge laid on an estate for the use of another estate belonging to another proprietor. Hence one speaks of a "servient" and a "dominant" estate; for instance, the right of passage over an estate in order to use better another estate. The essence of this legal institution is that the obligation imposed upon the proprietor of the servient estate passes over with the estate to any succeeding proprietor of the servient estate, and the corresponding right to any succeeding proprietor of the dominant estate. The obligation is, as it were, fixed on the servient, the right on the dominant estate. Analogously, a state servitude is an obligation referring to the territory of a state, as, e.g., the obligation not to fortify a certain place, imposed upon a state with the effect that any other state succeeding to the territory automatically also succeeds to this obligation; the corresponding right passes automatically to any state succeeding to the territory of the state in the favor of which the obligation is established. Whether such obligations and rights inherent to the state territory can be established by treaties is doubtful.[40] If they are possible, they certainly con-

---

[40] In the *North Atlantic Coast Fisheries* Arbitration between Great Britain and the United States of America (Tribunal of the Permanent Court of Arbitration, 1910; Scott, Hague Court Reports [1916], p. 160) the tribunal rejected the contention of the United States that the liberties of fishery, granted to the United States by a treaty of 1818, constituted a servitude in their favor over the territory of Great Britain. The tribunal was unable to agree with this contention *inter alia* because "the doctrine of international servitude in the sense which is now sought to be attributed to it originated in the peculiar and now obsolete conditions prevailing in the Holy Roman Empire of which the *domini terrae* were not fully sovereigns; they holding territory

stitute an exception to the principle that treaties impose duties and confer rights only upon the contracting states. For the state which succeeds to the territory in which the obligation is inherent is obliged by a treaty to which it is not a contracting party, and the state which succeeds to the territory in which the right is inherent becomes the subject of a right through a treaty to which it is not a contracting party.

2. Treaties by which territorial changes are established, espe-

under the Roman Empire, subject at least theoretically, and in some respects also practically, to the courts of that Empire; their right being, moreover, rather of a civil than of a public nature, partaking more of the character of *dominium* than of *imperium*, and therefore certainly not a complete sovereignty. And because in contradistinction to this quasi-sovereignty with its incoherent attributes acquired at various times, by various means, and not impaired in its character by being incomplete in any one respect or by being limited in favor of another territory and its possessor, the modern State, and particularly Great Britain, has never admitted partition of sovereignty, owing to the constitution of a modern State requiring essential sovereignty and independence"; and "because this doctrine being but little suited to the principle of sovereignty which prevails in States under a system of constitutional government such as Great Britain and the United States, and to the present international relations of sovereign States, has found little, if any, support from modern publicists. It could therefore in the general interest of the community of nations, and of the parties to this treaty, be affirmed by this tribunal only on the express evidence of an international contract . . . ."

In the *Wimbledon Case* (Publications of the Permanent Court of International Justice, Series A, No. 1) Germany refused to the English steamship *Wimbledon*, carrying munitions for Poland which then was at war with Russia, passage through the Kiel Canal, in spite of Article 380 of the Peace Treaty of Versailles, which provided: "The Kiel Canal and its approaches shall be maintained free and open to the vessels of Commerce and of war of all nations at peace with Germany on terms of entire equality." The Court (1923) stated: "In order to dispute, in this case, the right of the [*Wimbledon*] to free passage through the Kiel Canal under the terms of Article 380, the argument has been urged upon the Court that this right really amounts to a servitude by international law resting upon Germany and that, like all restrictions or limitations upon the exercise of sovereignty, this servitude must be construed as restrictively as possible and confined within its narrowest limits, more especially in the sense that it should not be allowed to affect the rights consequent upon neutrality in an armed conflict. The Court is not called upon to take a definite attitude with regard to the question, which is moreover of a very controversial nature, whether in the domain of international law, there really exist servitudes analogous to the servitudes of private law." The Court arrived at the conclusion that "the respondent, Germany, wrongfully refused passage through the Canal to the [*Wimbledon*]."

Creation and Application of International Law 347

cially treaties of cession, insofar as all the other states are not allowed to occupy the ceded territory after its evacuation by the ceding state and are obliged to consider the ceded territory after its occupation by the cessionary as legally belonging to the latter.

3. Treaties by which a new state is erected and at the same time duties are imposed upon this state, which is not a contracting party to this treaty: Danzig (Treaty of Versailles); Vatican City (Lateran Treaty); Free Territory of Trieste (Peace Treaty with Italy).

4. Treaties constituting an international organization and stipulating that amendments to the treaty become binding upon all members by a majority vote of a collegiate body composed of members, or by ratification by a majority of the members as e.g., Articles 108 and 109 of the Charter of the United Nations and Article 36 of the Constitution of the International Labor Organization.[41]

5. Multilateral treaties to which the overwhelming majority of the states are contracting parties, and which aim at an international order of the world, such as the Covenant of the League of Nations or the Charter of the United Nations.

Article 17 of the Covenant of the League of Nations provided: "In the event of a dispute between a Member of the League and a State which is not a Member of the League, or between States not Members of the League, the State or States not Members of the League shall be invited to accept the obligations of membership in the League for the purposes of such dispute, upon such conditions as the Council may deem just. . . . If a State so invited shall refuse to accept the obligations of membership in the League for the purposes of such dispute, and shall resort to war against a Member of the League, the provisions of Article 16 shall be applicable as against the States taking such action." Since Article 16 stipulates sanctions for the violation of the obligation not to resort to war, Article 17 extends this obligation to nonmembers, which means that the Covenant claims to be binding upon states not contracting parties to this treaty.

Article 2, paragraph 6, of the Charter provides that the Organiza-

---

[41] Cf. *supra*, p. 337.

tion shall ensure that states which are not members of the United Nations act in accordance with the principles laid down in Article 2, so far as may be necessary for the maintenance of international peace and security. One of the most important principles is the obligation to refrain from the threat and use of force and to settle international disputes by peaceful means. By authorizing the Organization to ensure that nonmembers act in conformity with the Charter, this treaty empowers the Security Council to take enforcement actions—as sanctions—against nonmembers acting in violation of obligations imposed upon members, and thus extends these obligations to nonmembers. That means that the Charter claims to be valid for states not contracting parties to this treaty.

The restriction of the personal sphere of validity of contractual norms establishing obligations, i.e., the principle that treaties—apart from the above-mentioned exceptions—can impose obligations only upon the contracting states is the consequence of the principle of the sovereignty of the state, which—as it is usually understood—implies that a state cannot be legally bound without its consent. It is, however, a characteristic tendency of modern international law to restrict this principle. Treaties imposing obligations upon third states have been generally recognized in a steadily increasing measure.

(b) Treaties Conferring Rights upon Third States.[42] The principle at the basis of the restriction of the personal sphere of validity of contractual norms establishing obligations is not involved in the question of the personal sphere of validity of contractual

---

[42] In the *Case concerning Certain German Interests in Polish Upper Silesia* (*supra*, p. 329) the Permanent Court of International Justice (1926) stated: "A treaty only creates law as between the States which are parties to it; in case of doubt, no rights can be deduced from it in favor of third States" (p. 29). In the *Case of the Free Zones of Upper Savoy and the District of Gex* (*supra*, p. 325) the Permanent Court of International Justice stated: "It cannot be lightly presumed that stipulations favorable to a third State have been adopted with the object of creating an actual right in its favor. There is however nothing to prevent the will of sovereign States from having this object and this effect. The question of the existence of a right acquired under an instrument drawn between other States is therefore one to be decided in each particular case: it must be ascertained whether the States which have stipulated in favor of a third State meant to create for that State an actual right which the latter has accepted as such" (pp. 147f.).

Creation and Application of International Law 349

norms establishing rights. By conferring a right upon a third state a treaty cannot infringe upon the so-called sovereignty of the state that is not a contracting party to the treaty. A treaty can confer a right upon a third state only by imposing an obligation upon a state that is a contracting party to this treaty. The only rule restricting the personal sphere of validity of contractual norms resulting from the principle of sovereignty is the rule that a treaty can impose obligations only upon the contracting States; and this rule is by no means affected by a treaty conferring a right upon a third state. As a matter of fact, there is no principle of positive international law excluding treaties in favor of third states. Such treaties are as follows:

1. Treaties by which state servitudes are established by creating rights for the successor to the dominant state, though not a contracting party to the treaty.

2. Treaties establishing the protection of minorities and opening to states that are not contracting parties to the treaty the possibility of invoking a court against violations of the treaty stipulations, such as the treaties concluded by the Principal Allied and Associated Powers with Poland, signed June 28, 1919; with Czechoslovakia, signed September 10, 1919; with the Serb-Croat-Slovene State, signed September 10, 1919; with Rumania, signed December 9, 1919; with Greece, signed August 10, 1920.

3. Treaties concluded between two states concerning a canal or a strait stipulating that the canal or the strait shall be open to vessels of all nations, as, for instance, the Hay-Pauncefote Treaty between Great Britain and the United States of 1901 and the Hay-Varilla Treaty between the United States and Panama concerning the Panama Canal of 1903, or the treaty between Argentina and Chile of 1881, concerning the Strait of Magellan.

4. The Peace Treaty of Versailles contains in Article 109 provisions in favor of Denmark; in Article 116, provisions in favor of Russia; and in Article 358, provisions in favor of Switzerland, although all the three states were not contracting parties to the treaty.

5. The Peace Treaty with Italy (signed on February 10, 1947) contains in Article 76 provisions in favor of "any of the United

Nations which broke off diplomatic relations with Italy and which took action in cooperation with the Allied and Associated Powers," without being contracting parties to the treaty.

If treaties are interpreted and applied in accordance with the intention of the contracting parties, the authorities competent to apply a treaty are bound to apply also a stipulation in favor of a third state, provided that the stipulation expresses the intention of the contracting parties, as long as the stipulation is not amended or abolished in conformity with international law. The usual objection against the validity of a stipulation in favor of third states—that it can be amended or abolished without the consent of the latter—misses its aim. Exactly the same situation exists with respect to rights established by the national law of a state. Nobody doubts that by municipal law rights are conferred upon individuals, although the law conferring these rights can be amended or abolished by the lawmaker without the consent of the subjects of these rights.

(c) *Treaties Imposing Duties and Responsibilities upon Private Individuals.* A treaty concluded between two or more states authorizing or obliging the contracting parties to execute sanctions against individuals who have committed certain delicts determined by the treaty directly imposes international obligations and responsibilities upon individuals, whether they are citizens of the contracting state or not. Examples of such treaties are given in the section dealing with individuals as subjects of international law.[43]

(d) *Treaties Conferring Rights upon Private Individuals.* Treaties by which private individuals are authorized to invoke an international tribunal for the protection of certain interests directly confer international rights upon private individuals. Such treaties are referred to in the section dealing with individuals as subjects of international law.[44]

---

[43] Cf. *supra*, pp. 140ff.

[44] Cf. *supra*, pp. 140ff. In the *Zoppot Street-Crossing Case* (Annual Digest 1933–1934, Case No. 104) the Danzig High Court (1934) held: "It may be conceded that, in principle, international agreements do not, as such, create rights and duties for private persons like the plaintiff. But in exceptional cases the effect of an international agreement may, in accordance with the intention of the parties, be such as to create rights and duties for private persons and

Creation and Application of International Law 351

(3) TRANSFORMATION OF TREATIES INTO NATIONAL LAW. From the principle that the binding force of an international treaty concerns the contracting states only, and not their subjects, it is usually inferred that it is necessary to transform an international agreement into national law in order that the former may reach private individuals.[45] Some writers even maintain that such transformation is necessary to make a treaty binding upon the organs of the state. They argue that since the subjects of international law are states, treaties can have effect only on states as such. If treaties refer to the subjects or organs of the contracting states, providing, e.g., for actions to be performed by the subjects or by definite organs of the contracting states, especially by their courts, the states must take the steps necessary to make the provisions of the treaty binding upon their subjects and organs. Otherwise the treaty cannot be executed. What steps are necessary will depend

to confer jurisdiction in respect of them on national courts. Whether this is so depends on the object and meaning of the particular treaty. The intention of the parties, which is to be deduced from the content of the agreement and the way in which it is applied, is in every case decisive."

[45] Thus, e.g., in the *Czechoslovak Agrarian Reform (Swiss Subjects) Case* (Annual Digest 1925–1926, Case No. 5) the Supreme Administrative Court of Czechoslovakia (1926) stated that international treaties, although they were also a source of law, created law only as between contracting states. In cases when their stipulations concerned the rights and duties of the subjects of the contracting states, the treaty as such could only bind the contracting states to incorporate corresponding provisions into their municipal law, and thus make the stipulations of the treaty binding also in the municipal sphere. As regards the Czechoslovak State, the official publication of the treaty was not sufficient to fulfill this obligation. For this purpose the stipulations of the treaty must be promulgated in the form required by the Constitution as provisions of the Czechoslovak legislative power, i.e., as a law or a decree. And in the *Rhineland Ordinances Case* (Annual Digest 1925–1926, Case No. 7) the German Reichsfinanzhof (1926) stated that international law, including international conventions, was binding upon courts and individuals only so far as it had been transformed into municipal law. But, in *Eheleute K. v. Deutsche Reichsbahn-Gesellschaft* (Annual Digest 1929–1930, Case No. 226) the German Reichsgericht (1929) stated with respect to a treaty concluded by Germany and Poland that the Convention of April 21, 1921, was concluded in pursuance of the provisions of the Treaty of Versailles. It had therefore become part of internal German law. It might be invoked if the particular provision, having regard to its content, purpose, and wording, was calculated to produce an effect in the sphere of private law. No further measures in the nature of international or municipal acts were needed.

on the constitution of the state concerned. A simple publication of the treaty in the official gazette may suffice, but it may be necessary to insert the content of the treaty into a statute adopted by the legislative organ.

As pointed out[46] this view can hardly be maintained without restrictions. Every norm of international law, and especially every treaty imposing an obligation upon a state, stipulates an action to be performed by some organ of the state. The state can manifest its existence only through acts performed by its organs. If international law in general and treaties in particular obligated only the state as such and not definite organs of the state, international law would obligate nobody. Hence every treaty would require some kind of transformation into national law. But there can be no doubt that in the practice of states the norms of general international law are applied and many treaties are executed by the competent organs of the states without any such transformation, especially treaties providing for actions of the state to be performed by that organ which is called the government—the Head of State and the cabinet. Such are, e.g., treaties of alliance and arbitration treaties. If a norm of international law is to be applied by the government of the state, most writers do not consider a transformation necessary because they identify the state with its government. Then there is no reason to consider transformation of a treaty necessary if the treaty is to be applied by administrative organs subordinate to the government, which may order them to apply the treaty, unless such order is interpreted to constitute a transformation of international into national law. If a treaty imposes upon a state an obligation which can be fulfilled only by a legislative act, this act is, as pointed out,[47] no transformation of international into national law undertaken for the purpose of making the application of the treaty possible, but the direct application of the treaty by the competent organ.

The situation is different when the provisions of a treaty are to be applied by the courts of the contracting state, independent of its government, and if the constitution of the state authorizes the

---

[46] Cf. *supra*, pp. 114ff., 194f.
[47] Cf. *supra*, p. 195.

Creation and Application of International Law 353

courts to apply only law created by the legislative organs of the state. Then, true transformation of the treaty into a statute is certainly necessary. But it is possible that the constitution of a state contains a provision according to which treaties concluded by the state in conformity with its constitution are to be considered as binding upon the organs and subjects of the state and especially upon its courts, in the same way as statutes or other legal norms created by the lawmaking organs of the state, without any publication of the treaty or other kind of transformation being necessary.

Thus, e.g., the Constitution of the United States contains the provision (Article VI, section 2) that "all treaties made, or which shall be made, under the authority of the United States, shall be the supreme law of the land; and the judges in every State shall be bound thereby, anything in the Constitution or laws of any State to the contrary notwithstanding." This provision may be interpreted to mean that every treaty concluded by the United States is applicable by the competent organs of this state in the same way as statutes adopted by the legislative organ, the Congress.

It is further possible that a treaty, according to its own terms, shall be directly applied by the organs of the contracting states, without any transformation into national law being necessary.[48] Then transformation is nevertheless necessary if the treaty is to be applied by the courts and if the courts, according to the constitution of the state concerned can apply only law created by the legislative organs of the state.[49] Many constitutions provide that

---

[48] This has been recognized by the Permanent Court of International Justice in its advisory opinion No. 15; cf. *supra*, p. 195.

In *S. Papadopoulos, of Pera v. N. V. Koninglijke Nederlandsche Stoomboot-Maatschappij, of Amsterdam* (Annual Digest 1927–1928, Case No. 285) the Court of Appeal, Amsterdam (1928) held that the Treaty of Lausanne not only binds the governments of the contracting states in the exercise of their sovereign rights, but also directly concerns the rights and interests of their subjects, so that the treaty forms part of the law of the states concerned; that Article 137 of the treaty obviously tends to accept the decisions and orders of the occupying powers as definitely clothed with legal effect, and that, therefore, the subjects of the contracting states are equally bound to respect the legal situation thus created. Cf. also *Eheleute K. v. Deutsche Reichsbahn-Gesellschaft, supra*, p. 351

[49] In *Foster v. Neilson* (2 Peters 314) the Supreme Court of the United States (1829) declared: "Our constitution declares a treaty to be the law of the land. It is, consequently, to be regarded in courts of justice as equiva-

all, or certain, treaties must be approved by the legislative organ in order to be valid. Such approval is no transformation; it is participation of the legislative organ in the conclusion of the treaty, that is to say, participation in the creation of international law. Whether a treaty concluded with the approval of the legislative organ requires transformation into a statute or a decree of the executive depends on the constitution of the state concerned. As pointed out, the necessity of transformation is a question of national not of international law.

(4) BEGINNING AND END OF THE VALIDITY OF THE TREATY. The territorial sphere of validity of a norm created by an international treaty is, as a rule, the territories of the contracting states. The temporal sphere of validity is the time during which the conventional norm is valid. It is the question as to the beginning and the end of the validity of the treaty.

A treaty enters into force at the moment when the concordance of will of the parties has been reached, in other words, when the procedure by which the contractual norm is to be created has been terminated. The beginning of the validity of the treaty as a norm coincides with the end of the procedure we call "treaty." At that moment the treaty assumes binding force. The binding force of the treaty manifests itself in that the contracting parties cannot unilaterally free themselves from the obligations stipulated by the treaty, unless the treaty itself authorizes each party to withdraw under definite conditions determined by the treaty. That such a treaty is in force means that the parties cannot unilaterally free themselves from the norms determining the conditions under which withdrawal is permitted. If the parties are unconditionally

---

lent to an act of the legislature, whenever it operates of itself, without the aid of any legislative provision. But when the terms of the stipulation import a contract—when either of the parties engages to perform a particular act, the treaty addresses itself to the political, not the judicial department; and the legislature must execute the contract, before it can become a rule for the court." In *Attorney-General for Canada v. Attorney-General for Ontario* the Judicial Committee of the Privy Council (1937 Law Reports A. C. 326) held: "Within the British Empire there is a well established rule that the making of a treaty is an executive act, while the performance of its obligations, if they entail alteration of the existing domestic law, requires legislative action."

Creation and Application of International Law 355

allowed to withdraw from the treaty, then there is no sufficient reason to assume the existence of a treaty binding upon the parties.

A treaty, it is true, may fix a date for its coming into force. This date may be after or prior to the termination of the procedure by which the treaty is concluded, for instance, a date after or prior to ratification; in the latter case the ratification has retroactive effect. But if a treaty contains such a provision, at least this provision must enter into force at the moment when the treaty-making procedure has been terminated; otherwise it could not have legal effect.

That the treaty has entered into force does not necessarily mean that the parties are obliged to perform the treaty immediately. For the treaty may contain a provision to the effect that the performance of the treaty is suspended by a condition or by a date. A condition is a future uncertain event on the occurrence or nonoccurrence of which the performance of the treaty depends; a date is a fixed point of time, that is, a certain future event with the occurrence of which the performance has to begin. Even if the performance of the treaty is suspended in this way, the treaty must enter into force immediately after it has been concluded (the treaty-making procedure has been terminated); otherwise its provision concerning the suspension of the performance could not have legal effect.

The validity of a conventional norm or, what amounts to the same, the binding force of a treaty, may be terminated by a fact determined directly by general international law, as, for instance, by another treaty concluded by the same contracting parties, or by a fact determined by the treaty itself, as, for instance, by the expiration of the time for which the treaty has been concluded. We may distinguish two different groups of facts terminating the validity of the norm created by a treaty.

The termination of the binding force may be the effect of an act performed by one of the contracting parties, or by all of them, with the intention of obtaining this effect, or by a fact different from such an act. As far as the first method of termination is concerned, the following principles apply: Except where otherwise expressly provided in the treaty itself, the norm created by the treaty is valid until abrogated by another treaty concluded by the same contracting parties. This kind of termination is usually designated by the expression "dissolution of a treaty by mutual consent." Such dissolution is legally excluded if the treaty is concluded for all time. Treaties concluded for all time are, for instance, treaties by which a federal state is established.

There is, however, another opinion according to which a treaty concluded for all time may be dissolved by mutual consent of the contracting parties. This interpretation is possible but not necessary. It is based on the idea that the states, even after having concluded a particular treaty for all time, retain the power of concluding treaties (which is not the case if by the treaty a federal state is established, the component states of which have no power to conclude treaties); and as the contracting states retain this power, they can conclude a treaty by which the eternity clause of a previous treaty is abrogated. The first-mentioned interpretation, according to which a treaty concluded for all time, and that means with the stipulation that the treaty cannot be dissolved by mutual consent, is based on the idea that the parties have by treaty renounced the possibility of applying the rule authorizing them to conclude treaties with respect to the subject matter of the treaty concluded for all time. The same double interpretation applies, in principle, to the case of a treaty concluded for a period of time that has not yet expired. If, however, in such a case, it is not possible to assume that the contracting parties have renounced the possibility of dissolving the treaty by mutual consent, this possibility cannot be denied; provided the treaty is interpreted according to the ascertainable intention of the parties.

As pointed out, a treaty may be abrogated by unilateral withdrawal on the part of a contracting state. This, however, is possible only if the treaty determines the condition under which unilateral withdrawal is permitted. Such condition may be an act of denunciation, that is a formal declaration of the intention to withdraw from the treaty, and this declaration may have the effect of terminating the validity of the treaty immediately or only after a certain period of time. The possibility of such withdrawal may be assumed even if it is not expressly stipulated but if it corresponds to the ascertainable intention of the contracting parties.

Such an intention cannot be assumed if a treaty according to its terms is concluded for all time or with the intention of establishing an everlasting condition of things, such as peace treaties, boundary treaties, the Kellogg-Briand Pact, the Charter of the United Nations, and the like. The Covenant of the League of Nations contained express provisions authorizing the members to withdraw by a unilateral act from the League, and that means, from the treaty constituting the League. Article 1, paragraph 3, provided: "Any Member of the League may, after two years' notice of its intention so to do, withdraw from the League, provided that all its international obligations and all its obligations under this Covenant shall have been fulfilled at the time of its withdrawal"; and Article 26, paragraph 2, stipulated that in case an amendment to the Covenant came into force any member which did not consent to the amendment could signify its dissent, in which case "it shall cease to be a Member of the League."

The Charter of the United Nations, as pointed out, does not contain a provision authorizing the members to withdraw, by a unilateral act, from the Organization. But Commission I of the San Francisco Conference adopted a resolution to the effect that a member of the United Nations may withdraw from the Organization in case of "exceptional circumstances." Examples of such exceptional circumstances are mentioned as follows: if "the Organization was revealed to be unable to maintain peace or could do so only at the expense of law and justice; . . . if an amendment to the Charter comes into force in which the Member has not concurred and which it finds itself unable to accept; if an amendment duly accepted by the necessary majority in the Assembly or in a general conference fails to secure the ratifications necessary to bring such amendment into effect."[50] Since the text of this resolution is not inserted into the Charter, it has no legal effect. From a strictly legal point of view, the members of the United Nations have no right of withdrawal from the Organization.

The validity of conventional norms may be terminated by a fact different from an act performed by one or by all of the con-

---

[50] The United Nations Conference on International Organization, Doc. 1178, I/2/76 (2), pp. 5f.

tracting parties with the intention of obtaining this effect (dissolution by mutual consent, notice). Such facts are as follows:

1. The happening of a certain or an uncertain event, that is to say, a *terminus ad quem,* or a resolutive condition fixed by the treaty itself.

2. The performance of all the obligations stipulated by the treaty, for instance, a treaty of cession after the ceded territory has been evacuated by the ceding state and occupied by the cessionary. The illegal nonperformance of the obligation stipulated by a treaty does not terminate its validity. If a bilateral treaty stipulates mutual obligations, that is to say, if it imposes obligations upon both the contracting parties, and if one of the parties does not fulfill its treaty obligation, the other party has the choice between two possibilities: to fulfill its own obligation and take the measures provided by general international law in case of an international delict, or to cancel the treaty on the ground of non-fulfillment on the part of the other state. Some writers maintain that the right to cancel the treaty exists only if essential stipulations of the treaty are violated by the other party. In case of a multilateral treaty, nonfulfillment of its provisions by one party does not authorize one of the other parties to cancel the treaty, each party being obliged to comply with the treaty in relation to all the other parties. The treaty remains in force, but the parties to the treaty may, as a reprisal, refuse to fulfill their obligations under the treaty in relation to that party which has violated the treaty.

3. The fact that the execution of the treaty becomes impossible subsequent to its conclusion; if, for instance, a state has ceded by a treaty an island to another state, and this island disappeared by an earthquake before the execution of the treaty. If impossibility of execution terminates the validity of a treaty, the non-execution (of the treaty) is not considered to be illegal and consequently does not entail an obligation of reparation.

4. In the case of a bilateral treaty, the fact that one of the two contracting parties ceases to exist.

(5) THE CLAUSULA REBUS SIC STANTIBUS. According to a widespread opinion, a treaty ceases to be valid as the effect of a vital

Creation and Application of International Law

change of circumstances; or, as this principle is usually formulated, according to the *clausula rebus sic stantibus* ("Clause concerning vital change of circumstances"). In order to justify the principle that a contracting party to a treaty can withdraw unilaterally from the treaty or, what amounts to the same, declare that it considers itself no longer bound by the treaty if the circumstances under which it has concluded the treaty or adhered to it have essentially changed, some writers maintain that if the change of circumstances is so essential that compliance with the treaty could impair the very existence of the state, the latter cannot be considered as bound by the treaty. Its fundamental right to existence is stronger than its obligation under the rule *pacta sunt servanda*. They sometimes refer to the fact that the principle in question is recognized by many national legal orders which permit a person to cancel a contract for the reason that the circumstances under which it has been concluded have essentially changed.

But there exists an important difference between the *clausula rebus sic stantibus* as part of national law and the same principle as part of international law. Under national law an objective and impartial authority is established to decide the question as to whether a vital change of circumstances has taken place, whereas under general international law the parties to the treaty are themselves competent to decide this question. The most serious argument against the doctrine that, according to a rule of international law, a treaty loses its validity when the circumstances under which it had been concluded have essentially changed, is this: that it is the function of the law in general and treaties in particular to stabilize the legal relations between states in the stream of changing circumstances. If circumstances did not change, the binding force conferred upon treaties by the law would be almost superfluous. The *clausula rebus sic stantibus* is in opposition to one of the most important purposes of the international legal order, its purpose of stabilizing international relations.

As a matter of fact, it is hardly possible to prove that the *clausula* is part of positive international law. When in 1870 Russia tried to withdraw unilaterally from the Treaty of Paris of 1856, which imposed upon Russia the obligation not to maintain a fleet in the

Black Sea, the parties to the Treaty of Paris in a conference held at London in 1871 adopted the following declaration: "It is an essential principle of international law that no power can free itself from obligations imposed upon it by a treaty or modify its terms, except with the consent of the contracting parties by means of an amicable agreement." This is an open rejection of the *clausula rebus sic stantibus*. The relatively few cases in which states have referred to essential change of circumstances to justify their noncompliance with treaty obligations may be interpreted simply as violations of international law rather than as evidence of the *clausula rebus sic stantibus* as a rule of positive international law. As a matter of fact, no international tribunal has, until now, unreservedly confirmed the existence of this rule.[51]

(6) EFFECT OF WAR ON TREATIES. A state of war does not affect the validity of treaties concluded for war or during war (such as treaties regulating the conduct of war, armistice treaties, and the like). As to other treaties, no unanimity exists. Many writers maintain that a distinction must be made between treaties to which only the belligerents and treaties to which also nonbelligerents are contracting parties. The validity of the former is terminated by the outbreak of war; the latter may be suspended by the belligerents. In this case, the peace treaty may contain provisions concerning the continuance of these treaties with or without modifications.

(7) REVISION OF TREATIES. By revision of a treaty a procedure of changing the content of a treaty for the purpose of adapting it to changed circumstances is understood. Article 19 of the Covenant of the League of Nations attempted to deal with this problem: "The

---

[51] The decision of the Permanent Court of International Justice in the *Case of the Free Zones of Upper Savoy and the District of Gex* (*supra*, p. 325) is sometimes quoted as confirming the *clausula rebus sic stantibus*. In this case France referred to the clause in order to free itself from a treaty obligation. But the court, without recognizing the *clausula* as a rule of positive international law, declared only that France failed to prove an essential change of circumstances.

In *Rothschild & Sons v. Egyptian Government* (Mixed Court of Appeal in Egypt, 1926; Annual Digest 1925–1926, Case No. 14) the Mixed Court of First Instance (1925) held that the *clausula rebus sic stantibus* in international law applies only to contracts and obligations of an indefinite duration, and not to those which have a specific fixed and limited duration.

Creation and Application of International Law 361

Assembly may from time to time advise the reconsideration by Members of the League of treaties which have become inapplicable, and the consideration of international conditions whose continuance might endanger the peace of the world." This provision did not confer upon the League the power to revise treaties. The advice of the Assembly to reconsider a treaty had no binding force. Besides, Article 19 of the Covenant has never been applied. The Charter of the United Nations does not contain an express provision concerning revision of treaties. But Article 14 authorizes the General Assembly to "recommend measures for the peaceful adjustment of any situation, regardless of origin, which it deems likely to impair the general welfare or friendly relations among nations, including situations resulting from a violation of the provisions of the present Charter setting forth the Purposes and Principles of the United Nations." This provision may be applied for the purpose of treaty revision. Under Article 14 the General Assembly may recommend the revision of a treaty creating a situation likely to impair the general welfare and friendly relations among nations. The recommendation of the General Assembly has no binding force. But whereas the advice of the Assembly of the League could be made only by a unanimously adopted decision, the recommendation of the General Assembly of the United Nations requires only a two-thirds majority vote.

(8) CONFLICT BETWEEN TREATIES. Two treaties may conflict with each other. With regard to such conflict we have to distinguish two different cases: (1) the two conflicting treaties are concluded by the same contracting parties; and (2) the two conflicting treaties are concluded partly by different contracting parties, for instance: State A concluded a treaty with State B, and later on State A concludes a treaty with State C, by which A assumes obligations incompatible with its obligations under its treaty with B. If the two treaties are concluded entirely by different parties, no conflict is possible. A treaty concluded between A and B cannot conflict with a treaty concluded between C and D.

1. Conflicting treaties concluded by the same contracting parties. If the conflicting treaties are concluded by the same contracting parties, according to general international law the rule *lex posterior*

derogat priori ("the subsequent law abrogates the preceding law") applies. However, a treaty may contain a provision which corresponds to another principle—the principle *lex prior derogat posteriori* ("the preceding law abrogates the subsequent law"). Then the subsequent treaty, if incompatible with the preceding treaty, is to be considered as null or annullable. This is the meaning of a treaty concluded for all time. A special problem is the conflict between a multilateral treaty and a later treaty concluded only by a part of the contracting parties to the former. It may be argued that the preceding treaty is abrogated by the subsequent treaty in the relation among the parties to this treaty; but it may also be argued that each party to a multilateral treaty is entitled to demand that all the other parties remain bound by the treaty as long as it is not abolished or modified by another treaty concluded by all contracting parties.

A multilateral treaty may contain an express provision to the effect that the contracting parties are forbidden to enter into an agreement with one another inconsistent with the terms of the former. Then the conclusion of such a treaty is a violation of a previous treaty obligation and the treaty thus concluded is null or annullable. Article 20 of the Covenant of the League of Nations provided: "The Members of the League severally agree that this Covenant is accepted as abrogating all obligations or understanding *inter se* which are inconsistent with the terms thereof, and solemnly undertake that they will not hereafter enter into any engagements inconsistent with the terms thereof." The first part is superfluous, for the abrogation of the previously concluded treaties takes place according to general international law. The second part refers not only to treaties among parties to the Covenant but also to treaties concluded by parties to the Covenant and other states. Article 8 of the North Atlantic Treaty of April 4, 1949, stipulates: "Each Party declares that none of the international engagements now in force between it and any other of the Parties or any third State is in conflict with the provisions of this Treaty, and undertakes not to enter into any international engagement in conflict with this Treaty." According to its wording, the first part has a mere declaratory character. If the declaration is true, it is

Creation and Application of International Law 363

superfluous; if it is not true, it has no legal effect. The second part refers not only to treaties entered into among the parties to the Atlantic Treaty, but also to treaties concluded by parties to the North Atlantic Treaty with third states, just as the second part of Article 20 of the Covenant referred not only to treaties entered into among members of the League of Nations but also to treaties entered into by members with nonmembers. This problem is considered below.

2. Conflicting treaties concluded partly by different parties. If State A concludes a treaty with State C which is inconsistent with an earlier treaty concluded between State A and State B, both treaties are valid according to general international law. If State A fulfills one of the two treaties, it violates the other with all the legal consequences of a treaty violation. Some writers on international law maintain that the conclusion of a treaty inconsistent with an earlier treaty is an illegal act and as such cannot have a legal, i.e., a law-creating effect. Consequently the later treaty is null and void. This theory is based on the principle *ex injuria jus non oritur*. But this principle, as pointed out,[52] if it is valid at all, is valid only with many exceptions, so that it is hardly possible to base on it the nonvalidity of the later treaty. Besides, the conclusion of a treaty inconsistent with a previously concluded treaty is an illegal act only if this treaty contains a provision imposing upon the contracting parties the obligation not to conclude a subsequent treaty inconsistent with it. Such obligation cannot be deduced from provisions establishing other obligations. And even if a treaty contains a provision forbidding the conclusion of inconsistent treaties such as the Covenant of the League of Nations or the North Atlantic Treaty, this provision can be violated only by the parties to the treaty containing the provision, not by a state which is a party to the subsequent but not to the precedent treaty. In respect to this state the conclusion of the subsequent treaty is certainly not an illegal act.

Sometimes it is argued that two treaties inconsistent with each other cannot be valid at the same time because they constitute a logical contradiction, and that such contradiction is impossible

---
[52] Cf. *supra*, pp. 216, 293.

within a legal system or, what amounts to the same, is incompatible with the necessary unity of the law. However, the fact that two conflicting treaties concluded partly by different parties are both considered to be valid is not incompatible with the unity of the law if this unity is conceived of as a logical unity.[53] The conflict in question is not a logical conflict; it does not imply statements which logically contradict one another. For the statement that the two treaties in question are in conflict with each other means this: If State A fulfills its treaty with B, State C is authorized to direct a sanction against A; and if it fulfills its treaty with C, B is authorized to direct a sanction against A. These two statements are in no logical contradiction. Of course, the situation is not satisfactory. It is true that Great Britain protested when in 1878 Russia and Turkey concluded the Preliminary Treaty of Peace of San Stefano, which was inconsistent with the Treaty of Paris of 1856 and the Convention of London of 1871, and that this protest was justified. But this does not mean that the Preliminary Treaty of San Stefano was, according to general international law, null and void.

In case a state assumes by a treaty an obligation in conflict with an obligation it has assumed by an earlier treaty with a third state, it has, under general international law, the choice between fulfilling the earlier treaty in violation of the later treaty and fulfilling the later treaty in violation of the earlier treaty. By a general convention codifying and reforming the law of treaties, the rule could be laid down that in case of such a conflict the execution of the earlier treaty shall take priority over the execution of the later treaty, and that the party damaged by the nonexecution of the later treaty shall be entitled to an indemnity. But this implies that the later treaty is to be considered as valid. For only if a treaty is valid is its nonfulfillment illegal; and the obligation of reparation presupposes an illegally caused damage.

Article 103 of the Charter provides: "In the event of a conflict between the obligations of the Members of the United Nations under the present Charter and their obligations under any other international agreement, their obligations under the present Char-

---

[53] Cf. *infra,* pp. 424ff.

Creation and Application of International Law 365

ter shall prevail." This provision refers to treaties concluded prior to the coming into force of the Charter as well as to treaties concluded afterward; and it refers to treaties concluded between members of the United Nations as well as to treaties concluded between members and nonmembers. In contradistinction to Article 20 of the Covenant, Article 103 of the Charter does not establish an obligation of the members not to conclude treaties inconsistent with the Charter. The provision that in case of conflict the obligations under the Charter shall prevail may be interpreted to mean that the fulfillment of these obligations shall take priority over the fulfillment of the obligations under any other treaty. This provision can be binding upon a nonmember that is a party to the treaty inconsistent with the Charter only if the Charter is interpreted, in conformity with Article 2, paragraph 6, as a treaty binding upon third states. As to treaties to which only members are contracting parties, Article 103 is superfluous. Such treaties, if preceding the Charter, are abrogated by the Charter, and, if subsequent to the Charter, are null and void or annullable because they attempt to amend the Charter, and an amendment to the Charter is valid only if enacted in conformity with Articles 108 and 109.

5. *Decisions of International Agencies*

In addition to custom and treaties, decisions of international agencies, especially judgments of international tribunals, are sources of international law. General international law does not institute such agencies. It leaves the application of the norms imposing obligations and conferring rights upon states to these very states. It is just in this respect that general international law proves to be a highly decentralized legal order. Centralization, that is, the establishment of special organs for the application of international law, is possible only by treaties.

In applying a pre-existent general norm of customary or conventional international law to a concrete case, such an international agency may create an individual norm of international law.[54] But

---
[54] Cf. *supra*, pp. 303f.

a special organ established by a treaty may also be competent to create general legal norms binding upon the parties to the treaty. The agency established by a treaty is an organ of the international community constituted by the treaty, the contracting parties being the members of this community. The organ competent to create general legal norms may be composed of representatives of all the parties to the treaty establishing the organ, or, what amounts to the same, of all the members of the community constituted by the treaty; or only of representatives of some of them. It may have the power to create general legal norms by a unanimous decision, or by a majority-vote decision, so that the norms thus created are binding also upon a state the representative of which voted against them. A general norm adopted by a unanimous decision of an international organ composed of representatives of all parties to the treaty establishing the organ is not different from a norm created by a treaty entered into by the states upon which the norm is binding. But if the norm is adopted by a majority-vote decision of an organ, composed of representatives of all parties to the treaty establishing the organ, and especially by the majority-vote decision of an organ composed only of representatives of some of the parties to this treaty, the creation of the norm assumes the character of legislation.

An international community may have central organs endowed with such legislative power. Under the Charter of the United Nations, the General Assembly as well as the Security Council has a restricted legislative power.[55] If, however, the centralization of the organization, especially the centralization of the power to create general legal norms binding upon the members, exceeds a certain degree, the international community is transformed into a national community, a state, and the law created by the central organ ceases to be international law; it assumes the character of national law. The transformation of a confederation of states into a federal state is an example.

The law created by international agencies, especially by decisions of international tribunals established by treaties, derives its validity from these treaties, which, in their turn, derive their

---

[55] Cf. *supra*, pp. 198ff.

validity from the norm of customary international law, *pacta sunt servanda*. The norms of customary international law represent the highest stratum in the hierarchical structure of the international legal order. The basis, that is, the reason of validity, of customary international law, is, as pointed out, a fundamental assumption, a juristic hypothesis called the basic norm; it is the assumption that international custom established by the practice of states is a law-creating fact. It is the norm presupposed by a juristic interpretation of international relations: that states ought to behave according to custom established by the practice of states.[56]

B. THE APPLICATION OF INTERNATIONAL LAW

1. Settlement of International Disputes by Agreement

International agencies are especially established for the peaceful settlement of disputes between states. A dispute exists if one state claims that the other should behave in a certain way, and the latter rejects the claim of the former. International disputes may be settled by an agreement of the parties to the dispute, or by the decision of an international agency binding upon the parties.

The agreement may be brought about by direct negotiations of the parties, or by the friendly intervention of a third state or some third states, called good offices or mediation. The purpose of both procedures is to bring about an agreement of the parties to the dispute. Some writers speak of mediation, in contradistinction to good offices, if a third state (or some third states) tries to bring about an agreement of the parties to the dispute on the basis of concrete proposals made by the mediator. In both cases the suggestions made to the parties to the dispute are not binding. In the Hague Convention for the pacific settlement of international disputes of 1907 the contracting parties assume the obligation to have recourse, in case of a dispute, before an appeal to arms, "as far as circumstances allow, to the good offices or mediation of one or more

---

[56] Cf. *infra*, pp. 417ff.

friendly Powers" (Article 2). Article 3 provides: "Powers strangers to the dispute have the right to offer good offices or mediation even during the course of hostilities. The exercise of this right can never be regarded by either of the parties in dispute as an unfriendly act."

If the dispute arises from a difference of opinion on points of fact it may be submitted to an international commission of inquiry established by a special agreement between the parties to the dispute. The function of the commission of inquiry is restricted to a statement of facts. The parties to the dispute may or may not accept this statement. Article 35 of the Hague Convention for the pacific settlement of international disputes, which provides for an international commission of inquiry and which contains rules for a detailed procedure of the commission, stipulates: "The report of the commission is limited to a statement of facts, and has in no way the character of an award. It leaves to the parties entire freedom as to the effect to be given to the statement."

If the commission is competent not only to ascertain disputed facts but also to make recommendations for the settlement of the dispute, one speaks of conciliation. As to the composition of a commission of conciliation, the provision of Article 14 of the treaty signed by Germany and Switzerland at Berne, December 3, 1921, is typical: "The contracting parties shall appoint one member each of their own choice, and nominate three other members by mutual agreement. These three members shall not be nationals of the contracting parties, nor shall they be domiciled on their territory, nor employed in their service. The contracting parties shall by mutual agreement elect the president from among these three members." Settlement of the dispute is brought about only if the parties accept the recommendations of the commission, which implies that they come to an agreement.

2. Settlement of International Disputes by Organs of the League of Nations and of the United Nations

a. *By the Council.* According to Articles 12 and 15 of the Covenant of the League of Nations the members were obliged to submit their disputes either to an international tribunal or to the Council.

Creation and Application of International Law 369

Submission to an international tribunal presupposed agreement of both parties to the dispute. In case no agreement to submit the case to a tribunal could be reached, each of the parties was entitled to submit the case to the Council, and, if the case was submitted to the Council by one party, the other party was obliged to recognize the jurisdiction of the Council. Article 15, paragraph 1, of the Covenant provided: "If there should arise between Members of the League any dispute likely to lead to a rupture, which is not submitted to arbitration or judicial settlement in accordance with Article 13, the Members of the League agree that they will submit the matter to the Council. Any party to the dispute may effect such submission by giving notice of the existence of the dispute to the Secretary-General, who will make all necessary arrangements for a full investigation and consideration thereof."

The Council was supposed first to "endeavor to effect a settlement of the dispute" by bringing about an agreement of the parties. If, however, the dispute could not be settled in this way, the Council was authorized to settle the dispute by making a recommendation to the parties. But only a recommendation unanimously agreed to by the members of the Council other than the representatives of the parties to the dispute gave the recommendation of the Council a legal effect. This effect consisted in that war against the party which complied with the recommendation was prohibited. Article 15, paragraph 6, stipulated: "If a report by the Council is unanimously agreed to by the members thereof other than the Representatives of one or more of the parties to the dispute, the Members of the League agree that they will not go to war with any party to the dispute which complies with the recommendations of the report." By the wording of this provision, war against the party which did not comply with the recommendations was not excluded. Nor was war excluded in case none of the parties complied with the recommendations of the Council. In case no unanimous recommendation could be reached by the Council, war was expressly permitted by the Covenant. Article 15, paragraph 7, ran as follows: "If the Council fails to reach a report which is unanimously agreed to by the members thereof, other than the Representatives of one or more of the parties to the dispute, the Members of the League reserve to themselves the right to take such action as they shall consider necessary for the maintenance of right and justice."

There was even a third case where war was not expressly excluded by the text of the Covenant. Article 15, paragraph 8, stipulated: "If the dispute between the parties is claimed by one of them, and is found by the Council, to arise out of a matter which by international law is solely within the domestic jurisdiction of that party, the Council shall so report, and shall make no recommendation as to its settlement."

According to the text of the Covenant it was doubtful whether war was forbidden in all cases where it was not expressly permitted (Article 15, paragraph 7) or only in the case where it was expressly prohibited (Article 15, paragraph 6).

Under Article 15, paragraph 9, the Council was authorized to refer to the Assembly a dispute submitted to it. The Council was bound to refer the dispute to the Assembly at the request of either party to the dispute provided that such request was made within fourteen days after the submission of the dispute to the Council.

b. *By the Security Council.* Article 1, paragraph 1, of the Charter of the United Nations stipulates: "The Purposes of the United Nations are . . . to bring about by peaceful means, and in conformity with the principles of justice and international law, adjustment or settlement of international disputes or situations which might lead to a breach of the peace." Since the employment of force is, in principle, reserved to the Organization, the members are obliged to settle their conflicts by peaceful means. Article 2, paragraph 3, provides: "All Members shall settle their international disputes by peaceful means in such a manner that international peace and security, and justice, are not endangered."

This obligation is specified by the provisions of Chapter VI of the Charter, which bears the title "Pacific Settlement of Disputes" but which deals also with the adjustment of situations which have not the character of a dispute.

Article 33, paragraph 1, provides: "The parties to any dispute, the continuance of which is likely to endanger the maintenance of international peace and security, shall, first of all, seek a solution by negotiation, enquiry, mediation, conciliation, arbitration, judicial

Creation and Application of International Law

settlement, resort to regional agencies or arrangements, or other peaceful means of their own choice."

If the parties are not able to settle their dispute by peaceful means of their own choice, Article 37 applies: "1. Should the parties to a dispute of the nature referred to in Article 33 fail to settle it by the means indicated in that Article, they shall refer it to the Security Council. 2. If the Security Council deems that the continuance of the dispute is in fact likely to endanger the maintenance of international peace and security, it shall decide whether to take action under Article 36 [recommend appropriate procedures or methods of adjustment] or to recommend such terms of settlement as it may consider appropriate."

Although, according to the wording of Article 37, paragraph 1, the parties shall refer the dispute to the Security Council, which could be interpreted to mean that both parties must agree to submit the dispute to the Council, the intention of those who drafted this provision was that each of the parties should have the power to bring the dispute before the Council. If the dispute is brought before the Council in this way, the Council has first to decide whether the dispute is in fact likely to endanger the maintenance of international peace and security. This the Council can do by investigating the dispute under Article 34. If the result of its investigation is that it deems the continuance of the dispute as a danger to the peace, the Council has the choice between two steps: it may make a recommendation of appropriate procedures or methods of adjustment, that is to say, it may recommend to the parties to settle their dispute by one of the means indicated in Article 33; or the Council may recommend terms of settlement. In both cases the Council can make only recommendations, which are not legally binding on the parties to the dispute. But none of the parties is allowed to enforce its claim against the other party. If the parties do not accept the recommendation of the Security Council the dispute remains unsettled. But under Article 39 the Security Council may determine that nonacceptance of its recommendation constitutes a threat to the peace or a breach of the peace, and then the Council may take enforcement action in order to maintain or restore peace, that is to say, the Council may enforce its recommendation. In this case, its recommendation has binding force upon the parties; and that means that it is not a mere "recommendation."

A dispute may be brought before the Security Council also under Article 38, which provides: "Without prejudice to the provisions of Articles 33 to 37, the Security Council may, if all the parties to any dispute so request, make recommendations to the parties with a view to a pacific settlement of the dispute." The words "to any dispute" must be interpreted to mean that Article 38 refers to disputes to which Article 33, paragraph 1, does not refer, namely, disputes the continuance of which is not likely to endanger the maintenance of international peace and security. If a dispute is likely to endanger the maintenance of international peace and security, the parties are obliged, before referring it to the Security Council, to seek a solution by peaceful means of their own choice. Only if the dispute is not of such a nature may the parties agree to refer it directly to the Security Council, which in this case is authorized to recommend terms of settlement.

A dispute may be brought before the Security Council not only by the parties to the dispute but also by the Security Council itself. Article 34 stipulates: "The Security Council may investigate any dispute, or any situation which might lead to international friction or give rise to a dispute, in order to determine whether the continuance of the dispute or situation is likely to endanger the maintenance of international peace and security."

If the investigation made under Article 34 has the result that the Security Council determines that the continuance of the dispute or situation is likely to endanger the maintenance of international peace and security, the Security Council may apply Article 33, paragraph 2, which stipulates: "The Security Council shall, when it deems necessary, call upon the parties to settle their dispute by such means [the means indicated in Article 33, paragraph 1]."

Although this provision precedes Article 34 referring to investigation, the Council can apply Article 33, paragraph 2, only after having applied Article 34. For the "call" in accordance with Article 33, paragraph 2, refers only to disputes determined by Article 33, paragraph 1, that is to say, the disputes "the continuance of which

Creation and Application of International Law

is likely to endanger the maintenance of international peace and security"; and to determine that a dispute is likely to endanger the maintenance of international peace and security, an investigation under Article 34 is necessary.

Article 34 refers not only to the settlement of disputes but also to the adjustment of other situations. A dispute exists, as pointed out, if one state has made a claim against another state and the other state has rejected this claim. A situation which has not the character of a dispute may endanger international peace and security; it may even constitute a breach of the peace. For instance, a civil war within a state may be a situation which endangers international peace, without being a dispute between two states; or an act of aggression committed by one state against another constitutes a breach of the peace, without being preceded by a dispute between the states concerned.

If the investigation made under Article 34 has the result that the Security Council determines that the dispute or the situation is likely to endanger the maintenance of international peace and security, the Council may, instead of applying Article 33, paragraph 2 (call upon the parties to settle their dispute by means of their own choice), apply Article 36, which runs as follows: "1. The Security Council may, at any stage of a dispute of the nature referred to in Article 33 or of a situation of like nature, recommend appropriate procedures or methods of adjustment. 2. The Security Council should take into consideration any procedures for the settlement of the dispute which have already been adopted by the parties. 3. In making recommendations under this Article the Security Council should also take into consideration that legal disputes should as a general rule be referred by the parties to the International Court of Justice in accordance with the provisions of the Statute of the Court."

According to paragraph 1 of this article the Security Council is authorized only to "recommend appropriate procedures or methods of adjustment," that is to say, one of the means of peaceful settlement indicated in Article 33, paragraph 1; the Council is not authorized to recommend "terms of settlement." The Security Council is authorized to recommend "terms of settlement"—according to the wording of Chapter VI—only in case the dispute (not a situation) has been brought before the Council by the parties to the dispute under Article 37 or Article 38, or if the Council has under Article 39 determined the existence of a threat to or a breach of the peace. Recommendation of appropriate procedures or methods must be clearly distinguished from recommendation of terms of settlement, on the one hand, and of the call upon the parties to settle their dispute by peaceful means under Article 33, paragraph 2, on the other. To call upon the parties to settle their dispute by peaceful means is to be interpreted to mean to remind the parties in general of their obligation established by Article 33, paragraph 1. To recommend appropriate procedures or methods of adjustment means to recommend a definite procedure or method, as, for instance, conciliation or arbitration. Hence the provision of Article 36, paragraph 2, that the Security Council should take into consideration any procedures for the settlement of the dispute which have already been adopted by the parties.

The distinction between legal and nonlegal, that is, political disputes referred to in Article 36, paragraph 3, will be discussed in another connection.[57] That the parties should as a general rule refer legal disputes to the International Court of Justice is not a strict obligation. It is only a suggestion made by the Charter. Submission of a dispute to the International Court of Justice is possible only on the basis of a voluntary agreement reached by all the parties to the dispute.[58]

A dispute or another situation may also be brought before the Security Council by any member of the United Nations or even by a nonmember state. In this respect Article 35 stipulates: "1. Any Member of the United Nations may bring any dispute, or any situation of the nature referred to in Article 34, to the attention of the Security Council or of the General Assembly. 2. A state which is not a Member of the United Nations may bring to the attention of the Security Council or of the General Assembly any dispute to which it is a party if it accepts in advance, for the purposes of the dispute, the obligations of pacific settlement provided in the present Charter.

---

[57] Cf. *infra*, pp. 380ff.
[58] Cf. *infra*, p. 391.

Creation and Application of International Law

3. The proceedings of the General Assembly in respect of matters brought to its attention under this Article will be subject to the provisions of Articles 11 and 12."

Under Article 35 a member may bring not only a dispute but also any other situation the continuance of which is likely to endanger the peace, before the Security Council or the General Assembly; a nonmember state, only a dispute to which it is a party. In case the dispute or the situation has been brought before the Council under Article 35, the Council may, or may not, investigate the dispute or the situation under Article 34, and, after having investigated the matter, apply Article 36, that is to say, recommend appropriate procedures or methods of adjustment (not terms of settlement).

A dispute or any other situation which endangers peace may also be brought before the Security Council by the Secretary-General. Article 99 provides: "The Secretary-General may bring to the attention of the Security Council any matter which in his opinion may threaten the maintenance of international peace and security."

When the Secretary-General has brought to the attention of the Council a dispute or another situation under Article 99, the Security Council may, or may not, institute an investigation under Article 34; after having investigated the dispute or the situation, the Council may apply Article 36.

Finally, a dispute or another situation may be brought before the Security Council by the General Assembly. Article 11, paragraph 3, provides: "The General Assembly may call the attention of the Security Council to situations which are likely to endanger international peace and security." The term "situations" may be interpreted to include disputes. The Assembly is obliged to bring a dispute or another situation before the Security Council in case the dispute or the situation under discussion by the Assembly is of such a nature that action is necessary. This is provided by Article 11, paragraph 2.

The parties to a dispute under consideration by the Security Council may be members of the United Nations or nonmembers; they may or may not be members of the Security Council. In this respect Article 32 provides: "Any Member of the United Nations which is not a member of the Security Council or any state which is not a Member of the United Nations, if it is a party to a dispute under consideration by the Security Council, shall be invited to participate, without vote, in the discussion relating to the dispute. The Security Council shall lay down such conditions as it deems just for the participation of a state which is not a Member of the United Nations." As to the voting procedure in the Security Council, Article 27, paragraph 3, stipulates that in decisions under Chapter VI (and under paragraph 3 of Article 52, that is to say, in decisions by which the Security Council refers a local dispute, i.e., a dispute between states that are members of a regional organization, to a regional agency), the member of the Security Council that is a party to the dispute "shall abstain from voting." This provision does not apply to decisions referring to situations not having the character of disputes.

As to the settlement of disputes and adjustment of other situations, there exists a concurring jurisdiction of the Security Council and the General Assembly. Article 10 authorizes the Assembly to discuss any questions or any matters within the scope of the Charter and to make recommendations to the members of the United Nations or to the Security Council, or to both, on any such questions or matters. These questions or matters may be disputes or other situations which are likely to endanger international peace and security. Article 11, paragraph 2, authorizes the General Assembly to "discuss any questions relating to the maintenance of international peace and security brought before it by any Member of the United Nations, or by the Security Council, or by a state which is not a Member of the United Nations in accordance with Article 35, paragraph 2 . . . ." The Assembly has the power to "make recommendations with regard to any such questions to the state or states concerned or to the Security Council or to both." By "questions," disputes or situations may be understood. In order to avoid conflicts between the recommendations made by the Assembly and the recommendations made by the Council, Article 12 provides that the General Assembly shall not make any recommendation with regard to a dispute or situation "while the Security Council is exercising in respect to any dispute or situation the functions assigned to it in

Creation and Application of International Law 377

the present Charter." The jurisdiction of the Assembly with respect to the settlement of disputes and adjustment of situations is referred to also in Article 14, which provides that "the General Assembly may recommend measures for the peaceful adjustment of any situation, regardless of origin, which it deems likely to impair the general welfare or friendly relations among nations . . . ." It should be noted that no provision exists analogous to that of Article 32, authorizing nonmember states parties to a dispute to participate in the discussion of the dispute in the General Assembly, and no provision analogous to Article 27, paragraph 3, excluding parties to a dispute from voting in the General Assembly.

3. Settlement of International Disputes by International Tribunals

a. *Arbitration and judicial settlement.* Totally different from the settlement of a dispute by an agreement of the parties, brought about by direct negotiation between the parties or by good offices, mediation, commission of inquiry, commission of conciliation, or by recommendations made by organs of the League of Nations or the United Nations, is the settlement of a dispute by the decision of an international agency.

If states submit a dispute to the decision of an international agency, they are obliged to execute the decision even if they do not consent to it. The international agency may or may not have the character of a tribunal. An international agency, that is, an agency created by an international agreement, is a tribunal (1) if the members of the agency are judges, (2) if the agency is competent to settle international disputes by applying international law, and (3), in case the agency is a collegiate organ, if it is competent to settle the dispute by a majority-vote decision.

The individual or the individuals appointed to settle the dispute are judges in the true sense of the term if they are independent, especially independent of the governments which have appointed them. That means that they are not legally bound by instructions with respect to the decision to be adopted by the tribunal. If they are independent, they are not representatives of the states which have appointed them. If they are not legally independent because they are legally bound by instructions referring to the content of their decision, they are representatives of the appointing state, agents of the appointing state, not judges. If the international agency is competent to settle the conflict by applying other principles than those of positive international law and—in case the agency is a collegiate organ—not by majority but by unanimous vote, it is usually not called a tribunal. The terminology, however, is not very consistent. An international agency competent to settle a conflict by majority vote may be called a tribunal, even a court, and may nevertheless be authorized to apply—under certain circumstances—other principles than those of positive law. Thus, for instance, the International Court of Justice may decide a case *ex aequo et bono* ("according to principles of equity") if the parties agree thereto (Article 38 of the Statute of the International Court of Justice).

The tribunal may consist of one individual or it may be a collegiate body. The parties to the dispute may, by agreement, confer upon the head of a third state, its minister of Foreign Affairs, the president of its supreme court, or any other person the power to settle the dispute by a decision binding upon them. If the tribunal is a collegiate body, it is usually composed of an uneven number of judges. A typical composition of an international tribunal is the one suggested by Article 45 of the Hague Convention for the pacific settlement of international disputes: each party appoints two members of whom one only shall be its national. These members together choose the fifth member.

The settlement of a dispute by the decision of an international tribunal is usually called arbitration, and the agreement entered into for this purpose, a treaty of arbitration. Such a treaty may be concluded after a dispute has arisen, and only for the settlement of this dispute. It may be concluded with respect to disputes which will arise in the future, either for the settlement of a definite category of disputes or for all disputes which may possibly arise between the contracting parties. By a treaty the parties may assume only the obligations to establish a tribunal in case a dispute arises, and to submit to this tribunal a dispute or disputes which may

Creation and Application of International Law 379

arise in the future; or they may immediately establish a tribunal and agree to submit to this tribunal a dispute or disputes which may arise in the future.

If the tribunal is competent to decide not only one dispute which has arisen prior to the establishment of the tribunal but an indefinite number of disputes which may arise after its establishment, the tribunal has a more or less permanent character. Such a permanent international tribunal may be established, not by a treaty concluded between the parties to an existing or future dispute, but by a number of states with the intention of giving to the contracting parties the opportunity to submit their disputes to this tribunal by a special agreement to be concluded by the parties to the dispute in each case as it arises; and the members of the tribunal may be appointed by an organ of the international community of which the tribunal is an organ. Such a permanent tribunal was the Permanent Court of International Justice established by the Protocol of Signature signed at Geneva, December 16, 1920, replaced now by the International Court of Justice established by the Charter of the United Nations.

It is usual to speak of judicial settlement of disputes in contradistinction to arbitration, in order to distinguish between decisions of these two courts and decisions of other international tribunals (e.g., in Article 12 of the Covenant and Article 33 of the Charter). But the difference between arbitration and judicial settlement of a dispute does not concern the function of the two Courts and other international tribunals, but their organization. The judges of the Permanent Court of International Justice were elected by the Assembly and the Council of the League of Nations, the judges of the International Court of Justice are elected by the General Assembly and the Security Council, whereas the members of other international tribunals—so-called tribunals of arbitration—are appointed partly directly, partly indirectly, by the states that are parties to the dispute or disputes to be settled by the tribunals.

The jurisdiction of an international tribunal is determined by the treaty establishing the tribunal. A permanent tribunal may have compulsory jurisdiction. Such compulsory jurisdiction exists if the treaty establishing the tribunal imposes upon the contracting parties the obligation to recognize the jurisdiction of the tribunal in every case in which they are involved, whether the case is brought before the tribunal by one of the parties or by an organ of the international community of which the tribunal is an organ, or in any other way determined by the treaty. Under general international law no state is obliged to submit a dispute with another state to an international tribunal. Such submission requires agreement of the parties to the dispute.[59]

As to the norms to be applied by an international tribunal, it is the existing customary and conventional international law which the tribunal, in settling the dispute, has to apply, unless the constituent treaty stipulates that the tribunal has to apply other norms, as, e.g., principles of equity or justice, and the like.

b. *Legal and political disputes.* According to a widespread opinion, existing international law is not applicable to all possible disputes between states, since there are disputes which, by their very nature, cannot be settled by the decision of an international tribunal applying existing international law to the dispute. Such disputes, frequently excluded in treaties of arbitration from the jurisdiction of international tribunals established by these treaties, are disputes which affect vital interests, or the independence, or the honor of a party to the dispute. The practice of states to exclude from the jurisdiction of international tribunals certain categories of disputes is backed by a doctrine according to which there exists an essential difference between legal and political disputes; in close connection with this difference a distinction is made between justiciable and nonjusticiable disputes.

The opinion prevails that only legal disputes are justiciable and hence suitable for submission to arbitration or judicial settlement, whereas political disputes can be settled only by the use of force

---

[59] In its advisory opinion in the *Eastern Carelia Case* (Publications of the Permanent Court of International Justice, Series B, No. 5, p. 27) the Permanent Court of International Justice (1923) stated: "It is well established in international law that no State can, without its consent, be compelled to submit its disputes with other States either to mediation or to arbitration, or to any other kind of pacific settlement. Such consent can be given once and for all in the form of an obligation freely undertaken, but it can, on the contrary, also be given in a special case apart from any existing obligation."

Creation and Application of International Law 381

or by agreement brought about by direct negotiation of the parties or by other means, especially conciliation. There exist treaties by which the parties assume the obligation to submit legal disputes to arbitration or judicial settlement, but political disputes to conciliation, as for instance the Treaty of Conciliation and Arbitration, signed by Germany and Switzerland at Berne, December 3, 1921, and the so-called Locarno Treaties, that is, the Treaties of Conciliation and Arbitration signed by Germany on the one hand and by Belgium, Czechoslovakia, France, and Poland, on the other hand, at London, December 1, 1925. But there are also treaties which stipulate that political disputes, if conciliation does not lead to an agreement of the parties, shall be submitted to arbitration or judicial settlement to be decided in accordance with principles other than those of positive international law, as, e.g., the treaty signed by Norway and Sweden, at Oslo, November 2, 1925, which provided that legal disputes shall be submitted to the Permanent Court of International Justice, and that other disputes, provided that they have first been submitted to conciliation, shall be submitted to arbitration to be settled in accordance with the principles of law and equity; or the treaty signed by Belgium and Sweden at Brussels, April 30, 1926, which provided that all legal disputes shall be submitted to the Permanent Court of International Justice, but other disputes to conciliation; and if conciliation does not lead to an agreement of the parties, to an arbitral tribunal which shall decide the dispute *ex aequo et bono*. The Charter of the United Nations provides for settlement of disputes by agreement of the parties brought about by negotiation, enquiry, mediation, conciliation, or recommendation by the Security Council or the General Assembly, but stipulates in Article 36, paragraph 3, that "legal disputes should as a general rule be referred by the parties to the International Court of Justice," without excluding the possibility of submitting such disputes to another international tribunal (Article 95).

The legal or political character of a dispute does not depend, as the traditional doctrine seems to assume, on the nature of the dispute, that is to say, on the subject matter to which the dispute refers, but on the nature of the norms to be applied in the settlement of the dispute. A dispute is a legal dispute if it is to be settled by the application of legal norms, that is to say, by the application of existing law. It is a political—that means not a legal—dispute if it is to be settled by the application of other norms—such as principles of equity, justice, and the like. Under general international law the states are obliged to settle their disputes in conformity with existing international law, but they are not obliged to submit their disputes to the decision of an international agency. They may or may not submit the dispute to such an agency; if they do so, they are free to determine what norms the agency has to apply—norms of existing international law or other norms. If a dispute to be settled by the application of norms other than those of existing international law is called a political dispute, it should not be overlooked that the difference between legal and political disputes is only a relative one. If the dispute is settled on the basis of a treaty by an agency, especially by a tribunal, authorized to settle the dispute by applying norms of justice, equity, and the like, the decision of the tribunal constitutes an individual legal norm, the parties to the dispute being legally obliged to comply with it. In such a case the difference between a legal and a political dispute is only the difference between a dispute to be settled by pre-existing international law and a dispute to be settled by international law to be created by the tribunal for the settlement of this dispute.

The usual definition of legal disputes is the one adopted by the so-called Locarno Treaties, referred to above.[60] In Article 1 of these treaties legal disputes are defined as "disputes of every kind . . . with regard to which the parties are in conflict as to their respective rights." This formula is not quite satisfactory, because it refers only to "rights," and "rights" may or may not be "legal" rights; and especially because it does not refer to legal obligations, which are in the first place involved. One state has a right only if the other has a corresponding obligation; and there is a dispute only if one claims to have a right and the other denies to be under a corresponding obligation. The legal character of a dispute depends on the attitude of the parties: whether one party justifies its claim

---

[60] Cf. *supra*, p. 381.

Creation and Application of International Law 383

and the other party rejects this claim by referring to existing international law.

If the parties to a dispute—to any dispute whatsoever—do not agree that this dispute shall be settled by the application of existing international law, there is no possibility of such a settlement by an international tribunal applying existing international law. But that does not mean that existing international law is not at all applicable to the dispute.[61] It certainly is applicable, and the parties are obliged to apply it if they do not agree to apply norms other than those of existing international law. If the statement that a political dispute is not justiciable means only that it cannot be settled by the decision of an international tribunal, then every dispute is not justiciable if the parties do not agree to submit it to a tribunal competent to settle it in accordance with existing international law. If, however, the statement that a dispute is not justiciable means that existing international law cannot be applied to it because of the very nature of the dispute, then there is no dispute which is not justiciable. There are only two possibilities: Existing international law imposes upon one of the parties, as the defendant, the obligation to behave in conformity with the claim of the other party, as the plaintiff; then in applying existing international law the tribunal has to decide the case in favor of the plaintiff. Or existing international law does not impose upon the defendant the obligation to behave as the plaintiff claims; then, again in applying existing international law, the tribunal has to decide the case in favor of the defendant, that is to say, to reject the claim of the plaintiff. What is not forbidden by the law is permitted by the law. If a state has no obligation to behave in a certain way, it is legally free to behave as it pleases.

Hence there is no dispute which by its very nature is excluded from the possibility of settlement by a decision applying existing international law. But the application of existing international law may, from one point of view or from another, be considered as not satisfactory. This may be a reason for not submitting the dispute to an international tribunal, but it cannot be a reason for excluding the application of existing international law to the settlement of

---

[61] Cf. *supra*, p. 306.

the dispute by the parties themselves, unless there is an agreement between them to have the dispute settled by the application of other norms.

Besides, the statement that the application of existing law is not satisfactory is a highly subjective, moral-political value judgment which may be set forth with respect to any legal norm of any legal order. As a rule, the application of existing law to a conflict of interests is always satisfactory to one and unsatisfactory to the other party. And even if it is admitted that existing international law is, from an objective point of view, unsatisfactory in many respects, such deficiency of international law can in no case justify the view which is at the basis of the distinction between justiciable and non-justiciable disputes: that there are conflicts between states which by their very nature cannot be solved by the application of existing international law.

This view is in close connection with the doctrine, considered in another connection,[62] that there are gaps in the law. Very characteristic in this respect is the General Act for the Pacific Settlement of International Disputes adopted by the Ninth Assembly of the League of Nations on September 26, 1928, which stipulated that legal disputes shall be submitted to arbitration or judicial settlement, and that other disputes, provided that conciliation does not lead to an agreement of the parties, shall be submitted to an arbitral tribunal, which shall apply the rules enumerated in Article 38 of the Statute of the Permanent Court of International Justice; which means the rules of existing law.[63] But it is added: "In so far as there exists no such rule applicable to the dispute, the tribunal shall decide *ex aequo et bono*." The General Act presupposes that there are cases to which the existing law is not applicable because this law does not contain a rule referring to the case, in other words, that there are gaps in the law.[64]

---

[62] Cf. *supra*, pp. 304ff.

[63] Cf. *infra*, pp. 393f.

[64] The Resolution 268 (III)A (Restoration to the General Act of September 26, 1928, of its original efficacy) adopted by the General Assembly at its 199th Plenary Meeting on April 28, 1949, instructed the Secretary-General "to prepare a revised text of the General Act," including certain amendments mentioned in the resolution, "and to hold it open to accession by States, under

If, however, the principle is recognized that what is legally not forbidden is legally permitted, a so-called gap in the law does not constitute a logical impossibility of applying the law, but a moral-political insufficiency of the existing law. Such defect may be due not only to the fact that the existing law does not establish an obligation which is considered to be desirable, or does establish an obligation which is considered to be too narrow, but also to the fact that the existing law does establish an obligation which is considered as undesirable or as too broad, from the point of view of a moral-political evaluation of the law. But traditional doctrine, not very consistently, assumes a gap in the law only in the first case. However, in both cases the existing law is logically applicable; and its nonapplication cannot be justified by the nature of the case, that is to say, by qualifying the case as one which by its very nature is nonjusticiable.

The erroneous view that the legal character of a dispute, and hence is justiciability, depends on the subject matter to which the dispute refers led to a definition laid down in Article 13 of the Covenant of the League of Nations: "1. The Members of the League agree that whenever any dispute shall arise between them which they recognise to be suitable for submission to arbitration or judicial settlement, and which cannot be satisfactorily settled by diplomacy, they will submit the whole subject-matter to arbitration or judicial settlement. 2. Disputes as to the interpretation of a treaty, as to any question of international law, as to the existence of any fact which, if established, would constitute a breach of any international obligation, or as to the extent and nature of the reparation to be made for any such breach, are declared to be among those which are generally suitable for submission to arbitration or judicial settlement." This formula was taken over by

---

the title 'Revised General Act for the Pacific Settlement of International Disputes.'" The amendments mentioned in the resolution "will only apply as between States having acceded to the General Act as thus amended and, as a consequence, will not affect the rights of such States, parties to the Act as established on 26 September 1928, as should claim to invoke it in so far as it might still be operative." The provision of the General Act referred to above is amended only insofar as the words "Permanent Court of International Justice" are replaced by "International Court of Justice."

the Statute of the Permanent Court of International Justice and the Statute of the International Court of Justice. The latter refers in Article 36, paragraph 2, to "legal disputes" and enumerates as such disputes concerning the matters mentioned in Article 13, paragraph 2, of the Covenant.

This enumeration is, logically, very problematical, since one of the enumerated matters, "any question of international law," covers the three others. Besides, if the parties to a dispute agree to submit it to the International Court of Justice or another international tribunal competent to settle the dispute in accordance with existing international law, the dispute is a legal dispute whatever its subject matter might be; and if they do not agree that the dispute shall be decided in accordance with existing international law, the dispute is not a legal dispute, even if it concerns the interpretation of a treaty or the question of reparation. In addition, if the parties submit the dispute to the Court but agree that the Court shall decide the case *ex aequo et bono* in conformity with Article 38, paragraph 2, of the statute,[65] the dispute is not a legal dispute, neither within the meaning of the usual definition nor within the meaning of the definition suggested in this treatise.

c. *Settlement of disputes by the International Court of Justice.* (1) THE PERMANENT COURT OF ARBITRATION AND THE PERMANENT COURT OF INTERNATIONAL JUSTICE. The first attempt to establish a permanent international tribunal was made by the Hague Convention for the pacific settlement of international disputes. According to Article 20 of the original Convention of 1899, the contracting parties undertook "to organize a Permanent Court of Arbitration, accessible at all times and operating, unless otherwise stipulated by the parties, in accordance with the rules of procedure laid down in the Convention." By Article 41 of the Convention of 1907 the contracting parties agreed to maintain this Court. According to Article 44 of the Convention of 1907, "Each contracting Power selects four persons at the most, of known competency in questions of international law, of the highest moral reputation, and disposed to accept the duties of arbitrator. The persons thus selected are inscribed, as members of the Court, in a list which shall

---

[65] Cf. *infra*, p. 393.

Creation and Application of International Law 387

be notified to all the contracting Powers by the Bureau. . . . The members of the Court are appointed for a term of six years. These appointments are renewable." Article 45 stipulates: "When the contracting Powers wish to have recourse to the Permanent Court for the settlement of a difference which has arisen between them, the arbitrators called upon to form the tribunal with jurisdiction to decide this difference must be chosen from the general list of members of the Court. Failing the direct agreement of the parties on the composition of the arbitration tribunal, the following course shall be pursued: Each party appoints two arbitrators, of whom one only can be its national or chosen from among the persons selected by it as members of the Permanent Court. These arbitrators together choose an umpire." The so-called Permanent Court of Arbitration was nothing but a list of persons out of which the judges forming a tribunal of arbitration could be chosen. The purpose of the convention was, as Article 41 expressly stated, to facilitate an immediate recourse to arbitration of international differences, not to establish directly a working tribunal.[66]

This has been done by the Covenant of the League of Nations and, on its basis, by a special treaty, the so-called Protocol of Signature of the Statute of the Permanent Court of International Justice, of December 16, 1920. Article 14 of the Covenant author-

---

[66] On December 20, 1907, five Central American states, Costa Rica, Guatemala, Honduras, Nicaragua, and Salvador, signed at Washington a convention for the establishment of a Central American Court of Justice. The court was composed of five judges, one being appointed by each of the contracting states (Article VI). The convention imposed upon the parties the obligation to submit to the court "all controversies or questions which may arise among them, of whatever nature and no matter what their origin may be, in case the respective Departments of Foreign Affairs should not have been able to reach an understanding" (Article I). The court should "also take cognizance of the questions which individuals of one Central American country may raise against any of the other contracting Governments, because of the violation of treaties or conventions, and other cases of an international character; no matter whether their own Government supports said claim or not; and provided that the remedies which the laws of the respective country provide against such violation shall have been exhausted or that denial of justice shall have been shown" (Article II). The court was established for a period of ten years (Article XXVII). After this period expired in 1918, the court ceased to exist. As to the full text of the convention, cf. *2 American Journal of International Law* (1908), Supplement, pp. 231ff.

ized the Council to "formulate and submit to the Members of the League for adoption plans for the establishment of a Permanent Court of International Justice." The draft statute of the Court, prepared by an advisory committee of jurists appointed by the Council, after examination by the Council, was approved by a resolution of the Assembly on December 13, 1920. This resolution provided that the statute "shall be submitted within the shortest possible time to the Members of the League of Nations for adoption in the form of a Protocol duly ratified and declaring their recognition of this Statute. . . . The said Protocol shall likewise remain open for signature by the States mentioned in the Annex to the Covenant." (In this annex the states were mentioned which were intended to be the original members of the League, and the states which were invited to accede to the Covenant.) The Permanent Court of International Justice, established on this basis, was not an organ of the League of Nations, but of a community different from the League, constituted by the Protocol of December 16, 1920. Not all members of this community were members of the League and not all members of the League were members of this community.

(2) THE INTERNATIONAL COURT OF JUSTICE. The Permanent Court of International Justice was replaced by the International Court of Justice, an organ of the United Nations. The statute of this Court, which forms an integral part of the Charter of the United Nations, is almost identical with the Statute of the Permanent Court of International Justice. The main provisions of the new statute are as follows:

(a) Organization of the Court. "The Court shall be composed of a body of independent judges, elected regardless of their nationality from among persons of high moral character, who possess the qualifications required in their respective countries for appointment to the highest judicial offices, or are juris-consults of recognized competence in international law" (Article 2). "The Court shall consist of fifteen members, no two of whom may be nationals of the same state" (Article 3, paragraph 1). "The members of the Court shall be elected by the General Assembly and by the Security Council from a list of persons nominated by the national groups in the Permanent Court of Arbitration, . . ." (Article 4, paragraph 1). A "national group" is formed by the persons (four at the most) selected by the contracting parties to the Hague Convention for the pacific settlement of international disputes according to Article 44 of this convention.[67] "In the case of Members of the United Nations not represented in the Permanent Court of Arbitration, candidates shall be nominated by national groups appointed for this purpose by their governments under the same conditions as those prescribed for members of the Permanent Court of Arbitration by Article 44 of the Convention of The Hague of 1907 for the pacific settlement of international disputes" (Article 4, paragraph 2). No national "group may nominate more than four persons, not more than two of whom shall be of their own nationality. In no case may the number of candidates nominated by a group be more than double the number of seats to be filled" (Article 5, paragraph 2). "Before making these nominations, each national group is recommended to consult its highest court of justice, its legal faculties and schools of law, and its national academies and national sections of international academies devoted to the study of law" (Article 6). "The Secretary-General shall prepare a list in alphabetical order of all the persons thus nominated" and "submit this list to the General Assembly and to the Security Council" (Article 7). "The General Assembly and the Security Council shall proceed independently of one another to elect the members of the Court" (Article 8). "At every election, the electors shall bear in mind not only that the persons to be elected should individually possess the qualifications required, but also that in the body as a whole the representation of the main forms of civilization and of the principal legal systems of the world should be assured" (Article 9). "Those candidates who obtain an absolute majority of votes in the General Assembly and in the Security Council shall be considered as elected" (Article 10, paragraph 1). "The members of the Court shall be elected for nine years and may be re-elected; provided, however, that of the judges elected at the first election, the terms of five judges shall expire at the end of three years and the terms of five more judges shall expire at the end of six years" (Article

---

[67] Cf. *supra*, pp. 367f., 378.

13, paragraph 1). "The Court shall elect its President and Vice-President for three years; they may be re-elected" (Article 21, paragraph 1). "The seat of the Court shall be established at The Hague. This, however, shall not prevent the Court from sitting and exercising its functions elsewhere whenever the Court considers it desirable" (Article 22, paragraph 1). "The Court shall remain permanently in session, except during the judicial vacations, the dates and duration of which shall be fixed by the Court" (Article 23, paragraph 1). The independence and impartiality of the judges is guaranteed by the following provisions: "No member of the Court may exercise any political or administrative function, or engage in any other occupation of a professional nature" (Article 16, paragraph 1). "No member of the Court may act as agent, counsel, or advocate in any case. No member may participate in the decision of any case in which he has previously taken part as agent, counsel, or advocate for one of the parties, or as a member of a national or international court, or of a commission of enquiry, or in any other capacity" (Article 17, paragraphs 1 and 2). "No member of the Court can be dismissed unless, in the unanimous opinion of the other members, he has ceased to fulfil the required conditions" (Article 18, paragraph 1). "The members of the Court, when engaged on the business of the Court, shall enjoy diplomatic privileges and immunities" (Article 19). "Every member of the Court, shall, before taking up his duties, make a solemn declaration in open court that he will exercise his powers impartially and conscientiously" (Article 20). "If, for some special reason, a member of the Court considers that he should not take part in the decision of a particular case, he shall so inform the President. If the President considers that for some special reason one of the members of the Court should not sit in a particular case, he shall give him notice accordingly. If in any such case the member of the Court and the President disagree, the matter shall be settled by the decision of the Court" (Article 24). Judges who are of the nationality of the parties to the case before the Court are not excluded from sitting in the case. But if "the Court includes upon the Bench a judge of the nationality of one of the parties, any other party may choose a person to sit as judge. Such persons shall be chosen

Creation and Application of International Law 391

preferably from among those persons who have been nominated as candidates as provided in Articles 4 and 5. If the Court includes upon the Bench no judge of the nationality of the parties, each of these parties may proceed to choose a judge as provided in paragraph 2 of this Article" (Article 31, paragraphs 2 and 3). This is the institution of "national judges."

(b) Competence of the Court. "Only states may be parties in cases before the Court" (Article 34, paragraph 1). Neither individuals as private persons nor international organizations have access to the Court. The Court is open to the members of the United Nations, which are all parties to the Statute, the Statute being an integral part of the Charter. Article 93 of the Charter expressly stipulates: "All Members of the United Nations are *ipso facto* parties to the Statute of the International Court of Justice." The same article provides: "A state which is not a Member of the United Nations may become a party to the Statute of the International Court of Justice on conditions to be determined in each case by the General Assembly upon the recommendation of the Security Council." In this way Switzerland became a party to the statute without becoming a member of the United Nations, that is to say, a party to the Charter of the United Nations in the wider sense of the term (including the statute). In conformity with Article 93 of the Charter, the statute stipulates that the Court shall be open to the states parties to the statute (Article 35, paragraph 1). But the Court is open also to states which are not parties to the statute within the meaning of Article 93 of the Charter. The conditions under which the Court is open to such states shall be laid down "by the Security Council, but in no case shall such conditions place the parties in a position of inequality before the Court" (Article 35, paragraph 2).

The parties to the statute (members and nonmembers of the United Nations) are not obliged to submit disputes to the Court. But they may do so. A case may be brought before the Court by a special agreement of the parties to the dispute. In this way any dispute whatsoever may be submitted to the Court. Such a special agreement is not necessary and the case may be brought before the Court by a written application addressed by one party to the

Court (Article 40, paragraph 1), if the parties to the dispute have previously made a declaration determined in Article 36 of the statute, which provides: "The states parties to the present Statute may at any time declare that they recognize as compulsory *ipso facto* and without special agreement, in relation to any other state accepting the same obligation, the jurisdiction of the Court in all legal disputes concerning: a. the interpretation of a treaty; b. any question of international law; c. the existence of any fact which, if established, would constitute a breach of an international obligation; d. the nature or extent of the reparation to be made for the breach of an international obligation" (Article 36, paragraph 2). This declaration "may be made unconditionally or on condition of reciprocity on the part of several or certain states, or for a certain time" (Article 36, paragraph 3).

The jurisdiction of the Court recognized by a declaration made under Article 36, paragraph 2, of the statute is not a true compulsory jurisdiction as it is called in this article. For, if a state which has made such a declaration brings a dispute with another state before the Court by a unilateral application in conformity with Article 40 of the statute, the other party is obliged to recognize the jurisdiction of the Court only if it, too, has made the same declaration. That means that the jurisdiction of the Court in this case is based, not on a special agreement referring to this concrete case, but on a general agreement of the parties to the dispute constituted by their declarations made under Article 36, paragraph 2. Declarations under Article 36, paragraph 2, of the statute have been made by several states, some of them under reservations which deprive them of almost all practical value.[68]

---

[68] Thus, e.g., the United States recognized the jurisdiction of the Court in disputes concerning the matters enumerated in Article 36, paragraph 2 of the statute "*Provided,* that this declaration shall not apply to a. disputes the solution of which the parties shall entrust to other tribunals by virtue of agreements already in existence or which may be concluded in the future; or b. disputes with regard to matters which are essentially within the domestic jurisdiction of the United States of America as determined by the United States of America; or c. disputes arising under a multilateral treaty, unless (1) all parties to the treaty affected by the decision are also parties to the case before the Court, or (2) the United States of America specially agrees to jurisdiction; and *Provided further,* that this declaration shall remain in force for a period of

Creation and Application of International Law 393

As to the law to be applied by the Court, Article 38 of the statute provides: "1. The Court, whose function is to decide in accordance with international law such disputes as are submitted to it, shall apply: a. international conventions, whether general or particular, establishing rules expressly recognized by the contesting states; b. international custom, as evidence of a general practice accepted as law; c. the general principles of law recognized by civilized nations; d. subject to the provisions of Article 59, judicial decisions and the teachings of the most highly qualified publicists of the various nations, as subsidiary means for the determination of rules of law. 2. This provision shall not prejudice the power of the Court to decide a case *ex aequo et bono,* if the parties agree thereto."

That the Court has to apply the existing conventional and customary law (clauses [a] and [b]) is self-evident and did not need to be stipulated. As to "the general principles of law recognized by civilized nations" (clause [c]), it is doubtful whether such principles common to the legal orders of the civilized nations exist at all, especially in view of the ideological antagonism which separates the communist from the capitalist, and the autocratic from the democratic legal systems. If the Court assumes that a general principle of law recognized by civilized nations exists, the question arises under what conditions the Court is supposed to apply this principle to the case at hand. If there is a treaty to which the states involved in the dispute are contracting parties, and if the treaty refers to the dispute, the treaty is to be applied (clause [a]). If there is no treaty, general customary international law is to be applied. This, as pointed out, is always possible. But clause (c) evidently presupposes the idea that there are gaps in international law. That means that the Court is authorized to apply a rule which the Court considers to be a general principle of law in case the Court deems the application of particular conventional or general customary international law not satisfactory, which implies an almost unlimited discretion on the part of the Court.

It is, however, doubtful whether the framers of the statute

---

five years and thereafter until the expiration of six months after notice may be given to terminate this declaration." That the jurisdiction of a court recognized under these reservations is not "compulsory" is quite evident.

really intended to confer upon the Court such an extraordinary power. Article 38, paragraph 1, expressly stipulates that the function of the Court is "to decide in accordance with international law." Hence it might be argued that "the general principles of law" are applicable only if they are part of international law, and that means part of the law referred to in clauses (a) and (b) of Article 38. Then, clause (c) is superfluous. Clause (d) does not refer to rules of international law to be applied by the Court; it establishes only a principle of interpretation. Article 59, to which clause (d) refers, stipulates that the decision of the Court has binding force only between the parties and only in respect to the particular case. Hence a decision of the Court cannot have the character of a precedent.

(c) Procedure of the Court. "The procedure shall consist of two parts: written and oral. The written proceedings shall consist of the communication to the Court and to the parties of memorials, counter-memorials and, if necessary, replies; also all papers and documents in support. . . . The oral proceedings shall consist of the hearing by the Court of witnesses, experts, agents, counsel, and advocates" (Article 43, paragraphs 1, 2, and 5). "The hearing in Court shall be public, unless the Court shall decide otherwise, or unless the parties demand that the public be not admitted" (Article 46). "All questions shall be decided by a majority of the judges present. In the event of an equality of votes, the President or the judge who acts in his place shall have a casting vote" (Article 55). "The judgment shall state the reasons on which it is based. It shall contain the names of the judges who have taken part in the decision" (Article 56). "If the judgment does not represent in whole or in part the unanimous opinion of the judges, any judge shall be entitled to deliver a separate opinion" (Article 57). "The judgment is final and without appeal. In the event of dispute as to the meaning or scope of the judgment, the Court shall construe it upon the request of any party" (Article 60). "An application for revision of a judgment may be made only when it is based upon the discovery of some fact of such a nature as to be a decisive factor, which fact was, when the judgment was given, unknown to the Court and also to the party claiming revision, always provided that such ignorance was not due to negligence. . . . The applica-

Creation and Application of International Law 395

tion for revision must be made at latest within six months of the discovery of the new fact. No application for revision may be made after the lapse of ten years from the date of the judgment" (Article 61, paragraphs 1, 4, and 5). The provision of Article 60 of the statute, that the decision of the Court is without appeal, is not consistent with the provision of Article 94, paragraph 2, of the Charter, that in case any party fails to comply with the decision of the Court, the other party may have recourse to the Security Council, which may settle the case in a way different from the decision of the Court. This provision will be discussed later.[69]

(d) Advisory opinions. Article 96 of the Charter authorizes the General Assembly and the Security Council to request the Court "to give an advisory opinion on any legal question. Other organs of the United Nations and specialized agencies, which may at any time be so authorized by the General Assembly, may also request advisory opinions of the Court on legal questions arising within the scope of their activities." Article 65 of the statute authorizes the Court to "give an advisory opinion on any legal question at the request of whatever body may be authorized by or in accordance with the Charter of the United Nations to make such a request. Questions upon which the advisory opinion of the Court is asked shall be laid before the Court by means of a written request containing an exact statement of the question upon which an opinion is required, and accompanied by all documents likely to throw light upon the question."

d. *Execution of decisions of international tribunals.* When states by a treaty of arbitration submit their dispute to an international tribunal, they assume the obligation to comply with the decision of the tribunal. There are, however, conditions under which a State is justified in not complying with the decision of an international tribunal. It is generally recognized that the decision of an international tribunal may be considered to be null and void or annullable if the tribunal has transgressed the competence conferred upon it by the treaty of arbitration (excess of jurisdiction).[70] But

---

[69] Cf. *infra*, p. 397.

[70] The cases are very rare in which parties to a dispute submitted to an international tribunal refused to comply with its decision. Such cases are the North-Eastern Boundary dispute between Great Britain and the United States,

who is competent to interpret the treaty of arbitration in this respect? The contracting states, parties to the dispute, or the tribunal, or both?

According to the principle that he who has to apply a legal norm is competent to interpret the norm, each contracting party is competent to interpret the treaty of arbitration insofar as that party has to apply the treaty by executing the decision of the tribunal. But the tribunal, too, is competent to interpret the treaty of arbitration since it has to apply the treaty by making the decision. The treaty conferring jurisdiction upon the tribunal may have the meaning that the contracting parties have renounced their right to interpret the treaty with respect to the competence of the tribunal. If, however, that renunciation is not expressly stipulated, the contracting parties are in a position to insist on their right to interpret the treaty of arbitration, and to declare not to be bound by the decision if the tribunal has transgressed its competence. As long as the contracting parties have the right to interpret the treaty of arbitration with respect to the competence of the tribunal, the execution of the decision depends, actually, on their good will. Misuse of the right of interpretation is excluded only if the parties renounce this right by conferring upon the tribunal the exclusive right to interpret the stipulations of the treaty determining its competence. The Statute of the International Court of Justice provides that "in the event of a dispute as to whether the Court has jurisdiction, the matter shall be settled by the decision of the Court" (Article 36, paragraph 6). Hence no party to a dispute can declare a decision of the Court as null and void because the Court has—according to the opinion of the party—transgressed its competence (jurisdiction).

---

decided by the King of Holland, 1831; the boundary dispute between Bolivia and Peru, decided by the President of Argentina, 1909; the dispute concerning the Orinoco Steamship Company between the United States and Venezuela, decided by Mr. Barge, whose decision was annulled by a tribunal of the Permanent Court of Arbitration, 1910; the dispute between Hungary and Rumania concerning certain claims by Hungarian citizens in connection with an agrarian reform in Rumania, decided by the Rumano-Hungarian Mixed Tribunal, 1927. In all these cases the reason for noncompliance with the arbitral decision was excess of jurisdiction of the tribunal. Cf. Oppenheim, *op. cit.*, II, § 16.

Under general international law, noncompliance with the decision of an international tribunal constitutes an international delict which entails all the consequences provided for by general international law. The party whose right is violated by the other party's failure to comply with the decision of the tribunal is authorized to resort to reprisals or war against the delinquent. Under the Charter, self-help in such a case is excluded. Only the Security Council has the power to use force against the delinquent state, and only if the Council under Article 39 considers noncompliance with the decision of the tribunal as a threat to or breach of the peace. The situation is slightly different in case of noncompliance with a judgment of the International Court of Justice. In this respect Article 94 of the Charter stipulates expressly an obligation to comply with the decision of the Court. If, however, "any party to a case fails to perform the obligations incumbent upon it under a judgment rendered by the Court, the other party may have recourse to the Security Council, which may, if it deems necessary, make recommendations or decide upon measures to be taken to give effect to the judgment." That means that the Security Council has the choice between two different procedures. It may give effect to the judgment of the Court, especially by taking enforcement measures against the state which fails to comply with the judicial decision. But the Security Council may also, if it deems necessary, make recommendations to the parties concerning the settlement of the dispute. According to the wording of Article 94, the Council in making such recommendations is not bound by the decision of the Court; its recommendations may differ from this decision.[71] The Council may even enforce its recommendation if it considers noncompliance with it as a threat to or breach of the peace. The rule of Article 27, paragraph 3, of the Charter, that members of the Security Council which are parties to a dispute under consideration by the Council shall abstain from voting, does not apply to decisions taken under Article 94.

---

[71] This is the interpretation of Article 94 given by the representative of the Department of State in the *Hearings before the Committee on Foreign Relations of the United States Senate on the Charter of the United Nations* (79th Cong., July 9–13, 1945), pp. 285ff.

V.
INTERNATIONAL AND NATIONAL LAW

A. THE DIFFERENCES BETWEEN INTERNATIONAL AND NATIONAL LAW

International law, as has been shown in the first part of this treatise, is law in the same sense as national law, for it is a coercive order, a set of norms providing for socially organized sanctions to be executed as reactions against delicts. But international law differs from national law in many respects. Whereas the main sanctions established by international law are reprisals and war, the sanctions of national law are punishment and civil execution. The difference which exists between punishment and civil execution constitutes the differentiation of national law into criminal and civil law; but the difference between reprisals and war does not justify a division of international law into two branches analogous to criminal and civil law. International law—at least insofar as the bulk of its norms is concerned—does not show that dualistic structure so characteristic of national law. However, punishment and civil execution are not completely missing in international law. Exceptionally, there are norms of general as well as of particular international law which provide for punishment and civil execution,[1] so that the difference between the two legal orders, with respect to the sanctions they provide, is only a relative, not an absolute, one.

In close connection with this difference is the fact that in international law collective responsibility prevails, whereas in national law individual responsibility is prevalent, as well as the fact that the collective responsibility constituted by the specific sanctions of international law—reprisals and war—is, as far as the responsible individuals are concerned, absolute responsibility, whereas the individual responsibility constituted by the specific sanctions of national law—punishment and civil execution—is, as a rule, responsibility based on fault. But neither is individual responsibility based on fault excluded from international law, nor collective and absolute responsibility from national law. In this respect, too, the difference between international law and national law is only a relative one.

---
[1] Cf. *supra*, p. 124.

A striking diversity results from the fact that the spheres of validity of international law are, in principle, unlimited, whereas national law, as the law of a state, is valid only for a definite territory and during a definite period of time. But the traditional view that international law is valid only for states as juristic persons, whereas national law is valid for individual human beings, has proved to be wrong. There is no difference between international and national law with respect to the subjects of the obligations and rights established by the two legal orders. The subjects are in both cases individual human beings. But whereas the national legal order determines directly the individuals who, by their behavior, have to fulfill the obligations or may exercise the rights, the international legal order leaves to the national legal order the determination of the individuals whose behavior forms the content of the international obligations and rights. The obligations and rights which the state has under international law are the obligations and rights which individuals have in their capacity as organs of the state; and these individuals are determined by national law, the law of the state. But, just as there are, exceptionally, norms of international law imposing obligations and conferring rights, not upon states as juristic persons, but directly upon individuals, there are norms of national law imposing obligations and conferring rights upon juristic persons, and thus only indirectly upon individuals. Again, the two legal orders differ only in degree, not in essence.

The most important difference between international and national law consists in the fact that the former is a relatively decentralized, the latter a relatively centralized coercive order. This difference manifests itself in the methods by which the norms of the two orders are created and applied. Custom and treaties, the main "sources" of international law, are decentralized methods; the main source of national law, legislation, is a centralized method of creating law. In contradistinction to national law, which confers upon tribunals the competence of applying the law and upon special organs the exclusive power to use force in executing the sanctions, there are under general international law no special organs for the application of the law and especially no central agencies for the execution of the sanctions. These functions are left to the states, which are subjects of international law. But under particular international law, the creation as well as the application of the law may be—and actually is—centralized; and this process of centralization is steadily increasing by the establishment of international organizations instituting international tribunals and international executive agencies.

B. THE RELATIONSHIP BETWEEN INTERNATIONAL AND NATIONAL LAW (MONISM AND PLURALISM)

1. The Monistic and the Pluralistic Theory

The foregoing analysis of international law has shown that most of its norms are incomplete norms which require implementation by norms of national law.[2] Thus the international legal order is significant only as part of a universal legal order which comprises also all the national legal orders. The analysis has further led to the conclusion that the international legal order determines the territorial, personal, and temporal spheres of validity of the national legal orders, thus making possible the coexistence of a multitude of states.[3] We have, finally, seen that the international legal order restricts the material sphere of validity of the national legal orders by subjecting them to a certain regulation of their own matters that could otherwise have been arbitrarily regulated by the state concerned.[4]

It is from the standpoint of international law that its connection with national law and hence with a universal legal order is seen in the preceding analysis. But, however strange it may seem, most theorists of international law do not share this monistic view. In their construction of the relationship between international and national law they do not proceed from international law as their

---

[2] Cf. *supra*, pp. 192ff.
[3] Cf. *supra*, pp. 206ff.
[4] Cf. *supra*, pp. 240ff.

starting point. International law and national law are, in their opinion, two separate, mutually independent legal orders that regulate quite different matters and have quite different sources.

This dualism or—taking into account the existence of numerous national legal orders—this pluralism contradicts, as we have seen, the content of international law, since international law itself establishes a relation between its norms and the norms of the different national legal orders. The pluralistic theory is in contradiction to positive law, provided international law is considered to be a valid legal order. And yet the representatives of this theory accept international law as positive law.

But the pluralistic view is untenable also on logical grounds. International law and national law cannot be different and mutually independent systems of norms if the norms of both systems are considered to be valid for the same space and at the same time. It is logically not possible to assume that simultaneously valid norms belong to different, mutually independent systems.

The pluralists do not deny that the norms of international law and the norms of national law are simultaneously valid. On the contrary, assuming both legal orders to be valid simultaneously, they assert that the one is valid independently of the other; which means that no relation exists between the two systems of valid norms. This, however, as we shall see, implies a contradiction.

2. *The Subject Matter of National and of International Law*

The mutual independence of international and national law is often substantiated by the alleged fact that the two systems regulate different subject matters. National law, it is said, regulates the behavior of individuals, international law the behavior of states. We have already shown that the behavior of a state is reducible to the behavior of individuals representing the state. Thus the alleged difference in subject matter between international and national law cannot be a difference between the kinds of subjects whose behavior they regulate.

The pluralistic interpretation is also supported by the assertion that, whereas national law regulates relations that have their seat within one state, international law regulates relations which transcend the sphere of one state. Or, as it is also put, whereas national law is concerned with the "internal" relations, the so-called "domestic affairs" of the state, international law is concerned with the "external" relations of the state, its "foreign affairs." One visualizes the state as a solid, space-filling body, with an interior structure and exterior relations to other subjects. When we try to find the thought behind the metaphor, and to formulate it without employing a metaphor, we arrive at the conclusion that the thought is wrong.

For it is impossible to distinguish the so-called "domestic affairs" from the "foreign affairs" of the state as two different subject matters of legal regulation. Every so-called domestic affair of a state can be made the subject matter of an international agreement and so be transformed into a foreign affair. The relation between employers and employees, for instance, is certainly an "internal" relationship within the state, and its legal regulation a typical "domestic" affair. But as soon as a state concludes a treaty with other states concerning the regulation of this relationship, it becomes a foreign affair. If we discard the spatial metaphor, we thus find that the attempted distinction between the subject matters of national and international law is a mere tautology. The so-called "domestic affairs" of a state are, by definition, those which are regulated by the national law; the "foreign affairs" are, by definition, those which are regulated by international law. The assertion that national law regulates domestic affairs, and international law foreign affairs, boils down to the truism that national law regulates what is regulated by national law, international law what is regulated by international law.

Still there remains a certain truth in the statement that international law is "interstate" law, whereas national law is, so to speak, one-state law. But, as pointed out,[5] this differentiation does not concern the subject matter; it concerns the creation of international and national law. Whereas national law is created by acts of one state alone (or by acts which are not acts of state), international

---

[5] Cf. *supra*, pp. 201f.

law is usually created by the cooperation of two or several states. This holds true of customary international law as well as of conventional international law.

There are, it is true, certain matters specific to international law, matters which can be regulated only by norms created by the collaboration of two or several states. These matters are—as pointed out[6]—the determination of the spheres of validity of the national legal orders and the procedures of creating international law itself. But there is no subject matter which can be regulated only by national law and not by international law. Every matter that is, or can be, regulated by national law is open to regulation by international law as well. It is therefore impossible to substantiate the pluralistic view by a difference in subject matter between international and national law.

3. The "Source" of National and of International Law

In support of the pluralistic theory, it has been argued that the different systems of norms come from different sources. The term "source" of law is another metaphorical expression which, as we have seen,[7] carries at least two different connotations. A "source" of law is, on the one hand, a procedure by which norms are created; on the other hand, the reason why norms are valid. Let us, to begin with, see how the argument fares if the term is understood in the former sense.

The distinction between two "sources" of law refers to the distinction between custom and legislation (in the wider meaning of any statutory, that is, conscious and deliberate, creation of law).[8] When one regards custom as a source of law, one presupposes the principle that the individuals ought to behave as they customarily behave. When one considers legislation (in the wider sense) as a source of law, one assumes that the individuals ought to behave as special organs authorized to create law by their acts ordain or as the individuals themselves agree to behave. Legislation, in the

---

[6] Cf. *supra*, p. 202.
[7] Cf. *supra*, pp. 303f.
[8] Cf. *supra*, pp. 307ff.

International and National Law 407

usual narrower sense, is only a special case of statutory creation of law, namely, the creation of a general norm by a special organ. But an individual norm, too, may have the character of statutory —in contradistinction to customary—law, as, for instance, a judicial decision or a norm created by contract or treaty.

As pointed out, both methods of creating law, the customary and the statutory law, occur in international as well as in national law. General international law, it is true, does not recognize legislation and lawmaking by the judiciary, the two most important methods of creating norms in the modern state. But courts and legislative organs can be created by treaty, which is itself a method of creating statutory law. The decisions of an international court are norms of international law, and so also are certain decisions of the General Assembly or the Security Council of the United Nations which bind the members of the Organization and thus are analogous to statutes of national law. Nothing prevents the creation by treaty of a collegiate international organ that is competent to pass majority resolutions binding upon the states parties to the treaty. If the centralization effected by the treaty does not go too far, such decisions would still be norms of international law (without having at the same time the character of national law).

Since in international law, legislation and judicial lawmaking are possible only on the basis of a treaty, and the binding force of treaties is based on a rule of customary international law, it may be said that the primary source (in the sense of method of lawmaking) of international law is custom and treaty, whereas the primary source of national law is custom and legislation. Further, it is true that custom and treaty, creating international law, involve the cooperation of two or several states, whereas custom and legislation creating national law are functions of the subjects or organs of one state only. The methods of lawmaking are thus, in this respect, different in national and international law; but this is not a difference in principle. The difference between custom and legislation as sources of national law is far greater than that between a treaty of international law and a contract of national law. And even if national law were created in a totally different way from that in which international law is created—which is not the case—such a difference in the sources would not mean that the norms created in different ways belong to different and mutually independent systems.

4. The Reason of Validity of National and of International Law

a. *The reason of validity of the national legal order determined by the international legal order.* The expression "source" of law is, as we have seen, sometimes understood to mean simply the reason why a norm is valid. If this is the meaning of the term, the argument that international and national law are separate systems because they have separate "sources" amounts to the statement that the ultimate reason of validity of national law is different from that of international law.

In this way the problem as to the relation between national and international law has already been formulated, especially in German literature. But the answer usually offered—that the validity of national law has its reason in the "will" of one state, whereas the validity of international law is based on the "combined wills" of several states—is only an anthropomorphic metaphor. A critical analysis discloses that the metaphor hides an empty tautology.

In order to answer the question whether the reason of validity of national law is or is not different from that of international law, and consequently, whether national and international law are different and mutually independent legal orders or form one universal normative system, in order to reach a decision between pluralism and monism, we have to consider the general problem of what makes a norm belong to a definite legal order, what is the criterion according to which several norms form one and the same normative system.[9]

Several norms belong to the same legal order if all derive their validity from the same basic norm. The question why a norm is valid necessarily leads back to an ultimate norm whose validity we do not question. If several norms all receive their validity from

---
[9] Cf. my *General Theory of Law and State* (1945), pp. 110ff.

the same basic norm, then—by definition—they all form part of the same system. The question why a norm is a norm of American law or of international law is thus a question of the basic norm of the American and of the international law. To determine the relationship between national and international law, we have to examine whether the norms of the two legal orders derive their validity from different basic norms or from the same basic norm.

According to the nature of the basic norm we may distinguish two different principles constituting the unity of a normative order or a normative system: a static and a dynamic principle. According to the static principle, the norms are valid, and that means we assume that the individuals whose behavior is regulated by the norms ought to behave as the norms prescribe, by virtue of their contents—their contents having an immediately evident quality that guarantees their validity; or, in other terms, the norms are valid because of their inherent appeal.

The norms have this quality because their validity is derivable from a higher, i.e., more general norm, as the particular is derivable from the general. The validity of the higher norm is itself self-evident, or, at least, presumed to be so. Such norms as one must not lie, one must not deceive, one must keep one's promise follow from a general norm prescribing truthfulness. From the norm one must love one's neighbor, such norms as one must not hurt one's neighbor, one must help him in need, and so on, may be deduced. If it is asked why one has to love one's neighbor, the answer will perhaps be found in some still more general norm, let us say, the postulate that one has to live in harmony with the universe. If that is the most general norm of whose validity we are convinced, we will consider it as the ultimate or basic norm. Its validity may appear so obvious that one does not feel any need to ask for the reason for its validity.

The various norms of such a normative system are implied in the basic norm, as the particular is implied in the general. Therefore all the particular norms are obtainable by means of an intellectual operation, namely, by the inference from the general to the particular. The principle constituting the unity of this normative system is of a static nature. It is characterized by the fact that not only the validity but also the contents of the norms forming the normative system can be derived by an intellectual operation from the basic norm presupposed to be self-evident.

The validity of a particular norm may, however, be derived from a basic norm in another way. A child, asking why he must not lie, might be given the answer that his father has forbidden him to lie. If the child should further ask why he has to obey his father, the reply would perhaps be that God has commanded that a child obey his parents. Should the child put the question why one has to obey the commands of God, the only answer could be that this is a norm beyond which one cannot look for a more ultimate norm. That norm is the basic norm providing the foundation for a system the unity of which has a dynamic character. The validity of all the norms of this system is derived from the basic norm, but not their contents. The contents of its various norms cannot be obtained from the basic norm by any intellectual operation. The basic norm merely establishes a certain authority, which may well in turn vest norm-creating power in some other authorities. The norms of a dynamic system have to be created through acts by those individuals who have been authorized by a higher norm to create norms. This authorization is a delegation. Norm-creating power is delegated from one authority to another authority; the former is the higher, the latter the lower authority. The basic norm of a dynamic system is the fundamental rule according to which the norms of the system are to be created. A norm forms part of a dynamic system if it has been created in a way determined in the last analysis by the basic norm. A norm does belong to the religious system just given by way of example if it is created by God or originates in an authority having its power from God, delegated by God. The basic norm of the dynamic type determines the validity, but not the contents, of the norms forming the normative system. Whereas according to the static principle, the validity as well as the contents of the norms of the system can be derived from the basic norm by an intellectual operation, according to the dynamic principle only the validity, not the contents, of the norms can be derived from the basic norm by an intellectual operation. The contents of the norms must be determined by acts

International and National Law

of authorized individuals, that is to say, the norms must be created in a way determined by the basic norm. They are valid if they are created in this way, in other words, if they are created in conformity with the basic norm, whatever their contents may be.

The static and the dynamic principle may be combined in one and the same system. The reason for the validity of the norm that we shall love our fellow men, may be the norm that we shall comply with the norms created by God, provided that God has actually established the norm that we shall love our fellow men. But from the norm that we shall love our fellow men many special norms may be deduced, as the particular from the general, by a mere mental process.

A legal order is a dynamic system of norms. Since, as pointed out, the law regulates its own creation, a norm belongs to a definite national legal order if it is created in a way determined by another —a superior—norm of this order. To the question why a certain act of coercion, for instance the fact that one individual deprives another individual of his freedom by putting him in jail, is a legal act, the answer is: Because it has been prescribed by an individual norm, a judicial decision. To the question why this individual norm is valid as part of a definite legal order, the answer is: Because it has been created in conformity with a criminal statute. This statute, finally, receives its validity from the constitution, since it has been established by the competent organ in the way the constitution prescribes.

If we ask why the constitution is valid, perhaps we come upon an older constitution. Ultimately we reach some constitution that is historically the first and that was laid down by an individual usurper or by some kind of assembly. The validity of this first constitution is the last presupposition, the final postulate, upon which the validity of all the norms of our legal order depends. It is postulated that one ought to behave as the individual or the individuals who laid down the first constitution have ordained. This is the basic norm of the national legal order under consideration. It is not a norm of positive law; it is a norm which we presuppose when we interpret social relations in legal terms, when we speak of delict and sanction, obligations, responsibilities, rights, jurisdiction, and the like. The basic norm is a hypothesis of juristic thinking, the fundamental condition under which our juristic propositions are possible. We may or may not accept this hypothesis because we may or may not interpret human relations as legal relations; we may consider them as mere relations of cause and effect. But if we consider them as legal relations, and that means if we consider them as regulated by a legal order, then we presuppose that the historically first constitution, on which this legal order is established, is a binding norm, that men ought to behave in conformity with that constitution. This presupposition is the basic norm. Only upon this presupposition are the declarations of those to whom the constitution confers norm-creating power binding legal norms. It is this presupposition that enables us to distinguish between individuals who are legal authorities and other individuals whom we do not regard as such, between acts of human beings which create legal norms and acts which have no such effect. All these legal norms belong to one and the same legal order because their validity can be traced back— directly or indirectly—to the first constitution. They are valid if they have been established, and they cease to be valid if they have been abolished in the way determined in the last analysis by the first constitution. This is the principle of legitimacy. That the first constitution is a binding legal norm is presupposed, and the formulation of the presupposition is the basic norm of the national legal order.

But the principle of legitimacy is not the only principle which applies when we answer the question as to the validity of legal norms. For if we analyze our judgments concerning the validity of legal norms, we find that we presuppose the first constitution as a valid norm only under the condition that the legal order established on the basis of this constitution is, by and large, effective, that is to say, that it is actually applied and obeyed. This becomes manifest in case of revolution.

Suppose that a group of individuals attempts to seize power by force in order to remove the legitimate government in a hitherto monarchic state and to introduce a republican form of government. If the group succeeds, if the old order ceases and the new order

International and National Law

begins to be effective because the individuals whose behavior the new order regulates actually behave, by and large, in conformity with the new order, then this order is considered as a valid order. It is now according to this new order that the actual behavior of individuals is interpreted as legal or illegal. But this means that a new basic norm is presupposed. It is no longer the norm according to which the old monarchical constitution was valid, but a norm according to which the new republican constitution is valid, a norm endowing the revolutionary government with legal authority. If the revolutionaries fail, if the order they have tried to establish remains ineffectual, then, on the other hand, their undertaking is interpreted, not as a legal, a law-creating act, not as the establishment of a constitution, but as an illegal act, namely, as the crime of treason, and this according to the old monarchic constitution and its specific basic norm.

If we attempt to make explicit the presupposition on which these juristic considerations rest, we find that the norms of the old order are regarded as devoid of validity when the old constitution and, therefore, the legal norms based on this constitution, the old legal order as a whole, have lost their efficacy; when the actual behavior of men no longer conforms to this old legal order. Every single norm loses its validity when the total legal order to which it belongs loses its efficacy as a whole. The efficacy of the entire legal order is a necessary condition for the validity of every single norm of the order. A *conditio sine qua non,* but not a *conditio per quam.* The efficacy of the total legal order is a condition, not the reason, for the validity of its constituent norms. These norms are valid not because the total order is effective, but because they are created in conformity with the constitution. But this constitution is supposed to be a valid norm only on the condition that the total order, established in conformity with it, is effective. The norms of this order cease to be valid, not only when they are annulled in conformity with the constitution, but also when the constitution ceases to be considered as a valid norm, which is the case when the total order established in conformity with the constitution ceases to be effective. It cannot be maintained that, legally, men ought to behave in conformity with a certain norm if the total legal order, of which that norm is an integral part, has lost its efficacy. The principle of legitimacy is restricted by the principle of effectiveness.

That does not mean that the principle of legitimacy is identical with the principle of effectiveness. There is still a difference between the "is" and the "ought," between the way men actually behave and the way men legally ought to behave. There are—and there must be—still cases where an individual actually does not behave as he ought to behave under the law, cases where an individual acts "contrary to the law," in violation of the law. The fact that the legal order as a whole is by and large effective does not mean that every individual acts always and without exception in conformity with the law, that no norm of this legal order is ever "violated."

Also for another reason the assumption that a legal order is valid only if it, as a whole, is by and large effective does not mean that validity is identical with effectiveness, that the "ought" is, so to speak, absorbed by the "is," and that it is consequently meaningless to ask how men ought to behave, the only question being how men actually behave. The principle that a legal order, as a whole, must be by and large effective in order to be valid is itself a norm. We may formulate this norm as follows: Men ought to behave in conformity with a coercive order which, as a whole, is by and large effective. This is a norm of positive international law, the principle of effectiveness prevailing within this law. It is implied in the rule usually formulated in the statement that according to international law an effective and independent government is the legitimate government of a state. That means that, according to international law, an actually established authority is the legitimate government, the coercive order enacted by this government is the legal order, a valid legal order, and the community constituted by this order is a state in the sense of international law, insofar as this order is, by and large, effective. According to international law, the constitution of a state is valid only if the legal order established on the basis of this constitution is, by and large, effective. It is this general principle of effectiveness, a positive norm of international law, which, applied to an individual national legal order, provides the basic norm of this

International and National Law 415

national legal order. Thus the basic norms of the different national legal orders are themselves based on a general norm of the international legal order. If we conceive of international law as a legal order to which all the states (and that means all the national legal orders) are subordinated, then the basic norm of a national legal order is not a mere presupposition of juristic thinking, but a positive legal norm, a norm of international law applied to the legal order of a concrete state. Thus the international legal order, by means of the principle of effectiveness, determines not only the spheres of validity, but also the reason of validity of the national legal orders. Since the basic norms of the national legal orders are determined by a norm of international law, they are basic norms only in a relative sense. It is the basic norm of the international legal order which is the ultimate reason of validity of the national legal orders, too.

A higher norm may determine not only the organs and the procedure by which lower norms are to be created but also, to a certain extent, the contents of these norms. But a higher norm may restrict itself to empower an authority to create lower norms at its own discretion. It is in the latter manner that international law forms the basis of the national legal order. By stipulating that an individual, or a group of individuals who are independent and able to obtain permanent obedience for the coercive order they establish for a certain territory and the individuals living thereon, are to be considered as the legitimate government of the community constituted by this order, and by stipulating that this community is a state in the sense of international law, and the coercive order constituting it, its national law, international law "delegates" the national legal order whose sphere of validity it thereby determines.

b. *Revolution and* coup d'état *as law-creating facts according to international law.* In determining the reason of validity of the national legal orders, international law regulates the creation of national law. This is clearly illustrated in the case, repeatedly mentioned here, where the constitution of a state is changed not in the way prescribed by the constitution itself, but violently, that is, by a violation of the constitution. If a monarchy is transformed into a republic by a revolution of the people, or a republic into a monarchy by a *coup d'état* of the president, and if the new government is able to maintain the new constitution in an effective manner, then this government and this constitution are, according to international law, the legitimate government and the valid constitution of the state. This is the reason why we have stated, in another connection,[10] that victorious revolution and successful *coup d'état* are, according to international law, law-creating facts. The assumption that the identity of a state is not affected by revolution or *coup d'état* as long as the territory and the population remain by and large the same is possible only if a norm of international law is presupposed recognizing victorious revolution and successful *coup d'état* as legal methods of changing the constitution.

The identity of the state implies the identity of the national legal order; and the identity of the national legal order is its continuity. Whereas from the point of view of the national legal order its continuity is destroyed by revolution or *coup d'état,* these facts have, from the point of view of international law, no effect on the continuity of a national legal order, the territorial and the personal sphere of validity of which have not essentially changed. There is no doubt, for instance, that the Russian state that existed under the tsarist constitution and that now exists under the bolshevist constitution and under the new name of Union of Soviet Socialist Republics is the same state; and that the law of that state, in spite of the essential changes which have taken place as an effect of the bolshevist revolution, is still the Russian law, just as the state and the law of France, in spite of the fundamental changes effected by the French Revolution of 1789, have not ceased to be the French state and the French law. Such an interpretation is not possible if we, ignoring international law, do not go beyond the Russian and the French constitutions as they existed at a given moment. If we do not consider the state and its law from the point of view of the international legal order, the identity of the Russian state and that of the French state and the continuity of the Russian law and that of the French law become incomprehensible. If the situation is judged from the point of view of the national legal order, the state

---

[10] Cf. *supra*, p. 264.

International and National Law

and its law remain the same only as long as the constitution is intact or changed according to its own provisions. That is the reason why Aristotle taught "that when the constitution (πολιτεία) changes its character and becomes different, the State too remains no longer the same."[11]

This view is inevitable if one tries, as Aristotle did, to comprehend the nature of the state without regard to international law. Only because modern jurists—consciously or unconsciously—presuppose international law as a legal order determining the existence of the state in every respect according to the principle of effectiveness, do they believe in the continuity of national law and the legal identity of the state in spite of a violent change of constitution.

c. *The basic norm of international law.* Since national law has the reason for its validity, and hence its "source" in this sense, in international law, the ultimate source of the former must be the same as that of the latter. Then the pluralistic view cannot be defended by the assumption that national and international law have different and mutually independent "sources." It is the "source" of national law by which that law is united with international law, whatever may be the "source" of this legal order. Which is the source, then, that is, the basic norm, of international law?

To find the source of the international legal order, we have to follow a course similar to that which led us to the basic norm of the national legal order. We have to start from the lowest norm within international law, that is, from the decision of an international tribunal. If we ask why the norm created by such a decision is valid, the answer is furnished by the treaty in accordance with which the tribunal was instituted. If, again, we ask why this treaty is valid, we are led back to the general norm which obligates the states to behave in conformity with the treaties they have concluded, a norm commonly expressed by the phrase *pacta sunt servanda*. This, as pointed out,[12] is a norm of general international law, and general international law is created by custom constituted by acts of states. The basic norm of international law, therefore, must be a norm which countenances custom as a norm-creating fact,

---

[11] Aristotle *Politics* iii, 1276b.
[12] Cf. *supra*, p. 314.

and might be formulated as follows: The states ought to behave as they have customarily behaved. Customary international law, developed on the basis of this norm, is the first stage within the international legal order. The next stage is formed by the norms created by treaties. The validity of these norms is dependent upon the norm *pacta sunt servanda,* which itself is a norm belonging to the first stage of general international law, which is customary law. The third stage is formed by norms created by organs which are themselves created by treaties, as for instance decisions of the Security Council of the United Nations or of the International Court of Justice or of tribunals of arbitration.

d. *The historic and the logico-juristic view.* The custom by which international law is created consists in acts of states. Thus, one might object, there must have been states before there could be any international law. But how can national law derive its validity from international law if the rise of the latter presupposes the existence of the former? The fact that customary international law exists does not necessarily imply that the existence of states preceded the existence of international law. It would be quite possible that primitive social groups developed into states simultaneously with the development of international law. The fact that tribal law is, at least, not a later product than intertribal law[13] allows such a conjecture. But even if the existence of states really preceded the existence of international law, the historical relation between national and international legal orders does not preclude the logical relation which, it is maintained, exists between their reasons of validity.

As long as there was no international law, the reason of the validity of national law was not determined by international law. If international law does not exist, or is not presupposed to exist as a legal order obligating and authorizing the states, the principle of effectiveness is not a norm of positive law but only a hypothesis of juristic thinking. When, however, an international law arose—that is to say, when legal norms created by the cooperation of two or more states came into existence—and the principle of effectiveness became a part thereof, the national legal orders were brought

---

[13] Cf. *supra,* p. 8.

International and National Law

into that relationship to international law which is asserted by the monistic theory.

5. Conflicts between National and International Law

International law and national law are not, so it is said, parts of one normative system, because they can, and in fact do, contradict each other. When a state enacts a statute which is contrary to some norm of international law, this statute may nevertheless be considered as valid. Simultaneously with the norm of national law, the norm of international law remains valid. According to the critics of the monistic theory, this situation involves a logical contradiction. If it were a logical contradiction, they would undoubtedly be right in their conclusion that national and international law do not form one normative system. But the contradiction is only apparent.

In case of a conflict between an established norm of international law and a more recent statute of national law, the organs of the state do not necessarily have to consider the statute as a valid norm. It is quite possible that the courts are empowered to refuse to apply such a statute, just as they are sometimes competent to refuse to apply an unconstitutional statute. And the same holds true in case of a conflict between a statute and a subsequent treaty. It may be that under the constitution of the state concerned, the treaty, and not the statute, has to be applied.[14] The question as to

---

[14] The French Constitution (*Journal Officiel*, October 28, 1946) contains the following provisions: "ARTICLE 26. Diplomatic treaties duly ratified and published shall have the force of law even when they are contrary to internal French legislation; they shall require for their application no legislative acts other than those necessary to ensure their ratification. ARTICLE 27. Treaties relative to international organization, peace treaties, commercial treaties, treaties that involve national finances, treaties relative to the personal status and property rights of French citizens abroad, and those that modify French internal legislation, as well as those that involve the cession, exchange or addition of territories shall not become final until they have been ratified by a legislative act. No cession, no exchange and no addition of territory shall be valid without the consent of the populations concerned. ARTICLE 28. Since diplomatic treaties duly ratified and published have superior authority to that of French internal legislation, their provisions shall not be abrogated, modified or suspended without previous formal denunciation through diplomatic channels. Whenever a treaty such as those mentioned in Article 27 is concerned,

whether in case of a conflict between national and international law the one or the other prevails can be decided only on the basis of the national law concerned; the answer cannot be deduced from the relation which is assumed to exist between international and national law. Since according to positive national law it is not excluded that in case of a conflict between this law and international law the former is to be considered as valid, we shall here assume that the state organs are bound to apply national law, even if it is contrary to international law.[15]

---

such denunciation must be approved by the National Assembly, except in the case of commercial treaties." Cf. also Article 25 of the Constitution of the Federal Republic of Germany, quoted *supra*, p. 195.

[15] In *Mortensen v. Peters* (Great Britain, High Court of Justiciary of Scotland, 1906, 8 Session Cases 93) the Court stated: "In this Court we have nothing to do with the question of whether the Legislature has or has not done what foreign powers may consider a usurpation in a question with them. Neither are we a tribunal sitting to decide whether an Act of the Legislature is *ultra vires* as in contravention of generally acknowledged principles of international law. For us an Act of Parliament duly passed by Lords and Commons and assented to by the King, is supreme, and we are bound to give effect to its terms."

In *The Zamora* (*supra*, p. 237) the Judicial Committee of the Privy Council declared: "It cannot, of course, be disputed that a Prize Court, like any other court, is bound by the legislative enactments of its own sovereign state. A British Prize Court would certainly be bound by acts of the imperial legislature. But it is none the less true that if the imperial legislature passed an act the provisions of which were inconsistent with the law of nations, the Prize Court in giving effect to such provisions would no longer be administering international law. It would in the field covered by such provisions be deprived of its proper function as a Prize Court. Even if the provisions of the act were merely declaratory of the international law, the authority of the court as an interpreter of the law of nations would be thereby materially weakened for no one could say whether its decisions were based on a due consideration of international obligations, or on the binding nature of the act itself. The fact, however, that the Prize Courts in this country would be bound by acts of the imperial legislature affords no ground for arguing that they are bound by the executive orders of the King in Council. . . ."

In the *Georges Pinson Case* (Annual Digest 1927–1928, Case No. 4) the French-Mexican Mixed Claims Commission (1928) held: National courts of justice, being an emanation of the sovereignty of each particular state, *may* indeed be (not, must necessarily be) obliged to enforce or apply municipal law, even when they consider the latter to clash with international law; this depends upon the principles consecrated by the national public law of the state concerned. International tribunals, however, as organs of the law of

International and National Law

The conflict between an established norm of international law and one of national law is a conflict between a higher and a lower norm. Such conflicts occur within the national legal order without the unity of this order thereby being endangered. A so-called "unconstitutional statute" is a typical example. That a statute is "unconstitutional" does not mean that it is null and void *ab initio*. It means only that if a competent court ascertains that a statute is not in conformity with certain provisions of the constitution, the statute may be annulled either only for the concrete case before the

---

nations, must neglect even the constitution of a state in favor of international law.—In the *Greco-Bulgarian "Communities" Case* the Permanent Court of International Justice (1930) held in an advisory opinion that "it is a generally accepted principle of international law that in the relations between Powers who are contracting Parties to a Treaty, the provisions of municipal law cannot prevail over those of the treaty." (Publications of the Permanent Court of Justice, Series B, No. 17, p. 32)

In *The Over The Top* (15 Federal Reporter, 2d Series 842) the United States District Court, D. Connecticut (1925) stated: "There is one ground only upon which a federal court may refuse to enforce an act of Congress and that is when the act is held to be unconstitutional. The act may contravene recognized principles of international comity, but that affords no more basis for judicial disregard of it than it does for executive disregard of it." Cf. also *Chung Chi Cheung v. The King, supra,* p. 233f., *infra,* p. 433.

In *Totus et al. v. United States et al.* (Annual Digest 1941–1942, Case No. 1) the United States District Court, Eastern District of Washington, 1941, held that a treaty concluded June 9, 1855, between the United States and the Yakima Nation of Indians was superseded by an act of Congress (the Selective Training and Service Act of 1940). The court stated: "It has long been recognized that the Congress has the right and the power to repeal a treaty or any provision thereof .... The rule is stated in *Thomas v. Gay* (169 U.S. 264, 18 S. Ct. 340, 42 L. Ed. 740), as follows: 'The effect of treaties and acts of Congress, when in conflict, is not settled by the Constitution. But the question is not involved in any doubt as to its proper solution. A treaty may supersede a prior act of Congress, and an act of Congress may supersede a prior treaty.' That the rule applies to Indian treaties as well as others was clearly determined in the *Cherokee Tobacco Cases* (11 Wallace 621, 20 L. Ed. 227)."

In *French National Railway Company v. Chavannes* (Annual Digest 1943–1945, Case No. 87), however, the Court of Appeal of Aix, France (1943), held with respect to the Convention of Rome of November 23, 1933, with which the French law of July 27, 1940, was in conflict: "The Convention of Rome is an international treaty which binds the States parties to it until such time as they withdraw therefrom in the form and after the giving of the notice provided by the Treaty itself, and no one of the High Contracting Parties can withdraw therefrom of its own accord." Cf. also *In re Riera et al.* (Colombia, Supreme Court, 1944; Annual Digest 1943–1945, Case No. 73.)

court, the latter being authorized not to apply the statute in this case, or for all possible cases, the court concerned or a special court being authorized to put the statute out of force. But as long as the statute is not annulled it remains valid. The constitution must be interpreted to provide that a statute enacted by the legislative organ is to be considered as valid as long as it is not annulled in the way prescribed by the constitution. Hence as long as it is not annulled there exists no logical contradiction between the constitution and the so-called unconstitutional statute. That a lower norm, as one says, "does not correspond" to a higher norm, in reality means that the lower norm is created in such a way, or has such content, that, according to the higher norm, it may be abrogated in another than the normal way; but, as long as the lower norm is not abrogated, it remains a valid norm, and that, according to the higher norm. The meaning of the latter is to render possible this abrogation.

The fact that a higher norm determines the creation or the content of a lower norm, however, may signify only that the organ which created the lower norm "not corresponding" to the higher norm is liable to a personal sanction. Then the norm created by the responsible organ will not be abrogated. In both cases there is no logical contradiction between the higher norm and the lower norm which does "not correspond" to the former. Illegality of a norm means possibility of abrogating the norm or inflicting a sanction upon the norm-creating organ.

The framing of a norm violating a higher norm may be a delict to which the legal order attaches a sanction. From our earlier considerations, it is clear that the occurrence of a fact does not logically contradict the norm which makes it a delict. The delict is not in contradiction to law; it is not a negation of law; it is a condition determined by law.[16] Thus there is no logical difficulty in acknowledging that valid legal norms may arise out of a delict. The principle *ex injuria jus non oritur* may belong to a given positive legal order, but does not necessarily do so. In its general form, it is not a logical but a political postulate. The creation of a valid constitu-

---

[16] Cf. *supra*, p. 7.

tion by revolution or *coup d'état* is a clear proof of this. The making of a certain norm may—according to a higher norm—be a delict and expose its author to a sanction, but the norm itself may—again according to the higher norm—be valid, valid not only in the sense that it may remain valid as long as it is not annulled, but also in the sense that it may not be voidable merely because of its origin in a delict.

This is exactly the case in the relationship between international and national law. International law usually obligates a state to give its norms certain contents in the sense that if the state enacts norms with other contents, then the state is liable to an international sanction.[17] A norm that, as one says, is enacted in "violation" of general international law remains valid even according to general international law. General international law does not provide any procedure by which norms of national law that are "illegal" (from the standpoint of international law) can be abolished. Such a procedure may be established by particular international law or by national law.

If the contents of norms of a national legal order are determined by international law, it is in an alternative sense only. The validity of norms with contents other than those prescribed is not excluded. Such norms are discriminated against only insofar as the act of making them is made an international delict. But neither the international delict, consisting in the making of the norm, nor the norm itself, is in logical contradiction to international law, any more than the so-called unconstitutional statute is in logical contradiction to the constitution. And just as the validity of "unconstitutional" statutes does not, therefore, affect the unity of the national legal order, so the validity of a national statute "violating" international law does not affect the unity of the legal system comprising both. The exponents of the pluralistic theory are thus mistaken when they think it possible to disprove the unity of national and international law by pointing at possible contradictions between the two.

---

[17] This is the meaning of the principle usually formulated in the statement that a state cannot invoke its national law to justify its violation of international law. Cf. the case of the *Treatment of Polish Nationals*, . . . *supra*, p. 195.

6. The Unity of National and International Law as a Postulate of Legal Theory

a. *The possible relationship between two systems of norms.* The unity of national and international law is an epistemological postulate. A jurist who accepts both as sets of valid norms must try to comprehend them as parts of one harmonious system. This is a priori possible in either of two different ways. Two sets of norms can be parts of one normative system because one, being an inferior order, derives its validity from the other, a superior order. The inferior order has its relative basic norm, and that means—if it is a dynamic system—the basic determination of its creation, in the superior order. Or two sets of norms form one normative system because both, being two coordinate orders, derive their validity from one and the same third order, which, as a superior order, determines not only the spheres but also the reason for their validity, and that means—if it is a dynamic system—the creation of the two inferior orders.

The procedure of creation and hence the reason of validity of an inferior order can be determined by a superior order directly or indirectly. The superior order can either itself determine the procedure in which the norms of the inferior order are to be created, or merely empower an authority to create norms for a certain sphere at its own discretion. The higher order is said to "delegate" the lower order. Since the relative basic norm of the inferior orders is part of the superior order, the inferior orders themselves can be conceived of as partial orders within the superior as a total order. The basic norm of the superior order is the ultimate reason of validity for all the norms, including those of the inferior orders.

The relationship of international and national law must correspond to one of these two types. International law can be superior to national law or vice versa; or international law can be coordinated with national law. Coordination presupposes a third order superior to both. Since there is no third order superior to both, they themselves must be in a relationship of superiority and inferiority. Entirely excluded is the possibility that they should exist side by

International and National Law 425

side, one independent of the other, without being coordinated by a superior order.

The pluralistic theory, which asserts this to be the case, invokes the relationship between law and morality in support of its assertion. These two normative systems are, it is true, independent of one another insofar as each has its own basic norm. But the very relationship between law and morality shows that two normative systems cannot be simultaneously considered as valid unless they are thought of as parts of a single system.

b. *The relationship between positive law and morality.* Let us consider the case of a conflict between a norm of positive law and a norm of morality. Positive law can, for instance, stipulate an obligation to render military service, which implies the duty to kill in war, whereas morality, that is to say, a certain moral order, unconditionally forbids killing. Under such circumstances, the jurist would say that "morally, it may be forbidden to kill, but that is irrelevant legally." From the point of view of positive law as a system of valid norms, morality does not exist as such; or, in other words, morality does not count at all as a system of valid norms if positive law is considered as such a system.[18] From this point of view, there exists a duty to perform military service, no contrary duty. In the same way, the moralist would say that "legally, one may be under the obligation to render military service and kill in war, but that is morally irrelevant." That is to say, law does not appear at all as a system of valid norms if we base our normative considerations on morality. From this point of view, there exists a duty to refuse mili-

---

[18] In *The Antelope Case* (cf. *supra,* p. 310) the United States Supreme Court in examining the question as to whether slave trade was illegal, after having admitted that slave trade "is contrary to the law of nature," declared: "Whatever may be the answer of a moralist to this question, a jurist must search for its legal solution, in those principles of action which are sanctioned by the usages, the national acts, and the general assent, of that portion of the world of which he considers himself as a part, and to whose law the appeal is made. If we resort to this standard as the test of international law, the question, as has already been observed, is decided in favor of the legality of the trade. Both Europe and America embarked in it; and for nearly two centuries, it was carried on without opposition, and without censure. A jurist could not say, that a practice thus supported was illegal, and that those engaged in it might be punished, either personally, or by deprivation of property."

tary service, no contrary duty. Neither the jurist nor the moralist asserts that both normative systems are simultaneously valid. The jurist ignores morality as a system of valid norms, just as the moralist ignores positive law as such a system. Neither from the one nor from the other point of view do there exist simultaneously two duties which contradict one another. And there is no third point of view.

To consider law and morality from one and the same point of view as simultaneously valid orders is possible only if one order is thought of as "delegating" the other. Positive law frequently refers to a certain system of morality, at least to regulate certain particular human relations; and many systems of morality acknowledge—with more or less extensive reservations—existing positive law. The delegated part of morality is part of positive law, and the delegated part of law is part of morality. To consider law and morality from one and the same point of view as valid orders, or, what amounts to the same thing, to accept law and morality as simultaneously valid systems, means to assume the existence of a single system comprehending both.

All quest for scientific knowledge is motivated by an endeavor to find unity in the apparent multiplicity of phenomena. Thus it becomes the task of science to describe its object in a system of consistent statements, that is, statements not contradicting each other. That is true also for the sciences of law and morality, sciences whose objects are norms. Contradictions are also banned within the sphere of these sciences. Just as it is logically impossible to assert both "A is" and "A is not," so it is logically impossible to assert both "A ought to be" and "A ought not to be." What is valid can be described only in phrases like "You ought to . . . ". It is in such terms that the jurist describes the system of supposedly valid legal norms, and the moralist describes the system of supposedly valid moral norms. Two norms which by their significance contradict and hence logically exclude each other cannot be assumed to be simultaneously valid. It is one of the main tasks of the jurist to give a consistent presentation of the material with which he deals. Since the material is presented in linguistic expressions, it is a priori possible that it may contain contradictions. The specific function of

International and National Law

juristic interpretation is to eliminate these contradictions by showing that they are merely sham contradictions. It is by juristic interpretation that the legal material is transformed into a legal system.

c. *Collision of duties.* Against our thesis that two contradictory norms cannot both be valid, one might argue that, after all, there are such things as collisions of duties. Our answer is that terms like "norm" and "duty" are equivocal. On the one hand, they have a significance that can be expressed only by means of an ought-statement (the primary sense). On the other hand, they are also used to designate a fact which can be described by an is-statement (the secondary sense), the psychological fact that an individual has the idea of a norm, that he believes himself to be bound by a duty (in the primary sense), and that this idea or this belief (norm or duty in the secondary sense) disposes him to follow a certain line of conduct. It is possible that the same individual at the same time has the idea of two norms, that he believes himself bound by two duties which contradict and hence logically exclude each other: the idea of a norm of positive law, for instance, which obligates him to render military service, and the idea of a norm of morality which obligates him to refuse to render military service. The statement describing this psychological fact, however, is no more contradictory than, for instance, the statement that two opposite forces work at the same point. A logical contradiction is always a relation between the meaning of judgments or statements, never a relation between facts. The concept of a so-called conflict of norms or collision of duties means the psychological fact of an individual's being under the influence of two ideas which motivate him in opposite directions; it does not mean the simultaneous validity of two norms which contradict one another.

d. *Normativity and factuality.* The failure to distinguish between the two senses of words like "norm" and "duty" is the main reason why one does not realize that two sets of valid norms must always be parts of one single system. If the word "norm" is used (in its secondary sense) to express the fact that individuals have the idea of norms, that individuals believe themselves bound by norms and are motivated by such ideas, if the term "norm" means an "is," not an "ought," then it is possible to assert that there exist norms which contradict each other, and to assert that there "exist" side by side complexes of norms which are not parts of one and the same system of norms. But the norms of which these statements speak are an object of psychology and sociology, not of juristic theory. The latter is not concerned with what ideas and beliefs people actually have, for instance, with regard to military service, but with the question whether or not people legally ought to perform—are obliged to perform—military service, that is, with norms in the primary sense. A sociologist or psychologist may observe that some people believe themselves to be obliged, that others believe the opposite, and that some oscillate between the two views. A sociologist or psychologist sees only the factual, not the normative aspect of law and morality. He conceives of law and morality as a complex of facts, not as a system of valid norms. He cannot, therefore, furnish any answer to the question whether one ought to render military service. That question can be answered only by the jurist or the moralist who considers law or morality as a system of valid norms, which he describes by propositions about what men ought to do, and not by statements about what men actually do, or actually believe they ought to do. It is the point of view of normativity, not that of factuality.

7. *Primacy of National Law or Primacy of International Law*

a. *National and international personality of the State.* It is the law as a system of valid norms, not the law as a complex of facts, to which must be referred all that has been said here about the necessity of comprehending national and international law as elements of one universal system. This tendency toward establishing unity in the plurality of legal norms is immanent in all juristic thinking. And this tendency prevails even in the theory of those who advocate the pluralistic construction. Usually, they do not deny that the state is a subject of international law as well as of its own national law. A legal personality is constituted by a legal order; it exists only as constituted by a legal order. If, then, there were no unifying relation between international and national law, the state, in its capacity as person of international law, would have to be an entity totally separate from the state in its capacity as person of national law. From the juristic point of view, there would then exist two different states under the same name, two Frances, two United States, and so on—a France of national law, and a France of international law, and so on. This absurd consequence is not accepted by the pluralists.

Sometimes, it is true, the pluralists assert that the international and the national personality of the state are distinct.[19] But they mean only that one and the same state has both an international and a national personality, just as a human being has both a moral and a juristic one. It has never been disputed that it is the same Mexico that concludes a treaty with another state in the sphere of international law, and that executes this treaty in the sphere of national law. Take, for instance, a treaty by which one state is obliged to naturalize citizens of another state only on the condition that they be released from their nationality by the other state. Then it is obviously the same state that, as a subject of international law, has concluded the treaty and, as a subject of national law, enacts a statute by which acquisition and loss of nationality are regulated according to the treaty. It is possible to say that a human being has both a legal and a moral personality, and that these personalities, as two different qualities of the same human being, are not identical. For the human being is a biologicophysiological unit, and as such the substratum of these two different personalities. That the same human being "has both a legal and a moral personality" is a metaphorical way of expressing the fact that the behavior of the same human being—as a certain biologicophysiological unit—is subject both to legal and to moral norms.

But the state is no biologicophysiological unit, not even a sociological one.[20] The relation between state and law is radically different from that between individual and law if the state is conceived

---

[19] Dionisio Anzilotti, *Cours de droit international* (1929), pp. 54, 405. This author is a consistent advocate of the pluralistic theory. Therefore he says, speaking of the term "state": "The term 'State' signifying . . . the subject of a national legal order, determines a subject entirely different from the State as the subject of international law."

[20] Cf. *supra*, pp. 100ff.

of as a social order. If the state is conceived of as an acting person or as a subject of obligations, responsibilities, and rights, the statement that law regulates the behavior of the state means that law regulates the behavior of individuals in their capacity as organs of the law or, what amounts to the same, as organs of a community constituted by the law. If, however, the state is conceived of as a social order, it is not, like human individuals, an object of legal regulation, but is the legal regulation itself, a specific legal order. The state is believed to be an object of regulation only because the anthropomorphic personification of this order leads us first to liken it to a human individual and then to mistake it for a superhuman individual.

This inadmissible hypostatization is the source of the belief that the state, as well as an individual, can have two personalities. If the state is not—as is a human being—the object of legal regulation, but this regulation itself, a legal order, then the identity of the state is the identity of a legal order. The pluralists do not deny the identity of the state as the common substratum of its personality of international as well as national law. They cannot deny that it is the same state that, for instance, according to international law, is obliged to declare war before the commencement of hostilities against another state, and that, according to its constitution, actually issues a declaration of war. But if they have to describe the legal reality without the aid of an anthropomorphic personification, they have to admit that the identity of the state is not the identity of a substratum different from the order regulating it, but is, instead, the identity of the order regulating the behavior of individuals in their capacity as organs of this order. The identity of the state as subject of international law and as subject of national law means that, finally, the international legal order obligating and authorizing the state, and the national legal order determining the individuals who, as organs of the state, execute its international duties and exercise its international rights, form one and the same universal legal order.

b. *Transformation of international into national law.* If one assumes that national and international law are disconnected systems of norms, then one must also assume that norms of international law cannot be directly applied by the organs of a state, and that the latter, especially the courts, can apply directly only norms of national law. If a norm of international law—for instance, an international treaty—is to be applied by the courts of a state, the norm, according to this view, first has to be transformed into national law by a legislative act creating a statute or an ordinance having the same content as the treaty.[21] This consequence of the pluralistic theory does not tally with the actual content of positive law. As pointed out, international law needs transformation into national law only when the constitution of the state requires such transformation.

Hence the question whether a transformation of international law into national law is necessary can be answered only by an analysis of positive national law, not by a doctrine of the nature of international or national law or of their mutual relations. By deducing the general necessity of transformation from the alleged independence of national from international law, the pluralistic theory comes into conflict with positive law and thus proves its inadequacy.

c. *Only one national legal order as system of valid norms.* If the pluralists were consistent, if they really considered national and international law, like law and morality, as two different and mutually independent orders, they would have to desist from considering both international and national law as systems of simultaneously valid norms. Just as the jurist ignores morality,[22] the moralist law, so the international jurist would have to ignore national law, and the national jurist international law. A theorist of international law would have to accept national law, a theorist of national law, conversely, international law, only as a fact, not as a system of valid norms. The exponents of the pluralistic theory, however, regard national and international law as two systems of norms which are valid simultaneously, and they have to do so, since the international legal order is meaningless without the national legal order, and the legal existence of the state cannot be understood without

---

[21] As to transformation in general, cf. *supra*, pp. 194ff., as to transformation of conventional international law into national law, cf. *supra*, pp. 351ff.

[22] cf. *supra*, pp. 425ff.

taking into consideration the international law determining this existence.

Should one decide to consider national law as alone valid, one would have to choose one national order as the only system of valid norms. What has been said of the relationship between international and national law holds also concerning the relationship between the various national legal orders. Validity can be simultaneously predicated of two national legal orders only if they are thought of as forming one single system. International law is the only legal order that could establish such a connection between them. If national and international law are disconnected, the various national legal orders, therefore, must also be disconnected. A theorist adhering to the pluralistic view thus would have to pronounce one national legal order—for instance that of his own state—as the only valid legal order.

To recognize the social order of one's own group as being the only true "law" is a typically primitive view, comparable to the view that only the members of one's own group are true human beings. In the language of some primitive tribes, the term designating "human being" is the same as that by which the members of the tribe designate themselves, in contradistinction to members of other tribes. Originally, the ancient Greeks considered only their own *polis* as a legal community, dismissing all foreigners as outlawed barbarians. Even today, one is inclined not to accept the social order of another community as "law" in the full sense of the word, especially when the order embodies political principles different from one's own.

d. *The recognition of international law.* Since, on the one hand, the validity of national law is considered to be a matter of course, and, on the other hand, it is hardly possible to deny outright the validity of international law, the pluralists have recourse to a hypothesis by which they—unintentionally—nullify the mutual independence of national and international law that they wish to uphold. By this hypothesis, they also establish a normative relationship between the various national legal orders and thus reopen the possibility of considering both the international and all the national legal orders as systems of valid norms. We refer to the well-known statement that international law is valid for a state only if it is "recognized" by the state.[23]

This is, as pointed out,[24] by no means a rule of positive international law. Positive international law does not make its validity for a state dependent upon recognition by this state. When a new state comes into existence, this state, according to international law, immediately receives all obligations imposed and all rights conferred upon a state by this legal order, independently of whether or not the state recognizes international law. According to international law itself, it is not necessary to prove that a state has consented to a norm of general international law in order to be able to assert that, in a concrete case, this state has violated an obligation, or another state has infringed upon the former's right, stipulated by the norm in question. A norm of international law which makes its own validity for the state dependent upon its recognition by the state is logically impossible because the validity of such a norm presupposes a validity of the international law independent of its recognition.

A different question is whether the legal existence of a state is dependent upon recognition by other states. This question has been answered in the affirmative in a previous chapter.[25] Some authors assume that recognition of international law by the state to be recognized is an essential condition of its recognition as a

---

[23] In *The Over The Top* (*supra,* p. 421) the Court stated: "International practice is law only in so far as we adopt it, and like all common or statute law it bends to the will of the Congress." In *Chung Chi Cheung v. The King* (cf. *supra,* p. 233) the Judicial Committee of the Privy Council (1939) stated: "It must be always remembered that, so far, at any rate, as the Courts of this country are concerned, international law has no validity save in so far as its principles are accepted and adopted by our own domestic law. There is no external power that imposes its rules upon our own code of substantive law or procedure. The Courts acknowledge the existence of a body of rules which nations accept amongst themselves. On any judicial issue they seek to ascertain what the relevant rule is, and, having found it, they will treat it as incorporated into the domestic law, so far as it is not inconsistent with rules enacted by statutes or finally declared by their tribunals."

[24] Cf. *supra,* p. 154.

[25] Cf. *supra,* pp. 264ff.

state. However, as pointed out, international law itself does not, and cannot, prescribe its recognition on the part of the states as a condition for its validity for the states. International law only makes its application to the relation between two communities dependent on the fact that they mutually recognize one another as states. It is positive international law itself that gives the recognition of one state by another its characteristic legal effects. Thus, mutual recognition of communities as states presupposes the validity of international law.

The recognition of a community as a state is an act provided by positive international law. The recognition of international law by a state—as a recognition of its validity for that state—is not, and cannot be, provided by international law. But if the legal interpretation of social relations starts from a definite national legal order, international law can be conceived of as a system of valid legal norms only if the national legal order, which is the starting point of this interpretation, delegates international law, and, hence, international law is part of this national law; just as moral norms can be considered as valid from the point of view of a definite national law only if they are delegated by this law and, hence, form part of this law, although no moral order makes its validity dependent on delegation by a legal order. This is the true meaning of the thesis advocated by the followers of the pluralistic doctrine: international law is valid for a state only if it is recognized by that state. "Recognition of international law by a state" is the figurative expression of "delegation of international law by a national law." Such recognition—according to the doctrine of the pluralists—may be performed tacitly or expressly. A tacit recognition of international law by a state is assumed if it is evidenced by conclusive actions on the part of the state, such as sending and receiving diplomatic agents, entering into international agreements, and the like. There is an express recognition of international law by a state if the law of that state contains a provision to the effect that the international law is to be considered as part of the national law concerned, or that the law-applying organs, especially the courts, are also bound to apply international law according to its inherent meaning. As

International and National Law

a matter of fact, the laws of some states contain provisions of this kind.[26]

e. *Primacy of national or primacy of international law.* The assumption that international law is valid for a state only if it is recognized by that state refers to international law as it actually exists. As to the content of international law, it remains exactly the same whether its validity for a definite state is assumed to depend or not to depend on its recognition by that state. The assumption that international law is valid for a state only if it is recognized by the State refers to the reason of validity of international law. The meaning of this assumption is that international law is valid for the same reason that national law of the state is valid, that is to say, that the reason of validity of international law is the basic norm of the law of the state, i.e., the basic norm of the national legal order. Expressed in the usual language of personification, the "will" of the state, which is the reason for the validity of its national law, is also the reason for the validity of international law. If international law is valid for a state, it is valid because the state so wills, and this "will" of the state is manifested in its tacit or express recognition of international law. By such recognition the state makes international law part of its own law. This doctrine prevails in Anglo-Saxon jurisprudence.[27]

---

[26] Cf. Article 25 of the Constitution of the Federal Republic of Germany, *supra*, p. 195. Sometimes only conventional international law, that is, the law created by treaties to which the state is a contracting party, is delegated by the law of that state. Thus, for instance, Article VI of the United States Constitution, quoted *supra*, p. 353. Cf. also the provisions of Articles 26–28 of the French Constitution, *supra*, p. 419.

[27] In *The Paquete Habana* (United States, Supreme Court, 1900, 175 U.S. 677) the Court stated: "International law is part of our law, and must be ascertained and administered by the courts of justice of appropriate jurisdiction, as often as questions of right depending upon it are duly presented for their determination." In *West Rand Central Gold Mining Co., Ltd. v. The King* (*supra*, p. 315) the Court declared with respect to this principle: "It is quite true that whatever has received the common consent of civilized nations must have received the assent of our country, and that to which we have assented along with other nations in general may properly be called international law, and as such will be acknowledged and applied by our municipal tribunals when legitimate occasion arises for those tribunals to decide questions to which

The doctrine that international law is valid as part of national law seems to be inevitable where the national law contains an express provision to the effect that international law shall be applied by the competent organs of the state, as the above-mentioned constitutions of the United States, of Germany, and of France. But this is not the case. If the legal interpretation of the social relations does not start from a definite national law, but from international law—and nothing in the content of the one or the other can prevent the jurist from taking as the starting point of his construction either the one or the other—the assumption that the international legal order is valid only if delegated by a national legal order (an assumption which is not and cannot be based on a provision of positive international law) is superfluous. Then the question is whether the organs of the state can apply international law only if it is transformed into national law, or also without such transformation. The answer to this question depends, as pointed out,[28] on the content of the national legal order. If the latter contains a provision to the effect that international law shall be applied by the competent organs of the state, such as the above-mentioned provisions of the American, French, and German constitutions, this provision must be interpreted, not as a recognition of international law by the state (or a delegation of international law by national law), but as a transformation, a general transformation of international into national law. Such transformation, as pointed out, is necessary if the constitution authorizes the organs of the state to apply only national law. But the validity

---

doctrines of international law may be relevant. But any doctrine so invoked must be one really accepted as binding between nations, and the international law sought to be applied must, like anything else, be proved by satisfactory evidence, which must shew, either that the particular proposition put forward has been recognized and acted upon by our own country, or that it is of such a nature, and has been so widely and generally accepted, that it can hardly be supposed that any civilized State would repudiate it. . . . that the law of nations forms part of the law of England, ought not to be construed so as to include as part of the law of England opinions of text-writers upon a question as to which there is no evidence that Great Britain has ever assented, and *a fortiori* if they are contrary to the principles of her laws as declared by her Courts."

[28] Cf. *supra*, p. 195.

International and National Law   437

of international law, if the legal interpretation starts from international and not from national law, is independent of its applicability by the organs of the state. If the organs of the state do not apply it because they are not authorized by national law to do so, the state is, under the valid international law, responsible for such violation of the law. If the starting point of the legal construction is a definite national legal order—or, as it is usual to say, the law of a definite state—and hence international law is valid only as part of the law of that state, then a violation of international law by that state is possible only if the state has recognized international law. But, practically, there is no difference in this respect between the interpretation by those who start from the international and those who start from the national law. For the latter actually assume that all states—at least tacitly by entering into international relations—have recognized international law.

If, as in this treatise, the legal construction proceeds from international law as a valid legal order, the reason of validity of international law cannot be found in the "will" of the state for which international law claims to be valid. The reason of validity of international law is its own basic norm, as formulated in a previous connection. On the other hand, the reason for the validity of the national legal orders can be found in the international legal order.[29] According to these two different ways of approaching the law—the national as well as the international law—two different views of the relationship between the two orders must be accepted. If we start from the international legal order, then the national legal orders are delegated by, and in this sense are inferior to, the international legal order, which is to be considered as superior to the national legal orders and forms, together with them, one universal legal system. If we start from a definite national legal order, international law must be delegated by national law in order to be conceived of as a valid legal order; then international law is not considered as superior to national law but as forming part of national law. If international law is considered as part of national

---

[29] Cf. *supra,* pp. 408ff.

law, it is necessary, as pointed out,[30] to distinguish between national law in a wider sense of the term—comprising, as part of it, international law—and national law in a narrower—in its specific —sense, not comprising international law. There is no follower of the doctrine of the supremacy of national law, who does not differentiate between national and international law, although he declares international law as part of national law and consequently as national law. That international law is considered to be valid only as part of national law means that the unity of the two is established by this approach, too. To guarantee this unity is, in fact, the essential purpose of the doctrine which considers international law as valid for a state only if recognized by that state, but at the same time assumes that all states have, at least tacitly, recognized international law. The difference between the two approaches consists only in that the one presupposes the primacy of international law over national law, the other, the primacy of national over international law. But both have a monistic character, and do not differ as to the content of international law; they differ only as to the reason of validity of international and of national law.

8. Sovereignty [31]

a. *Sovereignty as a quality of a normative order.* The most important consequence of the theory which assumes the primacy of national law is that the national legal order which is the starting point of the whole construction can be considered as the supreme authority and hence as sovereign in the original sense of the term "sovereignty". For the national legal order is presupposed to be the supreme order, above which no other legal order exists. This is also the final result of the pluralistic theory which, since it is not able to maintain its thesis that international law and national law are valid independently of each other, turns into a monistic doctrine. Its followers refuse to consider international law as a legal order above the national legal orders. Hence in dealing with international law as a valid legal order, they must assume that inter-

---

[30] Cf. *supra*, p. 206.
[31] Cf. *supra*, pp. 155ff., 225, 315f., 348.

national law is valid for a state only if recognized by this state, or, what amounts to the same, recognized in the national law of this state. That means that they accept the doctrine of the supremacy of national over international law. By assuming the supremacy of national over international law, or, what amounts to the same, by assuming that international law is valid only as part of national law, they abandon the dualism of national and international law, and hence juristic pluralism. We may, therefore, conjecture that the real purpose of the pluralistic doctrine is not so much to assert the mutual independence of national and international law, but rather to maintain the idea that national law, and that means a definite national legal order, is not subordinated to international law and hence may be considered to be the supreme legal authority.

Insofar as by the term "state" a social order, especially a national legal order, is understood, the idea that the national legal order is the supreme legal authority may be expressed in the statement that the state is sovereign. This is the usual way to speak of sovereignty. But if the state as juristic person is in question—the state as subject of national or international obligations, responsibilities, and rights—then the state cannot be considered as sovereign in the sense of supreme authority. For the state as subject of obligations, responsibilities, and rights must always be considered as subjected to a legal order—national or international—which imposes or confers upon the state, and that means upon individuals in their capacity as organs or members of the legal community, the obligations, responsibilities, and rights concerned. As subjected to a legal order, even to its own, i.e., the national legal order, the state cannot be considered as a supreme legal authority. The usual argument that the state can always change its own law and hence stands "above" its law is utterly wrong. The statement that the state can change its law means only that individuals determined by the law can change the law in a procedure likewise determined by the law. These individuals in changing the law are completely subjected to the law and stand in no way above it. Whether international law is considered to be superior to national law, or part of national law, the state as juristic person cannot be considered as sovereign. As subject of the law, the state—and that means the individual acting in his capacity as organ of the legal community—cannot be a supreme authority because it is no "authority" at all.

"Authority" is usually defined as the right or power to issue obligating commands. The actual power of forcing others to a certain behavior does not suffice to constitute an authority. The individual who is or has the authority must have received the right or power to issue obligating commands, so that other individuals are obliged to obey. Such a right or power can be conferred upon an individual only by a normative order. Authority is thus originally the characteristic of a normative order. As pointed out in a previous connection,[32] only a normative order can be "sovereign," that is to say, a supreme authority, the ultimate reason for the validity of norms which one individual is authorized to issue as "commands" and other individuals are obliged to obey. Physical power, a mere natural phenomenon, can never be "sovereign" in the proper sense of the word. As attributed to physical power, "sovereignty" could only mean something like the property of being a first cause, a *prima causa*. But the idea of a *prima causa* is a contradiction in terms. If, according to the principle of causality, every phenomenon has to be considered as the effect of a cause, every phenomenon which is considered to be the cause of an effect must be considered to be at the same time the effect of another cause. In the infinite chain of causes and effects, that is to say, within natural reality, there cannot be a first cause, and, therefore, no sovereignty.

The state in its capacity as legal authority must be identical with the national legal order. That the state is sovereign means that the national legal order is an order above which there is no higher order. The only order that could be assumed to be superior to the national legal order is the international legal order. The question whether the state is sovereign or not thus coincides with the question whether or not international law is supposed to be an order superior to national law.

That an order is "superior" to another order is, as we have pointed out,[33] a figurative expression. It means that we derive the reason of validity of one order from another order which, therefore, is

---

[32] Cf. *supra*, p. 109.
[33] Cf. *supra*, pp. 102ff., 424f.

supposed to be the superior order. That an order is a supreme order means that we do not derive its reason of validity from another as a superior order. The problem of the sovereignty of the state is not the problem whether a natural object does or does not have a given property. It cannot be answered in the same way as, for instance, a question concerning the specific weight of a metal, that is to say, by observation of natural reality. The answer to the question as to whether the state as a legal order is or is not sovereign, that is to say, the supreme legal authority, is not a statement about a fact; it is an assumption made by the one who interprets the legal phenomena. The result of our analysis was that international law, through its principle of effectiveness, determines the sphere and reason of validity of national law; and thus the superiority of international law to national law seems to be imposed by the content of the law itself. But international law determines the sphere and reason of validity of national law only if international law is supposed to be valid; and our analysis proceeded from the assumption that international law is a valid legal order. However, from the point of view of the recognition theory which starts from national law as a valid legal order, international law is valid only if recognized by the state or, what amounts to the same, if international law is delegated by the law of the state, i.e., the national legal order. After the state has recognized international law and international law thus becomes part of national law, international law, by its very content, determines the sphere of validity of the national legal order. But since this result is brought about only by recognition of international law on the part of the state, international law determines only, as part of national law in the wider sense, the sphere of validity of the national law in a narrower, the specific, sense of the term. That is to say, national law determines, i.e., limits the sphere of validity of those of its norms which form the national law in a narrower sense. Since international law is supposed to be valid only as part of national law, it has its reason of validity in national law. Hence, according to this view, the basic norm of the national legal order is the absolute supreme source of the validity of all law, so that the state as a legal order can be conceived of as sovereign, i.e., as the supreme legal authority.

If it is admitted that sovereignty of the state means only that the state as a legal order is the supreme legal authority, then sovereignty is not a fact which can or cannot be observed and ascertained. The state neither "is" nor "is not" sovereign in the sense that a body "is" or "is not" heavier than another. The state can only be presupposed to be or not to be sovereign; and this presupposition depends upon our approach to the legal phenomena. If the legal construction—as in this treatise—proceeds from international law as a valid order, which implies the primacy of this law over national law, then the state as a national legal order "is not" sovereign in the sense of being the supreme legal authority. Then the state as a national legal order can be sovereign only in the relative sense that no other order but the international legal order is superior to the national legal order, so that the state as the national legal order is subjected directly to the international legal order only.[34] If, on the other hand, the legal construction proceeds from a national legal order, which implies the primacy of national law, then the state as a national legal order "is" sovereign in the original absolute sense of the term, being superior to any other legal order, including international law which, by delegation, becomes part of national law.

b. *Sovereignty as exclusive quality of one legal order only.* If the phenomena of law are interpreted from the point of view of the primacy of national law, one national legal order only can be conceived of as sovereign. Only that national legal order can be presupposed to be sovereign which is the starting point of the whole construction. The necessary relationship between this order and the other national legal orders can be established only by international law, and only if it is admitted that international law determines the spheres of validity of the national legal orders. However, according to this view, international law is valid only if delegated by national law, or, what amounts to the same, is recognized by the state, which is sovereign because the international legal order is considered as part of the national legal order. Since the other national legal orders derive their validity from international law, they have to be considered as inferior to that national legal

---

[34] Cf. *supra*, pp. 110ff., 114.

order which first is, and which, therefore, alone can be presupposed to be, sovereign. This national legal order, through the medium of international law which is part of it, comprises all the other national legal orders "delegated" by the international legal order. The national legal order in the narrower sense of the term (not comprising the international legal order) which is the starting point of this construction, and all the other national legal orders are limited in their respective spheres of validity by the international legal order, supposed to be part of the national legal order, starting point of the construction. They can be created and modified only according to their own constitutions. But international law which, as part of one national legal order, guarantees the other national legal orders this relative sovereignty, has—from the point of view of this interpretation—its reason of validity in the national legal order from which the interpretation proceeds. Only this national legal order which, with respect to the reason of validity, not with respect to the contents of other national legal orders, presents itself as the universal legal order, is absolutely sovereign, and this means that only this national legal order is sovereign in the original sense of the term. If we speak of a national legal order as of a state, then the sovereignty of one state excludes the sovereignty of every other state.

This is an inevitable consequence of the recognition theory based on the assumption of the primacy of national law. Most exponents of this view, however, do not think it out to its last consequences. They conceive the world of law as a number of isolated national legal orders, each of which is sovereign and each of which contains international law as part of it. This is another type of legal pluralism. Since it is not possible to maintain that international law and national law are valid independently of each other and since international law is considered to be valid as part of national law, the validity of each national legal order is maintained to be independent of that of all the other national legal orders. For reasons that have already been explained, this type of legal pluralism, too, is logically impossible. There would, incidentally, on this view, exist as many numerically different international legal orders as there are states or national legal orders. It is, however, logically possible that different theorists interpret the world of law by proceeding from the primacy of different national legal orders or, what amounts to the same, from the sovereignty of different states. Each legal theorist may proceed from the primacy of his own national law, i.e., from the sovereignty of the state to which he belongs. Then he has to consider the international law, which establishes the relations between his own national law and the other national legal orders, as well as those national legal orders as parts of his own national law, the law of his own state conceived of as a universal legal order. This means that the picture of the world of law would vary according to what national law is made the basis of the interpretation. Within each of these systems established on the assumption of the primacy of national law, only one national law, or only one state as a national legal order, is sovereign; but in no two of them would this be the same national law or, what amounts to the same, the same state.

9. *The Philosophical and Juristic Significance of the Two Monistic Interpretations*

a. *Subjectivism and objectivism.* The assumption of the primacy of national law is a parallel to the subjectivistic philosophy which, in order to comprehend the world, proceeds from the philosopher's own ego and, hence, interprets the world as the will and idea of the subject. This philosophy, proclaiming the sovereignty of the ego, is incapable of comprehending another subject, the non-ego, the *tu* claiming to be also an ego, as an equal being. The sovereignty of the ego is incompatible with the sovereignty of the tu. The ultimate consequence of such a subjectivistic philosophy is solipsism.

The assumption of the primacy of national law is state subjectivism. It makes the state, i.e., the national law, which is the starting point of the construction, the theorist's own national legal order, i.e., the state to which he belongs, the sovereign center of the world of law. But this philosophy of law is incapable of comprehending other states, that is, other national legal orders, as equal to the philosopher's own state, and that means, as legal beings which are sovereign too. The sovereignty of the state-ego is incompatible with the sovereignty of the state-tu. The ultimate consequence of the primacy of national law is state solipsism.

The ego and the tu can be conceived of as equal beings only if our philosophy proceeds from the objective world within which both exist as parts, and neither of them as sovereign centers of the whole. Similarly, the idea of the equality of all states can be maintained only if we base our interpretation of legal phenomena on the primacy of international law. The states as legal orders can be considered as equal only if they are not presupposed to be sovereign, because they are equal only insofar as they are equally subjected to one and the same international legal order.

The primacy of international law and the primacy of national law are two different answers to the question as to the reason for the validity of the two legal orders. The description of their content by the science of law is not affected whether the validity of national law be based on international law or the validity of international law be based on national law. The international obligations and rights of the states are exactly the same whether the one or the other of the two interpretations is accepted. The fact that the positive law of a certain state declares the international legal order a part of its national legal order cannot prevent legal theory from assuming that the validity of international law does not depend upon a recognition on the part of the state, that is, from accepting the primacy of international law. Nor does the fact that positive international law determines the sphere and the reason of the validity of the national legal order prohibit the assumption that international law is valid for a state only if recognized by this state, which implies the assumption of the primacy of national law.

b. *Wrong use of the two assumptions.* The two interpretations—which are merely two different ways of comprehending all legal phenomena as parts of a single system—it is true, are sometimes misused as the basis for assertions about the content of positive law. From the assumed primacy of national or international law one attempts to draw conclusions which oppose the actual content of the positive law. Thus, according to those who presuppose the primacy of national law, the sovereignty of the state implies that the state is not always bound by treaties which it has concluded with other states; or that the state cannot be subjected to the compulsory jurisdiction of an international court; or that it cannot be obligated against its will by majority resolutions of collegiate international organs; or that national law cannot have its origin in a procedure of international law; or, especially, that the sovereignty of the state is incompatible with the idea that its constitution is created by an international treaty; and so on. These are all questions which cannot be answered by deductions from the concept of sovereignty but only by an analysis of positive law; and positive law shows that all the assertions quoted here are inaccurate. Those who accept the hypothesis of the primacy of international law, however, are just as mistaken when they maintain that international law overrides national law, that a norm of national law is null if it is not in conformity with international law. This would be the case only if there existed a positive norm providing a means of annulling a norm of national law because of its nonconformity with international law. General international law, at any rate, does not contain any such norm.

Each of the two monistic interpretations may be accepted or rejected in the face of any empirically given stipulations of positive national or international law—simply because they do not carry any implications in that respect.

c. *The choice between the two hypotheses.* In our choice between the two hypotheses we are as free as in our choice between a subjectivistic and an objectivistic philosophy. As the choice between the latter cannot be determined by natural science and has no effect on it, so the choice between the former cannot be made for us by the science of law and has no effect on it. The choice between the primacy of international law and the primacy of national law is, in the last analysis, the choice between two basic norms: the basic norm of the international and the basic norm of the national legal order. As pointed out,[35] the basic norm of a legal order is a hypothesis of juristic thinking, not a norm of positive law. Such a hypothesis may or may not be accepted. It must be accepted only if one wishes to interpret social relations as legal relations. But

---

[35] Cf. *supra,* pp. 314, 408ff.

such interpretation is only possible, not necessary. As we are free to accept or not to accept the hypothesis of a basic norm, we are free to choose between the basic norm of international law and the basic norm of a national law as the fundamental basis of our interpretation of the world of law.

It may be that our choice, though not determined by the science of law, is guided by ethical or political preferences. A person whose political attitude is that of nationalism and imperialism may be inclined to accept as a hypothesis the basic norm of his own national legal order; in other terms, he may proceed on the primacy of national law. A person whose sympathy is for internationalism and pacifism may be inclined to accept as a hypothesis the basic norm of international law and thus proceed from the primacy of international law. From the point of view of the science of law, it is irrelevant which hypothesis one chooses. But from the point of view of politics, the choice may be important since it is tied up with the ideology of sovereignty.

Even if the decision between the two hypotheses is beyond science, science still has the task of showing the relations between them and certain value systems of an ethical or political character. Science can make the jurist aware of the reasons for his choice and the nature of the hypothesis he has chosen, and so prevent him from drawing conclusions which positive law, as given in experience, does not warrant.

INDEX

INDEX

Absolute responsibility, and culpability, 11 ff.
  of the state and responsibility based on fault (culpability), 122 f.
Accession to treaties, 340 f.
Acquisition of state territory, 213 ff.
Act of state, 117 ff.
  as problem of imputation, 117 f.
  indirect responsibility for, 131 f., 235 f.
Action against former enemy states under the Charter of the United Nations, 62
Acts, of illegitimate warfare, 129
  performed at superior command, 136
  of private persons injurious to foreign states, 126 f.
Adjustment of situations (not having the character of disputes) by organs of the United Nations, 370 ff.
Advisory opinions of the International Court of Justice, 395
Agencies, international, decisions of, 365 ff.
Aggression, war of, 30
Agreement, executive, under constitution of the United States, 317, 323
Air Convention, International (1919), 226
Air space, 225
Air warfare, 81
Aliens, and citizens, 210 ff., 243
  treatment of, 213 ff.
Amendments, to the Charter of the United Nations, 337
  to the Covenant of League of Nations, 337
Application and creation of international law, 301 ff.
Arbitration and judicial settlement, 377 ff.
Argentina and Chile, treaty between concerning the Strait of Magellan (1881), 344
Armed attack under the Charter of the United Nations, 61 f.
Armed force, war as use of, 29 ff.
Armed forces, exterritoriality of, 232
Ascertainment of a legally relevant fact, recognition as, 267, 269 f.
Assembly, General of the United Nations, 178 f.
Authority, legal, and legal science, 6
Aviation, International Civil, Conference (1944), 226

Basic norm, of international law, 314, 417 f.
  of a legal order, concept of, 314, 408 ff.
Basis of international law, common consent of the States as, 152 ff., 311 ff.
Beamtenabkommen, 143

Beginning and end of the validity of treaties, 354 ff.
Belgium-Sweden, Treaty of Arbitration (1926), 381
Belligerency, recognition of, 292
Belligerent occupation, 73 f.
Belligerent power, recognition of insurgents as, 291 ff.
Bellum justum principle, 33 ff.
  in the Covenant of the League of Nations, 39 f.
  in the Kellogg-Briand Pact, 42 f.
  and neutrality, 84 ff.
  in positive international law, 38 ff.
  and principle of nonintervention, 64
  in the Treaty of Versailles, 38
Blockade, breach of, 128
Blood revenge, 8, 10, 16
Bohemia and Moravia, so-called Protectorate of, 168 f.
Bombardment, obligation to warn authorities before, 131
Boundaries of the territory of the state, 208 ff., 213
British Togoland, Trusteeship Agreement for, 167
Brussels Treaty for Collective Self-Defense (1948), 62, 353 f.

Calvo clause, 244
Capitulations, 235
Central American Court of Justice, 387
Centralization, and decentralization of the legal order, 8 f., 14 f., 35, 100 ff., 104, 168 ff., 402 f.
  and efficacy of a legal order, 108
Charter of the United Nations *see* United Nations
Church, the, as subject of international law, 159, 322
Citizens, and aliens, 210 ff., 243
  right of the state to protect its own, 245 f., 247
Citizenship (nationality), 248 ff.
  acquisition and loss of, 250 f.
  multiple, 251 ff.
Civil Aviation Conference, International (1944), 226
Civil execution as sanction of civil law, 5 f.
Civil sanctions, 5 f.
Civil war and international war, 32
Codification of International Law, Hague Conference on the Progressive (1930), 222

Coercion, as element of the law, 5 f., 100
  as the "political" element, 100
  sanctions as acts of, 4
Coercive acts not having the character of sanctions, 13
Coercive order, law as a, 5 f., 100
Collective responsibility, and individual responsibility, 9 ff., 98 f., 122 f.
  in international law, 116 ff., 401
Collective security and self-help, 15 f.
  under the Covenant of the League of Nations, 40 f.
Collective self-defense under the Charter of the United Nations, 58 ff.
Collision of duties, 427
Common international law, *see* General international law
Communities not having the character of states, as subjects of international law, 158 ff.
Communities of states as subjects of international law, 168 ff., 323
Community, imputation of acts of organs to the, 13 f., 98 f., 107 f.
  international, decentralization of, 22, 36, 402 f.
  as government of a state, 112
Compulsory jurisdiction, of international tribunals, 379 f., 392
  of the International Court of Justice, 392 f.
Conciliation, settlement of international disputes by, 368
Concordats, 159, 322
Conditional ratification of treaties, 332 f.
Conditional recognition, 275
Condominium, 218 f.
Confederation of states, 171 ff.
Conflict, between a higher and a lower norm, 421 f.
  of laws (private international law), 254 ff.
  between national and international law, 419 ff.
  of nationality, Hague Convention concerning questions relating to, 253
  between treaties, 361 ff.
Consent, common, of the states as basis of international law, 152 ff., 311 ff.
  mutual, dissolution of treaties by, 356
Constitution, concept of, 151
Constitutionality of treaties, 324 f.
Continuity of the national legal order and identity of the state, 259 f., 416 f.
Contraband of war, 79, 128
Contract, social, doctrine of, 153, 314 ff.
Conventional international law, 313 f., 317 ff.
Corporation, as juristic person, 98 ff.
Counterwar and war, 28 f.
Coup d'état and revolution as law-creating facts, 264, 415 ff.
Courts, international, *see* International tribunal
Covenant of the League of Nations, *see* League of Nations
Creation and application of international law, 301 ff.
Crimes against peace, 135 f.
Criminal law, 5 f.
Criminal sanctions, 5 f.

Culpability and absolute responsibility, 11 ff.
Custom, as evidence of law, 309 f.
  as a law-creating fact, 308 ff.
  and legislation, differences between, 308
  as source of international law, 307 ff.
Customary international law, as basis of conventional international law, 313 f.
  binding force of, 311 ff.
  reason of validity of, 314 ff.
Customary and statutory law, 307 ff.

Damage, obligation to repair, and responsibility, 11, 120
Decentralization, and centralization of the legal order, 8 f., 14 f., 36, 100 ff., 104, 168 ff., 402 f.
  of the international community (law), 22, 36, 402 f.
Decisions of international agencies, 365 ff.
Declaration concerning the neutralization of the Swiss Confederation (1815), 85
Declaration of Paris (1856), 78 f., 87
Declaration (draft) on the rights and duties of states, 158
Declaration by the United Nations (1942), 176
Declaration, Universal, of Human Rights, 144 ff.
Declaration of war, 67
Defense, war of, 30
Definition of law, 3 ff., 16, 100
Definition of international law, 3, 101
De jure and *de facto* recognition, 275 ff.
Delict, concept of, 5 f., 7, 13, 19
  international, 1 ff., 19 ff.
  and sanction, 6
  as violation of the law, 7, 19
Delinquency, international, 119
Delinquent, concept of, 5, 8
Denial of Justice, 246
Denunciation of treaties, 356 f.
Diplomatic envoys, exterritoriality of, 230 f.
  inviolability of, 242 f.
Disputes, international, settlement of, by agreement, 367 f.
  by conciliation, 368
  by good offices, 367 f.
  by the International Court of Justice, 386 ff.
  by international tribunals, 377 ff.
  by mediation, 367 f.
  by negotiation, 367 f.
  by organs of the League of Nations and of the United Nations, 368
Disputes, justiciable and nonjusticiable, 380 ff.
  legal, under the Charter of the United Nations, 385 f.
  legal and political, 380 ff.
Dissolution of treaties by mutual consent, 356
Domestic jurisdiction, under the Charter of the United Nations, 62 f., 196 ff.
  under the Covenant of the League of Nations, 196 ff.
  exclusive, 191 f.

Index

Domestic jurisdiction, (national) and international jurisdiction, 191 ff.
Dualism (pluralism) and monism, 403 ff.
Duties, collision of, 427
Duty (obligation), concept of, 7 f.
Dynamic and static systems of norms, 409 ff.

Economic and Social Council of the United Nations, 182
Effectiveness, principle of, 214 f., 289 f., 412 ff.
Efficacy, and centralization of a legal order, 108 f.
  of the national legal order as power of the state, 106 f.
  and validity of a legal order, 110, 413 f.
Elements of the state, 206 ff., 257 ff.
Enemy states, action against former enemy states under the Charter of the United Nations, 62
Enforcement measures, under the Charter of the United Nations, 46 ff.
  under the Covenant of the League of Nations, 40 ff.
  sanctions as, 4 ff.
Equality, as a fundamental right of the state, 155 f.
  before the law, 155
Espionage, 129, 238
Ex injuria jus non oritur, 216, 293, 363, 422
Exclusive domestic jurisdiction, 191 f.
Exclusive international jurisdiction, 202
Execution of decisions, of the International Court of Justice, 397
  of international tribunals, 395 ff.
Executive agreements under the Constitution of the United States, 317, 323
Exile, government in, 288 ff.
Existence, as right of the state, 155
Exterritoriality, 228 ff., 243
Extradition, 249 f.
Extraterritorial jurisdiction, 235

Factuality and normativity, 427 f.
Fault (culpability), responsibility based on, 11 ff.
Federal state, 111, 168 ff., 219
  sovereignty in, 113
Final Act of the International Civil Aviation Conference (1944), 226
Final Act of the Hague Conference on the Progressive Codification of International Law (1930), 222
Flag, illegal use of, 126
Force, armed, as element of law, 3 ff.
  threat or use of, effect of, on treaties, 326 f.
  use of, under the Charter of the United Nations, 44 ff.
  war as use of, 29 ff.
Force monopoly, of the legal community, 13 ff., 17, 101 f.
  centralization of, under the Charter of the United Nations, 44 ff.
Freedom of the sea, 125, 224 f.
Fundamental rights of the state, 148 ff.
  deduced from the personality of the state, 150 ff.

as principles presupposed by international law, 150 ff.

Gaps in the law, 304 ff., 384
General Act for the Pacific Settlement of International Disputes (1928), 384 f.
General Assembly of the United Nations, 178 f.
General (common) international law, 19, 95 f., 188 ff.
  and particular international law, 188 ff.
  See also International law
General participation clause, 65
Geneva Convention (1949), 66, 71
Germany and Czechoslovakia, agreement between concerning the Protectorate of Bohemia and Moravia (1939), 168 f.
Germany and Poland, convention between concerning Upper Silesia (1922), 142
Germany and Switzerland, Treaty of Conciliation and Arbitration between (1921), 368, 381
Good offices, settlement of international disputes by, 367 f.
Government, in exile, 288 ff.
  international community as government of a state, 112
  nonrecognition of, 282 ff.
  recognition of, 279 ff.
  recognition of, by the United Nations, 284 f.

Hague Conference on the Progressive Codification of International Law, Final Act (1930), 222
Hague Convention concerning certain questions relative to the conflict of nationality laws (1930), 253
Hague Convention for the Pacific Settlement of International Disputes (1907), 367 f., 378, 386 f., 389
Hague Conventions (1907), 65 ff., 72 ff., 77 ff., 82, 128 ff.
Havana, Convention of (1928), 231
Hay-Pauncefote Treaty (1901), 349
Hay-Varilla Treaty (1903), 349
Head of state, concept of, 230
  exterritoriality, 230 f.
  inviolability, 242
High seas, 219 ff.
Human rights, in the Charter of the United Nations, 143 ff.
  and fundamental freedoms, convention for the protection of (Rome, 1950), 148
Human Rights, Universal Declaration of, 144 ff.
Humanity, crimes against, 135 f.

Identity of the state, 259 ff., 416 f.
Immunity from jurisdiction (exterritoriality), 228 ff., 243
Impartiality of neutral states, 82, 84
Impenetrability of the state, 218
Implementation of international law by national law, 192 ff.
Imputation, act of state as problem of, 117 f.

Imputation, of the acts of an organ to the community, 13 f., 98 f., 107 f.
state as point of, 107 f., 117 f.
Independence as a characteristic of the state, 110 f., 156
Individual, as subject of international law, 114 ff., 124 ff., 130
as subject of international obligation and responsibility, 124 ff.
as subject of international right, 140 ff.
treaties conferring rights on, 350
Individual responsibility, for acts of state, 131 f., 235 f.
and collective responsibility, 9 ff., 98 f., 122 f.
in international law, 124 ff., 401
Inferiority and superiority, meaning of, 102 f., 424 f., 440 f.
Inquiry, commission of, 368
Insurgency, recognition of, 292
Insurgents, recognition of, as belligerent power, 291 ff.
Intention, 11 f.
Inter-American Treaty of Reciprocal Assistance, 61 f., 335
International agencies, decisions of, 365
International Air Convention (1919), 226
International Civil Aviation Conference, Final Act (1944), 226
International community as government of a state, 112
International Court of Justice, 379
advisory opinions of, 395
competence of, 391 ff.
compulsory jurisdiction of, 392 f.
execution of decisions of, 397
organization of, 388 ff.
procedure of, 394 f.
settlement of international disputes by, 386 ff.
Statute of, 388 ff.
International courts, see International tribunal
International delicts, 1 ff., 19 ff.
International delinquency, 119
International disputes, settlement of, see Disputes, international, settlement of
International jurisdiction, exclusive, 202
and national (domestic) jurisdiction, 191 ff.
International Labor Organization, 185 ff.
International law, basic norm of, 417 f.
common consent of the states as basis of, 152 ff., 311 ff.
communities not having the character of states as subjects of, 158 ff.
communities of states as subjects of, 168 ff., 323
conventional, 313 ff., 317 ff.
creation and application of, 301 ff.
custom as source of, 307 ff.
customary, as basis of conventional international law, 313 f.
binding force of, 311 ff.
reason of validity of, 314 ff.
decentralization of, 22, 36, 402 f.
definition of, 3, 201
delicts under, 19 ff.

determination of the spheres of validity of the national legal orders, according to, 203 ff., 207 ff.
doctrine of social contract in, 314 ff.
function of, 203 ff.
general (common), 19, 95 f., 188 ff.
and treaties, conflict between, 344
implementation of, by national law, 192 ff.
individuals as subjects of, 114 f., 124 ff., 130
jus cogens and *jus dispositivum* in, 344
and national law, conflicts between, 419 ff.
differences between, 401 ff.
reason of validity of, 408 ff.
relationship between, 108 ff., 191 ff., 205 ff., 403 ff.
source of, 406 ff.
subject matter of, 404 ff.
unity of, 424 ff.
national law created by an act of, 111
natural, 154 f.
nature of, 1 ff.
as part of national law, 109, 195, 206, 313, 435 ff.
particular, 19, 96, 188 ff.
primacy of, 428 ff., 435 ff.
as primitive law, 22, 36, 139
private (conflict of laws), 254 ff.
Progressive Codification of, Hague Conference on (1930), 222
recognition of, 109, 154, 313, 432 ff.
responsibility under, absolute and based on fault, 122 f.
collective, 116 ff., 401
individual, 124 ff., 131 f., 235 f., 401
retroactivity of, 95 f., 137
sanctions in, 1 ff., 19 ff., 401
self-help under, 23
sources of, 303 ff., 307 ff., 417 f.
sphere of validity, see Sphere of validity, of international law
state as subject of, 100 ff., 110 ff., 114, 152
statelike communities as subjects of, 161 ff., 322
subjects of, 96 ff., 114 ff., 402
transformation of, into national law, 194 ff., 430 f.
treaties as sources of, 317 ff.
as true law, 18 ff.
International legislation, 321 f., 365
International Military Tribunal (Nuremberg), 138, 238 f.
International obligation, individual as subject of, 124 ff.
state as subject of, 115 ff.
International organization, 172
League of Nations as, 174 ff.
United Nations as, 174 ff., 176 ff.
International personality and national personality of the state, 428 ff.
International Prize Court, Convention concerning (1907), 140
International responsibility, individuals as subjects of, 124 ff.
states as subjects of, 116 ff., 122
International rights, individuals as subjects of, 140 ff.
states as subjects of, 139 ff.
International sanctions, 1 ff., 19 ff., 401

Index

International tribunal, concept of, 377 f.
  execution of decisions of, 395 ff.
  for the Far East, charter of the, 138 f.
  jurisdiction of, 379 f.
  jurisdiction of, compulsory, 379 f., 392
  permanent, 379, 386 f.
  power of, 139 f.
  settlement of international disputes by, 377 ff.
Internationalization of the law, 202
Interpretation of treaties, 320 f.
Intertemporal law, 96
Intervention, 63 f.
Inviolability, privilege of, 242 f.
Italy, Peace Treaty with (1947), 148, 347, 349

Japan, Peace Treaty with (1951), 166
Judicial settlement and arbitration, 377 ff.
Jurisdiction, over citizens and aliens, 210 ff.
  domestic, see Domestic jurisdiction
  extraterritorial, 235
  immunity from, 228 ff., 243
  international, exclusive, 202
  of international tribunals, 379 f.
    compulsory, 379 f., 392
  of a state over another state, 125, 133, 134, 235 ff.
Jurisprudence, historical school of, 309 f.
  sociological school of, 309 f.
Juristic person, concept of, 97 f.
  corporation as, 98 ff.
  and physical (natural) person, 97 ff.
  responsibility of, 99 f.
  as subject of law, 96
Jus cogens and jus dispositivum in international law, 89, 323, 344
Justice, denial of, 246
Justiciable and nonjusticiable disputes, 380 ff.

Kellogg-Briand Pact, 29 ff., 39 ff., 42 ff., 86 ff., 294, 357
  bellum justum principle in, 42 f.
  neutrality under, 86 ff.
  self-defense under, 60
  war within the meaning of, 29
Korea, war in, 50, 53, 55

Labor Organization, International, 185 ff.
Lateran Treaty (1929), 159 f., 347
Lausanne, Peace Treaty of (1912), 67
Law, as a coercive order, 5 f., 100
  concept of, 3 ff., 16, 101, 108
  criminal, 5 f.
  customary and statutory, 307 ff.
  definition of, 3 ff., 16, 100
  gaps in the, 304 ff., 384
  international, see International law
  internationalization of, 202
  intertemporal, 96
  and morals, difference between, 5
  national, see National law
  natural, doctrine of, 149 f., 241, 310 f., 315 f.
  and nature as objects of science, 6 f.
  of nature and rule of law, 6 f.
  and peace, 17 f.

positive, and morality, relationship between, 425 ff.
primitive, 8 f., 10 f., 12, 16, 36, 100
  and a religious order, difference between, 5
  rule of, 6 f.
  source of, concept, 303 f.
  and state, 102 ff., 106 f.
  subjects of, 96 ff.
  violation of, 7, 19
Law-making treaties, 319 f.
League of Nations, Covenant of, 29 ff., 39 ff., 53 ff., 85 ff., 162 ff., 174 ff., 294, 330, 335, 336 ff., 347, 357, 361 ff., 368 ff., 379, 385 f.
  bellum justum principle in, 39 f.
  binding on third states, 347
  domestic jurisdiction under, 196 f.
  enforcement measures under, 40 ff.
  mandate system in, 162 ff.
  neutrality under, 85 ff.
  sanctions under, 40 ff.
  self-defense under, 60
  self-help under, 3
  self-help and collective security under, 40 f.
  war within the meaning of, 29
League of Nations, as international organization, 174 ff.
  settlement of international disputes by, 368 ff.
  and United Nations, differences between, 53 ff., 180, 199 f., 338
  withdrawal from, 337 f.
Legal authority and legal science, 6
Legal disputes under the Charter of the United Nations, 385 f.
Legal norm and rule of law, 6 f., 18
Legal order, centralization and decentralization of, 8 f., 14 f., 36, 100 ff., 104, 168 ff., 402 f.
  as a coercive order, 5 f., 100
  efficacy and validity of, 110, 413 f.
  spheres of validity of a, 91 ff.
  unity of, 408 f.
Legal and political disputes, 380 ff.
Legal and political recognition, of a community as a state, 267 ff.
  of a government, 279 ff.
Legal and political treaties, 320
Legal prohibition, 7
Legation, right of, 231
Legislation and custom, differences between, 308
Legislation, international, 321 f., 365
Legitimacy, principle of, 412 ff.
Liability, see Responsibility
Locarno Treaties (1925), 381 f.
London Agreement for the Prosecution of War Criminals (1945), 133 ff., 238 f.
London Convention (1871), 364
London, Declaration of (1871), 360
London Protocol (1936), 80
London, Treaty of (1930), 80

Malice, 11 f.
Mandates, 162 ff.
Maritime belt, 219 ff.

Material sphere of validity, of international law, 190 ff.
of the national legal order, determined by international law, 240 ff.
Mediation, settlement of international disputes by, 367 f.
Men-of-war, exterritoriality of, 232
Military Tribunal, International (Nuremberg Trial), 138, 238
Minorities, treaties establishing the protection of (1919–1920), 349
Monism and pluralism (dualism), 403 ff.
Monopoly of force of the legal community, 13 ff., 17, 101 f.
Morality and positive law, relationship between, 425 ff.
Multiple citizenship (nationality), 251 ff.

National (domestic) and international jurisdiction, 191 ff.
National law, continuity of, and identity of the state, 259 f., 416 f.
efficacy of, as power of the state, 106 f.
implementation of international law by, 192 ff.
international law, created by an act of, 111
as part of, 109, 195, 206
see also International law and national law
as legal order, sphere of validity of determined by international law, 203 ff., 207 ff.
in a narrower sense (not comprising international law), and in a wider sense (comprising international law), 206, 438
primacy of, 428 ff., 435 ff.
transformation, of international law into, 194 ff., 430 f.
of treaties into, 351 ff.
National legal order, see National law
National personality and international personality of the state, 428 ff.
National waters, 223
Nationality, see Citizenship
Nationality (citizenship), 248 ff.
conflict of, Hague Convention relating to questions of (1930), 253
Natural international law, 154 f.
Natural-law doctrine, 149 f., 241, 310 f., 315 f.
Natural (physical) and juristic person, 97 ff.
Naturalization, 249
Nature of international law, 1 ff.
Nature and law as objects of science, 6 f.
Negligence, 11 f.
Negotiation, settlement of international disputes by, 367 f.
Neutrality, 81 ff.
and *bellum justum* principle, 84 ff.
under the Charter of the United Nations, 87 ff.
under the Covenant of the League of Nations, 85 ff.
under general international law, 81 ff.
under the Kellogg-Briand Pact, 86 ff.
permanent, 85

Neutralization of the Swiss Confederation, Declaration Concerning (1815), 85
Nonintervention, under general international law, 63 f.
in matters of domestic jurisdiction under the Charter of the United Nations, 62 f., 196 ff.
right of the state to, 157
Non sub homine sed sub lege, 104
Nonrecognition, of a community as a state, 274 f., 284
of a government, 282 ff.
of illegally established situations (Stimson doctrine), 293 ff.
Norm, basic, of international law, 314, 417 f.
basic, of a legal order, concept of, 408 ff.
legal, 6 f.
validity of, 7
Normative order, concept of, 6 f.
Normativity and factuality, 427 f.
Norms, conflict between, 421 f.
systems of, static and dynamic, 409 ff.
systems of, possible relationship between two, 424 f.
North Atlantic Defense Treaty (1949), 61, 362 f.
Norway and Sweden, Treaty of Arbitration between (1925), 381
No-state's land (stateless territory), 214 f., 225
Nuremberg Trial, 138, 238 f.

Obligation (duty), concept of, 7 f.
primary and substitute, 22
of reparation, 20 f.
and responsibility, 9 ff.
Obligations, international, individual as subject of, 124 ff.
state as subject of, 115 ff.
subjects of, 96, 114 ff., 402
Occupation, belligerent, 73 f.
Open sea, 219 ff., 223 ff.
Opinions, advisory, of the International Court of Justice, 395
Option, 251
Order, coercive, law as a, 5 f., 100
legal, see Legal order
normative, concept of, 6 f.
public (policy), 240
Organ, imputation of its acts to the community, 13 f., 98 f., 107 f.
Organization, international, 172
League of Nations as, 174 ff.
United Nations as, 174 ff., 176 ff.
"Ought," the, 6 f.
and the "is," 414 f., 427 f.

Pacific Settlement of International Disputes, General Act for the (1928), 384 f.
Pacta sunt servanda, 96, 190, 314, 319, 417 f.
as basic norm of international law, 316
Pacta tertiis nec nocent nec prosunt, 345
Pactum de contrahendo, 342 f.
Paris, Declaration of (1856), 8 f., 81
Paris, Pact of, see Kellogg-Briand Pact
Paris, Treaty of (1856), 359 f., 364
Participation clause, general, 65
Particular international law, 19, 96, 188 ff.

Index

Particular international law, and general (common) international law, 188 ff.
Peace, crimes against, 135 f.
  and law, 17 f.
  treaty, 27, 32, 67 ff.
People of the state as personal sphere of validity of the national legal order, 206 ff., 227 ff.
Permanent Court of Arbitration, 386 f.
Permanent Court of International Justice, 335, 379, 384, 386 ff.
  Protocol of Signature concerning the Statute of the, 335 f., 379
Permanent international tribunals, 379, 386 f.
Person, juristic, see Juristic person
  state as a, 100 ff., 152
Personal sphere of validity, of international law, 96 ff.
  of the national legal order determined by international law, 227 ff.
  of the national legal order as people of the state, 206 ff., 227 ff.
Personality of the state, concept of, 152
  national and international, 152 ff., 428 ff.
Physical (natural) and juristic person, 97 ff.
Piracy, prohibition of, 124 f.
Pluralism (dualism) and monism, 403 ff.
Poland and Free City of Danzig, convention between called *Beamtenabkommen*, 143
  convention concerning the railways within the territory of Danzig (1920), 143
Police action or war, 29
Political, coercion as the "political" element, 100
Political and legal, see Legal and political
Power, concept of, 105 f., 113
  state as, 105 ff.
  of the state as efficacy of the legal order, 106 f.
Preliminary treaty, 343
Prevention and retribution, 17
Primacy, of international law, 428 ff., 435 ff.
  of national law, 428 ff., 435 ff.
Primary and substitute obligation, 22
Primitive law, 8 f., 10 f., 12, 16, 36, 100
  international law as, 22, 36, 139
Private international law (conflict of laws), 254 ff.
Privateering, 78
Prize Court, International, Convention concerning an (1907), 140
Prize courts, 79
Prohibition, legal, 7
Prohibition of war, 33 ff.
Property, enemy property in war, 72 f., 78 f.
  and territorial supremacy (sovereignty), 216
Protection, of organs and citizens of foreign states, 241 ff.
  by the state of its own citizens, 245 f., 247
Protectorate, 111, 161 f., 168 ff.
Public order (*ordre public*), 240
Public vessels, exterritoriality, 232 f.
Punishment as sanction of criminal law, 5 f.

Ratification of treaties, conditional, 332 f.
  no contravention pending, 328 f.
  no obligation of, 328
  partial, 332 f.
  with reservations, 332 f.
  and signature, 327 ff.
Reason of validity of national and international law, 408 ff.
Rebus sic stantibus, 358 ff.
Recognition, as ascertainment of a legally relevant fact, 267, 269 f.
  of belligerency, 292
  of a community as a state, 154, 264 ff.
    by admission to the United Nations, 277 ff.
    legal and political, 267 ff.
  conditional, 275
  constitutive or declaratory, 267 ff.
  de jure and *de facto*, 275 ff.
  of a government, 279 ff.
    legal and political, 279 ff.
    by the United Nations, 284 f.
  of insurgency, 292
  of insurgents as belligerent power, 291 ff.
  of international law, 109, 154, 313, 432 ff.
  of illegally established situations (Stimson doctrine), 293 ff.
  with retroactive force, 277
  withdrawal of, 274 f.
Regional arrangements under the Charter of the United Nations, 62
Registration of treaties, 338 ff.
Religious order and law, difference between, 5
Remedies, local, exhaustion of, 247
Renunciation of War, Treaty for, see Kellogg-Briand Pact
Reparation, for injuries suffered in the service of the United Nations, advisory opinion of the International Court of Justice, 184
  obligation of, and responsibility, 11, 120 f.
  and sanction, 20 f.
  as substitute obligation, 20 f.
  in the Peace Treaty of Versailles, 38
Reprisals, 23 ff.
Reservations to treaties, 332 ff.
Respect, right of the state to, 157
Responsibility, absolute, and culpability, 11 ff.
  collective in international law, 116 ff., 401
  concept of, 9
  individual, for acts of state, 131 f., 235 f.
  and collective, 9 ff., 98 f., 122 f.
  in international law, 124 ff., 131 f., 235 f., 401
  international, individual as subject of, 124 ff.
  state as subject of, 116 ff., 122 f.
  subjects of, 96 ff., 114 ff., 402
  of a juristic person, 99 f.
  and obligation, 9 ff.
  to repair a damage, 11, 120 f.
  subjects of international, 114 ff.
  of the state, absolute and based on fault (culpability), 122 f.
  direct and indirect, 119 f.
  original and vicarious, 120
Retorsion, 25
Retribution and prevention, 17
Retroactivity of international law, 95 f., 137, 277
Revenge, 8, 10

Revision of treaties, 360 f.
Revolution and *coup d'état* as law-creating facts, 264, 415 ff.
Revolution, war compared with, 36 f.
Right, concept of, 8 f., 25
Rights, and duties of states, draft declaration on, 158
  fundamental, of the state, 148 ff.
  human, in the Charter of the United Nations, 143 ff.
    Universal Declaration of, 144 ff.
  international, individuals as subjects of, 140 ff.
  states as subjects of, 139 ff.
Rule of law, and law of nature, 6 f.
  and legal norm, 6 f., 18

St. Germain, Peace Treaty of, 261
Sanction, civil execution as, 5 f.
  concept of, 4
  and delict, 6
  and obligation of reparation, 20 f.
Sanctions, as acts of coercion (enforcement measures), 4 ff.
  under the Charter of the United Nations, 54, 56 ff.
  coercive acts not having the character of, 13
  under the Covenant of the League of Nations, 40 ff.
  socially organized, 4
  transcendental, 4
  criminal and civil, 5 f.
  international, 1 ff., 19 ff., 401
  as enforcement measures, 22 ff.
San Francisco Treaty for Collective Self-defense (1951), 62
San Stefano, Treaty of (1878), 364
Science, law and nature as object of, 6 f.
  legal, and legal authority, 6
Sea, freedom of the, 125, 224 f.
  open, 219 ff., 223 ff.
Secretary-General of the United Nations, 182 f.
Security, collective, and self-help, 15 f.
  under the Covenant of the League of Nations, 40 f.
Security Council of the United Nations, 179 ff.
Self-defense, 16, 30, 58 ff.
  collective, treaties for the organization of, 61 f.
  under the Covenant of the League of Nations, 60
  under general international law, 58 ff.
  individual and collective under the Charter of the United Nations, 58 ff.
  under the Kellogg-Briand Pact, 60
Self-help, 8, 14, 15
  and collective security, 15 f.
  under the Covenant of the League of Nations, 39 f.
  under general international law, 23
Self-preservation, right of, 58 f.
  right of the state to, 157
Servitude, concept of, 345
Settlement, judicial, and arbitration, 377 ff.
  pacific, of International Disputes, General Act for the (1928), 384 f.

Settlement, of international disputes, see Disputes, international, settlement of
Signature and ratification of treaties, 327 ff.
Simplified procedures of conclusion of treaties, 334 ff.
Situations (not having the character of disputes), adjustment of, by the United Nations, 370 ff.
Social contract, doctrine of, 153
  in international law, 314 ff.
Solidarity, social, as source of law, 309 f.
Source of law, concept of, 303 f.
Source of national and international law, 406 f.
Sources of international law, 303 ff., 307 ff., 417 f.
Sovereignty, 108 ff., 155 ff., 225, 315 f., 348, 438 ff.
  divided, 112 f.
  as exclusive quality of one legal order, 442 ff.
  external and internal, 112 f.
  in a federal state, 113
  as a fundamental right of the state, 155 f.
  as a quality of a normative order, 438 ff.
  territorial (supremacy), 216 f.
Sphere of validity, of international law, 93 ff.
  material, 190 ff.
  personal, 96 ff.
  temporal, 94 ff.
  territorial, 94 ff.
  of a legal order, 91 ff.
  of the national legal orders, determined by international law, 203 ff.
Spheres of validity of treaties, 342 ff.
State, act of, 117 ff.
  individual responsibility for, 131 f., 235 f.
  as problem of imputation, 117 ff.
State, birth and death of, 258 ff.
  as a centralized legal order, 100 f.
  competence of the, 240 ff.
  elements of the, 206 ff., 257 ff.
  equality and sovereignty as fundamental rights of the, 155 f.
  federal, 111, 168 ff., 219
    sovereignty in the, 113
  fundamental rights of the, 148 ff.
  governed by an international community, 112
  Head of the, concept of, 230
  identity of the, 259 ff., 416 f.
  impenetrability of the, 218
  independence of the, 110 f., 156
  jurisdiction of, over another state, 125, 133, 134, 235 ff.
  and law, 102 ff., 106 f.
  legal existence determined by international law, 203 ff.
  national and international personality of, 428 ff.
  nonrecognition of a community as, 274 f., 284
  as a normative order and as a person, 109
  organs of, competent to conclude treaties, 323 f.
  people of the, 206 ff., 227 ff.
  as a person, 100 ff., 152
  personality of the, 152 ff., 428 ff.

Index

State, as point of imputation, 107 f., 117 f.
  as power, 105 ff.
  recognition of a community as a, 154, 264 ff.
  responsibility of the, see Responsibility of the state
  right of the, to protect its own citizens, 245 f., 247
  rights of, fundamental, 148 ff.
  servitudes, 345, 349
  sovereignty of the, 108 ff., 155 ff., 225, 315 f., 348
    as a right, 155 ff.
  as subject, of international law, 100 ff., 110 ff., 114, 152
    of international obligations, 115 ff.
    of international responsibility, 116 ff., 122
    of international rights, 139 ff.
  termination of existence of, 75 f.
  territory of, acquisition of, 213 ff.
    boundaries of, 208 ff., 213
    in a narrower and in a wider sense, 212 ff.
    as territorial sphere of validity of the national legal order, 207 ff.
  time as element of the, 257 ff.
  of the Vatican City, 159 f.
Stateless territory (no-state's land), 214 f., 225
Statelessness, 251 ff.
Statelike communities as subjects of international law, 161 ff., 322
States, common consent of, as basis of, international law, 153 ff.
  communities of, as subjects of international law, 323
  confederation of, 171 ff.
  Rights and Duties of, Draft Declaration on the, 158
  succession of, 295 ff.
Static and dynamic systems of norms, 409 ff.
Statute, of the International Court of Justice, 388 ff.
  of the Permanent Court of International Justice, 384
  unconstitutional, 421 f.
Statutory and customary law, 307 ff.
Stimson doctrine, 293 ff.
Subject matter of national and international law, 404 ff.
Subjectivism and objectivism, 444 f.
Subjects, of international obligation and responsibility, 96 ff., 114 ff., 402
  of law, 96 ff.
  on whom treaties are binding, 344 ff.
Subjects of international law, 96 ff., 114 ff., 124 ff., 130, 402
  communities not having the character of states as, 158 ff.
  communities of states as, 168 ff., 323
  statelike communities as, 161 ff., 322
  states as, 100 ff., 110 ff., 114, 152
Submarine warfare, 80
Submarine Telegraph Cables, Convention for the Protection of (1884) 127 f.
Subsoil, 225

Substitute obligation, and primary obligation, 22
  reparation as, 20 f.
Succession of states, 295 ff.
Superior command, acts performed at, 136
Superiority and inferiority, meaning of, 102 f., 424 f., 440 f.
Supremacy, territorial, 216 f.
Suzerainty, 111
Systems of norms, possible relationship between two, 424 f.
Swiss Confederation, neutralization of, 85

Temporal sphere of validity, of international law, 94 ff.
  of the national legal order determined by international law, 257 ff.
Termination of treaties, 355 ff.
Territorial sphere of validity, of international law, 94 ff.
  of the national legal order determined by international law, 207 ff.
  of the national legal order as territory of the state, 206 ff.
Territorial supremacy (sovereignty), 216 ff.
Territorial waters, 219 ff.
Territory, stateless, 214 f., 225
Territory of the state, see State, territory of
Three-mile zone, 220
Time as an element of the state, 257 ff.
Transcendental sanctions, 4
Transformation of international into national law, 194 ff., 430 f.
Transformation of treaties into national law, 351 ff.
Treaties, accession to, 340 f.
  beginning and end of validity of, 354 ff.
  competence of state organs to conclude, 323 ff.
  conferring rights on private individuals, 350
  conferring rights on third states, 348 ff.
  conflict between, 361 f.
  conflicting with general international law, 344
  constitutionality of, 324 f.
  denunciation of, 356 f.
  dissolution of, by mutual consent, 356
  effect of threat or use of force on, 326 f.
  effect of war on, 360
  form of, 327 ff.
  imposing duties on third states, 345 ff.
  interpretation of, 320 f.
  law-making, 319 f.
  legal and political, 320
  objects of, 342 ff.
  pactum de contrahendo, 342 f.
  of peace, 27, 32, 67 ff.
  preliminary, 343
  ratification of, see, Ratification of treaties
  registration of, 338 f.
  revision of, 360 f.
  signature and ratification of, 327 ff.
  simplified procedures of conclusion of, 334 ff.
  as source of international law, 317 ff.
  subjects bound by, 344 ff.
  termination of, 355 ff.

Treaties, transformation of, into national law, 351 ff.
Treaty, concept of, 317 ff.
no contravention pending ratification, 328 f.
as law created by specific procedure, 342 ff.
as law-creating procedure, 322 ff.
spheres of validity of, 342 ff.
withdrawal from, 157, 356 ff.
Tribunal, international, concept of, 377 f.
for the Far East, Charter of, 138 f.
Military (Nuremberg), 138, 238 f.
Tribunals, international, *see* International tribunal
Trust territories, 162 ff.
Trusteeship Agreement for British Togoland, 167
Trusteeship Council of the United Nations, 182

Unconstitutional statute, 421 f.
Union, personal and real, 171
United Nations, Charter of, 29 ff., 39 ff., 44 ff., 53 ff., 87 ff., 143 ff., 162 ff., 176 ff., 331, 337 ff., 347 f., 357, 361, 363 f., 370 ff., 379, 381
adjustment of situations (not having the character of disputes), 370 ff.
action against former enemy states, 62
armed attack, 61 f.
binding on third states, 347 f.
centralization of the force monopoly, 44 f.
domestic jurisdiction, 62 f., 196 ff.
enforcement measures, 46 ff.
human rights, 143 ff.
individual and collective self-defense, 58 ff.
legal disputes, 385 f.
neutrality, 87 ff.
nonintervention in matters of domestic jurisdiction, 62 f., 196 ff.
regional arrangements, 62
sanctions, 54, 56 ff.
self-defense, individual and collective, 58 ff.
settlement of international disputes, 368 ff.
trusteeship system, 162 ff.
war under, 44 ff.
war within the meaning of, 29
Declaration by (1942), 176
Economic and Social Council, 182
General Assembly, 178 f.
as international organization, 174 ff., 176 ff.
and League of Nations, differences between, 53 ff., 180, 199 f., 338
recognition of a government by, 284 f.
recognition of a state by admission to, 277 ff.
resolution "Uniting for Peace" adopted by the General Assembly, 51 ff., 178, 182
Secretary-General, 182 f.
Security Council, 179 ff.
Trusteeship Council, 182
veto right of the permanent members of the Security Council, 155, 180
withdrawal from, 338, 357
United States and Colombia, treaty between concerning the Panama Canal (1903), 328
United States and Germany, treaty between for the restoration of friendly relations (1921), 68 f.
United States and Japan, treaty of September 8, 1951, 217 f.
"Uniting for Peace," resolution adopted by the General Assembly of the United Nations, 51 ff., 178, 182
Unity of legal order, 408 ff.
Unity of national and international law, 424 ff.
Universal Declaration of Human Rights, 144 ff.
Upper Silesia, Germano-Polish Convention concerning, 142

Validity, and efficacy of a legal order, 110, 413 f.
of a norm, 7
reason of, of national and international law, 408 ff.
spheres of, *see* Sphere of validity
Vatican City, State of the, treaty establishing the (1929), 159 f., 347
Versailles, Treaty of, 38 f., 132 f., 141, 147, 186 ff., 329, 347, 349
bellum justum principle in, 38
reparation in, 38
Vessels, public, exterritoriality, 232 f.
Veto right of the permanent members of the Security Council of the United Nations, 155, 180
Violation of the law, 7, 19
Volksgeist as source of law, 309 f.

War, of aggression and war of defense, 30
air warfare, 81
beginning and end of, 67 f.
belligerent occupation, 73 f.
bilateral or unilateral action, 26 ff.
under the Charter of the United Nations, 44 ff.
concept of, 25 ff.
contraband of, 79, 128
and counterwar, 28 f.
crimes, 128 ff., 133 ff.
criminals, London Agreement for the Prosecution of, 133 f., 238 f.
declaration of, 67
of defense, 30
as delict or sanction, 28 f.
effect of, on treaties, 360
enemy property in, 72 f., 78 f.
the individuals against whom the destructive acts of war may be directed, 70 f.
international and internal (civil), 32
just, doctrine of, 33 ff.
as a law-creating fact, 37 f.
legal meaning (interpretation) of, 26 ff., 33 ff.

Index

War, within the meaning, of the Charter of the United Nations, 29
   of the Covenant of the League of Nations, 29
   of the Kellogg-Briand Pact, 29
 means of destruction, 71 f.
 or police action, 29
 privateering, 78
 prize courts, 79
 prohibition of, 33 ff.
 purpose of, 31 f.
 regulation of the conduct of, 64 ff.
 Renunciation of, Treaty for the, *see* Kellogg-Briand Pact
 and revolution, 36 f.
 a status or an action, 26 f.
 submarine warfare, 80
 as use of armed force, 29 ff.
 warfare on the sea, 77 ff.
Warfare, acts of illegitimate, 129
Waters, national, 223
 territorial, 219 ff.
Withdrawal, from League of Nations, 337 f.
 of recognition, 274 f.
 from treaties, 157, 356 ff.
 from United Nations, 338, 357

Lightning Source UK Ltd.
Milton Keynes UK
UKHW041013080223
416578UK00011B/340